MODELLING AND SIMULATION METHODOLOGY
IN THE ARTIFICIAL INTELLIGENCE ERA

MODELLING
AND SIMULATION METHODOLOGY
IN THE
ARTIFICIAL INTELLIGENCE ERA

edited by

MAURICE S. ELZAS
Wageningen Agricultural University
The Netherlands

TUNCER I. ÖREN
University of Ottawa
Canada

BERNARD P. ZEIGLER
University of Arizona at Tucson
U.S.A.

1986

NORTH-HOLLAND
AMSTERDAM · NEW YORK · OXFORD · TOKYO

DR 9/3/87

© Elsevier Science Publishers B.V., 1986

ISBN: 0 444 70130 3

Published by:
ELSEVIER SCIENCE PUBLISHERS B.V.
P.O. Box 1991
1000 BZ Amsterdam
The Netherlands

Sole distributors for the U.S.A. and Canada:
ELSEVIER SCIENCE PUBLISHING COMPANY, INC.
52 Vanderbilt Avenue
New York, N.Y. 10017
U.S.A.

PRINTED IN THE NETHERLANDS

FOREWORD

In August 1978, Bernard Zeigler organized the first meeting ever to devote itself entirely to modelling and simulation methodology, at the Weizmann Institute of Science, in Rehovot, Israel.
The fact that almost 1500 copies were sold of the book that resulted from this meeting (Methodology in Systems Modelling and Simulation), can be considered to be an indication of the amount of interest in the methodological issues that govern simulation studies that had been dormant until then.
At this first meeting, the editors of the present book got to know eachothers' work in greater depth, and decided to try to organize this type of meetings on a recurrent basis at moments far enough apart to reflect the major developments in the fundamental concepts and methods of Modelling and Simulation.
In 1982 Tuncer Oren organized the next meeting at Ottawa University in Ontario, Canada. Again, judging by the reviews, the resulting book (Simulation and Model-Based Methodologies: An Integrative View), branded it as a most valuable event.
I have had the honor to organize the third meeting of the series in July, 1984, at a conference centre near to the Wageningen Agricultural University in the Netherlands.

The present volume emerged from this third Working Conference, but is not strictly a record of its proceedings. The book contains papers which were carefully selected from those delivered at the meeting, subjected to a rigorous refereeing process by the editors, and finally accepted only if it presented important ideas relevant to the main theme in a clear and readable manner.

This volume is divided into seven sections.
Section I. provides insight into the influence of the results of Artificial Intelligence research on Modelling and Simulation methodology, presents concepts that can foster the synergy between both fields, defines knowledge from a systems research viewpoint, inspects the knowledge representation aspects of models and investigates the value of machine learning for simulation studies.
Section II. is devoted to knowledge structures for Modelling and Simulation, the state-of-the-art means to implement them, the use of these structures to build new models from already stored components and restructuring techniques for some problems in order to allow easier solution.
Section III. addresses the important contributions that (symbolic) processing of the models themselves can make to the solution of problems that, until now, had to be tackled by hand or required an exceptional level of expertise in mathematical subjects quite remote from the prerequisite knowledge needed for most traditional modelling and simulation applications. Moreover the value of expert-system-like concepts for assistance in complicated simulation tasks is demonstrated.

Section IV. shows inroads into the resolution of the problems associated with the modelling of systems with variable structure. As well the theoretical, as the methodological and the practical aspects of new approaches are discussed.

The ever more important issues of model validation and quality assurance of simulation experiments receive renewed attention in Section V. The section indicates that new directions in this area can originate as well from a priori (advisory) standpoints as from a posterpriori (certification) points of view.

The increasing necessity to model systems that contain human actors, especially those in which these actors interact through some common organization, causes the authors in Section VI. to look for contributions from Artificial Intelligence for new approaches to these extremely hard modelling problems. The section contains contributions that offer ideas as well on project management aspects that are important for this type of studies.

Finally, Section VII. presents some novel developments in the area of practical tools which are applicable in a number of the subfields of simulation and make use of recent developments in computer science.

I would like to take this opportunity to express my sincere appreciation to all those that made the conference possible, especially Maarten Koeman of the Board of Wageningen University, Wim Smit of AKZO, and last -but certainly not least!- Elly Gordijn the secretary of my Department without whose help the whole venture would not have been possible.

I can not conclude this foreword without thanking my fellow editors for their most valuable help in all aspects of the conference and the preparation of this book. I certainly hope to be able to continue to work together with them on many future (methodological) occasions.

The final sentence is devoted to the patience and understanding of my beloved wife, Yetty, who may well have thought sometimes that I had left her to marry a book.

Maurice S. Elzas

Wageningen.

MAJOR CATEGORY INDEX

APPLICABILITY of ARTIFICIAL INTELLIGENCE to MODELLING & SIMULATION

      Chapters: I.3 - II.1 - II.3 - II.5 - III.1 - III.2 - III.3
               IV.1 - IV.3 - V.1 - V.2 - V.3 - VI.1 - VI.2
               VI.3 - VI.4 - VII.1

BASES, MODEL/KNOWLEDGE

      Chapters: I.3 - II.1 - II.2 - II.3 - III.3 - V.3

EXPERIMENTATION with MODELS

      Chapters: II.1 - II.2 - II.3 - III.2 - III.3 - IV.3 - IV.4
               V.3

MACHINE LEARNING

      Chapters: I.4 - IV.2 - IV.3 - IV.4 - V.2 - VI.2

MAN-MACHINE INTERFACES

      Chapters: I.3 - II.1 - II.4 - II.5 - III.1 - III.3 - V.3
               VI.4 - VI.5 - VII.3

METHODOLOGICAL ASPECTS

      Chapters: I.2 - I.3 - I.4 - II.2 - II.3 - II.5 - III.1
               III.4 - III.5 - IV.1 - IV.3 - IV.4 - V.1 - VI.2
               VII.2

MODEL MANIPULATION

      Chapters: I.3 - I.4 - II.1 - II.2 - II.3 - II.4 - II.5
               III.1 - III.2 - III.4 - IV.1 - V.3

SOFTWARE TOOLS

      Chapters: II.1 - II.2 - II.3 - II.4 - IV.3 - V.3 - VI.2
               VI.4 - VII.2 - VII.3

SYSTEMS RESEARCH CONCEPTS

      Chapters: I.2 - II.2 - III.1 - III.2 - III.4 - IV.1 - V.3
               VI.3 - VI.5 - VII.1

TABLE OF CONTENTS

FOREWORD   v

MAJOR CATEGORY INDEX   vii

SECTION I : SURVEY OF THE FIELD AND CONCEPTUAL BASES

    Chapter I.1 : The Kinship between Artificial Intelligence,
                   Modelling & Simulation: An Appraisal.
                   M.S. Elzas   3

    Chapter I.2 : System Knowledge: a Definition and its
                   Implications.
                   B.P. Zeigler   15

    Chapter I.3 : The Applicability of Artificial Intelligence
                   Techniques to Knowledge Representation in
                   Modelling & Simulation.
                   M.S. Elzas   19

    Chapter I.4 : Implications of Machine Learning in
                   Simulation.
                   T.I. Ören   41

SECTION II : STRUCTURES FOR KNOWLEDGE-BASED MODEL PROCESSING

    Chapter II.1 : Relations between Artificial Intelligence
                   Environments and Modelling & Simulation
                   Support Systems.
                   M.S. Elzas   61

    Chapter II.2 : Entity-Based Structures for Modelling and
                   Experimental Frame Construction.
                   J.W. Rozenblit, B.P. Zeigler   79

    Chapter II.3 : Knowledge-Based Model Storage and
                   Retrieval: Problems and Possibilities.
                   D.L. Kettenis 1Ø1

    Chapter II.4 : An Approach to Model Composition from
                   Existing Modules.
                   C.R. Standridge   113

    Chapter II.5 : Structuring of Linear Optimization Problems.
                   U. Maschtera, W. Schneider   121

SECTION III: SYMBOLIC PROCESSING IN SIMULATION

Chapter III.1: Model Components for Symbolic Processing
               by Knowledge Based Systems:
               The STIPS Framework.
               F.R. Pichler   133

Chapter III.2: Possibilities for Expert Aids in
               System Simulation.
               A.W. Jones   145

Chapter III.3: Applications of Expert Systems Concepts
               to Adaptive Experimentation with Models.
               A. Jávor   153

Chapter III.4: World View Based Discrete Event Model
               Simplification.
               C.M. Overstreet, R.E. Nance   165

Chapter III.5: Transforming a Discrete-Event System
               into a Logic Programming Formalism.
               W.A. Zajicek   181

SECTION IV : VARIABLE STRUCTURE- AND LEARNING-MODELS

Chapter IV.1 : Toward a Simulation Methodology for
               Variable Structure Modelling.
               B.P. Zeigler   195

Chapter IV.2 : Recent Developments in Learning
               Automata Theory and Their Applications.
               N. Baba   211

Chapter IV.3 : Knowledge Seeking in Variable
               Structure Models.
               P. Hogeweg, B. Hesper   227

Chapter IV.4 : Use of Explicit Constraints to Evaluate
               a Potentially Unique, Neural Model for
               Single-Interval Concept Manipulation.
               R. Martin   245

SECTION V   : ARTIFICIAL INTELLIGENCE IN SIMULATION QUALITY
              ASSURANCE

Chapter V.1 : Artificial Intelligence in Quality Assurance
               of Simulation Studies.
               T.I. Ören   267

Chapter V.2 : An Exploration of Possibilities for
               Expert Aids in Model Validation.
               R.G. Sargent   279

Chapter V.3 : MAGEST: a Model-Based Advisor and
               Certifier for GEST Programs.
               Z.K. Aytaç, T.I. Ören   299

SECTION VI : ARTIFICIAL INTELLIGENCE TECHNIQUES IN
MODELLING OF ORGANIZATIONAL PROBLEMS

Chapter VI.1 : Artificial Intelligence and Modelling
of Societal Systems: A Synopsis.
M.S. Elzas 311

Chapter VI.2 : Applying Artificial Intelligence Techniques
to Strategic-level Gaming and Simulation.
P.K. Davis 315

Chapter VI.3 : A Model-Based Expert System for
Decision Support in Negotiating.
E.G. Roman, S.V. Ahamed 339

Chapter VI.4 : Expert Systems for Modelling of
Decision Support and Information Systems.
H.G. Sol 353

Chapter VI.5 : A Knowledge-Based Modelling Approach to
Office Form-Flow Systems.
A.M. Tjoa, G. Kappel, R.R. Wagner . . . 365

SECTION VII : RELATED TOOLS AND TECHNIQUES

Chapter VII.1: An Exploration of the Applicability of
Production Rule Based Techniques to
Process Modelling.
V.R. Voller, B. Knight 377

Chapter VII.2: Problems and Advantages of
Simulation in Prolog.
I. Futó, T. Gergely 385

Chapter VII.3: Graphic Interfaces for Modelling Systems
Y. Yamamoto 399

SUBJECT INDEX   405

SECTION I
SURVEY OF THE FIELD
AND
CONCEPTUAL BASES

Modelling and Simulation Methodology
in the Artificial Intelligence Era
M.S. Elzas, T.I. Ören and B.P. Zeigler (Editors)
© Elsevier Science Publishers B.V. (North-Holland), 1986

3

Chapter I.1

THE KINSHIP BETWEEN ARTIFICIAL INTELLIGENCE, MODELLING & SIMULATION:
AN APPRAISAL

M.S. Elzas

Agricultural University
Department of Computer Science
Wageningen/The Netherlands

The impact of Modelling & Simulation Methodology
research on the daily practice of the simulation
community is becoming clearly perceivable.
The same applies for the application of the results
of Artificial Intelligence research in a multitude of
computer related fields.
As both fields are strongly based on models, the fact
that these two computer-related areas are on the
brink of a period of synergy comes as a more or less
logical consequence.
There is an increasing interest of incorporating
methods and techniques developed by and for the
Artificial Intelligence community into Modelling &
Simulation methodology and practice.
This chapter therefore addresses, from a historical
perspective,: a) the basic nature of models in
Artificial Intelligence, b) their common aspects and
differences with simulation models, c) some potential
benefits of Modelling & Simulation methodologies for
Artificial Intelligence, d) some potential benefits
of state-of-the-art Artificial Intelligence
techniques for Modelling & Simulation.

1. INTRODUCTION.

Already in the very early days of the advent of the modern digital
computer, journalists and scientists alike have uttered speculative
ideas about the possibility that machines (especially programmable
ones) could be designed in such a way as to "behave intelligently".
The term "Artificial Intelligence" itself was first coined in 1947
by either von Neuman, Wiener or Rashevsky at a Symposium in Harvard
set up to explore - for the first time - the possible future impact
of programmable devices in this light.
The notion that is covered by this name originated though with Alan
Turing (in his lecture on "Intelligent Machinery", Sept. 1947)
(Turing 1947) and John von Neumann (who got interested - while on
the ENIAC project - in analogies between digital circuitry, the
human nervous system and certain mental processes), (von Neumann
1958). It was, however, E.C. Berkeley's book "Giant Brains or
Machines that Think" (Berkeley 1949) that first aroused public
awareness for the potential of computers in this area.

On the other hand the earliest computers (Kelvin 1872, Vannevar Bush 1927) were analog, specifically designed for simulation and already around in the 1930's. These were in effect computers that could be programmed in a 'conceptual way', meaning that models - or rather analogies of advanced mathematical and physical functions - could be directly programmed on these machines without necessity for any (unnatural) sequencing of operations. There was no great concern about which kind of operators had to be implemented or specific modelling methodology considerations because the hardware itself strictly limited the possibilities.

The fact that, around 1955, Selfridge decided to transpose simulation programs from analog computers to digital ones (mainly because of the size of the systems to be simulated) made it necessary - for the first time - to be able to argue about what exactly was being transposed, which functions were essential for simulation and how to use the far greater flexibility of representation on the digital computer (Selfrigde 1955).

Interestingly this was about the same moment at which the scientists interested in Artificial Intelligence also started to look into advanced programming methods for digital computers.

Although Grace Hopper had already published an early article on the feasibility of symbolic computation (Hopper 1952), even arithmetic statement translation posed such daunting problems on these early machines, that the feeling arose that it was absolutely necessary to know more about the conceptual side of languages and of reasoning about problem solving (Chomsky 1956).

This last subject gave rise to the concept that "heuristics" were an indispensable part of human problem solving. Newell, Shaw and Simon produced the first publication on this subject in 1957 (Newell et al. 1957).

The technique they proposed was:

1. to develop a conception of what one expects to find as a solution,
2. to use this conception to guide one in seeking, selecting and assign meaning to facts, and
3. to continually develop new, more adequate conceptions as problem solution proceeds.

One of their claims was that this procedure was a formal description of the approach that human beings followed in the process of discovery.

With other words: they had a model.

It took a visionary man like Richard Hamming, to describe already then - almost thirty years ago - the potential of tools and working habits that are emerging only now:

> *'In time, especially in fields where the basic theory*
> *is well understood, at least nine out of ten*
> *experiments will be done on computers, and only the*
> *interesting, suggestive experiments will be done in*
> *the laboratory to check the theoretical model...*
> *In the long run this change from the physical approach*
> *to the conceptual approach will revolutionize much of*
> *science and engineering and will keep the computers*
> *busy performing the clean-cut, idealized laboratory*
> *experiments whose interrelationships are too complex*
> *for the human mind to work its way through unaided,*
> *as well as the complex, messy situations that occur in*
> *engineering practice'* (Hamming 1958).

2. ARTIFICIAL INTELLIGENCE AND ITS MODELS

As pointed out in the introduction, after prospective inspection of
the possibilities to represent mental processes within stored
program machines, the pioneering days of Artificial Intelligence
were strongly influenced by the fact that early computers were
extremely hard to program and that higher level languages were not
yet mature enough to make their impact.
Therefore, moved along by enthusiasm caused by the early prospective
studies, the Artificial Intelligence community addressed the area of
problem solving techniques with the aim to facilitate the use of
computers in this way.
This meant in practice that research was in the first place focussed
on understanding the way in which human beings use facts (or data)
and preliminary knowledge while solving problems in practice
(Newell & Simon 1956). In doing so, one could naturally not avoid to
look into the problems of human kwowledge acquisition, organization
and storage, with other words the different aspects of (mechanical)
learning.
While mathematical problems and games gave - apparently - clean cut
and well structured problems to base this work on, the Artificial
Intelligence researchers soon found the mathematical discipline as
such was not adequately equipped to answer many of the emerging
questions. The link with cognitive psychology and epistomology
became mandatory.
In close cooperation with scientists from those fields, the theories
that were available there were converted into entities that could be
handled by computers.
Models again, in fact.
But rather special models.

In more or less the same way that the early digital simulation
programs and languages were based on a mimicry of the analog
computer (Brennan and Linebarger 1964) the models used by Artificial
Intelligence were a mimicry of strategies derived from theories
about human thought and problem solving, the goal of their
implementation being in the first place the verification of the
validity of those theories.
A formidable barrier than came in view: the difficulty in
communicating facts, theories and other knowledge to the "brain" of
general problem solvers, and the problems in communicating the
resulting conclusions back to the user.
Apart from creating an opening between the highly isolated field of
cognitive studies and computer architecture (all kinds of
sophisticated means were now needed to speed up communication like:
pattern recognition, computer generated pictures and sound), the
need to communicate gave rise to a new generation of models in order
to be able to work e.g. on natural language dialogues. Conceptual
models of expression in- and understanding of language came into
focus, (e.g. Bobrow's STUDENT (Bobrow 1968), Winograd's SHRDLU
(Winograd 1972), Weizenbaum's ELIZA (Weizenbaum 1966), Minsky's
publications on semantics (Minsky 1961)).
Though the work with these conceptual models the conclusion was
arrived at that a general theory of "intelligent" machine systems
was far too ambitious a goal in the short term.
Fortunately it was found that, under circumstances, it was possible
to isolate a "micro-world" out of the larger set of knowledge. In
such a micro-world knowledge about a clearly limited subject area
could be isolated from other, more general, knowledge and reasoning

strategies. Having come this far it was not so important anymore to accurately represent the processes that take place in the human mind.
Any strategy that yielded a reasonable solution valid for the specific micro-world under consideration came to be acceptable.
After some initial experiments, Feigenbaum - with DENDRAL and later METADENDRAL (Buchanan et al. 1969, Feigenbaum 1977) - achieved a breakthrough by providing a rather satisfactory system to help interpret measurement results from mass-spectrometers.
From this point on an apparent division has occured in Artificial Intelligence research. While work continues on the central issues closely connected with - the rather abstract - issues of cognitive systems and natural language interpretation, a large amount of effort has been put into building tools and practical examples of expert aids for certain micro-worlds, e.g. LOGO for certain teaching applications (Papert 1980) and Expert Systems for a multitude of complex diagnostic and consultation tasks (van Melle et al. 1981, Hayes-Roth et al. 1983). The latter effort has made intellectual and operational tools available that can bring new methods and techniques into being in the field of Modelling & Simulation, like Modelling & Simulation based on a priori domain knowledge, simulation of and with "autonomous systems", simulation query systems and other expert aids for model-building and simulation experiment management (Ören 1984a, Ören 1985).
These expert aids will in most cases be based on the experience gained with practical Expert Systems.
These Expert Systems are best suited for assistance in tasks for which normally thoroughly trained people, talented and experienced in some specialized problem domain, are needed.
With such a system interactive - consultative - access is provided to other people's accumulated skills and knowledge by means of a computer program and a suitable system to store, retrieve and consolidate items of knowledge. (Knowledge Bases, see e.g. Hayes-Roth et al. 1983, pp. 335-338).

3. CATEGORIES OF MODELS AND GOALS OF SIMULATION

For the purpose of being able to discuss the common aspects and differences of the use of models and the nature of simulation studies in Artificial Intelligence with reference to the general simulation field, a brief inventorisation of the possibilities that are encountered in these two fields seems appropriate.
Using the definitions proposed in Zeigler (1979) and Elzas (1984), we define a model to be "a compact representation of a real phenomenon which can generate a behavior comparable with some behavior of interest in the real system and moreover, a vehicle to make more evident key charateristics of an object under study".
Although everything which we call model can be made to fit this definition, the extent in which it realises compactness, comparable behavior, and displays key characteristics can vary greatly as is shown e.g. in Elzas (1984), Sargent (1984) and Zeigler (1984).
The mimicry models, which were mentioned before, display the characteristics of an analogy or a mental model of some real entity, and are judged on basis of behavior comparison with their direct meta-model (the analogy) and not specifically with reality.
Moreover, they are - at best - generative systems based on Zeigler's IOFO (Input/Output Function Observation) system specification level.

Therefore they do - in fact - not really have to represent any
sizeable part of reality, although they might very well show
similarities with it.
As long as human thought, knowledge acquisition and storage systems
are as extremely hard to 'measure' as they are now, models in
Artificial Intelligence and Expert Systems will not reach more
sophistication than Zeigler's IOFO's.
On the other hand, in most Simulation and Systems Research studies
the observation possibilities are such that one can reasonably
expect to be able to verify structural similarities between model
and reality. Therefore structured systems or networks of them form
the core of the model studies on this side of the fence (Zeigler
1984).
As was pointed out in Elzas (1980) one can only *claim* to gain more
understanding of the functioning of a real system through
simulation, if a minimum of structural similarity is achieved in the
model.
It is deemed quite possible that, if the Artificial Intelligence
community would have better access to some of the structural
modelling methodology developed by the simulation community, its
quest into the understanding of thought processes might be
accelerated.

Apart from the differences in the models that are being used, there
are also differences in the type of simulations that are carried
out. These can best be clarified by using a combination of the
definitions of goals for simulation studies as laid down by Karplus
(1976) and Weizenbaum (1976). These goals are:

a. without requiring knowledge about the structure of the real
   system:

   a1. understanding by imitation (*Mimicry-mode*)
   a2. generation adequate behavior based on whatever suitable
       principle one can find (*Generative-mode)*
   a3. testing theories based on analogies (*Theory-mode*)

b. Requiring some knowledge of the structure of the real system:

   b1. compute behavior based on input data (*Analysis-mode*)
   b2. identify structure based on I/O trajectory pairs
       (*Synthesis-mode*)
   b3. prescribe necesarry input trajectory for required
       behavior (*Control-mode*)

The simulation experience in the Artificial Intelligence community
is mainly concentrated in Class a. while the Simulation and Systems
Research communities have accumulated years of practice in Class b.
Their needs, however, span both worlds as is illustrated in fig. 1.

	A.I.	E.S.	Systems Analysis	System Design	Management & Control
a1. Understand	X		X		
a2. Generate	X	X		X	
a3. Test Theory		X			X
b1. Compute	X		X	X	
b2. Identify		X	X	X	X
b3. Prescribe					X

fig. 1: Simulation Mode Requirements

From this figure further possibilities of mutual assistance and synergy are derivable, as is discussed in the sequel.

4. SOME POTENTIAL BENEFITS TO ARTIFICIAL INTELLIGENCE

The state-of-the-art methods and tools in the area of Modelling & Simulation could benefit the "convential" Artificial Intelligence community in several ways.
In the first place the system-knowledge structuring tools, that have been developed in the simulation context (Zeigler 1979, Zeigler et al. 1980, Rosenblit 1984), can enhance the abilities of the Artificial Intelligence scientist by helping him to map the elements of knowledge he has about certain thought and/or problem solving processes, establishing their hierarchical interdependencies, helping him in pruning general knowledge elements which are unnecessary in certain micro-worlds, mapping semantic hierarchies in dialogue scenarios, etc.

In the second place approved and tested simulation model description techniques could provide better (crisper) representation for cognitive models.
The simulation means, methods and languages available with which it is possible te separate models from experiments like in GEST (Ören 1984b), test applicability of certain experiments (or experimental frames) to specific models (Zeigler 1979) and manage model-frame

pairs (Rosenblit 1984), would allow Artificial Intelligence to concentrate much more on the modelling of e.g. the reasoning or learning process, rather than be forced to reconstruct a complete new experiment with its embedded model every time the requirements change or progress is made.

Although much of the recommendations above are also valid for the Expert System builder and the Knowledge Engineer, additional advantage could be gained from Expert Systems if they would have embedded simulation models to guide their inferencing or improve the dialogue with the user. If these models moreover allow adaptation of parameters (or even better modification of their structure) while in dialogue mode, responses for comparison could be offered to the user of the Expert System in order to home in, in a more orderly fashion - and possibly with less time consuming heuristics -, on the problem at hand.

E.g. in case of a diagnosis system for complex machine malfunctions, the Expert System could require measurements to be made, read them in, compare with its embedded model, and adjust its parameters until the difference in response is such that the model represents the malfunctioning device within an acceptable margin of uncertainty.

A rather well known example of an Expert System for Automotive Troubleshooting (Hayes-Roth 1985), has to rely on a verbal description of time-dependent oscilloscope signals in order to discriminate between certain malfunctions. Therefore in representing knowlegde, Expert Systems, that until now have very little means to adequately represent dynamic variables, could profit from the experience available for this purpose in the simulation field.

5. SOME POTENTIAL BENEFITS TO MODELLING & SIMULATION

Ören (in Ören 1984a) has already offered a rather comprehensive taxonomy of feasable synergies of Artificial Intelligence and simulation. In the referenced publication he shows that Artificial Intelligence can contribute in several modules of a so called "Knowlegde-Based Modelling & Simulation System". He indicates that Artificial Intelligence can positively contribute to several aspects of model utilization:

- through a query system, with which the user could query a model about its behavior or an assembly of models (e.g. stored in a model base), about their common properties or their individual properties with reference to a specific problem
- through a Modelling system, within which facilities are offered to help create models for a specific problem in an already known domain; a collection of basic scientific law knowlegde which can be used to verify general consistency aspects of the model that is to be created and a model processing facility that allows symbolic manipulation of models
- through a Behavior processing system, within which behavior display and analysis can be facilitated.

Shannon (Shannon et al. 1985, Shannon 1985) proposes synergies which are closer to the ideas of heuristic problem solving developed in the early days of Artificial Intelligence (see also the Introduction to this Chapter). He proposes the creation of:

. Domain Knowlegde Bases, that contain an organized base of models
  and domain specific knowlegde whose partial knowlegde can be
  integrated to achieve a coherent model from partial models. These
  partial models being the collection of (parts of) previous models
  specialized, modified or augmented to serve the present modelling
  requirement. These new models are also expected to enrich the
  original store of models. Thus this specific Knowlegde Base
  gradually should know more - and be more usefull - for modelling
  tasks in the relevant domain
. Experimental Design Aids, offering expert advice on the way to
  design appropriate simulation experiments for evaluation,
  prediction, sensitivity, optimization and decision support tasks.
. Model Generator Systems, which - by making use of the two systems
  mentioned earlier - would be able to automatically compose the
  most appropriate model in a specific domain for a specific
  experimental goal.
  This naturally within the realm of the modelling knowledge
  already available in a system that, to be effective, should have
  been in use in the specific domain for quite some time, in order
  to have accumulated sufficient knowlegde for the specific study
. Input Data Management Systems, that can store, manipulate and
  retrieve data for specific modelling exercises within a fixed
  environment like a given manufacturing facility. In this way
  these standard data have to be collected only once for use by
  many models. The intelligence is needed in this case for
  establishing automatically which data are needed for a certain
  simulation experiment
. an Experiment Supervisor, which would watch the simulation run
  and be able to make its 'own' decisions on sample sizes, run
  duration and repetition, based on the nature of the experiment
  prescribed by the user.

Other synergies, which could be added to the suggestions made above
are:

- the use of symbolic processing software to investigate
  (approximate) analytical solutions for mathematical models that
  were already stored in the sytem (e.g.: steady state behavior
  estimates)
- natural language interfaces to advanced modelling systems (see
  e.g. Subramanian and Cannon 1981, whose work was based on Ören's
  GEST (Ören 1984b)
- and last (but not necessarily least) dialogue based simulation
  program generators, of which a few are emerging like KBS
  (McRoberts et al. 1985), MAGEST (Ören 1985), SEE-WHY (Fiddy 1981)
  and CM100 (Elzas 1986).

6. CONCLUSION

Both the Artificial Intelligence and the Simulation community use
MODELS as the main way with which they convey their knowlegde. The
methods and techniques used in modelling for these disciplines are
rather different, both can profit from the results obtained in the
other camp to improve their working conditions and advance the
state-of-the-art in their respective disciplines. Many ideas on how
to proceed are presented in the sequel of this book and in the work
that is continually going on to improve the methodologies in these
fields of research.

7. REFERENCES

NOTE: for all publications of historical importance the oldest retrievable reference has been selected.

Berkeley, E.C. (1949). Giant Brains or Machines that Think. John Wiley & Sons, New York.

Bobrow, D.G. (1968). Natural Language Input for a Computer Problem-solving System. In: Semantic Information Processing, Minsky, M. (Ed.), MIT Press, Cambridge, pp. 135-143.

Brennan, R.D. and R.N. Linebarger (1964). A survey of Digital Simulation: Digital Analog Simulator Programs. In: Simulation, Vol. 3, No. 6, pp. 22-36.

Buchanan, B., G. Sutherland and E.A. Feigenbaum (1969). Heuristic DENDRAL: A Program for Generating Explanatory Hypotheses in Organic Chemistry. In: Machine Intelligence, American Elsevier.

Chomsky, N. (1956). Three models for the description of Language. In: IRE Transactions on Information Theory, Vol. IT-2: Proceedings of the Sept. '56 Symposium on Information Theory.

Elzas, M.S. (1980). Simulation and the Progress of Change. In: Simulation with Discrete Systems: A State-of-the-art View. Ören, Shub, Roth (Eds.), IEEE, New York, pp. 3-18.

Elzas, M.S. (1984). System Paradigms as Reality Mappings. In: Simulation and Model-Based Methodologies: An Integrative View. Ören, Zeigler, Elzas (Eds), Springer-Verlag, Heidelberg, pp. 40-67.

Elzas, M.S., J. Dijkstra, E. Van der Veen and L. Goedhart (1986). Design Study for a system that generates Simulation programs from Entity Structures. Technical Report, Campus SoftWare, Wageningen (In Dutch).

Feigenbaum, E.A. (1977). The Art of Artificial Intelligence: Themes and Case Studies of Knowledge Engineering. In: Proceedings IJCAI-5 '77, pp. 1014-1020.

Fiddy, E. (1981). Understanding Dynamic Systems Using Pattern Recognition. In: Operations Research '81, Brans, J.P. (Ed.), North-Holland, Amsterdam, Conf. Abstracts.

Hamming, R.W. (1958). Frontiers in Computer Technology, In: Proc. 5th Computer Applications Symposium, Oct. '58, Armour Research Foundation of the Illinois Institute of Technology, Chicago,pp. 106-115.

Hayes-Roth, F., D.B. Lenat and D.A. Waterman (Eds.) (1983). Building Expert Systems. Addison-Wesley, Reading, Mass.

Hayes-Roth, F. Rule-Based Systems. In: Communications of the ACM, Vol. 28, No. 9, pp. 923.

Hopper, Grace M. (1952). The Education of a Computer. In: Proc.
    Pittsburgh Meeting of the ACM, May '52.

Karplus, W.J. (1976).The Spectrum of Mathematical Modelling and
    Systems Simulation. In: Simulation of Systems. Dekker, L (Ed.),
    North-Holland, Amsterdam, pp. 5-13.

McRoberts, M., M. Fox and N. Husain (1985). Generating model
    abstraction scenarios in KBS. In: Artificial Intelligence,
    Graphics and Simulation, Birtwistle, G. (Ed.), Simulation
    Councils Inc., San Diego, Ca., pp. 29-33.

Melle, W. van, A.C. Scott, J.S. Bennett and M.A. Peairs (1981). The
    Emycin Manual. Technical Report, Heuristic Programming Project,
    Stanford University.

Minsky, M. (1961). Descriptive Languages and Problem Solving. In:
    Proceedings '61 WJCC as reprinted in Loc. cit. sub Bobrow,
    pp. 419-422.

Neumann, J. von (1958). The Computer and the Brain. Yale University
    Press, New Haven, Conn.

Newell, A. and H.A. Simon (1956). The Logic Theory Machine. In: IRE
    Transactions on Information Theory, Vol. IT-2, No. 3.

Newell, A,. J.C. Shaw and H.A. Simon (1957). Empirical Explorations
    of the Logic Theory Machine: A Case Study in Heuristic. In:
    Proceedings Western Joint Computer Conference, Febr. '57,
    pp. 218-239.

Ören, T.I. (1984a). Model-Based Activities: A Paradigm Shift. In:
    Loc. cit. sub Elzas (1984), pp. 3-40.

Ören, T.I. (1984b). GEST: A modelling and simulation based on system
    theoretic concepts. In: Loc.cit. sub Elzas (1984), pp. 281-335.

Ören, T.I. (1985) Architecture of MAGEST: A knowledge-based
    modelling and simulation system. In: Simulation in Research and
    Development, A. Javor, (Ed.), North-Holland, Amsterdam.

Papert, S. (1980). Mindstorms, Children, Computers and Powerful
    Ideas. CN 5077, Basic Books Inc., New York.

Rosenblit, J.W. EXP- A Software Tool for Experimental Frame
    Specification in Discrete Event Modelling and Simulation. In:
    Proceedings .'84 SCSC, Simulation Councils Inc., San Diego, Ca.,
    pp. 967-981.

Sargent, R.G. (1984). Simulation Model Validation. In: Loc. cit. sub
    Elzas (1984), pp. 537-555.

Seflfrigde, R.G. (1955). Coding a General Purpose Digital Computer
    to Operate as a Differential Analyzer. In: Proceedings '55
    Western Joint Computer Conference, pp. 82-84.

Shannon,R.E., R. Mayer and H.H. Adelsberger (1985). Expert Systems
    and Simulation. In: Simulation, Vol. 44, No. 6, pp. 275-284.

Shannon, R.E., (1985). Models and Artificial Intelligence. Invited
    paper presented at Knowledge-Based Modelling and Simulation
    Methodologies Conference, Papendal, July '85.

Subrahmanian, E. and R.L. Cannon (1981). A Generator Program for
    Models of Discrete Event Systems. In: Simulation, Vol. 36,
    No. 3, pp. 93-101.

Turing, A.M. (1947), reprinted -after his death- as: Computing
    Machinery and Intelligence. In: Minds and Machines,
    A. Ross Anderson (Ed.), Prentice-Hall, Englewood Cliffs, 1964,
    from p. 11.

Weizenbaum, J. (1966). A Computer Program for the study of Natural
    Language Communication between Man and Machine. In:
    Communications of the ACM, Vol. 9, No. 1, pp. 36-44.

Weizenbaum, J. (1976). Computer Power and Human Reason. W.H. Freeman
    & Co., San Francisco, pp. 165.

Winograd, T. (1972). Understanding Natural Language. In: Cognitive
    Psycology, No. 3, Academic Press, New York, pp. 8-28.

Zeigler, B.P. (1979). Structuring principles for multifacetted
    system modelling. In: Methodology in Systems Modelling and
    Simulation, North-Holland, Amsterdam, pp. 93-135.

Zeigler, B.P., D. Belogus and A. Bolshoi (1980). ESP: An Interactive
    Tool for System Structuring. In: Proceedings EMCSR'80, Vienna,
    Hemisphere Press, New York.

Zeigler, B.P., (1984). Multifacetted Modelling and Discrete Event
    Simulation. Academic Press, London, Chapters 3, 15, 16 and 17.

Modelling and Simulation Methodology
in the Artificial Intelligence Era
M.S. Elzas, T.I. Ören and B.P. Zeigler (Editors)
© Elsevier Science Publishers B.V. (North-Holland), 1986

Chapter I.2

SYSTEM KNOWLEDGE: A DEFINITION AND ITS IMPLICATIONS

Bernard P. Zeigler

Department of Electrical and Computer Engineering
University of Arizona
Tucson, Arizona 85721

A definition of knowledge is given in the form of
criteria for a system's knowing about a class objects or relations. To illustrate the definition,
some types of knowledge involved in the modelling
and simulation enterprise are discussed. Such
considerations become important when considering
the design of intelligent agents capable of modelling each other.

Although the term "knowledge" is ubiquitously used in the artificial
intelligence literature, it is rarely given a precise definition.
In such contexts, it seems to connote facts and relationships that
can be manipulated by inferencing and problem solving procedures.
Yet there are many types of knowledge recognized in daily life, science and philosophy that do not seem to be encompassed by such a
connotation, at least at first glance. Distinctions in the kinds of
knowledge that a system may have will be increasingly important as
ambitions for machine intelligence become greater. Since such distinctions fail to be made with a loose approach to knowledge definition, we shall offer a first attempt at a definition which is oriented toward a pragmatic approach to incorporating intelligence into
systems.

We say that a system "knows about" a class of objects, or relations,
if it has an internal representation for the class which enables it
to operate on objects in this class and to communicate with others
about such operations. Thus, if a system knows about X, a class of
objects, or of relations on objects, it is able to use an internal
representation of the class in at least the following ways:

receive information about the class, generate elements in
the class, recognize members of the class and discriminate
them from other class members, answer questions about the
class, and take into account information about changes in
the class members.

The above list of criteria is a minimal one since one can extend it
to include additional desirable capabilities. For example, one can
add the ability to interrogate others in order to fill in any information perceived as lacking about a particular member of X.

It is doubtful that any system, human or artificial, each with its
own fallibilities, could be verified empirically as knowing about
some particular class under such a definition. Yet we can interpret the definition as presenting a goal for system design that will
be approximated as closely as design objectives require, and
resources and knowledge (the designer's) permit. Thus, "giving a
system knowledge about X" can be taken as a location for designing
into it the above-mentioned abilities concerning X to a degree that
must be specified ultimately in the design requirements for the

system to be constructed.

1. KNOWLEDGE RELATED TO MODEL SYNTHESIS

In these terms, let us consider three types of relationships that
can be "wired in" to a system: decomposition, taxonomic, and coupling. A system knows about decomposition if it has schemes for
representing the manner in which an object is decomposed into components, and can operate on, and communicate about, such schemes.
For example, consider a simulation program that was designed to reflect a decomposition of a complex system into simpler components.
While the designer can be said to know about the decomposition (according to the definition of knowing just given), the program does
not. The reason is that such a program consists only of executable
statements for generating the behavior of the components. It does
not have schemes for representing decompositions and cannot operate
on, nor communicate with others about, such schemes. However, the
program can be said to know about the behavior of the system being
modelled - to the extent that the model undelying it is valid, it can
generate this behavior and can answer certain "what if" questions
about the system relating to this behavior.

Consider in contrast, an intelligent system that knows about decomposition of the system just discussed. To satisfy the definition of
"knows about decomposition" such an intelligent system would have to
have a scheme for representing decompositions of the type employed
in designing the program. It would be able to accept a description
of such a decomposition, generate its own internal representation of
it, change this internal representation when receiving new information about the decomposition, and answer questions about the decomposition. Knowledge to this level of capability is a kind of "active"
documentation. More capability would enable the system to generate
a simulation program from its internal representation. To do this
would require knowledge of more than just the decomposition. It
requires the taxonomic and coupling knowledge mentioned earlier.

By taxonomic knowledge, we mean a representation for the kinds of
variants that are possible for objects <u>i.e.</u>, how objects may be categorized and sub-classified. For example, a system could know that
cars can be station wagons or sedans, and that the latter can be of
the two-door or four-door variety.

To construct a model of a system, models for the components of a
decomposition must be coupled together. Thus, the third kind of
knowledge that a system can have is that of coupling relationships
and constraints.

The system entity structure described in (Zeigler, 1984) provides
a knowledge representation scheme that encompasses the three kinds
of knowledge just discussed (see also chapter II.2 by Rozenblit and
Zeigler in this volume).

2. EMPIRICAL KNOWLEDGE ABOUT A SYSTEM

A kind of distinction not well characterized in the loose approach
mentioned above is that between empirical and formal knowledge. Empirical knowledge is usually associated with "facts" and formal knowledge with "inference rules" for manipulating these facts to generate
new ones. However, in modelling of real world systems, there is a
much more extensive inference chain between empirical knowledge acquired in observation of system behavior and the structure attributed

to it on the basis of such observed behavior. Indeed, there is a hierarchy of levels at which a system may be described (Zeigler,1984). According to our definition, these levels should also serve as levels at which knowledge about a system may be acquired, manipulated and communicated. Indeed, in another formulation, the hierarchy of system descriptions is called the epistemological hierarchy (Klir, 1985). The processes of acquiring knowledge at these levels, which constitute a significant portion of the overall effort in modelling and simulation, have been extensively considered by Zeigler (1984) and Klir (1985).

3. SYSTEM KNOWLEDGE ABOUT OTHER SYSTEMS

If we now shift our focus from the traditional one in which a human modeller is acquiring and utilizing knowledge about a system, to one in which an intelligent agent is similarly engaged, the full force of our definition of "system knowledge" may be appreciated. We now can envision systems that can know about other systems: *i.e.*, they can operated upon representations of other systems and communicate about these operations. Indeed, "knowledgeable" systems may construct, and communicate among themselves about, models of each other. The hierarchy of epistemological levels, and the processes for knowledge acquisition and manipulation, should provide a basis for designing agents of this kind. The considerations characterized by Elzas (1984) should then help in this regard.

Of course, such systems may model each other in order to better cooperate, or to more effectively compete, with one another. We have argued elsewhere that a pair of antagonistic agents, such as "smart missiles," cannot each possess valid models of the other: the loser is defeated precisely because of deficiences in its model about the winner (Zeigler, 1985). If for no other reason than discovering truths about one another, it seems that we should seek co-operative implementations of knowledgeable agents.

REFERENCES

Elzas, M. S. (1984), System Paradigms as Reality Mappings. In: Simulation and Model-Based Methodologies: An Integrative View, Springer-Verlag, Berlin, pp. 41-68.

Klir, G. J. (1985), Architecture of Systems Problem Solving, Plenum Press, New York, 539 p.

Rozenblit, J. W. and B. P. Zeigler, Entity-based Structures for Model and Experimental Frame Construction. Chapter II.2, this volume.

Zeigler, B. P. (1985), On the Concept of Validity for Model Embedded Systems, Proc. of 1985 Society for General Systems Research Meeting, San Francisco, Intersystems Press.

Zeigler, B. P. (1984), Multifaceted Modelling and Discrete Event Simulation, Academic Press, London, 300 p.

Modelling and Simulation Methodology
in the Artificial Intelligence Era
M.S. Elzas, T.I. Ören and B.P. Zeigler (Editors)
© Elsevier Science Publishers B.V. (North-Holland), 1986

Chapter I.3

THE APPLICABILITY OF ARTIFICIAL INTELLIGENCE TECHNIQUES TO KNOWLEDGE
REPRESENTATION IN MODELLING AND SIMULATION.

M.S. Elzas

Agricultural University
Department of Computer Science
Wageningen/The Netherlands

The developments in Artificial Intelligence and
Knowledge Engineering techniques during the last
few years has shown that succesfull prototypes of
Knowledge-Based systems can be constructed, using
general knowledge representation techniques - that
were developed by the Artificial Intelligence
community - in a restricted domain of human activity.
The main requirement on such a domain is that the
basic describing its knowledge - and the way in which
it is used - are limited in number and clearly
definable. Recent developments in Modelling &
Simulation Methodology have brought order and
structure into its terminology and its working
methods. This, in itself, makes the field a prime
candidate for investigation of applicability of
Knowledge Engineering techniques to an entire field.
In order to assess the possible implications of such
a development, this chapter first investigates
Modelling & Simulation with regard to Knowledge
Acquisition and Knowledge Structuring aspects. After
this review of activities, Knowledge Representation
methods like Entity Trees, Semantic Nets, Similarity
Nets and Entity Lattices will be discussed.
Finally some concepts (Classes, Rules and Frames)
will be described in the light of a synergy between
Modelling & Simulation and Artificial Intelligence.

1. INTRODUCTION

The increasing degree of activity in the area of Expert Systems has
helped discover the need for a "new" engineering discipline:
Knowledge Engineering. This discipline is expected to concentrate
its activities on the processes preceding the construction of
Knowledge Bases and Expert Systems. In order to operate adequately
- as a discipline - knowledge engineering will have to make new
- basic - inroads into knowledge acquisition and representation.
The basic tenets and axioms of this field are therefore still to be
discovered.

Notwithstanding this state of affairs it is not too early to inspect
the knowledge engineering aspects of Modelling & Simulation, because
the synergies detected in this way might help reinforce this
emerging discipline.

Modelling & Simulation is in an advantageous position for this task:
not only has the use of models always been a common aspect of
Simulation and Artificial Intelligence (see also Chapter I.1 of this
book), but also the type of application of knowledge engineering of
main importance to modelling and simulation falls within the
category of most succesfull applications of Expert Systems to date.
It is well known that Expert System techniques have been quite
succesfull in offering assistance in diagnostic and classification
problems. These are exactly the type of problems the modeller is
faced with in the initial stage of system analysis and model design.
Moreover, the fact that at that stage the entities he manipulates
can be considered to be static and deterministic in nature,
diminishes the risk of venturing outside of the domain of expertise
acquired within knowledge engineering to date (see e.g. Zeigler's
Chapter I.2). In stating this it is also fair to acknowledge that
this situation is not exceptional: the initial phase of analysis of
information systems in general, also displays some of these welcome
characteristics as is shown, e.g. in Simons and Wieringa (1986).

What has been said above about the knowledge engineering aspects of
modelling and simulation, can be extended to subjects in the area of
representation of characteristics of models - e.g. for model
retrieval - using formalisms that formerly were used exclusively in
the domain of Artificial Intelligence.
The massive investments in the construction of multi-facetted models
for all kinds of relevant applications forces the field into
reconsidering the state-of-the-art modelbuilding approaches, yet
another reason to investigate a neighbouring discipline for possible
advantageous synergies.

2. KNOWLEDGE ACQUISITION IN THE MODELLING CONTEXT

While the "normal" procedure of knowledge acquisition, in the
context of Expert Systems, is to extract all necessary knowledge
from (only) one expert through having him interviewed by a small
team of knowledge engineers; in the Modelling & Simulation context
the knowledge has to be extracted directly from a (perceived) real
system, by an (often quite large) multidisciplinary team of persons
experienced in modelling and/or simulation, but not necessarily
acquainted with professional information gathering or knowledge
acquisition techniques.
One of the possible outcomes of applying expert-system like
techniques to the Modelling & Simulation process might well
therefore be that several levels of knowledge - connected in a
hierarchy - might have to be handled. Thus while in the "normal"
situation only one level of knowledge is to be collected, in the
modelling context several levels of knowledge of several types have
to be collected and, moreover, sufficient information on how to
decide which knowledge to use if the different levels or types are
in conflict with eachother.
A simple example may clarify these points.

Assume that the modelling task is the multifacetted modelling of a
car. Members of the modelling team are e.g. mechanical engineers,
industrial engineers, aerodynamicists, market specialists and
automobile regulation experts.
According to established practice part of the team will endeavour to
undertake the "pure" modelling of the car and others will mainly

serve to formulate the questions that the modelling exercise will
have to yield answers to (they contribute to the design of the
experimental frames (Zeigler 1979)). One can state that the shape of
the car, the subject the industrial engineers are experts in, is
subservient to the functional requirements which are being modelled
e.g. by the mechanical engineers and the aerodynamicists.
Clearly decision rules are needed in case the respective models
clash in a conflict of interfaces - or even model design itself -
where e.g. the mechanical design does not fit within the body or the
aerodynamic properties of the chosen shape do not fall within the
maximum energy expenditure tolerances set by the marketing people.
Even if these conflicts are reconciled it might still be possible
that the legal and safety departments come up with "what if"
questions that cannot be answered by the model as it is, (Frames not
applicable to models (Zeigler 1979, pp. 121-124)). Today, the normal
procedure would be to iterate the system analysis and model design
activities until an acceptable solution is found. The application of
thorough, and adequately specialized, knowledge acquisition
techniques underpinned by appropriate knowledge processing software
(see e.g. Chapter II.1), can clearly make this whole process far
more efficient in time and satisfying in results.
The levels of knowledge mentioned above are not the only ones that
are relevant to such modelling processes. It is deemed to be clear
that items of "general knowledge" like basic laws of physiscs,
knowledge about dimension consistency principles, knowledge of
mathematical principles and numerical thechniques has to be acquired
and stored in such a fashion that it is applicable to a wide range
of models.
The same holds for many application oriented software tools which
can be subservient to the modelling or simulation tasks (see for
example Spriet and Vansteenkiste (1982), Chapter 6).

From what has been stated above it can be concluded that knowledge
in the Modelling & Simulation context does not form a unified and/or
homogeneous body like in most of the domains for which Expert
Systems have been developed.
The modelling and simulation context requires the modelling and
simulation knowledge engineer to be able to collect, reason about
and (re)organize knowledge that is stratified (not always in direct
meta- or meta-meta relationships) and multidisciplinary.
Some work on acquisition methodology has been done in this direction
in the area of information system analysis and design (e.g. by
Lundeberg e.a. (1978)), leading to the conclusion that on knowledge
acquisition methodology issues and practice the modelling and
simulation community could profit handsomely from cooperation, not
only with the Artificial Intelligence field, but also with the much
larger group of persons engaged in General Information Systems
Research.

3. KNOWLEDGE STRUCTURING

From the previous paragraph on knowledge acquisition considerations
one can deduce that the knowledge acquired in the initial stage of a
modelling exercise can be considered to be structured in a hierarchy
of epistomological levels, a hierarchy of decomposition into
disciplinary aspects and system substructures within these levels
and a hierarchy of frames and instances of (simulation) experiments
within these frames.

This stratified approach to knowledge structures is not unique to modelling and simulation. Work on the larger information and Expert Systems, which by nature have to handle a large amount of items of knowledge, has led to the rediscovery of entity structures by scientists in those fields (see e.g. Wieringa and Curwiel (1986) and Findler (1979)).

In this last reference thourough discussions can be found on rather recent developments in semantic nets and associative knowledge representation. Most of the work in this area is apparently oriented towards understanding of - and inferencing from - natural language scripts.

This field, quite naturally, is much wider and less specialized than Modelling & Simulation which has imbedded structures of its own, based on paradigms of General Systems Research augmented with some considerations that mainly cater for implementability and maintainability of models.

As an area of knowledge consisting of unconnected, single items, is hard to imagine, any attempt at structuring a body of knowledge must at least lead to partioning the body in smaller parts within which groups of items or objects, united by some common denominator,exist. Such partitioning is accepted state-of-the-art practice by now, as well in Artificial Intelligence (e.g. the Spaces and Vistas mentioned in Hendrix (1979)) as in Modelling & Simulation (Mathematical Model versus Experimental Frame: Oren and Zeigler (1979)).

Therefore, if one is to study the general principles of Knowledge Engineering for Modelling & Simulation, it might be worthwhile to look into possible partitioning/clustering ideas in Artificial Intelligence and evaluate their merits for Modelling & Simulation. Brachman (in Brachman (1979), p. 39) outlines some basic relational principles which are needed to allow sensible structuring of items of knowledge or ordering of concepts, while Zeigler in Spriet and Vansteenkiste (1982) proposes some novel structuring principles for systematic model decomposition.

These, and other, publications form the basis of the structuring elements presented in the sequel. Elaborating from Hendrix (1979), one can state that knowledge representation for Modelling & Simulation, based on structured conceptual objects (called entities in most areas of computer science nowadays), must account for the following - minimum - relationships:

1. the relationship between Entity and its Aspects or Specializations
2. the relationship between Entity and (at least) one of its decompositions
3. the Specialization structure of an Aspect (with other words the relation of an Aspect or Specialization with its sub-Aspects or sub-Specializations)
4. the relation between subsequent Entity decompositions
5. possible relationships between partial decompositions and sub-Aspects or -Specializations.

Zeigler's structuring paradigm is in accordance with all of these conditions, because his approach is, in essence, limited to wholly deterministic systems of which the (de-)composition is unequivocal and static. The fundamental relationship conditions outlined above are met, in Zeigler's case, by imposing strict hierarchy in the resulting decomposition tree, strict uniformity among sub-decompositions of tree-nodes (entities, aspects, specializations)

with the same name and strict adherence to alternation of modes.
(Meaning that a node that represents an entity must always first
branch out into aspects or specializations before leading to lower
echelon entity nodes and vice versa).
As an additional feature for systems in which multiple occurences
can be found of an entity with the same name and attribute-set, but
with a possible difference in attribute-values while in operation,
the concept of an entity-type was introduced by Zeigler in his 1982
publication (the other basic tenets of his structuring paradigm can
already be found in Zeigler (1979)).
Although effort is being put into developing methodologies for so
called "Variable Structure Systems" (see this book Chapters IV.1:
Zeigler, and IV.3: Hogeweg, Hesper), these mainly contribute to the
description of structures of models where either the variability
occurs according to a plan or strategy known beforehand (Zeigler) or
to reflect "optimal" structure search strategies embedded in the
model (Hogeweg).

These, naturally, are extremely relevant examples of systems of
which the structural "map" can change while the system is in
operation, but still represent a unique vision on candidate
components for such a system.
Now, in Modelling & Simulation like in Artificial Intelligence, the
composition of an object or item of knowledge is hard to establish
in a unique fashion for any realistic multifacetted system.
(Multifacetted meaning that these systems consist of many subsystems
which are essentially different in nature: in principle they are
depositories of multi- and inter-disciplinary knowledge).
So, in a similar fashion to the one with which the lack of objective
means to validate the truthfullness of some item of knowledge is
handled in Artificial Intelligence, the concept of approximately
correct decompositions of systems can be introduced in Modelling &
Simulation.
This implies that in such circumstances decompositions of systems
are not anymore unique, but "fuzzy", where the degree of certainty
of a certain decomposition is based on the strength of the evidence
supporting this specific decomposition. This evidence can be
constructed in one out of several ways: e.g. on basis of previous
structure-validation data (obtained through simulation and
identification processes), the number of times this decomposition
has been chosen over others when a model was used (assessed e.g. by
means of a model base monitor), the size (and qualifications) of the
team that established the decomposition (modelling by consesus?) or
simply the measure of belief in this representation put forward by
one or more users of the model. This then clearly implies that at
every node in any structure-tree there are a number of alternate
further decomposition paths, each with its respective degree of
certainty. The conjunction of all certainty factors for a chosen
decomposition path (or rather -tree as the structure has become a
multi-dimensional tree or -lattice in the meantime), yields a
certainty factor for the finally chosen model structure.
Such an enhancement of the-state-of-the-art system structuring tools
might very well alleviate some of the model base problems that
Kettenis indicates in Chapter II.3 of this book.
Of course the applicability of these enhancements depends strongly
on the strength of knowledge representation methods for this
purpose.

4. KNOWLEDGE REPRESENTATION REQUIREMENTS

It is deemed evident by now that the specific aspects of Modelling & Simulation knowledge acquisition and knowledge structuring impose some restrictive rules on knowledge representation possibilities, especially since the tools that will have to be developed will have to function on state-of-the-art computing machinery. (A good reference text on this subject viewed from the Expert Systems context is Negoita (1985)).
These representation requirements can be summarized as follows:

1. *Generality:* the basic elements of a knowledge representation scheme in the Modelling & Simulation context should be as application independent as possible, allowing liberal adaptation of the representation vehicle to the needs of the various disciplines which will participate in the model building and simulation activity. This implies:

   1a. basic construction elements for trees and lattices, general enough to describe all types of nodes encountered in the structures described above. (Example: the ITOC or item occurence of Belogus (1985) which possesses a name, attributes (=variables, parameters, conditions), mode (=entity, aspect, specialisation, type), substructure (=decomposition and associated certainty factors) and context (=aggregation relationships))

   1b. multifacetted access facilities, allowing divergence of nomenclature between the different classes of builders/users of the decomposition structure. (Example: the tolerance of multiple name referral to the same node by the use of synonims with completely equivalent status as well for ITOC's as for their attributes (Belogus loc.cit.), the use of labels for nodes in conjunction with a translation table (Zeigler 1984), the representation of these labels by icons etc.).

2. *Consistency:* the construction and utilisation requirements of a Modelling & Simulation knowledge representation scheme, dictate the presence of axioms which preserve the integrity of the structuring relationships under all circumstances of acquisition and utilization. This implies:

   2a. uniform interpretation of items with all their associated elements (e.g. name-sets are unique, items are uniquely bound to modes, variables and substructures)

   2b. strictly defined geometry and dependency rules (trees and lattices are graphs, their utilization in this context requires them to be directed graphs with unambiguous conventions as to the hierarchy of relationships, the nature of subsumptions (see also Finin and Silverman (1986), Corella (1986) and Ait-Kaci (1986)), antecedents <-> consequents routing, absolute location of nodes, traversing conventions (what is "up", "down", "left", "right", "front" or "back" and what is their reach? E.g., must moving left be restricted to branches referring to the node one is "under" or can it allow jumping into other decompositions?)

3. *Finiteness:* the knowledge representation scheme should guarantee that the trees or lattices that are built are not only finite in their number of nodes and branches but will also lead to a terminating path during traversing operations at inspection vs. retrieval time.

All these requirements have to be taken "sensu stricto", meaning that failure to comply with any one of the requirements will invalidate the knowledge representation scheme, either because it will not allow sufficiently powerfull representation or because the resulting structures will not be implementable or usable on a computer.
In fig. 1 a table is presented that checks the (potential) adherence to these requirements of several types of state-of-the-art knowledge storage and retrieval systems.
In the table CDBMS denotes the class of CODASYL database management systems, RDBMS the class of relational DBMS's, KBMS knowledge of base management systems (like Carnegie Mellon's CAT/SDMS or Stanford's KBMS, etc.), EDS stands for Expert Database Systems (Tentatively described in Smith (1986) and ESP for Belogus' and Zeigler's Entity Structuring Program (Schoenmakers (1986) and Belogus (1984)).

Requirement → Product ↓	1a	1b	2a	2b	3
CDBMS				ok	ok
RDBMS			ok	ok	ok
EDS		ok	ok	ok	?
KBMS	ok	?		ok	?
ESP		ok	ok	ok	ok

fig.1: Comparison of Knowledge Representation Abilities

From this table one can deduce that Expert Database Systems and Entity Structuring Programs come nearest to the requirements for Knowledge Representation in Modelling & Simulation.
However, the former do not exist yet and the latter are not yet general enough to support uncertainties, conditional decompositions and lattices.
Therefore it can be considered to be worthwhile to investigate other means of knowledge representation, like Semantic Nets, Similarity Nets and Entity Lattices in the following paragraphs.

5. SEMANTIC NETS

Semantic Nets have been used in Artificial Intelligence to represent
a variety of kinds of knowledge for a variety of applications.
Winston (1975) has shown that - using semantic nets - it is possible
to construct a program that is able to build up a structural
description of compound (but still: simple) geometrical objects
based on an initial knowledge of simple instances of selected basic
components in a specific domain.
As mentioned before Hendrix (1979) has shown that partitioning of
semantic nets allows the introduction of generalized concepts as
elements in the net. Hendrix's concept of a *space* is meant to
contain a partial net that has a specific (repeating) function in a
specific context. (E.g., a syntactic unit in a natural language
sentence.)
Such a *space* can thus be considered to be a kind of meta-node in a
semantic net. In a similar vein this idea was generalized further,
to allow meta-spaces or *vistas*, which then could represent certain
concepts about specific types of e.g. common properties of some
syntactic units in natural language sentences.
This vista concept is particularly usefull for machine understanding
of a *set* of sentences in one context, as these vistas can now be
used to find recurring syntactic units in connected phrases and thus
allow context-dependent interpretations to some extent (see also
Rich (1983)).

Coming back to Modelling & Simulation: it has been shown (e.g. in
Elzas (1984)) that the first - informal - description of a model is
mostly an ill-defined assembly of concepts and ideas, often
expressed in verbal or pictorial (schematic) form by a multidisciplinary team. The task of bringing this, rather vague and
incoherent, first *base model* description into a form amenable for
conversion into a formal model specification is often difficult and
time-consuming. Quite often shortcuts will be taken that tend to
omit parts of the model which the individual proponent finds hard to
describe in a formal way, thus potentially yielding a model
specification which does not make optimal use of the knowledge that
is available.
Partitioned semantic nets can be used to advantage to improve the
initial system-analysis/model-building process, as well in the case
that there is no specific previous knowledge about modelling such a
system as in the case that some knowledge is available (e.g. in a
model base).
A simple example might be usefull to clarify these concepts.

Assume a team consisting of an automotive engineer, a planning
officer of a bus company and a financial expert are discussing a
model for the design of a novel type of bus. At a certain point
during their exchange of ideas they all use the word *performance*.
Naturally, even when using the same word, they are not thinking
about identical concepts.
To the engineer *performance* is tied to the concepts {weight, power,
resistance, fuel-consumption, loading-state, geometrical dimensions,
etc.}.
To the planning officer *performance* is tied to the concepts
{reliability, (un)loading-time, manoeuvrability, mean-time-to-repair
maintenance-frequency, etc.}.
Finally to the financial expert the same word recalls concepts like
{return-on-investment, maintenance-costs, depreciation, etc.}.

It is deemed to have become clear by now that the semantic net notions of Spaces and Vistas are closely tied to the Modelling & Simulation notion of a decomposition structure containing a hierarchy of Aspects and/or Specializations.

In the example the Vistas (=highest level Aspects/Specializations) are clearly Engineering, Scheduling, Economy. First level sub-aspects are Automotive, Public Transportation and Capital-goods management. Only at the next level down one does meet Specializations which can be considered to be equivalent to Spaces, e.g. aerodynamics, mechanics, industrial design, traffic engineering, resource management etc.

Even without any access to a relevant model base an initial investment in the creation of a structured knowledge base that contains Spaces and Vistas that are appropriate for some specific composition of a modelling team could already allow some form of natural language dialogue based initial systems description parsing, leading to a rough outline of the type of queries to which the model should be able to propose an answer.

In some (even partially) adequate model base would be available and some structuring knowledge present, the recognition of (partial) models from the concepts used in the discussion could possibly lead a sophisticated system for modelling assistance to offer a "bibliography" of possibly adequate candidate-models that it has in store.

As a conclusion to this paragraph one can remark that, if one would endeavour to build a modelling-support system which is to have a natural language interface, a choice for a knowledge representation system which makes use of partitioned semantic nets can be profitable.

This would especially be true if the Vistas and Spaces in such a system allow a finer hierarchical subdivision commensurate with the hierarchy of Aspects and Specializations that is needed for modelling applications.

The other "understanding" aspects of such a natural language interface may, on the other hand, be quite a lot simpler than what is usually needed to interpret languages as the main function of such an interface is to look for references to already known models and entity structures.

6. SIMILARITY NETS

To facilitate the search for matching concepts when trying to use already stored knowledge, Minsky (1975) proposed a system consisting of a net of objects linked through a directed graph, where the links refer to resemblances between the items of knowledge represented by the objects in the net. These resemblances can be considered to be "driven" by the stored attributes of the objects. The resulting network is a lattice of partial orderings of concepts, where the sequencing is based on the degree of similarity between concepts. Once key knowledge elements have been stored in such a similarity net, traversals of such a net offer the possibility to adequately search for the nearest conceptual match to a specific query for an element of knowledge in the base, if some starting point can be given on basis of certain attributes of the element which fall within the class of the attributes that are associated with the objects in the similarity net.

An illustration of such a net and typical traversal paths is given in fig. 2. The example has been chosen on purpose for the illustration of the utility of semantic nets for Modelling & Simulation applications.

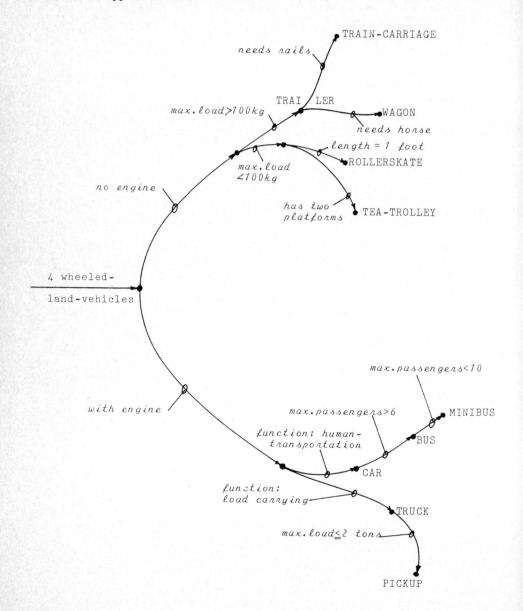

Fig. 2: Similarity Net for some 4-WHEELED LAND-VEHICLE Models.

The objects stored in the net are all vehicles of a certain class.
These vehicles form a sub-class of the general family of vehicles,
as is shown in the relevant specialization taxonomy tree in fig. 3.
Models of similar objects will mostly all have a (restricted) set of
attributes (e.g. variables) that are to be found in all members of
the model family.
In case of vehicles these attributes will almost certainly be
variables or parameters that describe: dimensions, geometry, mass,
speed, acceleration, trajectory (including the nature of its
medium), means of propulsion and load carrying capacity.
These attributes form prime candidates for specialization taxonomy
trees, as can be seen in the relevant illustration.

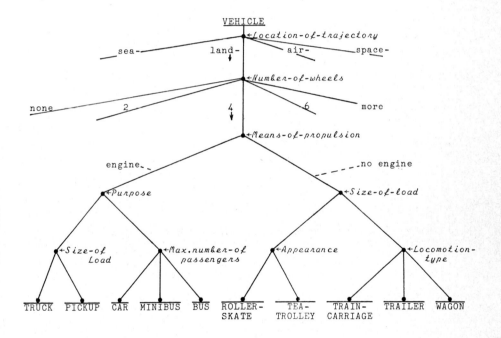

Fig. 3: A Specialization Taxonomy Tree for VEHICLE.

Specialization trees have some points in common with entity trees, but do not reflect the components and structure of the relevant models. They can rather be considered to be the cognitive structure that connects a family of entity structures of models of similar systems. In this way entity structures of related systems can be connected in a single (multi-dimensional) network of lattice, that can be traversed - for browsing and retrieval purposes - using a technique identical to the similarity net approach of Minsky.

Another way to look at the similarity between several models (or different decompositions of the same model) is to take into account the uncertainties inherent in the concepts that describe the modelled entity ot the degree of validity of certain model decompositions for a specific application.
As an illustration of the uncertainty in concepts, let us have a brief look at another example from the VEHICLE-world.
Assume the concept "selfpropelled" would have been used in fig. 3 instead of "with an engine". A discussion can arise immediately on the question if a quadricycle (4-wheeled vehicle propelled in the same way as a bycicle), would have to be classified under "selfpropelled" or not. The argument in favour - based on considerations of similarity - could be that, although a person is needed to actuate the pedals in the quadricycle in order to get it to move, a car is also not able to ride without a driver in control of accelerator- and brake-pedals.
The argument against would naturally be that human energy is the only source of power for the vehicle (except when going downhill or being pushed by the wind, of course!). Even the general (Webster) definition of "self-propelled": *moved forwards by One's or its own force or momentum* does not resolve the matter. Therefore any choice that is made can certainly not be given a certainty factor of 1! Similar situations can arise when comparing different decompositions of one and the same entity.

Take for example different models of the rear train of car-like vehicles as they could occur in a model base of an automotive industry. Consider three types of suspension: stiff axle and elliptic springs, independent suspensions (no axle), De Dion rear axle.
The first type of rear train arrangement is most common in trucks and similar heavy vehicles, the second type in normal modern sedans especially those with front wheel drive and the last category is quite common for sophisticated sportscars. This would be reflected in the knowledge structure that governs the specific body of rear train models.
Taking into account that the knowledge management system *knows* that there are different types of similars and can recognize them by means of a dialogue with the user, the model base management system will allocate certainty factors to the different models of the rear train depending on the type of vehicle that is being modelled.
E.g. if the type of vehicle for which a model is being built is a sportscar, the certainty associated to the rear train model consisting of a rigid rear axle and elliptic springs will be low, while the De Dion system would score quite high on the certainty scale.
In this way the user of the model base can be helped to find the *most obvious* types of (sub)model for his application.

Naturally this would require the existence of possibilities to traverse the model base along a path of a given certainty factor range.

The objects in the similarity net are, in such a case, not only linked by ties of *conceptual similarity* but also by ties of *comparable certainty*.

This makes the resulting similarity nets as well *dynamic* (in the sense of varying in composition depending on the application on hand) but also *three dimensional* because searches must be possible as well on basis of conceptual similarity as on basis of similar certainty.

A last point to be discussed under this heading is the question of *functional similarity* of (sub)models.

Through this type of similarity the likeness of the mathematical models of different (sub)systems or concepts can be expressed. Example: the same first-order differential equation can describe as well the behavior of an R-C network, a simple hydraulic system or a fermentation process in a finite environment, the well known biharmonic equation can describe an electronic oscillator, a simplified version of the partial differential equation of a vibrating string, etc.

It appears that this type of similarity is very hard to handle in a uniform way, as the research into model bases has shown, which - until now - has in a large extent been focussed on this approach (see also Kettenis' Chapter II.3 in this book).

Added to the difficulty of appropriately comparing mathematical models, without exactly knowing what they represent in real life, there is the problem that several mathematical representations of the same system can be considered - and proved - to be equivalent under certain circumstances. (See e.g. Zeigler (1984), pp. 56 and 63-65, where it is shown that the differential equation representation of a system can be mapped to a discrete event formalism).

Therefore, in the contrast to the general position being held before in the Modelling & Simulation community, studying the Artificial Intelligence achievements in storing and retrieving items of knowledge leads to the conclusion that model bases stand more chance of success if based on similarities that are connected to direct cognitive elements, rather than the mathematical formulation of models.

7. ENTITY LATTICES

In the previous paragraphs several ways of structuring system knowledge were presented, amongst others: Entity Structure Trees, Specialization Taxonomy Trees and nets of substructures for identical entities that have different degrees of validity (certainty) for different modelling applications: these shall be called Uncertainty Nets henceforward.

In a repository of modelling (and simulation) knowledge one must expect all these specific structures to be interconnected in order to allow searches of the relevant model-knowledge space to yield candidate models that fulfill some set of requirements of a user operating in a known environment.

Because of this, simple trees or other two dimensional network concepts, are no longer adequate for the (graphical) representation of the resulting object relationships. Therefore, taking into account that there are three components in the relationships: Specialization, Composition and Certainty (= validity for a specific case), the choice for a three dimensional graph - a LATTICE - as a means for representation of this knowledge structure is advocated.

The principle and main properties of such a lattice are illustrated
in fig. 4, using the VEHICLE examples that were discussed earlier on
in this Chapter.

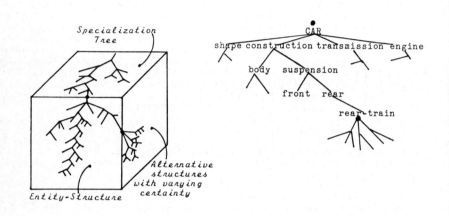

a) ENTITY-LATTICE   c) ENTITY-STRUCTURE

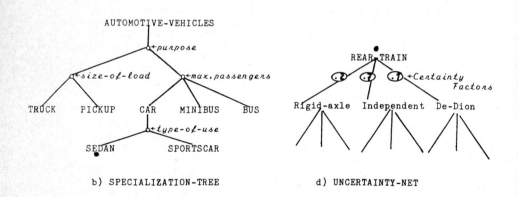

b) SPECIALIZATION-TREE   d) UNCERTAINTY-NET

Fig. 4: Structure and Components of Entity Lattices

In fig. 4-a) an illustration is given of the overall interconnection relationships, the dots on the "edges" of the presented lattice-section referring to the links between the different structuring types.
As can be seen these connection-dots come back in the different projections of the structure that are shown in fig. 4-b), c) and d). The fact that the dot in fig. 4-b) is located at *SEDAN* while fig. 4-c) starts with *CAR* requires some explanation and shows an interesting property of such a lattice. The basic reason of this - apparently odd - situation is that *Sedan* and *Sportscar* are just specific instances of the object *Car* while they have, by and large, identical entity structures. Moreover, the link between the specialization tree and the entity structure would take place at Aspect/Specialization level, and Aspects cannot be considered to be objects in the cognition sciences interpretation of this concept. Therefore, all links between the different types of structure have to take place at Entity-level to allow proper operation of the Similarity Net search procedures (see also previous paragraph). All this leads to the tentative conclusion that:

a. the STRUCTURE of the items of knowledge in realistic MODEL BASE management systems will have to be of the LATTICE type
b. this lattice structure should allow substructures of (at least) three kinds: SPECIALIZATION trees, ENTITY trees and UNCERTAINTY nets
c. the TOTAL model base should allow partitioning into SPACES (and possibly VISTAS) in order to allow the focus the knowledge from a specific viewpoint on a specific application domain (see examples used earlier on in this Chapter)
d. the different substructures in the lattices of the model base should be LINKABLE to eachother via ENTITIES, these being the key cognition elements
e. model bases should allow BROWSING (and thus retrieval of adequate models). This browsing can best be routed through SIMILARITY NETS which should at least reflect the status of the specialization tree and the uncertainty net for the application on hand.

8. CLASSES

The concept of CLASS as a higher principle that governs a set of objects with similar properties originated in the SIMULA simulation language (Dahl and Nygaard (1966)).
It was mainly introduced in that context to provide a vehicle to be able to dynamically instantiate processes that have a common nature (= common structure, attributes and interfacing properties). In this way SIMULA was the first simulation vehicle that introduced a kind of meta-knowledge concept in a Modelling & Simulation tool.
Recently, the same type of concept has emerged again, but this time in the Artificial Intelligence context.
Horn (in Horn et al. (1986)) uses the Class concept to group items of knowledge and (production) rules that have common properties together, in order to be able to apply knowledge of a more general level to relevant parts of the inference process in the VIE-PCX expert system shell.
Thus, also in Expert Systems, the concept of Class is introduced as a vehicle to cater for the management of elements of Meta-Knowledge. In this sense Classes have much in common with the Vistas mentioned earlier on, for they are both concepts that allow one to handle the

general knowledge about knowledge applicable to several problem
domains.
However, while Vistas are closely linked to the concept of keeping
specific elements of knowledge in focus, the more general Class
principle (e.g. by the fact that it is not tied to a specific method
of knowledge representation like Vistas to Semantic Nets), have the
power in them not only to keep some knowledge in focus but,
additionally, to establish reasoning processes about common elements
of knowledge of the objects which are on a lower level in the
knowledge hierarchy.
That is why the class concept can be used to advantage for
implementing general meta-knowledge (e.g. about the laws of physics,
mathematics, etc.) in knowledge storage and retrieval systems,
especially those in which there is no doubt as to which kind of
meta-knowledge is needed. Model bases in fact are amenable to this
criterium, and so one finds a fourth element that has to be catered
for in this type of knowledge depository.
The Class knowledge to be embedded in a model base can be thought to
tie in, by preference, to the top objects of the specialization
trees in order to provide the whole family of derivates with those
knowledge attributes which are essential for their kind.
Also sets of (production-) rules, that are geared to verifying the
consistency and correct application of the valiable meta-knowledge
in the models being stored, could be stored using the Class concept.
That, of course, would be a part of a model base management system,
and not of a model base in itself. Which then entails that the
different types of meta-knowledge have to be stored in such a way
that their elements can be used in exactly the same way by the
aforementioned production rules in the model base management system.
This task would require a complete reformulation of many basic laws
and axioms that are used by modellers on a daily basis, often even
intuitively.
Certainly a formidable task which will take great minds and long
years to accomplish.

9. <u>RULES</u>

By the simple term *rule* it is customary to denote the *production
rule* concept that Artificial Intelligence has borrowed from the
propositional calculus.
In fact production rules are not much different from the
IF..THEN..ELSE clause known from most programming languages, but
instead of operating on data, they operate on the presence or
absence of certain attributes of elements of knowledge.
A simple example will suffice to clarify their nature.

Imagine a tourist visiting Europe on a predetermined schedule,
knowing that on Tuesday his group will visit the capital of France.
If the tour has been on schedule all the time he can state *IF this
is Tuesday THEN this must be Paris* with a certainty factor very near
to 100 percent. (In the meantime it has naturally become clear that
we had 6 production rules in our little story, sequenced in such a
way as to make it an understandable anecdote: our inference
mechanism was embedded in the way the story was told!).

As outlined before rules could be used to advantage for checking
model-knowledge that is to be stored in the base against
meta-knowledge already available.

But that is not their only usefull function in Modelling &
Simulation. They will also play an essential role in selecting the
relevant alternative decompositions in the model base for a specific
application, can be used as a formalism to represent certain
discrete event systems (Broda and Gregory (1984) and Futó and
Gergely, Chapter VII.2 of this book) and may come to be used for the
construction of an automated tool to prune entity structures with
reference to the requirements of specific experimental (observation)
frames (Rosenblit and Zeigler (1985)).
Production rule mechanisms will also play an important role in the
model base management systems of the future as will be shown in the
next paragraph and in Chapter II.1 of this book.

10. FRAMES AND DEMONS

So far, two mechanisms have been presented that are commonly used in
Artificial Intelligence to represent specific elements of knowledge
and their relations in a retrievable form: semantic nets and
production rules.
However, general Modelling & Simulation practice shows evidence that
people do not always analyze systems-to-be-modelled from scratch and
then build entirely new models to represent those systems.
Instead of this, they have memorized in some way a sizeable
collection of models representing their past experience with systems
Modelling & Simulation.
To analyze a "new" system, they recall appropriate analogous system
models and specialize them using the key attributes of the system
currently under study.
A general mechanism especially designed (for the first time by
Minsky (1975)) for the computer representation of the same type of
general knowledge in Artificial Intelligence is the *FRAME*. The *frame*
is in principle an *object* (like the ones defined in LISP) that has
general attributes called *SLOTS* that can be filled with certain
(limited) attribute instantiations, and *DEMONS* which, in principle,
are procedural mechanisms that watch for some *slot-filling* condition
to become true and then activate some process conceptually
associated with this condition.
To a certain extent, these structures and their *demon-driven*
relations, can be seen as an extremely complex form of semantic net
nodes, but - through their inherent structure - they are far more
powerful.
For instance most *frame* implementations allow *recursive* application
of the concept. (Meaning that slots need not only be filled with
values or instances of attributes but can as well be filled by
(instances) of other frames describing other objects).
Associated with any slot there normally is a condition monitoring
mechanism that watches if the *filler* of a slot meets some predefined
set of restrictions.
Usually, in the absence of filler information to the contrary, each
slot can - automatically - be filled with some default value
corresponding with a "business as usual" situation.
To clarify all this let us examine a frame-technique to help the
tourist (from the rules-example) know in which city he is. A rather
involved (and hypothetical) approach has been chosen, just to be
able to use recursiveness, demons etc.
For the chosen recognition process three frames - each with three
slots - are needed as illustrated in fig. 5.

(Note that in this case the '=' sign is used to mean 'is the present instance of'.)

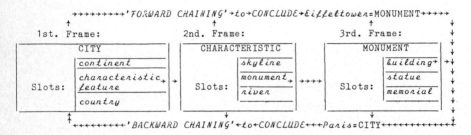

(Forward-chaining = reasoning from initial states to solution vicinity)

(Backward-chaining = reasoning back from approximate solution to initial state, if initial states do not match, ITERATE.)

Fig. 5: The Paris Frame Structure

The valid fillers for the diverse slots are as follows:

a) CITY-slots:
   continent : Europe, Asia, Africa, America
   characteristic-feature : has, has-not
   country : IF Europe=continent THEN France, Italy, England
              ELSE IF America=continent THEN United-States ELSE none.

b) CHARACTERISTIC-slots:
   skyline : true, false
   monument : true, false
   river   : present, not-present

c) MONUMENT-slots:
   building : Eiffeltower, Empire-State-building, Vatican-palace,
               St.Paul's-cathedral
   statue-of : Michiel-de-Ruyter, Abraham-Lincoln, Napoleon,
               Julius-Caesar
   memorial-type : war, peace, freedom

The inference-process, that makes use of demons, could e.g. work in the following way:

```
{ACTIVATE} CITY

    IF characteristic-feature {FILLED} 'has'
       THEN {ACTIVATE} CHARACTERISTIC

    IF monument {FILLED} 'true' THEN {ACTIVATE} MONUMENT

    IF building {FILLED} 'Eiffeltower'
       THEN {CONCLUDE} Eiffeltower=monument

    IF MONUMENT=monument
       THEN MONUMENT=CHARACTERISTIC .WHILE. Eiffeltower=MONUMENT
          THEN {CONCLUDE} Eiffeltower=CHARACTERISTIC

    IF Europe=continent .WHILE. Eiffeltower=CHARACTERISTIC
       THEN {CONCLUDE} Paris=CITY
```

Note the fact that, in the example, the frame concept cannot operate
on knowledge in isolation, but needs procedure-like enhancements to
make reasoning possible. In this case a kind of production rule
mechanism was used, but other procedural mechanisms can also be
envisaged.

It should also have become clear that, if nodes in networks are
described using a frame concept, network traversals can be
mechanised using demons and production rule type procedures.
They will possibly even play a central role in future model base
management systems. The reason for this being the frame's flexible
slot and demon interpretation possibilities and the attribute-driven
nature of modelling knowledge elements.
This principle can easily be illustrated by representing the
similarity net traversal of the VEHICLE world (depicted in figures 2
and 3), by making use of frames.
As is shown in fig. 6, all that is needed for this purpose is the
presence of appropriate attribute slots in a VEHICLE frame, together
with a simple demon/production rule of the general from:

```
    IF {slot X = filled with permissible attribute}
    THEN APPLY {slot X = instantiation process}
    ELSE {return to model base manager}.
```

The allowed attributes can e.g. be the following for this case:

```
geometry   : IF purpose = freight-carrying
                THEN number-of-platforms
             ELSE body-shape
dimensions: length, width, heigth
trajectory: x, y, z, omega, theta, phi (also implying all derivates)
medium     : sea, land, air
purpose    : personal-transportation, freight-carrying, both
Interface-with-medium: wheels, wings, hull
capacity   : number-of-persons, kg-of-freight
```

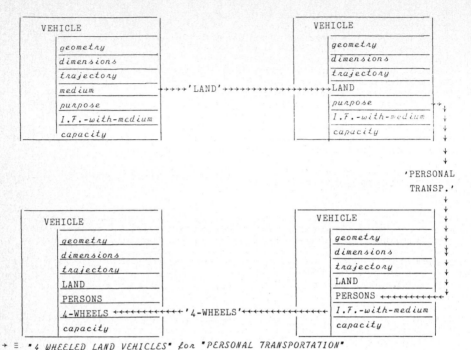

Fig. 6: Frames and the VEHICLE World

Only at the last stage (where the VEHICLE frame is tied to the entity structure of a specific instance) can the process need an instantiation of a frame with another name.
Also the node-objects in entity trees, and therefore in the corresponding uncertainty nets, can adequately be represented and structured through frames.
This offers the opportunity to utilize readily available Artificial Intelligence environments for the development of advanced model base management systems.
This subject will be reviewed in more detail in Chapter II.1 of this book. The present paragraph can, however, not be concluded before mentioning the fact that the frame concept has also been successfully used to implement discrete event simulation systems (see e.g. Fox and Reddy (1982) & Reddy and Fox (1982)).

11. CONCLUSION

It has been shown in this chapter that many of the principles developed in the Artificial Intelligence community for the acquisition and management of knowledge, can be advantageously applied to the area of Modelling & Simulation.

It has also been indicated that Modelling & Simulation is a prime candidate for this application because the elements of knowledge in this field form a well structured whole by nature.

Application of advanced knowledge structuring, model storage and (partial) model retrieval techniques have, however, been shown to require the adherence to certain strict structuring rules and the development of novel data structures (Entity Lattices). The meaning and consequences of introducing uncertainties in decompositions has been addressed in this context and shown to be amenable to integration in this structuring principle. Finally frames have been shown to be the most relevant form of knowledge representation for Modelling & Simulation.

12. REFERENCES

Ait-Kaci, H. (1986). The Subsumption as a Model of Computation. In: Expert Database Systems, Kerschberg, L. (Ed.), The Benjamin/Cummings Publishing Co., Menlo Park, pp. 115-139.

Belogus, D. (1984). Methodology and Software Tools for Modelling and Simulating Multifacetted Systems. Computer Science Ph.D.Thesis, Applied Mathematics Dept., Weizmann Institute of Science, Rehovot, Israel.

Brachman, R.J. (1979). On the Epistemological Status of Semantic Networks. In: Associative Networks, Findler N.V. (Ed.), Academic-Press, New York, pp.3-50 (especially p. 39).

Broda, K. and S. Gregory (1984). Paralog for Discrete Event Simulation. Research Report DOC84/4, Dept. of Computing, Imperial College of Science and Technology, London.

Corella, F. (1986). Semantic Retrieval and Levels of Abstraction. In: Loc.cit. sub Ait-Kaci, H. (1986), pp. 91-114

Dahl, O.J. and K. Nygaard (1966). Simula: A Language for Programming and Description of Discrete Event Systems. Technical Report, Norwegian Computer Center, Oslo.

Elzas, M.S. (1984). System Paradigms as Reality Mappings. In: Simulation and Model-Based Methodologies: An Integrative View, Oren, Zeigler, Elzas (Eds.), Springer-Verlag, Heidelberg, pp. 41-67.

Findler, N.V. (Ed.)(1979). Associative Networks. Academic-Press, New York.

Finin, T. and D.Silverman (1986). Interactive Classification. In: Loc.cit sub Ait-Kaci, H. (1986), pp. 79-90.

Fox, M.S. and Y.V. Reddy (1982). Knowledge Representation in Organization Modelling and Simulation: Definition and Interpretation. In: Proceedings of the 13th. Pittsburgh Conference on Modelling and Simulation, pp. 675-683.

Hendrix, G.G. (1979). Encoding Knowledge in Partitioned Networks. In: Loc.cit sub Findler, N.V. (1979), pp. 51-92.

Horn, W. et.al. (1986). VIE-PCX: The Vienna PC Expert System.
    Manual, 2nd edition, Austrian Research Institute for Artificial
    Intelligence of the OeSGK, Vienna.

Lundeberg, M., G. Goldkuhl and A. Nilsson (1978). Information System
    Development -A First Introduction to Systematic Approach. ISAC
    Specialist Report, University of Stockholm.

Minsky, M. (1975). A framework for Representing Knowledge. In: The
    Psychology of Computer Vision, Winston, P.H. (Ed.),
    McGraw-Hill, New York.

Negoita, C.V. (1985). Expert Systems and Fuzzy Systems. Benjamin/
    Cummings Publishing Co., Menlo Park, Ca, especially pp. 69-94.

Oren, T.I. and B.P. Zeigler (1979). Concepts for Advanced Simulation
    Methodologies. Simulation, Vol. 32, No. 3, pp. 69-82

Reddy, Y.V. and M.S. Fox (1982). Knowledge Representation in
    Organization Modelling and Simulation: A Detailed Example. In:
    Loc.cit. sub Fox and Reddy (1982), pp. 685-691.

Rich, E. (1983). Artificial Intelligence. McGraw-Hill, Singapore,
    pp. 329-338.

Rosenblit, J. and B.P. Zeigler (1985). Concepts for Knowledge-Based
    System Design Environments. In: Proc. 1985 Winter Simulation
    Conference, San Francisco, Ca.

Schoenmakers, H. (1986). E.S.P.-2, an Entity Structuring Program
    with Pruning Facilities. Technical Report, Computer Science
    Depts., Univ. of Arizona and Wageningen Univ.

Simons, J.L. and R.J. Wieringa (1986). The place of Expert Systems
    in a typology of information systems. Technical Report, Dept.
    of Computer Science, Wageningen University.

Smith, J.M. (1986). Expert Database Systems: A Database Perspective.
    In: Loc.cit. sub Ait-Kaci, H. (1986), pp. 3-16.

Spriet, J.A. and G.C. Vansteenkiste, (Eds.), (1982). Computer-aided
    Modelling and Simulation. Academic-Press, London.

Wieringa, R.J. and P.H. Curwiel (1986). Second report on FAD: The
    Farmer's Aid in plant disease Diagnosis. Technical Report,
    Dept. of Computer Science, Wageningen University.

Winston, P.H.(1975). Learning Structural Descriptions from Examples.
    In: Loc.cit sub Minsky, M. (1975).

Zeigler, B.P. (1979). Structuring principles for multifacetted
    system modelling. In: Methodology in Systems Modelling and
    Simulation, North-Holland, Amsterdam, pp. 93-135.

Zeigler, B.P. (1984). Multifacetted Modelling and Discrete Event
    Simulation. Academic-Press, London.

Modelling and Simulation Methodology
in the Artificial Intelligence Era
M.S. Elzas, T.I. Ören and B.P. Zeigler (Editors)
© Elsevier Science Publishers B.V. (North-Holland), 1986

Chapter I.4

IMPLICATIONS OF MACHINE LEARNING IN SIMULATION

Tuncer I. Ören

Computer Science Department
University of Ottawa
Ottawa, Ontario, Canada

Machine learning is a process by which a computer or a computer embedded system increases the quantity or enhances the quality of its knowledge processing ability or its knowledge about a system or about itself. In cognizant simulation, the modelling and simulation environment and/or the simulation system have cognitive abilities such as perception, interpretation, reasoning, explanation, goal setting, or learning. A taxonomy is developed to systematize different aspects of machine learning and to explore its implications in simulation. The criteria used are: 1) scope of learning, 2) initiative of the learner, 3) level of transformation of input knowledge, 4) frequency of learning, and 5) type of knowledge processing knowledge learned.

1. INTRODUCTION

Cognitive simulation has been used for a long time to simulate cognitive characteristics of humans. Currently, we are at the beginning of the development of cognizant simulation where the modelling and simulation environment and/or the simulation system have cognizant abilities such as perception, interpretation, reasoning, explanation, goal setting, and learning. In this article, a taxonomy is developed to systematize different aspects of machine learning and to explore its implications in simulation. Some views on artificial intelligence in simulation have been expressed in Ören 1984, Birtwistle 1985, Holmes 1985, Zeigler 1985, Elzas et al. 1986, Ören 1986a, Kerckhoffs and Vansteenkiste 1986, and Luker and Adelsberger 1986.

In simulation the role of computers is not limited to behavior generation. They can also be used for behavior processing, symbolic model processing, as well as modelling and knowledge based management for several types of knowledge which may exist in advanced simulation environments (Ören 1984,1985b). For these activities, computer assistance can be provided in increasing level of expertise as asssistant, consultant, advisor, certifier, and expert. However, expertise should not be considered a static entity. Machine learning can definitely enhance, computer expertise and can create new roles for computers.

Machine learning can be conceived as a special case of a systemic problem, i.e., response to stimuli. There are two categories of response of objects to stimuli: memoryless response and memory response. *Memoryless response* is transformation of a stimulus into an output without remembering the stimulus or its effects. There are two types of *mem-*

ory response depending on whether or not knowledge does or does not affect the future behavior of a system. Accordingly, there are two types of systems, i.e., knowledge acquisition and knowledge assimilation system.

Knowledge acquisition implies that some input knowledge is remembered and can be made available when necessary. In the case of knowledge acquisition systems, knowledge is remembered but does not affect the behavior of the system. Normally, data bases work this way; i.e., knowledge is memorized and can be given back, butthe knowledge processing ability of the data base management system is not affected by the knowledge contained in the data base.

Knowledge assimilation implies that the system remembers part or all of the stimuli knowledge and/or its implications and that the behavior of the system, i.e., its response to a future knowledge will be affected by the remembered knowledge. Learning is there fore synonymous with knowledge assimilation.

There is an interesting and common aspect of machine learning and simulation. One of the primordial characterstics of simulation is that models used in simulation are always memory models. Therefore, any simulation model remembers its past experience through its state variables which, in turn, affect the current behavior of the model.

2. ANALOGY BETWEEN TWO EVOLUTIONS

Machine learning is an important step in the evolution of machines and among other application areas, has definite implications in modelling and simulation. Discussion of some trends and analogies may help us have an appreciation of the possibilities for the future.

Use of machines has three distinct levels: mechanization, automation, and cybernation (Figure 1).

Mechanization is replacement of physical efforts of biological origin by machines. Any elementary machine such as a machine tool (e.g. a drill) can be given as an example.

Automation is formation of a series of systems into a self-regulating process. An assembly line is an example to automation which requires a higher degree of mechanization.

Cybernation is realization of a machine or a system which has cognitive abilities such as perception, reasoning, interpretation, explanation, goal setting, and learning. A programmable intelligent robot is an example to the early stage of cybernation.

There is an interesting analogy between the three levels of use of machines and the three levels of use of computers in modelling and simulation (Figure 2.)

Computerization of simulation is replacement of human knowledge processing efforts by computers in a simulation study and is analogous to mechanization. There are two groups of possibilities: 1) Any computerized simulation where behavior generation task has to be carried out by a computer. 2) Any computer-aided modelling and simulation system where model development and simulation program generation are aided/performed by a computer.
A *modelling and simulation environment* forms a series of modelling and simulation systems into a self-regulating system and is analogous to automation (or to operating systems in computers). In a computer-aided modelling and simulation system, automatic invoking of consistency checks of models with respect to a modelling formalism may be one of the several functions to be provided by a modelling and simulation environment.

Level	Explanation	Example:
Level 1: *Mechanization*	Replacement of physical efforts of biological origin by machines	An elementary machine e.g. a drill
Level 2: *Automation*	Formation of a series of systems into a self-regulating process (Requires a higher degree of mechanization)	An assembly line
Level 3: *Cybernation*	Building a machine or system with cognitive abilities such as: - perception, - interpretation, - reasoning, - explanation - goal-setting, and - learning.	Programmable intelligent robot

Figure 1. Evolution of level of use of machines.

Level	Explanation	Example
Level 1: *Computerization of simulation* (analogous to mechanization)	Replacement of human knowledge processing efforts by computers	- Any computerized simulation (behavior generation task is carried out by a computer) - Any computer-aided modelling and simulation (model development and simulation program generation are aided/ performed by a computer)
Level 2 *Modelling and simulation environment* (analogous to automation (or to operating systems in computers))	Formation of a series of modelling and simulation system into a self-regulating system	- In a computer-aided modelling and simulation system,.automatic invoking of consistency checks of models with respect to a modelling formalism
Level 3 *Cognizant simulation*	The modelling and simulation environment or the simulation system has cognitive abilities such as: - perception, - interpretation, - reasoning, - explanation, - goal-setting, and - learning	- Intelligent modelling and simulation environment - Expert modelling system - Simulation with intelligent models

Figure 2.   Analogy between levels of useage of machines and useage of computers in modelling and simulation

Cognizant simulation is the third level of use of computers in modelling and simulation. In cognizant simulation, the modelling and simulation environment and/or the simulation system has cognitive abilities such as perception, interpretation,reasoning, explanation, goal setting, and learning. Some examples to cognizant simulation are: intelligent modelling and simulation environment, expert modelling system, and simulation with intelligent models.

Cognizant simulation provides cognitive abilities to the simulation system and/or to modelling environment and is similar to cybernation which provides cognitive abilities to machines.

3. KNOWLEDGE PROCESSING MACHINES OR SYSTEMS AND SIMULATION

A *computer* is an instrument to execute computer programs. Like the duality of musical instruments and musical scores, there is a functional duality between computer programs and the machines which execute them. This functional duality implies that one of the entitics can be defined/developed without access to the other one. However, ultimately one needs simultaneous access to and compatibility of both of them. A computer program can exist as a software or firmware.

A *computer program* is a knowledge transducer (Ören 1986a). Like a multitute of signal transducers which are used in engineering disciplines, a computer program has input (stimulus) knowledge and output knowledge. The output knowledge from a computer program can be either a transformation of or knowledge about input knowledge.

In a computer program input and out knowledges can be:

- Numerical
- Textual (one or two dimensional)
- Graphical (still or moving)
    - Two-dimensional
    - Three-dimensional
        - Emulated on a two-dimensional surface
        - True 3-D picture generated via computer controlled laser pixels
- Audio (voice/speech)
- Tactile, and
- Other types of signals
    (including those connected to biological systems)
    - Coming from sensing devices or
    - Going to control devices.

Proper perception of computers and machines is essential in having a generalization of the concept of knowledge processing machines (or knowledge processing systems in general). A knowledge processing system can be either a computer or a computer embedded system. Primary function of a computer is knowledge processing and is normally used as a stand-alone system for this purpose.

There is a multitude of other machines or systems the primary objective of which is not knowledge processing. Computers can be embedded in such systems if knowledge processing ability can enhance their primary objectives. Depending on the case, one can use the terminology "computer embedded machine" or "computer embedded system." Figure 3 (adapted from Ören 1986a) categorizes several types of computer embedded systems such as knowledge-based, optimizing, reasoning, simulating, and multiparadigm computer embedded systems.

Stand-alone systems (primary objective is knowledge processing)	Computer	Instrument to execute programs

Computer-embedded system (machine)
 	
 (ces) or (cem)
 	
 (Primary objective is not knowledge processing but ability of knowledge processing enhances system performance)
	Knowledge-based system
	
	 (k-ces)
		- Camera reading directly
		   - film speed
		   - flash/lens characteristics

	Optimizing system (o-ces)	- Tracking missile - Vehicle-sensing road for traffic optimization
	Reasoning system (r-ces)	- Rule-base robot
	Simulating system (s-ces)	- Predictive displays generated via on-line simulation i.e., simulation with on-line data coming from host system and/or environment - submarines - air-traffic control - advanced decision center

	Multi-paradigm ces
	
	 (mp-ces)
		- Advanced/autonomous monitoring/ self-monitoring systems with abilities for
		   - computation,
		   - optimization,
		   - reasoning, and
		   - simulation
		
		 - e.g. autonomous and intelligent
		   - robot
		   - space station

Figure 3.   A generalization of knowledge processing machines and
a classification of computer embedded systems

There are two implications of this generalized view of knowledge processing machines in simulation: one is the concept of simulating system, the other one is the multiparadigm computer embedded system which may use simulation as one of the paradigms. Machine learning is applicable to both stand-alone computers and to computer embedded systems.

Figure 4 reveals an analogy between stand-alone and embedded use of computers and simulation. Stand-alone use of simulation for decision making has a definite use and usefulness. However, integrative simulation, i.e., integrative use of simulation and other knowledge processing techniques for man-in-the-loop decision systems and autonomous systems have yet to be explored. Oren et al. (1984) provides a guide for an integrative view of simulation and other model-based decision making techniques.

The ability to use different types of sensors is an important possibility for computers to receive knowledge directly from their environment, and has an implication for advanced simulation systems. A simulating system, i.e., a system with an embedded computer, which in turn has a simulation model which is used with on-line data, can learn from its environment the values of constant or time-varying parameters and can use them directly. This possibility has to be explored to enhance the usability and usefulness of integrative simulation for the realization of advanced integrative decision making systems.

4. MACHINE LEARNING

Machine learning is a process by which a computer or a computer embedded system increases the quantity or enhances the quality of its knowledge processing ability or its knowledge about the system or itself. A good reference on machine learning is Michalski et al (1983). Utgolf and Nudel (1983) is a good bibliography on the subject. The terms relevant to learning discussed in this article are given in Figure 5.

Machine learning requires the following functions and the corresponding elements and units.

- knowledge acquisition by a knowledge acceptor from the environment or from the system itself (for self-monitoring system),

- knowledge assimilation
(e.g. internalization and operationalization),

- storage and rearrangement of and access to knowledge,

- a performance element which uses the knowledge to perform its task.

One of the tasks of the learning element is to bridge the gap between the level at which the stimuli knowledge is received (from the environment or the system itself) and the level at which the performance element can use it to carry out its function.

Assimilation of knowledge necessitates that the knowledge processing system is affected by the simuli knowledge, i.e., that the future behavior of the knowledge processing system to some other stimuli will have the effect of the assimilated knowledge. Assimilated knowledge is latent knowledge until it is used. In a knowledge processing system, mere increase of the quantity of knowledge or enhancement of the quality of knowledge does not constitute learning if behavior of the knowledge processing system is not affected by the acquired knowledge.

For example, a knowledge acquisition system such as a computerized data base (as they are in mid 1980s) is not a learning system since it has no potential of being affected by the knowledge it has access to. However, a knowledge based system such as a camera

Type of use:	Use of computers	Use of simulation
Stand-alone use	Stand-alone use of computers for knowledge processing (stand-alone computer)	(Stand-alone) use of simulation for decision making (stand-alone simulation)
Embedded use	Integrative use of computers in computer-embedded systems (or machines) (embedded computer)	Integrative use of simulation and other knowledge processing techniques for - man-in-the-loop decision systems - autonomous systems (integrative simulation)

Figure 4. Analogy between trends of use of computers
and use of simulation

education
knowledge, high-level
knowledge, irrelevant
knowledge, latent
knowledge, level of
knowledge, low-level
knowledge, sample of
knowledge, transformation of input
knowledge, acquisition
knowledge, assimilation
learner, initiative of
learning, autonomous
learning, autosimulative
learning, deductive
learning, dynamic
learning, experiential
learning, frequency of
learning, goal-directed
learning, incremental
learning, inductive
learning, initial
learning, integrative
learning, introspective
learning, liberal
learning, machine
learning, meta-
learning, mosaïc
learning, observational
learning, outcome of
learning, passive
learning, rote
learning, scope of
learning, simulative
learning, static
learning, unsupervised
learning by abstraction
learning by analogy
learning by autosimulation
learning by being programmed
learning by direct memorization
learning by discovery
learning by experimentation
learning by generalization
learning by induction
learning by operationalization
learning by simulation
learning examples
learning from a teacher
learning from examples
learning from general case
learning from instruction
learning from observation
learning from self-monitoring
learning to learn
response, memory
response, memoryless
training, vocational

Figure 5. Terms relevant to learning discussed in this article.

which can directly read the speed of the film loaded in it, has the ability of getting knowledge about the characteristics of a component of the system and using the acquired knowledge to perform its function. Therefore, such a system (or machine) has learning ability. In such a simple case, the learned knowledge is the value of a parameter which remains constant until the film is replaced. In a simulating system such as a submarine control system, the learning element can get (through sensors) time varying environmental knowledge and can use it to generate predictive displays of the imminent trajectory of the submarine. In this case, the system learns time-varying values of the parameters.

5. A TAXONOMY OF MACHINE LEARNING

A taxonomy of machine learning is developed to systematize its different aspects and to explore its implications in simulation. The taxonomy is based on the following criteria:

- Scope of learning,
- Initiative of the learner,
- Transformation of input knowledge,
    - Level of transformation,
    - Nature of transformation,
- Frequency of learning, and
- Type of knowledge-processing knowledge learned.

5.1 A Taxonomy of Machine Learning Based on Scope of Learning

Based on the scope of learning, one can idenntify three types of learning. They are: meta-learning, goal-directed learning, and liberal learning.

Meta-learning is learning to learn and may be developed and embedded in machine learning systems to enhance their learning process.

Goal-directed learning (or vocational training) requires that all knowledge made available to the knowledge processing system or all knowledge assimilated by the knowledge processing system are task oriented which implies that learning is done to improve the performance of the system. Within the realm of vocational training, any knowledge which cannot contribute directly or indirectly to the performance of a task or set of tasks is irrelevant knowledge and, for the sake of effectiveness of the learning system, has to be avoided. This approach is valid for training technicians and for the current state-of-the-art of machine learning. (However, it is a pity to see university students who limit their knowledge acquisition to task related knowledge only).

Liberal learning (or education) is not limited to acquisition and assimilation of task related knowledge only. A creative knowledge processing system may associate knowledge, which could otherwise be considered latent knowledge, to create new applications or new application areas for multi-domain knowledge. Synthesis of knowledge belonging to different domaines requires the ability to detect analogies and explore the association of multi-domain knowledge.

From a pragmatic point of view, vocational training of computers and computer embedded systems is very important, regardless whether or not we use the term vocational training or attribute intelligence to knowledge processing machines.

From an exploratory point of view, it might be quite interesting to also work to educate computers and computer embedded systems and observe the effect of their ability to pro cess multi-domain knowledge. Computational ability to transpose knowledge from one domain to another, as explored in general system theories, might end up in interesting results.

5.2 A Taxonomy of Machine Learning Based on Initiative of Learner

There are two aspects of the initiative of the learner: 1) learner's role in the generation of the stimuli knowledge and 2) learner's role in the perception of the knowledge to be learned. Both of these aspects can be passive and active. Figure 6 summarizes a taxonomy of machine learning based on the initiative of the learner.

Passive perception of knowledge corresponds to passive generation of knowledge, i.e., the learner has no active role in the generation or preparation of the knowledge. Passive perception corresponds to learning from a teacher which might be a human or a system. Passive perception learning can be named *passive learning* (or learning examples) and can be achieved as learning by being programmed and learning from instruction.

Learning corresponding to *active perception* of knowledge can be called *autonomous learning* or unsupervised learning. There are two categories: 1) knowledge is expected, 2) knowledge is not expected but the knowledge processing system is able to handle (i.e., discern, interpret, evaluate, transform, assimilate) unexpected stimuli knowledge.

Autonomous learning of expected knowledge has two sub-categories corresponding to passive or active generation of the stimuli knowledge.

Autonomous learning of the expected and passively generated knowledge consists basically of two types of learning: learning from observation (or observational learning) and learning from self-monitoring (or introspective learning). In both of these cases stimuli knowledge is generated independent of the learning element but learner has an active role in knowledge perception.

An active learning element generates conditions which cause generation of knowledge to be processed (filtered) for learning. Autonomous learning of expected and actively generated knowledge consists of basically two types of learning: learning by experimentation on the real system, i.e., experiental learning, and learning by simulation, i.e., simulative learning.

In *learning by experimentation,* the learner has access to the real world as source of stimuli knowledge and sets up experimental conditions under which behavior of the real world is observed.

Simulative learning is learning by simulation. In simulative learning, the learner has three choices:

1) By having access to a model of the real world and setting up experimental conditions under which behavior of a specific model of the real world is observed, the learner may learn the behavior of the simulated system under different experimental conditions.

2) By developing models of the real world and simulating the real world under different experimental conditions, and after validation of the simulated model, the learner may infer not only about the behavior but also about the structure of the real system.

3) By using a copy of its own structure, a system can simulate itself (i.e., perform auto-simulation - similar to introspection) and can learn about its own behavior *under conditions set up* by itself *specifically for this purpose.* The use of autosimulation in learning corresponds to autosimulative learning.

Learning by discovery is autonomous learning where knowledge is not expected but knowledge processing system is able to handle, i.e.., discern, interpret, evaluate, transform, assimilate unexpected stimuli knowledge. Learning by discovery is applicable to both passive and active generation of stimuli knowledge.

In learning, examples are samples of knowledge and they can stem from several sources. All six types of autonomous learning, i.e., observational learning, introspective learn-

		learner's role in generation of stimuli knowledge	
		passive generation	active generation
Learner's role in the perception of the knowledge to be learned	passive perception (passive learning)	- learning by being programmed - learning from instruction - learning examples	
	Active perception (autonomous learning) (or unsupervised learning) — knowledge is expected	- learning from observation (observational learning) - learning from self-monitoring (introspective learning)	- learning by experimentation (experiential learning) - learning by simulation (simulative learning) - learning by auto-simulation (autosimulative learning)
	knowledge is not expected but knowledge processing system can handle (discern, interpret, evaluate, transform, assimilate) unexpected stimuli knowledge)	- learning by discovery	

Figure 6. A taxonomy of learning based on the initiative of the learner

ing, experiental learning, simulative learning, autosimulative learning, and learning by discovery are all special cases of learning from examples (or learning by induction) if the system has generalization ability. Otherwise the system may learn only specific examples.

5.3 A Taxonomy of Machine Learning Based on the Level and Nature of Transformation of Input Knowledge.

Level of knowledge is the degree of generality or domain of applicability of the knowledge.

Low-level knowledge is knowledge specific to a particular entity such as an object, attribute, relationship, or action.

High-level knowledge is abstract knowledge applicable to a class of entities or to several application domains.

A taxonomy of machine learning based on level and nature of transformation of input knowledge is given in Figure 7.

Learning by operationalization implies that there is a transformation of the nature of input knowledge which is knowledge-processing knowledge. In learning by operationalization the descriptive (i.e., declarative) knowledge-processing knowledge is transformed into operational knowledge-processing knowledge such as access oriented, data flow oriented, data-structure oriented, functional, procedural, object oriented, rule-based, or mixed-paradigm knowledge-processing knowledge.

Other learning situations where there is no transformation of the nature of input and output knowledge can be studied with respect to the correspondence of level of learned knowledge to the level of stimulus knowledge.

There are three cases: the learned knowledge is at the same level as, or at a higher level or lower level than the input knowledge.

Learning by direct memorization consists of rote learning and learning by analogy.

Rote learning is direct memoriation of knowledge without transformation of its level of generality and corresponds to the case where learned knowledge applies to the same entity of the same class as the stimulus knowledge or applies to entities of the same class. Referring to rote learning as "learning by memorization" is a tautology since all learning necessitates memorization.

In *learning by analogy* the learned knowledge applies to entities of another class.

Learning from examples or inductive learning consists of learning by generalization or learning by abstraction.

Learning by generalization is learning from examples where learned knowledge applies to more cases of the same class.

Learning by abstraction is learning from examples where learned knowledge applies to more than one class.

Learning from general cases (or deductive learning) is learning by specialization where there are two types of specialization of the learned knowledge: The learned knowledge applies to a smaller number of cases of the same class or to a smaller number of classes of the stimulus knowledge.

Transformation of input knowledge		Correspondence of level of learned knowledge to level of stimulus knowledge		Type of learning
		Same class	Another class	
Relative level of output (learned) knowledge to input (stimulus) knowledge	*Same level* (learning by memorization or learning examples)	- applies to - same entity of same class - entities of same class		rote learning
			- applies to entities of another class	learning by analogy
	Higher level (learning from examples or inductive learning)	- applies to more cases of same class		learning by generalization
			- applies to more than one class	learning by abstraction
	Lower level (learning from general case or deductive learning)	- applies to smaller number of cases of same class	- applies to smaller number of classes	learning by specialization
Nature of transformation input (stimulus) knowledge is descriptive (e.g. declarative) output (learned) knowledge is operational (e.g. - access oriented, - dataflow oriented, - data-structure oriented, - functional, - procedural, - rule-based, - mixed-paradigm)				learning by operation-alization

Figure 7.   A taxonomy of machine learning based on level and nature of knowledge transformation

5.4 A Taxonomy of Machine Learning Based on the Frequency of Learning

Based on the frequency of learning there are two types of machine learning: initial learning and incremental learning.

In *initial learning* (or initialization learning), the system gets its knowledge at once and thereafter the quantity and quality of useable knowledge is constant. Initial learning is static learning.

In *incremental learning* (or dynamic learning) a system learns at several instances. Therefore, quantity or quality of useable knowledge is not constant. There are two cases of incremental learning: mosaic learning and integrative learning.

Mosaic learning is addition of new knowledge without integrating or consolidating it in the previous knowledge that the system has. Addition of new knowledge may introduce contradiction or ambiguity to the knowledge base of the system.

Integrative learning is incremental learning where consistency checks and/or transformations of both input and existing knowledge can be performed at the occurrence of an input knowledge.

5.5 A Taxonomy of Machine Learning Based on the Type of Knowledge Processing Knowledge Learned

A knowledge processing system, regardless whether or not it is a stand-alone computer or a computer embedded system can improve its knowledge processing ability by learning.

The highlights of a taxonomy of machine learning based on the knowledge-processing knowledge learned is given in Figure 8. Basically, a cognizant simulation can learn three categories of knowledge-processing knowledge: 1) modelling and simulation knowledge for knowledge processing, 2) software engineering knowledge for knowledge processing, and 3) knowledge engineering knowledge for knowledge processing.

Modelling and simulation knowledge for knowledge processing consists of knowledge of model management, knowledge of symbolic model-processing , and knowledge of model behavior. Accordingly, one can identify learning model management (including learning to model), model referencing, model analysis, model transformation, and learn ing to represent, generate, and process model behavior.

Software engineering knowledge for knowledge processing consists of knowledge of programming environment and software tools as well as knowledge of software of life cycle. Accordingly, one can identify learning software engineering knowledge for programming environments and software tools and learning software engineering knowledge for software specification, generation/synthesis, understanding, monitoring, modification/transformation, improvement and optimization.

Knowledge engineering knowledge for knowledge processing consists of knowledge acquisition, assimilation, generation, transformation, internalization, dissemination and transformation.Accordingly, a system may learn corresponding knowledge-processing knowledge.

Type of learned knowledge processing knowledge		Type of learning
Modelling and simulation knowledge for knowledge processing	knowledge of model management	- learning model management - learning model referencing
	knowledge of symbolic model processing	- learning - model analysis - model transformation

	knowledge of model behavior, i.e.,
	- behavior
	  - representation
	  - generation
	  - processing
		- learning to
		  - represent behavior
		  - generate behavior
		  - process behavior

software enginering knowledge for knowledge processing	knowledge of programming environment/ software tools	- learning software engineering knowledge for programming environments

	knowledge of software life-cycle	- learning software engineering knowledge for software
		  - specification
		  - generation/ synthesis
		  - understanding
		  - monitoring
		  - modification/ transformation
		  - improvement/ optimization

knowledge engineering knowledge for knowledge processing	knowledge
	- acquisition
	- assimilation
	- transformation
	- generation
	- transmission
	- dissemination
		- learning to
		  - acquire knowledge
		  - assimilate knowledge
		  - transform knowledge
		  - generate knowledge
		  - transmit knowledge
		  - disseminate knowledge

Figure 8.   A taxonomy of machine learning based on the type of knowledge processing knowledge learned

Acknowledgement

The contents of this article and a few related ones have been developed during the academic year of 1984-85 while I was spending my sabbatical leave in Vienna, Austria jointly at the Institute of Statistics and Computer Science of the University of Vienna and at the System and Decision Sciences Program of IIASA - Institute for Applied Systems Analysis.

I would like to express my appreciation to Profs. G. Bruckmann and G. Vinek of the University of Vienna, and to Profs. A. B. Kurzhanski and A. Wierzbicki of IIASA for their invaluable considerations which helped make my sabbatical year a very productive one.

REFERENCES

Birtwistle, G. (Ed) (1985). Artificial intelligence, graphics, and simulation, SCS, La Jolla, CA, 119 p.

Elzas, M.S., T.I. Ören, and B.P. Zeigler (Eds) (1986). Modelling and simulation methodology in the artificial intelligence era, North-Holland, Amsterdam.

Holmes, W.M. (Ed) (1985). Artificial intelligence and simulation, SCS, San Diego, CA, 75 p.

Kerckhoffs, E.J.H. and G.C. Vansteenkiste (Eds) (1986). Artificial intelligence in simulation, SCS, San Diego, CA.

Luker, P.A. and H.H. Adelsberger (Eds) (1986). Intelligent simulation environ- ments, SCS, San Diego, CA, 167 p.

Michalski R.S., J.G. Carbonell, and T.M. Mitchell (Eds) (1984). Machine learning -- An artificial intelligence approach --, Springer-Verlag, Berlin, Germa- ny, 572 p. (Original edition by Tioga, Palo Alto, CA, is dated 1983).

Ören, T.I. (1984). Model-based activities: A paradigm shift. In: Simulation and model-based methodologies: An integrative view, T.I. Ören, B.P. Zeigler, and M.S. Elzas (Eds), Springer-Verlag, Heidelberg, Germany, pp. 3-40.

Ören, T.I. (1986a). Artificial intelligence and simulation. In: Proceedings of Artificial intelligence in simulation, Ghent, Belgium, 1985 Feb. 25-27. SCS, CA.

Ören, T.I. (1986b). Knowledge bases for an advanced simulation environment. In: Intelligent simulation environment, P.A. Luker and H.H. Adelsberger (Eds), Proceedings of SCS Conference on intelligent simulation environ- ments, San Diego, CA, 1986 Jan. 23-25, pp. 16-22.

Ören, T.I., B.P. Zeigler, and M.S. Elzas (Eds) (1984). Simulation and model-based methodologies: An integrative view, Springer-Verlag, Berlin, Germany, 651 p.

Utgoff, P.E. and B. Nudel (1984). Comprehensive Bibliography on Machine learning. In: Machine learning, R.S. Michalski, J.G. Carbonell, and T.M. Michell (Eds), Springer-Verlag, Berlin, Germany, pp. 510-549.

Zeigler, B.P. (Ed) (1985). Expert systems and simulation models, lecture notes of the seminar in expert systems and simulation models, the University of Arizona, Tucson, AZ, 1985 Nov. 18-19.

SECTION II
STRUCTURES
FOR KNOWLEDGE-BASED MODEL PROCESSING

Modelling and Simulation Methodology
in the Artificial Intelligence Era
M.S. Elzas, T.I. Ören and B.P. Zeigler (Editors)
© Elsevier Science Publishers B.V. (North-Holland), 1986

Chapter II.1

RELATIONS BETWEEN ARTIFICIAL INTELLIGENCE ENVIRONMENTS
AND
MODELLING & SIMULATION SUPPORT SYSTEMS

M.S. Elzas

Department of Computer Science
Agricultural University
Wageningen/The Netherlands

The typical, common, aspects of knowledge acquisition
and -representation in the field of Modelling &
Simulation and in Artificial Intelligence (see
Chapter I.3, this book), justify the expectation that
future Modelling & Simulation support systems will
use state-of-the-art Artificial Intelligence tools,
while being thoroughly based on the results of
research going on in the field of Systems Modelling &
Simulation Methodologies (see e.g. Zeigler et al.
(1979), Oren et al. (1984) and the present book).
In this Chapter it will first be shown that a large
degree of similarity exists between knowledge-
structuring paradigms for Modelling & Simulation and
their counterparts in Artificial Intelligence.
Then an overview will be given of the different
facilities that can form part of an Artificial
Intelligence environment, and a typology presented
of the different implementation forms available on
the market.
In the third place the utility of Modelling &
Simulation for Artificial Intelligence environments
and the necessary Artificial Intelligence tools for
Modelling & Simulation support will be discussed.
Then a (limited) evaluation of existing Artificial
Intelligence environments with respect to these
aspects is attempted.
Finally a set of recommendations is formulated for
future research into enhancements of these
environments to improve the synergy between the two
fields.

1. INTRODUCTION

In Section I. of this book the foundations of the intersection
between the methodological aspects of Artificial Intelligence and
Systems Modelling & Simulation Methodology have been highlighted.
The present Section focusses more on the actual implications of
these basic principles.
Therefore this first Chapter will endeavour to explore the practical
elements of mutual benefits within the state-of-the-art of these
disciplines.

If one succeeds to keep abreast of the large number of new
publications on Artificial Intelligence and Expert Systems, one
discovers that the latter ever more frequently include the
utilization of embedded simulation models in their inference
processes (see e.g. Faught (1986).
More often than not the dynamic models that are used in such a way
are of the Discrete Event type. In general because the most common
Artificial Intelligence tools and languages are best suited to
represent this type of system. This "uni-formalism" type of approach
need not be a serious shortcoming on its own. However, if these
models are inspected more critically one discovers that - by and
large - they do not comply with the state-of-the-art in Modelling &
Simulation methodologies and are more or less handicapped by the
restrictions of the environment in which they have to operate.
On the other hand, if one takes a close look at many of the most
used Modelling & Simulation tools, especially those associated with
specific languages, one discovers shortcomings as well. Most of
these can be avoided if the Modelling & Simulation community would
start building its tools using the techniques that have been almost
made to measure by many Artificial Intelligence teams and are
starting to become readily available and possibly: economically
interesting.
Indications on how to proceed can also be found in many places
elsewhere in this book.

2.   SIMILARITY in PARADIGMS

In Chapter I.3 (especially paragraphs 8, 9 and 10) basic elements,
that form the building blocks of knowledge manipulating systems,
were presented.
The great number of slight differences in terminology caused by the
participation of a whole gamut of disciplines in the development of
Artificial Intelligence, makes it difficult to choose adequate names
for the most elementary components of knowledge.
Instead of *object* (which term is also used for a frame-like concept
in the LOOPS shell), the lowest element in the knowledge hierarchy
will be called *subject* here (like in a subject of a conversation).

A *class-of-subjects* or any other structured conglomerate of such
items and associated rules or procedures, will hence be called a
block (of knowledge). As a matter of fact an extension to EMYCIN's
block concept, see van Melle (1980).
These blocks are items of knowledge about subjects and their
relation with each other and with the outer world. Therefore they
are a kind of meta-knowledge which consists of classes of subjects
(as defined in Chapter I.3) and the rules or frames that apply to
the subjects in these classes.
An example might be welcome to clarify this principle. Assume an
(extremely simple), two tiered, knowledge based system that is able
to answer questions on regulations that govern the construction of
houses with a certain type of utilization within certain types of
agglomerations (cities and villages).
Obviously the system will have to "know" the concepts *house*,
agglomeration, *construction*, *regulation*, *quantities*, *types*, etc.
The lowest level of the system, leading to a conclusion e.g. with
regard to the type of agglomeration, could look more or less like
this in a Rule-type system:

    IF *houses=many* THEN *agglomeration=city*.

In a frame oriented system we would need an *agglomeration* frame,
with a slot *houses*, where the permissible filler values could e.g.
be "many" or "few". The frame would moreover have to possess a demon
to instantiate *agglomeration* into *city* or *village*.
On top of this layer there is a block which "knows" all that the
lower layer knows, and moreover can recognize *types-of-utilization*
in order to generate commands that fetch the right type of
regulation. (It is deemed clear that blocks can use rule-sets,
frame-sets or any other applicable representation formalism).
Having defined this block notion, an epistemological structure can
now be built, as illustrated in fig. 1.

                              'KNOWN' FACTS
                                   |

Reasoning Systems: RELATIONS
                                   |
                                        Grouping by SUBJECT

Subject Structuring Systems: BLOCKS
                                   |
                                        Grouping by PROBLEM

Knowledge System: KNOWLEDGE BASES
                                   |
                                        Grouping by DOMAIN

Coupling of Knowledge Systems: META-KNOWLEDGE BASES
                                   |
                                        Grouping by SCIENCE

Theories: META-META KNOWLEDGE (BASES)
                                   |

                    Fig. 1: The Knowledge Epistemology

Note that the *blocks* concept introduced above is a more powerfull
construct than the *spaces and vistas* associated with semantic nets
that were discussed in paragraph 5 of Chapter I.3 of this book.
Blocks can be seen as independent (though limited) "mini" knowledge
bases that can be reapplied in another context as the one in which
they were created, and therefore can exist on their own, while
spaces and vistas are closely tied to the net of which they form a
participation.
An epistemological hierarchy for Systems Modelling was first
introduced by Klir in 1979 and further refined by Zeigler (1984a),
Klir and Elzas in 1984.
The gist of the common ground of these publications is shown in
fig. 2.

```
                         'OBSERVATION' DATA
                              |

Generative System:       EXPRESSIONS
                              |
                                    Grouping by ASPECT

Structure System:        SUBMODELS
                              |
                                    Grouping by ENTITY

I/O Systems:              MODELS
                              |
                                    Grouping by APPLICATION

Coupling of Systems:     META-MODELS
                              |
                                    Grouping by SYSTEM-THEORIES

Methodologies:           META-META-MODELS
                              |
```

Fig. 2: The Modelling Epistemology

It should be clear by now that there is a strong resemblance in the way knowledge can be hierarchically organized in ever more general ensembles as well in Systems Modelling as in Knowledge Engineering. Also the fact that both fields face similar problems when acquiring and applying knowledge, will foster the tendency to use eachothers tools.

A basic problem in knowledge engineering is the acquisition of the initial knowledge for some knowledge processing engine like an expert system.

In this situation, also taking into account that no standard acquisition procedures exist yet, a common concern with the modelling fraternity is the evaluation of consistency and certainty of the collected elements.

This problem can be tackled from many sides. A customary approach in knowledge- and information engineering is to organize interviews in such a way as to yield some basic guarantees. One parameter for this type of strategy is the number of persons being interviewed or participating in the modelling exercise. Basic paradigms, that are valid both for system analysis and knowledge engineering, then emerge:

- if only an *individual specialist* is consulted, there is little ground for realistic evaluation of uncertainties while inconsistencies can readily be cleared;
- if a set of *individual specialists* is interviewed, the possibility exists that unresolvable inconsistencies in knowledge will emerge, on the other hand uncertainties can be estimated;
- last, if an *interdisciplinary team* is chosen as a source of reference, then some uncertainties might be explainable but basic disagreements on key items may be found.

It is therefore evident that both Modelling & Simulation and Artificial Intelligence tools need means to handle uncertainties as well as inconsistencies to accomodate the consequences of these three different knowledge acquisition approaches, as the size of reference group is problem dependent and should not be imposed by the capabilities of the tool that is being used.

Another common aspect can be found in the aspirations for the role that automated tools should play for the non-expert user.
If one classifies the type of knowledge one needs to use such a tool for Modelling & Simulation or Artificial Intelligence applications into three categories:

1. operational knowledge (knowledge on how to operate the tool),
2. applicability knowledge (knowledge on how to apply the tool for a given problem), and
3. background knowledge (knowledge of the basic principles and of the construction of the tool),

one discovers that these differences suggest that three types of tools can be defined as well for Artificial Intelligence as for Modelling & Simulation which can be characterized by the distribution of knowledge between the user and the machine.

Both Artificial Intelligence and Modelling & Simulation developments display a trend to provide support systems that ask the user to learn the operational aspects of his support tool, but leave the higher classes of knowledge in the tool itself, offering ad hoc consultation and Artificial Intelligence guidance services when the user asks for it.
Thus we may conclude that, because there is evidence that Modelling & Simulation and Artificial Intelligence have basic, operational, elements in common, a number of tools and methods usefull for one are probably profitable for both.

3. COMPONENTS of ARTIFICIAL INTELLIGENCE ENVIRONMENTS

In this paragraph a more or less comprehensive overview will be given of the main functional elements that form the joint capability of state-of-the-art Artificial Intelligence environments.
Most practical environments only have a subset of these because some features are complementary and others are still in the research phase.
For basic elements of *knowledge representation*, frames and rules have already been mentioned in Chapter 1.3, however, one also finds systems that know *objects*. These objects can be seen as simplified versions of frames, in the sense that they can also have attributes (=slots) that can have values (=fillers) but miss facilities like recursive instantiation or demons.
Other systems provide facilities for logic programming using predicate calculus type mechanisms such as *Horn-clauses* (like in PROLOG). Although the subject representation capabilities are rather limited, Horn-clause systems offer the advantage that the inference mechanism is in fact fully controlable by the user.
On a higher level of items one finds *demons* (see e.g. Chapter I.3) and *messages*, which are programmable mechanisms to allow actions (like instantiations, value-transfer, proposition evaluation, etc.) on basis of filler types, attribute values, state conditions, etc.

At the *blocks* level, as defined before, classes of objects and/or frames can be found, as well as classes of rules (generally called *meta-rules*).

The meta-rules are very close to the *inference-engines* that most systems possess in order to be able to reach conclusions based on sets of rules and/or frames. (As said before Horn-clauses mostly include the inference mechanism). Meta-rules allow a user to modify or augment the *inference-strategy* inherent in the preprogrammed part of the environment.

Inference engines mostly include *search-mechanisms* in order to establish the sequence in which the stored knowledge is to be evaluated. In some cases these search algorithms can be accessed by the user or even adapted to his needs.

In a number of systems the inference engine uses a *scratchpad* or *blackboard* as a communication area between ongoing processes like instantiations, temporary conclusions, location in the knowledge hierarchy, etc.

Most systems have facilities to store the massive amounts of items needed for reasoning in some type of (easily searchable) background memory: *knowledge bases*.

These knowledge bases need some control mechanism that can operate closely together with the inference engine, because the latter determines search strategies and the *chaining* of evaluation operations. It has been shown in Chapter I.3, paragraph 10, that in many cases as well *forward reasoning* as *backward reasoning*, often augmented with *iteration* possibilities are needed to reach factual conclusions.

To get the knowledge adequately in some knowledge base a *knowledge editor* is needed that is as user-friendly as possible and makes use of typing capabilities as sparingly as possible. Tool components that promote these facilities are also very welcome once the knowledge system is to used e.g. for consultation purposes.

Therefore powerful forms of dialogue with the knowledge engineer and the other users should be possible.

Graphical interaction has a preferred position in this case above other means because of the possibility of extremely compact communication. Thus *icons* and *graphs* play an important role, as well as screen addressing input capabilities like *mouses*. Other important graphical capabilities are *windows* and *zooming and panning* of screen details.

Natural language dialogue possibilities stand at a premium, but are not wide spread because of remaining ambiguity problems and the heavy typing load involved.

Also, to benefit the knowledge engineer and the user alike, most systems offer *explaining facilities*, *tracers* and *monitors* to show the operator how the system reaches specific conclusions, and even (in some cases) how the knowledge space is searched.

A number of systems support the utilization of fuzzy knowledge by offering means to *handle uncertainties* and *manage probabilities*.

A few systems have imbedded facilities to interface with elements of importance for appropriate, production type, utilizations like: *databases* (in order to allow use of data already collected through other sources), *computer-networks* (in order to make use of important application program libraries residing elsewhere) and the *source-language* in which the system was written (in order to allow enhancement of the capabilities of the environment).

Three systems have some discrete event *modelling support* facilities (KBS for SRL: see McRoberts, et al. and Reddy et al. (1985); SIMKIT for KEE: see Klahr et al. (1980) and Faught (1986); and (as a special case for power systems) TOAST for OPS5: see Talukdar and Cardozo (1986)).

Some typical tasks, that normally should be supported in such an environment, are unfortunately not yet adequately catered for. To mention just a few obvious ones:

- very few systems have facilities to assist in *maintaining consistency* between different representations of similar knowledge or between several levels of the knowledge hierarchy
- knowledge base *maintenance facilities* are very seldom to be found,
- tools for performing automated *knowledge synthesis* tasks are almost non-existent,
- specific tools for *problem-decomposition assistance,* e.g. in the phase of knowledge-acquisition and -structuring, are yet to appear,
- and last, but not least, *general, cognitive modelling* tools and provisions for the inclusion of *dynamic knowledge components,* which are elements of knowledge that have time-dependent components (like e.g. dynamic simulation models or other programs directly generated by the knowledge system) are still to be seriously investigated as to general implementability and coupling possibilities.

4. TYPOLOGY of ARTIFICIAL INTELLIGENCE ENVIRONMENTS

From the description of components that was given above a generalized architecture of Artificially Intelligent knowledge manipulation systems can be distilled.
In such an architecture all essential facilities, as well for the user as for the *knowledge engineer*, have to be included, even if they are not always present all together in all systems available on the market.
Such an architecture is depicted in fig. 3:

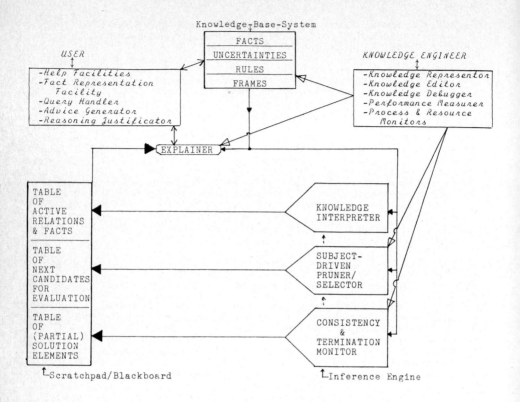

Fig. 3: Generalized Artificial Intelligence Environment
Architecture

From fig.3 and the prerequisite knowledge paradigms presented at
the end of paragraph 2, one can divide the types of Artificial
Intelligence environments in three categories:

- those that are *purely user-oriented* and require the user mainly
  to be knowledgeable about his problem and not - in any depth at
  least - about the tool he is using,
- *application oriented*, requiring the user to be at home in the
  (entire) application domain to which his problem belongs, and be
  aware of its general principles, in order to enlist appropriate
  assistance of the tool,

and, finally,

- those that provide adequate *facilities to build new tools* of the
  former kinds and therefore require the user to be conversant with
  many of the methods and techniques that form the general basis for
  the addressed family of computer tools.

In the case of Artificial Intelligence environments this
classification corresponds to a division in:

- consultation/advisory systems (where a considerable part of the
  problem-solving knowledge is supposed to reside in the tool), also
  commonly known by the name of *Expert Systems*,
- Artificial Intelligence workbenches that contain many of the
  elements needed to experiment with the principles of Expert
  Systems- like tools and allow the design and construction of new
  ones. This second class of systems is also known as *Expert System
  Shells* or *Artificial Intelligence Workstations*. This last name if
  strongly dependent on specific hardware. Quite a number of other
  Expert System development tools exist (e.g. OPS5, see Brownstone
  1985) that are more than a shell, though mostly not quite as
  powerful (especially with respect to interactive capabilities) as
  a workstation,
- general (mostly: hardware independent) Artificial Intelligence
  basic *building blocks* like special object-oriented languages
  (e.g. LISP and its dialects), special languages for propositional
  logic casu quo predicate calculus (e.g. PROLOG and its derivates),
  KBMS's (Knowledge Base Management Systems) and their associated
  software, Interactive Graphic hard- and software, etc.

Referring back to fig. 3: the first class of tools will contain most
of the elements depicted there in capital letters, though - in case
such a system resides in a small machine - often in a simplified
form, the access paths for the user are limited to those indicated.
Real (independent) knowledge base systems seldom occur in this
class, the knowledge often being embedded in one module in
conjunction with the inference mechanism.
Some of these simple systems allow a user to enter his own facts,
uncertainties and rules into the knowledge base, in this way
creating a kind of intermediate class tool.
Most Artificial Intelligence workbenches provide - at least - tools
for building knowledge structures (although often not in the form of
real - exchangeable - bases), modifying the available inference
mechanisms, enhancing explainer facilities and customizing the user
interfaces especially dialogue-contents and -presentation form.
In most systems of the third type all the elements have to be built
from scratch, at best with the assistance of already available
subroutines for some of the features shown in the figure.
Without much further argumentation it is supposed to be clear that
for creating "intelligent" Modelling & Simulation applications, the
best choice would be a type 2 (Artificial Intelligence workbench)
tool that has sufficient facilities to allow creation of the
additional features that are needed for this type of work, like:

- the creation of sophisticated (and often very voluminous)
  knowledge structures and associated KBMS's (based e.g. on entity
  lattices),
- provisions to use both rules and frames,
- allow forward and backward chaining,
- provide interfacing facilities, e.g. to databases (for storing
  measurement and simulation data), to languages like LISP or PROLOG
  (to create inference engine and knowledge structure extensions)
  and other (simulation) programs at runtime.

5. MUTUAL BENEFITS

When one starts to look critically at the possible synergies of
Artificial Intelligence and Modelling & Simulation, based - amongst
others - on Oren's comprehensive 1984 overview one finds that the
contributions differ quite considerably in nature depending on their
direction.
While apparently there is plenty of room for methodological
contributions from the side of Modelling & Simulation to basic
elements for the realization of more powerful Artificial
Intelligence systems; the function of Artificial Intelligence
achievements to the enrichment of Modelling & Simulation can by and
large be seen to be focussed primarily on improving the practical
applicability of methodical concepts, of which many have already
been suggested quite some time ago (see e.g. Oren and Zeigler 1979).

5.1 Benefits of Modelling & Simulation for Artificial Intelligence

The methodological ideas in Modelling & Simulation can contribute
positively to several aspects of the typical knowledge management
concepts and tools of Artificial Intelligence, like they are e.g.
present in Expert Systems.
Some of these aspects are:

- the *knowledge acquisition* process
- the *knowledge structuring & synthesis* concepts
- the methods for reasoning about *compatibility* between e.g. facts
  and knowledge elements
- techniques for the inclusion of *temporal knowledge* elements
  allowing dynamic model driven reasoning
- inherent manipulation of *numerical data*,
- techniques for *testing and validation* of knowledge systems.

In KNOWLEDGE ACQUISITION one of the most important problems for the
knowledge engineer is that there is no firm body of expertise on
which to base this activity. Therefore more often than not, this
process takes place in a more or less haphazard way and the
knowledge collected through interviews has to be made compatible and
complete by trial and error while entering it in the knowledge base,
often requiring extra iterations in the knowledge acquisition
process and thus requiring additional effort from the interviewees.
Experiments have shown that, using a vehicle much like an Entity
Structuring Program - ESP - (see Zeigler 1984b, pp. 344-348), this
situation can be considerably improved by allowing the interviewer
to structure his questions beforehand in an applicable knowledge

hierarchy and providing means to immediately evaluate dependencies and completeness of the answers by filling in the relations so obtained into a tree structure containing as well the names of the relevant subjects as their relevant attributes.
Very often such a structure can then be immediately used for building the knowledge base without requiring any extra processing iterations.

A similar tool can be used for KNOWLEDGE STRUCTURING & SYNTHESIS, once full use is made of the *blocks* concept that was introduced by van Melle in 1980 and extended in paragraph 2 of this Chapter.
As an additional feature for the ESP, a pruning facility (like the one described by Zeigler in 1984 (see Zeigler 1984b, pp. 272-281) and realized by Schoenmakers in 1986) is needed as well as some composition formalism, e.g. based on Zeigler's concept (Zeigler 1984, pp. 281-291).
In order to guarantee that such a methodology can be operationalized, the prime - addressable - elements of knowledge in the relevant knowledge base have to be blocks instead of individual rules, frames or concepts, because only blocks can be considered as being knowledge components that can more or less be freed from their (temporary) context.

When one gets to knowledge bases that can be *specialized* so as to be usable in different contexts, formalisms have to be created in order to be able to verify (or create) COMPATIBILITY between the newly assembled knowledge elements and the relevant context or set of facts.
For this purpose the Modelling & Simulation concept of Experimental Frames (see e.g. Rozenblit 1984) is almost optimally suited, mainly because the issues of compatibility between experimental frames and models have already been explored in detail. Experimental frames (see also Elzas 1984) can be considered to be the contexts in which certain specializations (hierarchies of aspect-specific submodels, see fig. 2) of models have to operate in order e.g. that a simulation with the model can answer certain questions given certain input conditions. The specification of such an experimental frame can then be used to select a specialized model composition out of a general model structure in order to obtain the requested - and necessary - elements for responding to its requirements.
In exactly the same - formal - vein *Experimental Contexts* can be defined for knowledge bases, that can be considered to be a kind of *cognitive models*, in order to select those cognition components (problem-specific blocks, in general, see fig. 1) which are needed to reason about facts within the context.
The main principles of this approach are to be found - mutatis mutandis - in the next Chapter (II.2) of this book.

The state-of-the-art in Artificial Intelligence has no operational concepts and facilities for representing TEMPORAL KNOWLEDGE that are worthwhile, being generally based on static knowledge.
That is: representing relations between knowledge components that do not possess any mechanism to display (time) dependent behavior other than the one inherent in the facts presented to it. A grossly simplified example to illustrate this point might be the following: consider a (hypothetical) expert system that is aware of the existence of Newton's laws of gravitation and is confronted with the falling apple problem. Based on the essential attributes (like: weight, starting-heigth and gravitational-constant) and assuming

that the system is so sophisticated that its production system can
include simple mathematical operations (which mostly is not yet the
case) then the system will be able to answer questions about
time-elapsed between start and end of fall, final-speed etc.
Detailed information about behavior during the fall will not be
obtainable unless special enhancements were provided for.
With other words such a system is - at best - able to know about and
display *point behavior*.
Now an essential paradigm in Newton's law is the smoothness, or
continuity, of the *trajectory* of the apple. In order to reconcile
the full knowledge with the real facts (or observations), e.g. for
an expert system to decide if the movement is Newtonian or not, the
knowledge system should "know" about trajectories. It should have
this knowledge not only in order to be able to display the
characteristics of such a behavior to its user, but more importantly
because the information content of the dynamics of the phenomenon is
much larger than what can be distilled from the exterior
characteristics of point behavior. For example if (speed dependent)
friction components have to be added at a higher cognitive level,
the earlier point behavior knowledge can not make any contribution
(=a whole new object will have to be built), while knowledge of the
properties of the trajectory (especially if in the form of any type
of dynamic model) will allow extension into higher, or more
detailed, cognitive levels and allow reasoning about the falling
apple at any time during the experiment. (E.g. if the apple would
stop in mid-air and pick up enough speed after that to land on time,
point behavior would still allow one to consider the motion to be
Newtonian, while trajectory behavior would allow proof to the
contrary).

The requirement for the inclusion of cognitive elements that can
vary in time, such as mentioned above, preferably making use of
(mathematical) models is not the only reason why manipulation of
NUMERICAL ENTITIES is important for Artificial Intelligence
environments.
Experience has shown that, e.g. for many relevant expert system
applications, it is of great importance to be able to reason about
sets of numerical values. On one hand to be able to interface the
knowledge base with sets of observational data (like e.g. in an air
polution risk advisory system that is being developed for the Dutch
Ministry of the Environment) making access to large data bases
essential. On the other hand to allow easy interfacing to a whole
scala of computational programs that are essential to either support
a diagnosis (like in the TOAST system that was referenced in
paragraph 3) or needed to evaluate numbers that are entered as
(part of) the facts that drive the inferencing.

Last, but not least, it is a rather well known fact that the testing
of a product produced with an Artificial Intelligence workbench
(like, e.g. an expert system) requires a long time and many sessions
with "prototype" users.
It might be very worthwhile to do this TESTING and VALIDATION using
simulation of models of the user's environment made by an
independent team, and applying validation techniques that have been
in use in Modelling & Simulation for a long time already (see
Sargent (1984) and Oren, Elzas, Sheng (1985)).

5.2 Benefits of Artificial Intelligence for Modelling & Simulation

The operational achievements in Artificial Intelligence environments,
which are becoming almost common property because of the recent
strong upswing in their application, have much to offer in helping
to realize many improvements in simulation support systems.
Many of such improvements have been high on the users' priority
lists for a considerable time, but have had to wait until now for
realization by means of the advances in Artificial Intelligence
systems.
Looking at Oren's 1984 publication and several of the Chapters in
this book, one can readily see that the main developments can be
expected in:

- improved *dialogue* facilities with Modelling & Simulation systems,
  especially those that have model bases,
- *Modelling & Simulation consultation* systems, that provide advice
  on *how* to use *which* models for *what* purpose,
- *symbolic model manipulation*, for comparing model formulation,
  searching for certain variables in simulation programs, extracting
  steady state (analytical) models from simulation models, etc.
- *model search* and *model inferencing* in/from assemblies of model
  components in model bases,
- automated *simulation program generation* from structured model- and
  experimental frame specifications.

Most of these issues have either been discussed in this Chapter and
Chapter I.3 or are handled elsewhere in this book (especially in
Sections II, III and V), therefore it is more useful to concentrate
on the requirements for Artificial Intelligence environments that
are essential for these developments.

The most important of these are:

- multiple knowledge representation formalisms, in any case
  including frames,
- flexible inference mechanism, preferably allowing both forward-
  and backward chaining
- easy interfacing with databases, either directly or through a
  network
- possibility to work with (large) knowledge bases on mass storage
- possibility to optimize knowledge structure for Modelling &
  Simulation application (e.g. for blocks, see paragraph 2 and
  entity lattices, see Chapter I.3)
- powerful dialogue capabilities, including good graphical
  capabilities
- easy – source language – interfacing with other program modules
  including possibility to generate and store programs (e.g. for
  simulation program generation).

6.   SURVEY OF EXISTING ARTIFICIAL INTELLIGENCE ENVIRONMENTS

In this paragraph a brief overview of contemporary Artificial
Intelligence environments is attempted with reference to the
requirements for Modelling & Simulation applications mentioned in
the previous paragraph.
The main criteria for inclusion of a system in the survey have been:
sophistication, operational state and (potential) availability.

NAME	SOURCE	MODELLING & SIMULATION ASPECTS
AGE	Stanford University	Supports many Artificial Intelligence mechanisms, no DB interface, no source interface.
ART	Inference Corp.	Viewpoints similar to blocks, graphics interface, rule compiler, no DB interface, no demons.
BABYLON	GMD, Bonn/FRG	All representation mechanisms, graphic interface, limited DB interface, source interface, no certainty factors.
CAT/SDMS	CCA & Carnegie Mellon Univ.	DB support, graphical database interface, limited to (powerful) rules, source interface.
EXPLAIN	Knowledge Engineering	rule based, mathematical representation, equation solving engine, limited DB interface.
HP-KL	Kewlett-Packard	Frame oriented, supported by DBMS, source interface.
KEE	Intellicorp	All representation mechanisms, potent graphic interface, rule compiler, no DB interface, no certainty factors, Discrete Event simulation module.
KBMS	Stanford Univ.	Intelligent processing in large databases models for interfaces, design, performance of advanced testing human knowledge base management systems.
LOOPS	Xerox	Integrates procedure-, object-, access- and rule-oriented mechanisms, extended source programming, no DB interface.

NAME	SOURCE	MODELLING & SIMULATION ASPECTS
OPS5	Digital Equipment	Powerfull, rule-based, easy interfacing with other languages, VAX-based, no dialogue, no graphics.
PRISM	Univ.of South Carolina	Object-oriented, intelligent DB support, integrity management.
SRL+	Carnegie Group	All representation mechanisms + DBMS-like schemata, DB support, no certainty factors, Discrete Event Simulation support incl. some model management facilities.
TAXIS	Univ. of Toronto	Object-oriented tool for design and construction of information systems, compiles into PASCAL.
UNITS	Stanford Univ.	Frames, rules and hierarchies, no DB support.

7. RECOMMENDATIONS FOR FUTURE RESEARCH

The contents of this Chapter added to the ideas already presented in Chapter I.3, suggest the need for further research on a whole series of Artificial Intelligence related subjects for Modelling & Simulation support systems.

Main items could be:

- new knowledge structures in Artificial Intelligence environments for Modelling & Simulation support systems (like the blocks mentioned in paragraph 2 of this Chapter and the entity lattices of Chapter I.3)
- construction of adequate browsing and selection mechanisms for the manipulation of model components in model bases (possibly using the similarity net concept described in Chapter I.3)
- design of experimental - frame - driven model composition algorithms, based on the selection procedures mentioned above,
- development of dialogue-based simulation program generators that make use of models composed by means of the methods mentioned above
- the possibilities for expert modelling assistance systems that can profer advice on best models for certain applications.

Of course many more subjects could be suggested, many users will, however, consider the above certainly more than worth waiting for.

8. REFERENCES

Brownstone, L. (Ed.) (1985). Programming Expert Systems in OPS5.
    Addison Wesley, Reading, Mass.

Elzas, M.S. (1984). System Paradigms as Reality Mappings. In:
    Loc.cit. sub Oren, et al. (1984), pp. 41-67

Faught, W.S. (1986). Applications of Artificial Intelligence in
    Engineering. In: Computer, Vol. 19, no.7, pp. 17-27.

Klahr, P., W.S. Faught and G.R. Martins (1980). Rule-Oriented
    Simulation. In: proc. 1980 IEEE Conference on Cybernetics and
    Society.

Klir, G.J. (1979). General systems problem solving methodology. In:
    loc.cit. sub Zeigler, et al. (1979), pp. 3-28

Klir, G.J. (1984). General Systems Framework for Inductive
    Modelling. In: Loc.cit. sub Oren, et al. (1984), pp. 69-90.

McRoberts, M. M.S. Fox and N. Husain (1985). Generating model
    abstraction scenarios in KBS. In: Proc. SCS Conference on
    Artificial Intelligence, Graphics and Simulation, San Diego,
    Ca., pp. 29-33.

Melle, W. van (1980. A Domain-Independent System that Aids in
    Constructing Knowledge-Based Consultation Programs. Stanford
    Heuristic Programming Memo HPP-80-22.

Oren, T.I. and B.P. Zeigler (1979). Concepts for advanced simulation
    methodologies. In: Simulation, Vol. 32, nr. 3, pp. 69-82.

Oren, T.I. et al. (1984). Simulation and Model-Based Methodologies:
    An Integrative View. Oren, T.I., B.P.Zeigler, M.S.Elzas (Eds.),
    Springer-Verlag, Heidelberg.

Oren,T.I. (1984). Model-Based Activities: A Paradigm Shift.
    In: Loc.cit. sub Oren, T.I. et al. (1984), pp. 3-40.

Oren, T.I., M.S. Elzas and G. Sheng (1985). Model Reliability and
    Software Quality Assurance in Simulation of Nuclear Waste
    Management Systems. In: Waste Management '85, Post, R.G. (Ed.),
    Vol. I, pp. 381-396, Tucson, Az.

Reddy, Y.V., M.S. Fox and N. Husain (1985). Automating the Analysis
    of Simulations in KBS. In: Loc.cit. sub McRoberts (1985), pp.
    34-40.

Rozenblit, J.W. (1984). EXP - A Software Tool for Experimental Frame
    Specification in Discrete Event Modelling and Simulation. In:
    Proc. 1984 Summer Computer Simulation Conference, Boston, pp.
    967-971.

Sargent, R.G. (1984). Simulation Model Validation. In: Loc.cit. sub
    Oren, et al. (1984), pp. 537-556.

Schoenmakers, H. (1986). ESP-2, an Entity Structuring Program with Pruning Facilities. Technical Report, Depts. of Computer Science, Univ. of Arizona and Wageningen Univ.

Talukdar, S.N. and E. Cardozo (1986). Artificial Intelligence Technologies for Power System Operations. Report EL-4323, Electric Power Research Institute.

Zeigler, B.P. et al. (1979). Methodology in Systems Modelling and Simulation. Zeigler, B.P., M.S. Elzas, G.J. Klir, T.I. Oren (Eds.), North-Holland, Amsterdam.

Zeigler, B.P. (1984a). System Theoretic Foundations of Modelling and Simulation. In: Loc.cit. sub Oren, et al. (1984), pp. 91-118.

Zeigler, B.P. (1984b). Multifacetted Modelling and Discrete Event Simulation. Academic Press, London.

Modelling and Simulation Methodology
in the Artificial Intelligence Era
M.S. Elzas, T.I. Ören and B.P. Zeigler (Editors)
© Elsevier Science Publishers B.V. (North-Holland), 1986   79

Chapter II.2

ENTITY-BASED STRUCTURES FOR MODEL AND
EXPERIMENTAL FRAME CONSTRUCTION

Jerzy W. Rozenblit and Bernard P. Zeigler

Department of Electrical and Computer Engineering
The University of Arizona
Tucson, Arizona 85721
U.S.A.

This chapter sets up a conceptual framework for
constructing knowledge-based environments to support
a model and simulation program development process.
The framework is based on the formal structures
underlying the multifacetted modelling methodology,
namely that of the system entity structure and
experimental frame. It is argued that these structures
represent the basic knowledge required to specify
models and experimental conditions in simulation
studies.

1. INTRODUCTION

The primary concerns of the modelling and simulation enterprise are the
construction of models of real world systems, computer simulation of
such models, and analysis of the simulation results. The ultimate
benefit of modelling is to improve and increase decision making
capabilities in engineering and business environments. The
methodologies offered by the discipline should be an inherent component
in computer-aided decision systems for management, control and design
(Sprague and Carlson, 1982; Elzas, 1982). The tools and activities
prescribed by such methodologies should enable the decision makers to
evaluate the effects of decisions before they are actually carried
out. The best - in terms of performance measures related to the system
under evaluation - intervention alternatives should be chosen and
deployed in the real system.

The choice of performance measures reflects the questions the decision
maker (be it an economist, a designer of a car, or a technician
supervising a manufacturing process) wants to ask about the system
under consideration. The questions translate into the objectives of
the simulation study that is undertaken to provide the answers about
the system. Therefore, it is important to recognize the importance of
the simulation objectives. They play the key role in orienting and
driving both the model building and design of simulation experiments.

In this chapter we shall focus on the objectives-driven model
development methodology (Zeigler, 1984) and its underlying formal
structures. We propose a systematic model and experimental frame
development methodology supported by adequate formal concepts. Our
framework corresponds to the deducive modelling approach proposed by
Elzas (1984). As defined by Elzas (1984) the deducive approach requires

some a priori knowledge of the structure of a real system. It also assumes the existence of a methodology for the construction of experimental frames from proposed alternative system decompositions, obtained through the deductive process.

We first address the problem of representing the fundamental structures for the model and experimental frame development. Then, we proceed to define procedures that employ these structures and facilitate the model construction process.

2. THE SYSTEM ENTITY STRUCTURE

To appropriately represent a family of possible model structures we need a representation scheme that embodies knowledge about the following three relationships: decomposition, taxonomy, and coupling. By knowing about decomposition we mean that the scheme has a means for representing the manner in which an object is decomposed into components.

By taxonomic knowledge, we mean a representation for the kinds of variants that are possible for an object. Such variants are termed specializations. To construct a model, the components identified in decompositions and specializations must be coupled together. Thus, the third kind of knowledge that our scheme should have is that of coupling relationships.

A formal object that conforms to the above specification is the system entity structure (Zeigler, 1982, 1984, Belogus 1985).

The system entity structure is based on a tree-like graph encompassing the boundaries and decompositions that have been conceived for the system (Zeigler, 1982, 1984). An entity signifies a conceptual part of the system which has been identified as a component in one or more decompositions. Each such decomposition is called an aspect. Thus entities and aspects should be thought of as components and decompositions, respectively. The system entity structure organizes possibilities for a variety of system decompositions and model constructions.

Both entities and aspects can have attributes represented by the so called attached variable types. When a variable type V is attached to an item occurrence I, this signifies that a variable I.V may be used to describe the item occurrence I. Thus, while an unqualified variable type such as LENGTH may have multiple occurrences in the entity structure, a qualified variable e.g. QUEUE1.LENGTH belongs to one and only one item occurrence, QUEUE1.

Among many important features of the system entity structure we would like to emphasize the following three:

a.) coupling constraints on the possible ways in which components (represented by entities) identified in decompositions (represented by aspects) can be coupled together are attached to aspects. This plays a crucial role in the hierarchical model construction process (Zeigler, 1984);

b.) there is a special type of decomposition called a multiple decomposition that allows for a flexible representation of multiple entities whose number in a model may vary;

c.) there is a special relation termed <u>specialization</u> which allows for representation of objects with individual attributes, yet inheriting the variables of a general class to which they belong. The specialization is modelled after the class concept of SIMULA and more recent object oriented languages.

Figure 1., depicts a system entity structure for an automobile. The triple vertical lines denote multiple decompositions while the double vertical lines stand for specializations. We shall refer to this entity structure throughout the ensuing sections.

The representation of attached variables as <u>item-name.variable-type</u> pairs has profound implications for design of modelling support environments. A data base of <u>generic variable types</u> should be an indispensable component of a software package for the system entity structure and experimental frame specification. The user of such a system faced with a modelling problem that falls into a certain general class e.g. queuing systems, would refer to the generic variable base and choose variable types suitable for the class his problem belongs to. The same concerns the specification of the appropriate experimental frames via the concept of the generic frame type. At this point we proceed to define the other fundamental concept in our framework that is the experimental frame.

3. <u>EXPERIMENTAL</u> <u>FRAME</u> <u>DEFINITION</u> <u>AND</u> <u>ITS</u> <u>STRUCTURAL</u> <u>REALIZATION</u>

Zeigler (1984) has laid down the groundwork for the modelling methodology in which the statement of objectives is operationalized in a definition of experimental frames. The experimental frame as initially perceived by Oren and Zeigler (1979) defines a set of circumstances under which a model of the real system is to be observed and experimented with. We would like to emphasize the importance of the experimental frame concept in the following contexts.

First, a frame in the objectives-driven methodology directs the model building process. It also facilitates meaningful simplification and stating of relations the modeller seeks to establish between two models (Zeigler, 1984).

Secondly, in the context of computer assistance for simulation, tools and architectures for the multifacetted modelling, the frame concept allows for a clear separation of the model and experimentation specifications. This in turn results in modular simulation software designs. Such designs should incorporate the model/experimental frame separation in that separate modules for model, experiment and execution control specification are provided. This conceptual framework has in fact found its realization in the new simulation systems and software for both continuous and discrete event systems (Oren, 1982; Pegden, 1982; Crosby, 1983; Javor, 1982; Kettenis, 1983).

In view of the recent efforts leading towards knowledge-based simulation environments, the experimental frame concept is directly related to the selective model instrumentation framework postulated by Reddy, Fox and Husain (1985). The key facility in that framework is a rule-based system whose task is to generate experimental modules by consulting a domain specific knowledge base.

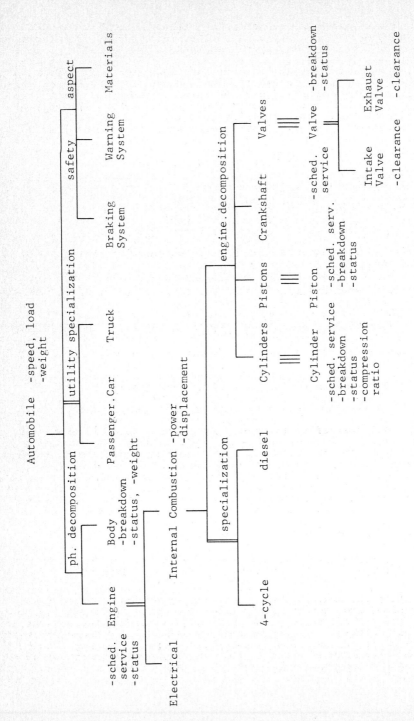

Figure 1. System Entity Structure for Automotive Modelling

Finally, the hierarchical frame specification (Rozenblit, 1985b) consolidates efforts to provide a unified framework for simulation of distributed, hierarchically specified systems.

Let us now briefly discuss the steps that lead to the specification of an experimental frame. The set of experimentation circumstances that we strive to define by means of a frame is perceived as consisting of four categories, namely: input, output, run control and summary variable sets. There are also constraints on the time segments of input and run control variables. Formally, the experimental frame is defined as follows:

$$EF=<T,I,O,C,W_I,W_C,SU,W_{SU}>$$

where

T is a time base
I is the set of <u>input variables</u>
O is the set of <u>output variables</u>
C is the set of <u>run control variables</u>
W_I is the set of <u>admissible input segments</u>, i.e. a subset of all time segments over the crossproduct of the input variable ranges
W_C is the set of <u>run control segments</u>, i.e. a subset of all time segments over the crossproduct of the control variable ranges.
SU is a set of summary variables
$W_{su}=\{s|\ s: I \times O \ --> \ SU.range\}$ is the set of <u>summary mappings</u>

The I/O data space defined by the frame is the set of all pairs of I/O segments:

$$D=\{(w,r)|\ w \in (T,X)\ ,\ r \in (T,Y)\ and\ dom(_w)=dom(_r)\}.$$

where X and Y are input and output value sets, respectively.

The reader is referred to (Zeigler, 1984) for a detailed exposition of the frame concept. Here we emphasize the meaning of the run control variables and segments. One should realize that they initialize the experiments and set up conditions for continuation as well as termination of simulation runs. The set of initialization conditions constitutes a subset of the control space called INITIAL. Similarly, the subset defined by the termination conditions is called TERMINAL. The run control segments can then be defined as follows:

$$W_C=\{m\ |m:\ <t_{initial},\ t_{final}>\ -->\ Z\ \}$$

where Z = crossproduct of the ranges of individual run control variables, and $m(t_{initial}) \in INITIAL$, $m(t_{final}) \in TERMINAL$.

We now relate the above definition of the experimental frame to the issue of simulation design. It is clear that a means of expressing a frame in the procedural form would greatly facilitate the generation of simulation programs. Other than the few simulation systems referenced above the state-of-the-art simulation languages do not capture the notion of experiment in a manner conducive to our description. However, prototypes for structural realization of experimental frames have been proposed by Zeigler (1984).

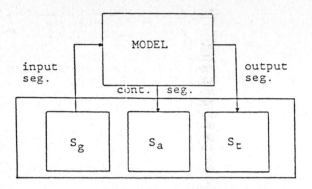

Figure 2. Structural Realization of an Experimental Frame

Employing the concepts of automata theory and the DEVS (discrete event system specification) formalism, Zeigler (1984) defines a DEVS generator, acceptor and transducer. The experimental frame E is then realized by a system S_E which is a parallel composition of systems S_I (an input segment generator or acceptor), S_C (a run control segments acceptor) and S_O (a composition of transducers, each of which realizes a summary mapping). Such a realization is depicted in Figure 2. Notice that the system S_E is coupled to the model of the system under study.

Accordingly, the resulting simulation program should consist of procedures representing the model and frame specifications, respectively. Such tripartite realization of an experimental frame provides a very flexible means for user specification of the experimental circumstances in a simulation study. Moreover, basic DEVS devices for standard operations e.g. computation of the average of values, acceptance of a constant segments, can be used as elements of the computer-aider environment for the simulation program generation.

In the context of the above definition an experimental frame employed in a simulation program applies to a specific problem and answers the questions directly addressed to that problem. In other words, the variables, segments and initialization/termination conditions are defined in such a way that the frame applies to the specific model under study. However, we would like the frame generation to be supported by knowledge-based environments. It is thus natural to conceive any frame realization as a concretization of a general experimental frame type. Such a general frame type can be regarded as a generic experimental frame for certain classes of problems and types of performance evaluation criteria. Such standard criteria would include input/output performance indexes, utilization of resources measures, reliability assessments etc.

Also, recall that the experimental frame concept is discussed in this paper in the context of the objectives-driven simulation methodology. Thus, it is necessary to view the simulation design from a perspective in which the model and experimental frame development are complimentary and mutually supportive processes. In the following section we present the concept of the generic frame type and discuss its role in the model development methodology.

4. THE CONCEPT OF GENERIC EXPERIMENTAL FRAME

As we have indicated in Section 3., a generic frame should be a general class from which an experimental frame specification for a simulation study under consideration could be derived. The generic frame is defined by means of unqualified generic variable types that correspond to the objective for which the simulation is undertaken. Thus, a generic frame should be only a template whose instantiation takes place after the simulation model has been constructed. With an objective we associate a performance index that allows for a final judgement of the simulation model with respect to that objective. A generic experimental frame is defined as the following structure induced by a performance index pi.

$$GEF_{pi} = \{IG, OG, W_{GI}, SU, W_{SU}\}$$

where: GEF_{pi} denotes a generic experimental frame for performance index pi and

      IG is the set of generic input variable types for pi
      OG is the set of generic output variable types for pi
      W_{IG} is the set of generic input segment types for pi
      SU is the set of summary variables
      W_{SU} is the set of standard summary mappings

Notice that we have decided not to include the set of run control variables and segments in the above definition. We feel that the execution control conditions for a simulation run should be specified after the relevant generic frame has been instantiated and the model is ready to be experimented with.

To illustrate how a generic frame type may be specified let us consider a simple example. In many classes of problems one of the standard simulation objectives is to obtain measurements concerning utilization of system's components. A common measure associated with this objective is often called utilization and is expressed as follows:

Utilization = (total time a component is active/total observation time)

Let us now define a generic frame type that corresponds to this performance measure. It is easy to notice that in order to record the utilization of a component we must monitor its status, i.e. whether it is active or idle. We also need to define input variables and segments in order to observe how the component responds to a sequence of tasks arriving at the system. Then, a generic frame Utilization can have the following form:

Generic Frame Type: UTILIZATION
    {comment: specifies a class of experimental frames for evaluation of component utilization in discrete event systems}

Generic Input Variables:
    Arrival with range {0,1} where 1 denotes an event of arrival, 0 is an empty event

Generic Output Variables:
    Status with range {0,1} where Status=0 denotes idle, Status=1 denotes active component

<u>Generic</u> <u>Input</u> <u>Segment</u> <u>Type</u>:
    InSeg_Arrival
        class: DEVS segment
        parameters: inter-arrival distribution type

    {comment: after the generic frame is instantiated the segment
    description is matched with the specification of standard
    experimental frame input generators, so the input segment can be
    realized as a DEVS generator;

<u>Generic</u> <u>Summary</u> <u>Variable</u>
    Utilization

    {comment: to obtain values for Utilization a standard DEVS
    transducer should be employed. Such a transducer will monitor the
    variable Status and record the ratio of time(Status=1)/
    Total.Elapsed.Time}

Other examples of generic experimental frame types for various
performance criteria are presented in (Rozenblit,1985).

In the context of the experimental frame generation, the generic frame
constitutes a skeleton from which the experimental modules are
constructed. We shall discuss this process, called instantiation, in
Section 7. In the model development aspect, the key role of generic
frames is to provide a means for selecting substructures of the system
entity structure which accommodate the modelling objectives i.e.,
contain all the attached variable types present in the generic
frames. This process is called <u>pruning</u> and will be explained in detail
in the next section.

We are now ready to incorporate the system entity structure and generic
frame types into the model and experimental frame development process.
Recall that the entity structure represents a family of model
structures (Zeigler, 1984) that are used in the model construction
process. Each such structure has attributes expressed by means of
variables and associated coupling constraints that restrict the way in
which the components of the structure can be connected together. Also,
it is important to remember that the simulation objectives are the
driving mechanism in the model construction process. We are simply
interested in obtaining the "simplest" (minimal, least complex) model
that is capable of answering our questions about the real system. Thus,
we need a means of extracting from the system entity structure all the
model structures that meet the simulation objective, or in more
specific terms, that accommodate the generic experimental frame
expressing that particular objective. Consequently, the extracted
model structures should support the instantiation of the generic frame
in which they have been obtained.

In the following section we propose a framework for the entity
structure-based model and experimental frame development.

5. <u>ENTITY</u> <u>STRUCTURE</u> <u>PRUNING</u> <u>FOR</u> <u>GENERATION</u> <u>OF</u> <u>MODEL</u> <u>STRUCTURES</u>

Given the system entity structure we are offered a spectrum of model
alternatives due to the multiplicity of aspects and specializations.
The question arises: "how can we meaningfully use the structure to
support the model development process?"

Assume that an entity structure has been transformed into a structure
with no specializations. Then, imagine that we traverse the structure
selecting a single aspect for each entity and zero or more entities for
each aspect. All selected entities carry their attributes with
them. The coupling constraint of the selected aspect is attached to the
entity to which this aspect belongs. The above process results in
decomposition trees (Zeigler 1982, 1984) that represent hierarchical
decompositions of models into components. We term such decomposition
trees model structures. The process that extracts the model structures
from the system entity structure is called pruning.

In what follows we present definition of the pruning process based on
the generic experimental frame concept. By pruning the system entity
structure with respect to generic frames we derive the following
benefits:

a.) a generic frame extracts only those substructures which conform
    to the modelling objectives. Thus, a number of model alternatives
    may be disregarded as not applicable or not realizable for a
    given problem.

b.) partial models can be formulated and evaluated. This may
    significantly reduce the complexity which would arise if we had
    to deal with the overall model. The generic frame concept may
    thus be viewed as an object that partitions the system entity
    structure into modelling objectives related classes.

c.) the evaluation of the models constructed from the pruned
    substructures is performed in corresponding experimental
    frames. Such frames are generated by instantiating the generic
    frames used to prune the system entity structure. Hence,
    automatic evaluation procedures could be employed in the
    simulation design process.

In terms of facilitating the pruning process itself, generic frames
automatically determine:

a.) the aspects that are selected for each entity

b.) the depth of the pruning process

c.) the descriptive variables of components

Having discussed the benefits afforded by the generic frame concept we
now proceed to define the pruning procedure.

The pruning procedure presented here is defined for pure system entity
structures, i.e., structures in which no specializations are
present. Rozenblit (1895) presents a suite of algorithms that transform
entity structures with specializations into pure system entity
structures.

For the pruning process it is enough to restrict the generic
experimental frame to the generic observation frame i.e.:

$$GOF = \{IG, OG\}$$

where IG denotes the set of generic input variable types, and OG is the
set of generic output variable types. By defining the observation
frame as above, we restrict its role to representing the behavioral
aspects of modelling objectives. As we have already indicated, there

are also objectives that constrain the structural aspects of the
project under consideration. Therefore, as we shall see in the next
section, in order to realize the structural constraints it will be
necessary to augment the model development with a process that we term
synthesis rule generation.

The pruning procedure is based on the depth first tree traversal. In
this procedure every entity in each aspect is searched for occurrences
of variable types that are present in the generic observation
frame. The entities are attached to the model decomposition tree as the
search progresses. At the same time the algorithm calls itself

recursively for each entity being searched. The complete pruning
procedure is given below:

Procedure Prune(E_j, CV_{GOF}, V_{GOF});
  { This procedure prunes the pure system entity structure and
    returns the model structures that accommodate the generic
    observation frame GOF. Multiple occurrences of a frame
    variable type are permitted in the model structures }

E_j - root of the pure entity structure
CV_{GOF} - set of variables of the generic frame GOF

              this set is used to check if all the frame
              variables are present in the pruned substructure
              initially CV_{GOF} = V_{GOF}
V_{GOF} set of input and output variable types of GOF

begin
  for each aspect $A_i \in E_j$ do
    begin

      for each entity $E_k \in A_i$ do
        begin

            attach E_k with all its variables as a child of TE_j;
            { TE_j denotes the root of the model structure being
              currently built }

            CV_{GOF} := CV_{GOF} - v_k;

            { update the current set CV_{GOF} by subtracting
              the variable types v_k such that v_k V_{GOF}
              and v_k is attached to E_k }

            if E_k has at least one variable type present in V_{GOF}
            then   mark this level in the model structure as the
                   last level at which variable types present in
                   the frame have been found;

        end; {of for each entity ... }

      attach the coupling constraint of the aspect A_i to TE_j;

```
      for each E_k ∈ A_i such that E_k has aspects do
         Prune(E_k, CV_GOF, V_GOF);


      if C_GOF is empty   { i.e. the frame is accommodated }
      then

         begin

            create a copy of the current model structure
            rooted by TE_j;

            { this copy will serve as a basis for model
              structure construction in the next aspect A_{i+1} }

            output the current model structure rooted by TE_j
            without the entities that appear below the level
            marked as the last level with frame variable type
            occurrence;

         end; {of if}

      update the current structure TE_j by cutting
      off the last level entities;

      { thus prepare the structure for pruning in the
        next aspect}

   end; {of for each aspect ... }

end. {of Prune}
```

To initialize the pruning process we follow the steps given below:

a.) in the system entity structure choose the entity E_i that represents the model you intend to evaluate (this entity will label the root of the model structure TE_i).

b.) create a dummy entity DE (with no variables) with a dummy aspect DA in which E_i is a subentity of DE.

c.) call Prune(DE, CV$_{GOF}$, V$_{GOF}$);

After the procedure has been executed we have to eliminate DE from all the model structures.

We have already indicated that the procedure Prune generates a set of model structures in the form of decomposition trees. Each such structure accommodates the generic observation frame GOF and constitutes a skeleton for a hierarchical model construction. Figure 3 illustrates the results of pruning of the system entity structure with respect to frame GOF.

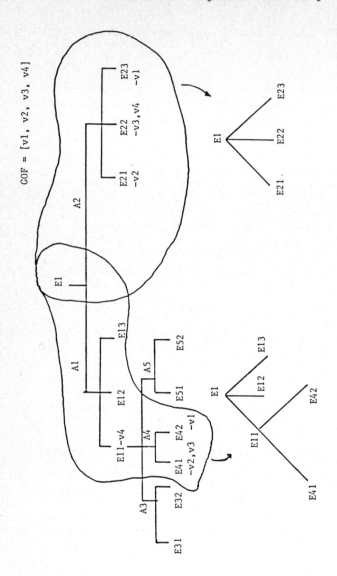

Figure 3. Pruning the System Entity Structure in the Generic Frame GOF and
Resulting Structures for Model Construction

In conclusion, the pruning process plays the major role in the selection of model alternatives that conform to the objectives. Thus the modelling space is meaningfully restricted to behaviorally feasible model structures. Having presented the framework for behavioral pruning, in the next chapter we proceed to establish rules for expressing the structural aspects of modelling objectives.

6. ENTITY STRUCTURE-BASED SYNTHESIS RULE SPECIFICATION

The pruning process described in the foregoing chapter restricts the space of possibilities for selection of components and couplings that can be used to realize a model. Thus we can assume that model development process may now be reduced to the synthesis problem (Zeigler, 1986). Synthesis involves putting together a system from a known and fixed set of components in a fairly well-prescribed manner. In the synthesis problem, we are modelling a rather restricted design process, one amenable to automation by extracting concepts and procedures from experts' knowledge and experience, augmenting them and molding them into a coherent set of rules. The rule development methodology that we propose for such a modelling enterprise is as follows:

*.) Restrict the modelling domain by pruning the system entity structure in respective generic observation frames.

*.) Examine the the resulting substructure and their constraints. Try to convert as many constraint relations as possible into the active from, i.e. into rules that can satisfy them. For those that cannot be converted into such rules write rules that will test them for satisfaction.

*.) Write additional rules, modify existing ones, to coordinate the actions of the rules (done in conjunction with the selected conflict resolution strategy).

In a synthesis problem, several kinds of constraints may come into play. Here, we focus on two types of constraints that influence the manner in which synthesis rules are specified. Assuming that a synthesis problem is appropriate for expert system design, there are known actions that can be taken to try to satisfy the performance constraints derived from the objectives and imposed standards. Indeed, an expert's procedural knowledge represents efficient procedures that are likely to achieve the goals and subgoals that arise in attempting to meet the performance requirements. The pruning process described in the previous section is an example of such an action. We see the following constraint classification emerging: some constraints are convertible to active form, i.e., they can be converted into actions intended to satisfy them. Other constraints are inherently passive, they do not motivate or guide action, they sit there demanding satisfaction. The question that now begs to be addressed is: assuming that it is possible, how can we convert a constraint to active form? We conceive of the synthesis problem as a search through the search space, the set of all pruned model structures. These are candidates for a solution to the problem. Our set of rules will take us from an initial state in this space to a goal state. The search should proceed by generating successive candidate structures in an efficient manner.

We can assume that for each active constraint we have a means of generating such candidates to test against the constraint. Call such an operator NEXT_IN_Ci.

The passive constraints have no corresponding operators and thus we can only test for their satisfaction. Failure causes backtracking if a state has been reached for which none of the operators can be applied. Instead of applying an operator and then testing if it has consumed more than what remains of an available resource, we can try to inhibit the application of operators that would bring about the resource depletion.

Let Con be a constraint that we wish to pretest. An operator, NEXT_IN_Ci will map a state s into the region satisfying Con if, and only if, Con(NEXT_IN_Ci(s)). To allow the operator to be applied safely we need to define <u>applicability</u> predicate, Ai such that:

$$Ai(s) \text{ if, and only if, } Con(NEXT\_IN\_Ci(s))$$

Thus a canonical rule scheme for a synthesis problem takes the following form:

RC If C satisfied on (state)
       then Output (state) as the solution

Rl If Cl is not satisfied
       Al is satisfied
       then state:=NEXT_IN_Cl(state)

  . . . .

Ri If Ci is not satisfied
       Ai is satisfied
       then state:=NEXT_IN_Ci(state)

  . . . .

Rn If Cn is not satisfied
       An is satisfied
       then state:=NEXT_IN_Ci(state)

The structures generated as results of behavioral pruning and structural synthesis should be used to construct models employing the hierarchical model construction methodology . We shall briefly describe the underlying concept of this framework and refer the reader for details to (Zeigler, 1984).

Recall that the pruned entity structures generated by the objectives-driven pruning represent minimal structures that have all the variables required by the generic observation frame. Many more variables may have to be employed by a model to fully express the nature of the system being modelled. Thus, we must assume that an expansion of the set of attached variables is possible to incorporate all the attributes requires by the model.

The next step in the model construction process is the so-called orientation and role designation i.e., selection of input, output, state variables and model parameters. Having established input/output orientation, we are in a position to couple components together in accordance with the coupling constraint associated with internal nodes of the structure. The formalism that enables us to uniquely specify models based in the hierarchies pruned from the system entity structure is called <u>composition</u> <u>tree</u> (Zeigler, 1984a).

Let us now gather the strands up and propose an environment to support the model and experimental frame development process. An example explicating the use of such an environment and its formal tools will follow in Section 8.

7. <u>ENVIRONMENT</u> <u>FOR</u> <u>SUPPORT</u> <u>OF</u> <u>MODEL</u> <u>AND</u> <u>FRAME</u> <u>DEVELOPMENT</u>

It has been our contention throughout the foregoing sections that the system entity structure and the concept of the generic frame type constitute the knowledge that can support the automatic specification of models and experimental frames. To discuss this argument we propose the following architecture to support such an automatic process.

As illustrated in Figure 4, the data base of simulation objectives specification is one of the major components of the system. It has to be well understood that the modelling objectives drive three processes in our methodology. First, the retrieval and/or construction of the system entity structure. Naturally, the modeller desires to obtain a family of model representations rather then a single model structure. A classic example would be the area of system design where a spectrum of design alternatives is sought for evaluation before the final design is chosen (Rozenblit, 1984b). Secondly, the objectives serve as a basis for definition of the generic frame types. Finally, the objectives understood in a somewhat broader context (e.g. as design requirements), imply a set of rules for the model synthesis and constraints on how the model components may be coupled. Therefore in the proposed architecture we introduce the base of synthesis rules and coupling constraints.

The ultimate purpose of the system represented in Figure 4, is to analyze and integrate the relationships concerning the objectives specification base, the generic frame, and system entity structure base to form an appropriate model and simulation experiment for the problem at hand. As Shannon, Mayer and Adelsberger (1985) point out, this presents an ideal problem for the application of expert systems technology.

Let us propose how such a system should operate given the knowledge represented by the aforementioned bases. First, we augment the system entity structure extraction with a synthesis rule-based pruning. The pruning procedure presented in Section 5 extracts the substructures that accommodate the simulation objectives from the behavioral standpoint. Actually, the nature of the generic frame concepts is intrinsically behavioral. Pruning the entity structure in a generic template results in models whose behavioral properties enable us to answer the questions of the simulation study. We feel however, that the class of models generated by pruning should be further restricted in order to account for the constraints imposed by the rules of synthesis (Rozenblit and Zeigler, 1985).

Both, structural and behavioral pruning applied to the system entity structure should result in model structures that we term candidates for hierarchical model construction. The term candidates implies that some checks for consistency and admissibility (in the sense of conformance to the objectives) should be performed at this stage. If the candidate is inadmissible or no candidates can be obtained by pruning, the process should be reiterated with possible user intervention. The

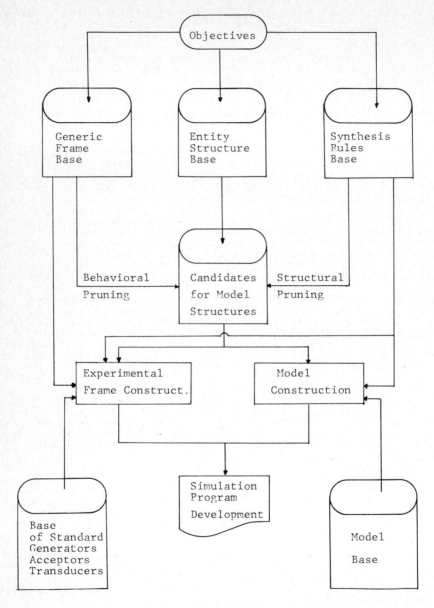

Figure 4. Environment for Support of Model and Frame Development

kinds of interventions we suggest are modifications or retrieval of the new system entity structure, enhancement of the generic experimental frame or modification of synthesis rules.

The system should construct models for the skeletons generated as a result of the structural and behavioral pruning. Such model construction is based on the composition tree formalism presented in (Zeigler, 1984). Again, the base of synthesis rules should be consulted for proper implementation of coupling constraints. At the same time the generic experimental template should be instantiated. We envision the instantiation as a three phase process.

In the first stage the variable types present in the template are assigned component names i.e. the names of entities to which these types are attached. However, since the pruning procedure proposed in Section 5., generates all occurrences of a given type, it is necessary to eliminate from the experimental frame those variables which are internally controlled in the model. Recall, that the pruning is guided only by the input and output generic types, therefore we have to be concerned with that type of variables. An appropriate scheme for elimination is to consult the synthesis rules and coupling constraints associated with the entities of the model candidate structures and proceed to filter out the internally controlled variable by applying a scheme similar to that of the coupling recipe defined by Wymore (1980).

Following Wymore's terminology we assert that the experimental frame induced by a generic frame type contains only those (input and output) variables that are free input and output variables. An input/output variable is free if it does not appear in any of the links of the coupling scheme. As this may be somewhat restrictive in the sense of limiting the observation space we can relax this constraint by allowing the frame to collect the data from some of the internally controlled output variables.

The third stage in the frame generation is to choose appropriate variables to serve as run control variables. We feel that this should be done by the user just before the model is ready to be run within the frame under consideration. The same concerns setting up the INITIAL and TERMINAL sets. The summary variables of the generic frame are directly applied in the experimental frame. They are simply instantiated with the names of the model components to which the modeller wishes them to apply.

Finally, in the context of the frame realization, a base of standard generators, acceptors and transducers should be available in the system. The retrieval of the appropriate modules from that base would be guided by the obtained experimental frame definition.

To illustrate the concepts discussed in the foregoing sections we now provide a simple example form the area of automotive design.

8. EXAMPLE - DEVELOPMENT OF DESIGN MODELS

Assume that an automotive company is designing a new model of a truck. To satisfy prospective customers who, among other things, require that a truck should be operational above 95% over its life cycle, the company has placed a very strong emphasis on the reliability aspect of the new model. Factors like: the number of scheduled inspections, the time it takes to complete an inspection, the time it takes to repair or replace a malfunctioning part etc., will play a major role in evaluating the new design. In general, the generic frame Utilization can be chosen to represent this particular behavioral design objective. A corresponding observation frame is given below:

<u>Generic</u> <u>Observation</u> <u>Frame</u>: Utilization.

Input variables:
    Scheduled.Service
    Breakdown

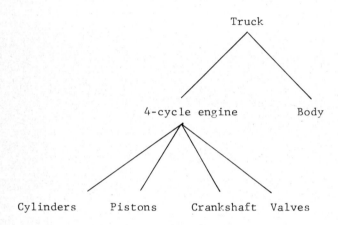

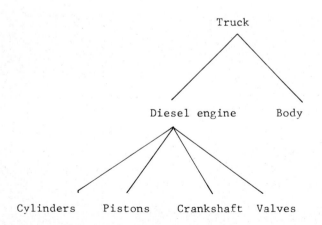

Figure 5. Model Structures Resulting from Pruning the Sytem Entity Structure of Figure 1.

Output Variables:
    Status (with range {In.Repair, In.Operation})

We should also list some other requirements and constraints concerning
the truck design. For example, the company may be restricted by the
technological standards to use only internal combustion, four cycle or
diesel engines.

In the first stage of the design process, a system entity structure
representing an automobile is proposed. Such an entity structure can
have the form depicted in Figure 1. As we can see there are several
aspects and specializations in the structure. Certainly, for the sake
of brevity, our automotive design is rather simple.

Given the design entity structure we first prune it with respect to the
observation frame Utilization. The safety aspect will be pruned out as
it does does not have the generic variable types present in our
observation frame. Pruning results in a total of six design model
structures with Passenger.Car and Truck as the root entities and Body,
4-cycle/diesel/electrical engine, as the entities representing the
components of decomposition.

As the design objectives and constraints dictate, the structures for a
passenger car are eliminated first. Further, the structure for a truck
with an electrical engine is disregarded. Finally, only the
configurations with a 4-cycle and diesel engines are deemed
admissible. They are shown in Figure 5.

The general truck design problem is now reduced to the synthesis of a
truck with a 4-cycle, internal combustion or diesel engine. We are now
ready to formulate the structural constraints and convert them into a
production rule scheme consistent with the canonical form presented in
Section 6.

 In our formulation we shall define synthesis rules for a very coarse
model of a truck. We shall assume that the following factors play a
major role in the synthesis process: first, we should restrict the
maximum capacity of the truck. Secondly, we assert that it is necessary
to synthesize an engine with enough power to set the truck (with
maximum load) in motion. We assume that in order to increase the
engine's power we can add cylinders in pairs. However, the number of
cylinders cannot be less than 4 and cannot exceed 16. Adding a pair of
cylinders also increases the volume of the engine i.e.:

    ENGINE.VOLUME = VOLUME.FACTOR * CYLINDER.VOLUME * CYLINDERS.NUMBER

The constraints associated with the physical decomposition of the
entity TRUCK can be formulated as follows:

1.) BODY.VOLUME >= ENGINE.VOLUME + LOAD.VOLUME

2.) ENGINE.POWER >= BODY.WEIGHT + MAXIMUM.LOAD

3.) BODY.VOLUME <= MAXIMUM.VOLUME   (capacity)

where MAXIMUM.VOLUME can be interpreted as a standard constraint
imposed by government regulations (due to restrictions on maximum axis
load on interstate highways) and the measures of load and weight are
given by the relations below:

LOAD = LOAD.VOLUME * WEIGHT.OF.VOLUME.UNIT

BODY.WEIGHT = BODY.VOLUME * WEIGHT.OF.VOLUME.UNIT

The constraints associated with the ENGINE synthesis have the form:

4.) CYLINDERS   must be coupled in pairs
                either in line or across from one another

5.) CYLINDERS.NUMBER ∈ [4, 16]

To convert the constraint to production rules we implement the
canonical scheme given in Section 6. As in the general approach rule RC
is the global constraint checker. Rules RC1 and RC2 are implemented as
local constraint satisfiers for constraints 1 and 2. Note, that the
resource constraints 3 and 5 have been formulated as pretests for
applicability of the rules. The production rule scheme is presented
below:

RC if ENGINE.POWER >= BODY.WEIGHT + MAXIMUM.LOAD
       BODY.VOLUME >= ENGINE.VOLUME + LOAD.VOLUME

    then
       Print "Truck Completed"

RC1 if BODY.VOLUME <= MAXIMUM.VOLUME - 1 VOLUME.UNIT
       BODY.VOLUME < ENGINE.VOLUME + LOAD.VOLUME

    THEN
       expand BODY.VOLUME by 1 UNIT
       update BODY.WEIGHT

RC2 if a pair of CYLINDERS is available
       ENGINE.POWER < BODY.WEIGHT + MAXIMUM.LOAD
    then
       add this pair of CYLINDERS to the ENGINE
       update ENGINE.VOLUME

After candidate structures that satisfy all the constraints have been
found, design models of the truck should be constructed and the
observation frame "Utilization" should be refined to an experimental
frame. Then, the resulting models can be evaluated via simulation
experiments.

9. CONCLUDING REMARKS

We have presented an approach to generate the model and experimental
modules for simulations in the objectives-driven modelling
environments. As we have shown, the model and experimental frame
development should be mutually supportive in the following sense: while
the basic objects representing the knowledge about the model and
experimental frame (i.e. the system entity structure and generic frame

type) can be conceived and developed separately, the construction of the model and experiment specification for a given problem is a process in which inferences from both objects should be drawn at the same time.

We hope that our approach will contribute to the ongoing discussion concerning the interfaces between modelling methodologies and expert system techniques, and that our subsequent research efforts will result in the fruition of the presented concepts in the form of expert simulation software support.

REFERENCES

Belogus D. (1985) "Multifacetted Modelling and Simulation: A Software Engineering Implementation", Doct. Diss., Weitzman Institute of Science, Rehovot, Israel.

Crosbie R.E., Hay J.L. (1983) "ISIM - A Simulation Language for CP/M Systems", in: Proc. of the Summer Computer Science Conference, Vancouver, July 1983.

Dekker L., Elzas M.S., (1984) "Methodology-Based Interactive Systems Modelling and Implementation", in Proc. of the 1984 Summer Simulation Conference, Boston, July 1984.

Elzas M.S., (1982) "The Use of Structured Design Methodology to Improve Realism in National Economic Planning", in Model Adequacy (ed. H. Wedde), Pergamon Press, London.

Elzas, M.S., (1984) "System Paradigms as Reality Mappings", in Simulation and Model-Based Methodologies: An Integrative View, (ed Oren, T.I., et al), Springer-Verlag, New York.

Kettenis D., (1983) "The COSMOS Modelling and Simulation Language", in Proc. of The First European Simulation Congress, Sept. 1983

Oren, T.I., Zeigler B.P. (1979) "Concepts for Advanced Simulation Systems", Simulation, 32,3 pp. 69-82.

Oren, T.I. (1982) "GEST - A Modelling and Simulation Language Based on Systems Theory Concepts", in: Simulation and Model Based Methodologies: An Integrative View, (ed. Oren T.I., et.al), Springer-Verlag .

Pegden D., (1982) "Introduction to Siman", Systems Modeling Corp., State College, Pensylvania.

Reddy Y.V., Fox M.S., Husain N., (1985) "Automating the Analysis of Simulations in KBS", in Proc. of the SCS Multiconference, San Diego, January 1985.

Rozenblit J.W., (1985a) "A Conceptual Basis for Integrated, Model Based System Design", Doct. Diss. Dept. of Computer Sci., Wayne State University, Detroit, Mi

Rozenblit J.W., (1985b) "Experimental Frames for Distributed Simulation Architectures", Proc. of the 1985 SCS Multiconference, San Diego, January 1985.

Rozenblit J.W., (1984) "Structures for a Model-Based System Design Environment", Technical Report, Siemens AG, West Germany (internal distribution).

Rozenblit J.W. and Zeigler B.P., (1985) "Concepts for Knowledge-Based System Design Environments", Proc. of the 1985 Winter Simulation Conference, San Francisco, December 1985.

Shannon R.E., Mayer R., Adelsberger H.H., (1985) "Expert Systems and Simulation", Simulation vol. 44, number 6, June 1985.

Sprague R.H., Carlson E.D. (1982) "Building Effective Decision Support Systems", Prentice Hall, N.J.

Wymore, W. (1980) "A Mathematical Theory of Systems Design", Tech. Report, College of Engineering, U. of Arizona.

Zeigler B.P. (1984a) "Structures for Model Based Simulation Systems", in: Simulation and Model-Based Methodology: An Integrative View, Springer-Verlag

Zeigler B.P. (1984) "Multifacetted Modelling and Discrete Event Simulation", Academic Press, London.

Zeigler B.P., (1986) "Expert Systems: A Modelling Framework", (in preparation)

Modelling and Simulation Methodology
in the Artificial Intelligence Era
M.S. Elzas, T.I. Ören and B.P. Zeigler (Editors)
© Elsevier Science Publishers B.V. (North-Holland), 1986

Chapter II.3

KNOWLEDGE–BASED MODEL STORAGE AND RETRIEVAL:
PROBLEMS AND POSSIBILITIES

Dirk L. Kettenis

Department of Computer Science
Agricultural University
Wageningen/The Netherlands

Depending on the level of detail needed to meet the
objectives of the simulation study one may formulate
several models of a system: continuous-change models,
discrete-change models, or combined-changed models,
linearized or non linearized models and so on.
A model base must reflect that situation.
The variety of models of one system complicates the
retrieval of models from a model base. Some tools to
choose a model are operational, but those tools
operate based on the static structure of a model. In
certain situations, the dynamic behavior of a model
is of interest in the model retrieval process.
A survey of the possible ways to include the dynamic
behavior of a model in the model retrieval process
is given.

1. INTRODUCTION

As reported by Roth, Gass and Lemoine, the U.S. Federal Government
annually used to spend half a billion of dollars on developing,
using and maintaining computer models (Roth, et.al., 1978).
Extrapolating this seven year old number to a figure valid for
the world at present, it seems to be an understatement to say that
worldwide a very large amount of money is involved in developing
models. To be able to save some effort in this respect, it is
necessary to have access to models or submodels developed earlier.
To be accessible, the models or submodels could be stored in a
number of domain specific model bases. Through the models, the
knowledge about a (sub)system is stored, so we may expect that the
access to the model base is limited to people working for the same
organization.

Modelbuilding is a process that is performed to learn something
about a real system. Through a model translated into a computer
program one may generate data, and these data may be used to check
if the model validly represents the real system. If the model does
not represent the real system to its full extent, the model must be
adapted. In this way the modelbuilding process functions as a
framework to gather information that hopefully leads to knowledge
about the real system. It is believed that the knowledge collected
during the modelbuilding process is the most important product of
that process. If one uses prespecified (sub)models, the personal
comprehension of the real (sub)systems is not enhanced in the same
extent it would be if one has built the complete model oneself.

On the other hand science would not have grown to the present level,
if scientists would not have been able to build on well understood
knowledge collected by former scientists. It is believed that
building a model based on not well understood submodels, will create
more problems than it will solve. Or in other words, to the opinion
of the author, models can not be treated as black boxes. However,
this does not imply that we can not have model bases consisting of
clearly written and well documented models.

2. KNOWLEDGE REPRESENTATION IN A MODEL

As a preliminary to the construction of a simulation model it is
necessary to abstract from the real system all those components and
their interactions, that are considered important enough for
inclusion in the model. The choice of which components will have
to be included in the model will be made by the model constructor
and depends on the objectives of the simulation study. So far as
the trajectory of model's descriptive variables is concerned there
are two major modelling approaches, continuous-change and discrete-
change. In this section the relation between the objectives of the
simulation and the model and modelformalism chosen will be discussed.

2.1 Continuous-change versus Discrete-change Modelling Methodology

The models that are built, are usually categorized into one of two
classes, based on the way the descriptive variables changes:

1. Continuous-change models, described either by ordinary or partial
   differential equations.

2. Discrete-change models, described either by difference equations,
   by a sequence of time-events or by a mixture of both or other
   modelling formalisms, such as finite state machines or Markov
   chain.

The partition of simulation models into these two classes results
from the different techniques applied rather than from the physical
world being divisible into two classes of dynamic systems. The type
of model a simulation practitioner selects depends, apart from the
discipline the modeller is familiar with, on the degree of
aggregation of individual phenomena. Continuous-change models are
useful when the behavior of the system depends more on the aggregate
flow of events than upon the occurrence of individual events. Choice
of a continuous-time or discrete-time modelling approach depends not
so much on the nature of the system, but mainly on the objectives of
the simulation. This can easily be shown in viewing the different
types of model used in traffic control (Cellier, 1979).
In the traffic control field one may study a system at three levels
of detail:

  a. Macroscopic level. A study at the macroscopic level results
     in entirely continuous-change models in which the single
     vehicle is not represented at all. State variables are traffic
     flow and its accompanying densities. Such models involve sets
     of coupled partial differential equations.

b. Microscopic level. A study at the microscopic level results
   in entirely discrete-change models with vehicles entering
   the considered system, traveling through it, e.g. from one
   intersection to the next with queueing situation in front of
   traffic lights etc.
   The dynamic behavior of every single vehicle, such as
   accelleration and stopping, is not included in the model.

c. Submicroscopic level. At this level the dynamic behavior of
   every single vehicle is described in detail. For example, the
   acceleration and stopping of every single verhicle is included
   in the model. This level leads to a model using a so called
   combined/dicrete approach leading to a combined-change model.

The physical system, however, is identical in all these cases.
The model of the system have been developed in a way suitable for
optimal fitting to the given simulation objectives.

2.2 Degree of Complexity of Models

Model construction being performed to learn something from the
real system, the construction phase will be followed by an
experimentation phase to validate the model. Validation leads to
new experimentation with the real system and may require more
modification or even rejection of the model. Ultimately, one or
more models are produced to meet the external objectives. The model
construction and in particular the level of detail in the model,
depends on the objectives of the modelling study. There is an
advantage to minimizing detail, since the simpler a model is, the
easier it is to construct, and the less expensive it is in computer
time and space; furthermore, the easier it is to calibrate since it
has fewer parameters. On the other hand, a more refined model is
likely to represent the real system with greater fidelity. The
result of these considerations will generally be that one constructs
a family of models at different complexity levels which can be
checked against each other, and against the real system.

Very often models, of varying degree of complexity, are applicable
in different situations. A realistic example can be found in control
theory applications. To be able to describe the transfer from one
equilibrium point of a real process to another equilibrium point,
a highly non-linear model is needed. Especially if the states before
and after the transfer are far apart.
To execute a simulation run with such a model takes a lot of
computer time. If one wishes to control the transfer process with
the help of a simulation, the significant amount of computer time
the simulation takes is often not prohibitive because in the real
process such a transfer will often also take a considerable time.
In the case the real process has to be controlled to stay in the
neighbourhood of a certain equilibrium point, the fluctuations can
be supposed to be very small. To be able to keep such a situation
under control, a fast reaction of the control mechanism is needed.
A simplified model is needed to be able to compute the state of
the system in the shortest possible time. A linearized model will
do a fine job in such a situation.

2.3 Conclusion

A model represents knowledge about a system, see also Chapter I.2
of this book. Knowledge can be defined as the combination of facts,
beliefs and heuristics. From the foregoing it might be clear that
the beliefs and heuristics may vary depending on goal, complexity
and the personality and experience of the modeller and so the
knowledge that is included in the model may vary accordingly. So,
even if it can be asserted that a model is based on knowledge of
the system, most often just a part of the knowledge is represented
in any particular model.

The simulation practitioner, willing to use a model residing in a
model base is confronted with a number of models describing a
(sub)system. Zeigler (1984) has studied the applicability of
experimental frames to models based on the input and output
variables of a model. An experiment is applicable to a model if the
experiment is derivable from the so called scope frame of the model.
Normally the applicability of an experimental frame to a model will
limit the number of candidate models. In certain situations the
dynamical behavior of the model is of interest in the model
selection process. Because the dynamical behavior is not taken into
account in the applicability of an experimental frame to a model,
it might be insufficient for selecting the proper model. Knowledge
of an expert is needed to choose the model that is most applicable
in the setting of the selected experiments. It is most likely that
if there is only one candidate model available in the model base,
chances are that that model is not appropriate for the objectives
of the simulation study.

3.   REPRESENTATION OF SYSTEM KNOWLEDGE

Let us assume that a model has been formulated well documented and
thoroughly tested. Such a model is of value to be stored in a model
base. From section 2 we have learned that not only the model must
be stored, but also - at least - the experimental conditions under
which the model is valid must be stored. Normally such a model is
parametric, so - among others - valid ranges of parameters must be
given. In this section we at first will discuss the possibilities
of a simulation language for model storage. Later on we will
investigate if the techniques for knowledge representation used in
Artificial Intelligence today may be of value for model storage.

3.1 Storage of Models Formulated in a Simulation Language

In principle, there is a diversity of reasons for building models.
In the scope of this paper models are built to experiment with on
a computer. Therefore, sooner or later, a simulation practitioner
will have to represent a formal model into a computer program.
Languages especially oriented to simulation applications are on the
market and are being developed. In spite of that, an important part
of the simulation applications are developed in general purpose
languages, among others FORTRAN as the most favorite one. In a model
written in such a general purpose language, the domain specific
knowledge is mostly buried in unreadable computer code where most
modelling assumptions are embedded and scattered throughout the
program. It is therefore obvious that a general purpose language

is not well suited to represent the knowledge about a system.
A language is a means of communication. In the special case of a
simulation language the communication is oriented to:

- the modeller during model development and later use of the model
- the computer
- the potential users of the model

In this way a simulation language serves three purposes, mainly as
documentation. For continuous-change models one may formulate a
model in mathematical notation. On the other hand one may use the
simulation language for that purpose if the model formulation in the
simulation language is close enough to the mathematical formulation
of the model. The simulation languages for continuous-change models
have evolved from explicit block oriented simulation languages, such
as MIMIC and CSMP 1130, via implicit block oriented simulation
languages, such as CSMP III and ACSL, to completely declarative
simulation languages, such as COSY (Cellier, 1979), GEST (Oren,
1971, 1984) and COSMOS (Kettenis, 1983, 1984). It is believed that
the last category of languages is very well suited to represent the
knowledge about a system that is stored in a model. This is mainly
based on the fact that in these languages the model formulation is
very close to the mathematical formulation of the model. This is
true for continuous-change models described through algebraic
equations and ordinary differential equations. Discontinuous-change
models (or piecewise continuous models) are also described by
differential equations and may have discontinuities in derivatives
and state variables. In contrast to the present day simulation
languages for continuous-change models, the declarative languages
provide for language constructs to describe discontinuous changes
in state or derivative variables in an easy and clear way. Systems
formulated through partial differential equations - that are systems
with more than one independent variable - cannot be described in
the implicit block oriented or declarative simulation languages.
The language elements to describe such partial differential
equations, normally, are not available in those languages.
It is possible to transform a model description through a partial
differential equation into a set of ordinary differential equations,
for example using the method of lines approach (Vemuri, 1981).
It is believed that a model developed using such an approach, cannot
be applied to document the system.

As we have seen before, a model stores the knowledge about a system.
Some of the knowledge will not be in the model, because the presence
of all the knowledge in the model is not necessarily the purpose of
the simulation study. A model represented in a simulation normally
stores a part of the knowledge. To be able to choose such a model it
is necessary to investigate the system knowledge represented in the
model first.

An advantage of a model base consisting of models stored in one
specific simulation language is that such models are usable without
processing. Such models can easily be coupled to other submodels to
form a part of a larger model, or can be used as complete model.
A disadvantage of such a model base is that models residing in the
model base can only be used in connection with that specific
language. Overstreet (1985) has developed a specification formalism
that allows computer generation of a simulation program in the three
world views of discrete-change models. That means that if the models
are stored using Overstreet's formalism, the computer is able to

generate a simulation program in the well known simulation languages like SIMULA, SIMSCRIPT and GPSS. The formalism developed by Overstreet applies just for discrete-change models.

ESP (Zeigler, 1982) is an interactive tool for system structuring. With the help of this program a system can be described from different points of view. The program can be used to develop the static structure of a family of models. The models can be stored in a model base in a hierarchical way, relations are stored basically in a tree structure. The ESP model base can be maintained easily by deleting or adding (sub)models. The ESP structure of a model can be used to extract a static structure of a lumped model that describes a certain facet of the system.
ESP may serve the purpose of (sub) model retrieval as far it concerns the static part of a model. The dynamic relations between the variables belonging to the static structure of the model are not included in the ESP model base. Because of that, the way certain relations are modelled cannot be taken into account in the selection procedure. Sometimes it will be sufficient to select upon the static structures of models, sometimes it will be necessary to take into account the way the state variables change, e.g. by a discrete-change model, a continuous-change model, or a linearized model, because that may influence the reliability of the results.

Calu suggests to store the mathematical operations in the model description in the form of a tree structure (Calu, et al., 1985). In fact Calu adds to the tree structure of ESP the mathematical relations between the variables of the model, as is done in the code generation phase of compilers. Tree structures are very close to the implementation of the model on the computer, but it is believed tree structures cannot be used to sufficiently document the model to enhance comprehension by the user. Some other authors store the model in a pictorial or graphical form. Graphical representations are comparable to the block oriented simulation languages, such as CSMP 1130 and TUTSIM. Such representations are excellent for typically small models, limited to approximately 10 to 20 equations. In some technological applications it is possible to represent larger models in a couple of smaller submodels of this limited size. In other applications, in general, it will not be easy to build submodels of this limited size. A modelling and simulation language that allows to represent relations in an almost mathematical form is, in general, therefore felt to be superior to represent models.

If the simulation language supports coupling facilities, such as GEST and COSMOS do, it is relatively easy to couple continuous-change submodels to other continuous-change submodels. For discrete-change models the situation is more complicated. In the first place, it is necessary to recall the different world views employed by discrete-change modelling: event scheduling (GASP, SIMSCRIPT), activity scanning (CSL, SIMON) and process interaction (SIMULA, COSMOS). In the event scheduling world view every piece of code describes one class of events only, the so called event routine. Several event routines together with some scheduling primitives form a model. Submodels representing an entity of the real system cannot be described as a whole. The activity scanning world view is comparable to the event scheduling in this respect. On the other hand, process description describes the whole life cycle of entity classes. All the events, that take place with an entity of the real system, will be localized in one process. Such processes can be seen as submodels and can be used as parts of a larger model. One may even distinguish a fourth world view: the transaction flow. Transaction flow languages (GPSS, SLAM and recently: SIMSCRIPT) are actually process languages, since they take a synoptic view of systems, but, as Shannon (1975), the author prefers to view them as a separate category because of their flow chart orientation. In transaction flow languages, sometimes also called the material flow oriented process approach, a model is described as the flow of active and transient entities, called transactions, through a framework of predefined passive server entities (facilities and storages). Languages supporting the transaction world view do not provide explicit facilities to couple submodels, and it is felt that the approach is not very well suited for the coupling of submodels which is the central condition for the succesful utilisation of model bases.

Continuous-change submodels communicate through signals, represented by variables in a simulation language. In principle the communication takes place in a continuous way, although the couplings may be discontinuous, that is to say: the couplings of the diverse output variables to the input variables may vary during the simulation experiment. Discrete-change submodels represented in the process world view communicate through variables, on the other hand the implicitly described events must be synchronized. To be able to synchronize the event handling of several submodels (processes) it is necessary to study carefully the formulation of the submodel, or the model must be augmented with documentation of the synchronization points.

Zeigler (1984) has developed a "user oriented language" for multi-component DEVS. In this language the synchronization points are represented in a clear way. Synchronization will be done through sending signals to the diverse components of the model.
For relatively simple models this method is shown to be very clear. This language is designed to be applied to "modelling in the large" applications. It is feared that in such applications, where the number of highly interactive components is relatively large, the redundancy in usage of variables to represent the synchronizing signals will tend to obscure the structure of the models.

For the moment, the conclusion of this paragraph is that model storage through a modern simulation language can be done easily for continuous-change models. Discrete-change models developed according to the process world view could be used, but synchro-nization of the events creates some problems. A drawback of a model base built in this way is that the models can only be used in an environment that supports one specific simulation language.

3.2 Knowledge Representation in Artificial Intelligence System

Artificial Intelligence applications, like an Expert System, are based on knowledge and reasoning with that knowledge. A lot of research effort, has been spent to develop techniques to store knowledge, and this research still continues (Rich, 1983). The presently available techniques can roughly be divided into two types:

- declarative methods, in which most of the knowledge is represented as a static collection of facts accompanied by a small set of general procedures for manipulating them, and

- procedural methods in which the bulk of the knowledge is
  represented as procedures for using it.

The knowledge structures used are among others: predicate logic,
semantic nets, frames, conceptual dependencies and scripts. Apart
from predicate logic, these structures - although they have
different names and have traditionally been used for separate
problems - are not radically different from each other. They share
the notion that complex entities can be described as a collection
of attributes and associated values. Knowledge representation
through predicate logic techniques can be used to represent simple
facts. The objects in those representations are so simple that much
of the structures of the world, and in the models of those, cannot
be described easily.
The "world" contains individual objects, subsystems, each of which
have several properties, including relationships to other objects.
It is often useful to collect those properties together to form a
single description of a complex object. One advantage of such a
scheme is that it enables a system to focus its attention on entire
objects without also having to consider all the other facts it
knows. In simulation, and in real life of course, objects are not
the only structured entities. Scenarios, or typical sequences of
events often occur. For this type of knowledge semantic nets, frames
and scripts may be applied. So far, we have discussed fairly static
ways of representing knowledge. Associated with each way of
knowledge representation there have been a small number of
procedures that manipulate the facts represented in the declarative
structures. An alternate approach is to expand the role of the
procedures, and simultaneously to contract the part played by the
static facts. This method is known as the procedural representation.
The shift to represent the knowledge more in procedural form does
not enlarge the complexity to be representable through this method
in relation to the declarative method. In practical applications,
very often, not just only one knowledge structure is used, but the
described methods of knowledge representation are used in
combination with each other.

The knowledge structures as described above have been applied to
real life problems. And as such it is believed that they can be used
to represent the knowledge represented in models. A complete model
is far too complex to be represented in one structure, e.g. a frame.
In a frame it might be possible to represent one single equation, or
a limited number of equations, if the frame concept implementations
that are available today are adapted in this sense. So it will be
necessary to decompose a model before it is possible to represent it
with the help of the knowledge structures available to-day. The
decomposition process is a non-trivial process, that only pays if
one wants to explain to the model user the model to its full extent.
Such an approach is taken by the EDORA Club (Pave, et al., 1985),
that is developing a computer-aided modelling system using ordinary
differential- and recurrence-equations with applications in
population dynamics. The purpose of a model base is, on the other
hand, more oriented to deliver "prefab" building blocks (submodels)
to be used in a simulation study. The decomposed model must be
translated into a routine efficiently executable by the computer,
otherwise it is believed that execution time of the models will grow
to an unacceptable level.
The translation is an easy process if the model is represented in a
simulation language.

4. MODEL OR SUBMODEL RETRIEVAL

Present day continuous-time simulation languages, such as ACSL and
CSMP, offer in a certain sense, submodel abilities in the form of
subroutines or macro's. These modules are relatively small and
uniquely defined submodels. Each user or user-community is able to
build its own library of submodels, and such a library may be seen
as a model base. In the most simple case of a relatively small
number of macro's, where just one macro represents one subsystem and
one subsystem is represented by one macro, retrieval may be done by
the name of the macro, giving the fact that, hopefully, the name
represents the meaning of the subsystem.

In section 2. we have explained that normally one has several models
of a real (sub)system, every model being applicable within a certain
experimental frame. As is illustrated in section 2.1., the models of
one system may be modelled according to the continuous-change or
discrete-change world view. Only a few simulation systems, like
COSMOS, provide for language constructs that allow the combination
of these two world views. A modeller confronted with a number of
models, all of them describing the same subsystem, has the problem
which one to choose.

The model base will consist of several (sub)systems. Each
(sub)system entry contains all the models of the subsystem available
in the model base. De Wael (1985) suggests that each model in the
model base is accompanied by the base frame of the model. All models
of one subsystem correspond with different questions that can be
asked about the subsystem and different experimental conditions.
A model can be applied if the experimental frame of the actual
situation is derivable (Zeigler, 1984) from the base frame of the
model.

De Wael claims that the derivability relation can be expressed
mathematically in function of the ranges of the different variables.
In practice, however, one will be confronted with models built
according to different formalisms (continuous-change, discrete-
change) and different levels of detail. If, in certain situations,
the dynamical behavior of the model must be taken into account, it
will be impossible to choose the right model only based on the
derivability relation.
The derivability relation, normally, will - however - limit the
number of candidate models (see also section 2.3).

In a situation where the number of candidate models is relatively
small, experimenting with the model may lead to the choice of a
model that fits the purpose best. A software system could be written
to experiment succesfully with many candidate models. Such an
approach can be very costly, because, in general, a large number of
simulation runs will have to be performed. In section 2. the
conclusion was that to be able to choose the right model one needs
knowledge of an expert, such as e.g. the person who has developed
the model. Normally such experts are not around at the time one
needs them, and especially in that situation an EXPERT SYSTEM could
be helpful. The Expert System represents the knowledge necessary to
be able to use the models residing in the model base, as a submodel
or as a complete model. Such an Expert System will guide the
potential user to choose the right model. The knowledge stored in

the model, in principle, will not be represented in the Expert
System. The Expert System can also advise on how to realize coupling
to another model and which point is of ultimate importance for
synchronizing the events described in the discrete event models
according to the process interaction world view.

5. CONCLUSION

The knowledge of systems modelled through continuous-change models
described by ordinary differential equations can be stored through a
declarative simulation language. To be able to store the knowledge
of systems described through partial differential equations by such
a language, suitable language elements must be included in those
languages. Present day discrete-change simulation languages can
cause problems when used for knowledge representation of systems.

In this paper, we have illustrated that a model base consisting of
a couple of models alone, will not be an operational help for the
modeller. Because of the fact that modelling is a multifacetted
discipline, the modeller needs a system that will advise the model
user to choose the right model. In this paper an Expert System is
suggested for that purpose. The applicability of experimental frames
to models and an ESP oriented model base may be a part of such an
intelligent system.

6. REFERENCES

Calu, J., L.De Wael, E.Esmeijer, E.J.H.Kerckhoffs, G.C.Vansteenkiste
    (1984).Knowledge-Base Aspects in Advance Modelling and
    Simulation. In: W.D. Wade (ed.) Proc. of 1984 Summer Computer
    Simulation Conference, SCS pp 1247-1253.

Cellier, F.E. (1979). Combined Continuous Discrete Simulation by use
    of Digital Computers: Techniques and Tools. PhD-Thesis, Swiss
    Federal Institute of Technology, Zurich/Switzerland.

Kettenis, D.L. (1983). The COSMOS Modelling and Simulation Language.
    In: W. Ameling (ed.), Proc. of the First European Simulation
    Congress 1983, Springer-Verlag, pp. 251-260.

Kettenis, D.L. (1984). Building Discrete Models with COSMOS. In:
    D.J. Murrau-Smith (ed.), Proc. of the 1984 UKSC Conference on
    Computer Simulation, Butterworth, London, pp. 47-56.

Oren, T.I. (1971). GEST: A Combined Digital Simulation Language for
    Large Scale Systems. In: Proc. of the Tokyo 1971 AICA Symposium
    on Simulation of Complex Systems, Tokyo, Japan, September 3-7
    pp. B-11/4.

Oren, T.I. (1984). GEST - a Modelling and Simulation Language Based
    on System Theoretic Concepts. In: T.I. Oren, M.S. Elzas and
    B.P. Zeigler (eds.), Simulation and Model-Based Methodologies:
    An integrative view. Springer-Verlag, pp. 281-335.

Overstreet, C.M., R.E. Nance (1985). A Specification Language to Assist in Analysis of Discrete Event Simulation Models. In: Communication of the ACM, Februari 1985, Volume 28, Number 2, pp 190-201.

Pave, A., F. Rechenmann (1985). Object-oriented Knowledge Representation for Computer-aided Modelling. In: E.J.H. Kerckhoffs, G.C. Vansteenkiste and B.P. Zeigler (eds.), Proc. of the Intern. Working Conference on Artificial Intelligence in Simulation, to be published by SCS, U.S.A.

Rich, E. (1983). Artificial Intelligence. McGraw-Hill International Book Comp., Singapore.

Roth, P.F., J.I. Gass and A.J. Lemoine (1978). Some considerations for Improving Federal Modelling. In: Proc. of 1978 Winter Simulation Conference, pp. 213-217.

Vemuri, V., W.J. Karplus (1981). Digital Computer Treatment of Partial Differential Equations. Prentice-Hall, pp. 305-331.

Shannon, R.E. (1976). Systems Simulation, the Art and Science. Prentice-Hall.

Wael, L. De (1985). A Knowledge-Based Tool for Model Construction. In: E.J.H. Kerckhoffs, G.C. Vansteenkiste and B.P. Zeigler (eds.), Proc. of the Intern. Working Conference on Artificial Intelligence in Simulation, to be published by SCS, U.S.A.

Ziegler, B.P., D. Belogus, A. Bolshoi (1982). ESP: an Interactive Tool for System Structuring. In: Proceedings of 1980 European Meeting on Cybernetics and Systems Research Hemisphere Press, N.Y.

Zeigler, B.P. (1984). Multifacetted Modelling and Discrete Event Simulation. Academic Press, London.

Modelling and Simulation Methodology
in the Artificial Intelligence Era
M.S. Elzas, T.I. Ören and B.P. Zeigler (Editors)
© Elsevier Science Publishers B.V. (North-Holland), 1986

Chapter II.4

AN APPROACH TO MODEL COMPOSITION
FROM EXISTING MODULES

Charles R. Standridge, Ph.D.

Pritsker & Associates, Inc.
P.O. Box 2413
West Lafayette, Indiana 47906
U.S.A.

1.0   INTRODUCTION

In general computer programming, software engineering techniques suggest that
programs be developed as a set of independent modules. Each module performs a
single, well defined function. Information is passed to and from the module
through a set of parameters. The computational aspects of the module are hidden
from a user, that is the module appears as a black-box. Modules which perform
commonly needed functions may appear in many programs.

These same principles may be applied to the development of models. Models can be
developed as a set of independent modules. Each module models a single, well
defined component of the system. Each independent module can be composed of other
such modules. Modules may be written to be useful in many models. For example,
model modules could be used to generically model the end of service in a single
server queue. The modules are built from capabilities commonly found in discrete
simulation languages: find the number of entities in a list (LENGTH_OF_LIST) and
change the status of a resource (CHANGE_STATUS). Figure 1 gives the modules. The
example assumes the user is responsible for event scheduling. While the example
is trivial, it does illustrate several points. The user passes information to the
module with two parameter values (QUEUE_ID, RESOURCE_ID). Two modules performing
single functions, end of service and start of service, are identified. The start
of service model can be re-used to help model the arrival of an entity to the
queuing system.

The effective management and manipulation of component modules is necessary for
their use in many models. In general data processing, database management
techniques are used for the organization and manipulation of large amounts of
data. Database management systems provide functions for manipulating data in
useful ways, for example subsets of data can be selected and different data sets
can be united. In a similar way, techniques for organizing and manipulating
collections of component models are needed. Such modelbase management systems
would assist in constructing component modules and composing models from these
existing components.

The state of support for building models from component modules varies among
simulation languages. Continuous simulation languages typically support the
development of modules. Sets of equations can be isolated and parameterized as a
component. A component model can be repeated many times in a single model or used
in a variety of models. GEST[9] typifies the state-of-the-art of component models
in continuous simulation language.

Discrete event modeling and simulation languages provide varying kinds of support for component models. Some discrete event languages, such as SIMSCRIPT [4] and SIMULA [3], are programming languages containing modeling and simulation capabilities. Component modules can be developed using standard software engineering techniques supported by the ability to dynamically create simulation entities. Other discrete event languages such as GASP IV [13] are libraries of subroutines. As component modules are developed, these can be used to augment the existing libraries. Again modules can be developed using standard software engineering techniques.

Capabilities for the development of modules in discrete event languages supporting the process interaction world view are not always well developed. Typical capabilities are found in Q-GERT [12], SLAM II [14], and SIMAN [11]. Fundamentally, these languages were not implemented with the composition of models from modules in mind. Limited capabilities for module development are provided. Modules must be specified internally to the models in which they are used. GPSS/H [1] is an implementation of GPSS where module development and use within models is supported.

The computer aided assistance of model composition from modules and module specification is in its infancy. Capabilities are beginning to appear as a part of modeling and simulation systems. Underlying formalisms for these systems are discussed by Zeigler [20]. Concepts for these systems are presented by Nance et al [6]. These systems typically assist in the model building and entry into the computer, simulation and statistical analysis and the presentation of results, including reports, graphs and animation.

MAGEST [10] assists in the construction of GEST models and in the simulation of these models. MAGEST employs a knowledge base consisting of the GEST morphology and knowledge obtained from and about user programs. MAGEST uses the knowledge base to assist in the specification of models, parameter sets and experiments. MAGEST performs checks and certifies GEST programs. Thus any GEST module in a modelbase can be certified to be correct.

Similarly, TESS [18] provides support for module development with SLAM II networks. A component network can be developed using a graphical model builder and stored in the TESS database. However, no parameters are allowed. Component networks can be included in a model. However, each occurrence of the component must be included in the desired position in the model. Each occurrence must be edited to specify parameters. A review of the basic concepts of model modules and their composition into models as discussed in the literature is presented. Issues of methodology are discussed. Illustrations of current capabilities and future possibilities are given.

2.0 CONCEPTS FROM THE LITERATURE

The literature presents three basic concepts about model composition from components:

1. The development of independent model modules which can be used in a variety of models;
2. The management of modelbases;
3. The composition of models from modules.

The need for component modules arises naturally. Simulation languages provide general capabilities applicable to a wide variety of systems. Typically, analysts work on a narrow class of systems such as steel making, batch manufacturing or computer design. As such analysts develop several models, common modules evolve.

In several publications, Ören and Zeigler have discussed concepts of model modules and their composition into models. In "Concepts for Advanced Simulation Methodologies" [7], the idea of a model file (modelbase) is presented. The model file consists of two parts--model structure and model output specification. Desirable manipulations of such a model file include decomposition into modules and inter-model comparison. Computer-aided coupling of component modules in either a time-variant or time-invariant manner is discussed.

Ören [8] gives four basic groups of possibilities for computer-aided modeling systems. The first of these is model generation/referencing including the retrieval of models and the combination of component modules. Insertion, deletion and modification of models is possible. Capabilities for searching models for specified properties are possible.

Zeigler [19] based on Ören [8] gives a five activity decomposition of the modeling and simulation process. The first of these activities is model generation/referencing. Models are built from scratch and/or by retrieving model modules from a model bank (modelbase). A second activity is model processing which includes manipulating models to produce documentation or check model specification correctness.

More extensive attention is paid to these concepts in Zeigler [20]. In this work, formal specifications for model modules and their combination into models are developed.

Nance et al [6] define model management system concepts. A model management system includes tools for accessing models and submodels and for constructing such models. A model management system includes a database management system for organizing and storing models.

Ketcham et al [2] presents the concept of a model frame consisting of a user interface for interactive model development, a modelbase for managing models and model modules, and a model translator for converting models to a form which can be simulated. Component modules can exist in several models. Models are built from modules using a system linker.

Standridge and Marshall [16] illustrate another kind of model composition from modules. In this case, the modules have no need to communicate with each other except that the results from one module can be used as inputs to another. The system presented by Standridge and Marshall is shown in Figure 2. Each component can be simulated independently with the results stored in a central database for later use in the simulation of another module. This allows one module to be simulated with different inputs without having to needlessly simulate the others. However, any feedback relationships between the modules are lost.

Due to space limitations this literature review has not been exhaustive. Representative articles which discuss basic ideas about component modules and composing models from components have been cited.

3.0 MODULES IN INTEGRATED SIMULATION SYSTEMS

Integrated simulation systems support the activities of a simulation project other than those supported by simulation languages. These activities include model entry, statistical analysis, graphics, animation and reporting.

One such system is TESS which supports modeling, simulation and statistical analysis and result presentation using SLAM II, MAP/1 [5] and GPSS/H [1]. TESS includes a framework for model development which provides some rudimentary capabilities for modular model development.

3.1 MODEL DEVELOPMENT SUPPORT

Integrated simulation systems can provide for the development of models using various formalisms such as:

1. general purpose simulation languages; such as SLAM II;
2. special purpose simulation languages; such as MAP/1;
3. diagrams of a system; lacking all the detail necessary for simulation, but useful for showing animation;
4. ICONs, each ICON is a single modeling symbol.
5. Definitions, the descriptions of the data input to or resulting from a simulation run.

Analysis of models can be performed using simulation and animation. ICONs are elementary symbols used in constructing diagrams. Driven by a list of the event occurrences of a simulation organized according to a definition, an animation shows the structure and dynamics of the simulation on a facility.

Figure 3 relates these formalisms. A set of ICONs is used in constructing a diagram. The diagram is the graph on which the animation is shown. Definitions describe the results to collect during the simulation of a model. The results can be displayed on the diagram in an animated form.

All information, including models, schematics, ICONs and definitions are stored in a central database. Many of each can be stored. SLAM II networks would provide a typical example of the use of the database. Direct access to network symbols by name or graphical location is provided through the use of database access paths. Three forms of a network are stored in the database. The graphical form feeds the user interface for editing. The executable form can be simulated by SLAM II. The encoded form is intermediate between the graphical and executable forms, providing for easier translation to the executable form.

Graphical model builders can provide for the entry and editing of models, diagrams and ICONs. Models and diagrams are built by selecting and locating ICONs on the terminal screen. The screen is a window on to a large wall on which the model or diagram is built.

Composition of models in any formalism can be done in two ways:

1. A new model may be built starting with an existing model.
2. An existing model may be explicitly included within another model.

Users may develop and simulate a model of each of several components of a system. Composition capabilities are used to build a single, large model of a system, adding feedback relationships between the components.

3.2   POTENTIAL CAPABILITIES

Several capabilities of integrated simulation systems are easy to envision.

1. Querying Model Modules. Database management systems have capabilities for user specified selection of data for reports and graphs. Since models are stored as data these same capabilities can be used to selectively report or graph parts of model modules. Typical model parts would include resource allocation and deallocation and queuing.
2. Model Module Relationships. Simulation systems maintain directories of models. Relationship information can be stored in this structure as well. Typical information would be which models are included in other models.
3. Mixing of Model Formalisms. Typically, both a model for analysis by simulation and a diagram for animation are developed. It would be worthwhile to develop a way to:

   1. simulate schematics;
   2. add ICONs to process-oriented models to provide more realistic looking models.

4.0   SUMMARY

Principles of modelbases and the development of models from modules have been well developed in the literature. These capabilities are utilized in continuous simulation languages and discrete event, programming languages such as SIMSCRIPT, SIMULA and GASP IV. The current structure and implementation of some existing process-oriented discrete simulation languages does not allow modular development capabilities to be easily added. The redesign of the implementation of these languages is in order. The GPSS/H reimplementation of GPSS has relieved the restrictions in this language.

The automation of model development from modules is beginning to appear in simulation systems such as TESS and MAGEST. The future will see more such systems and more sophisticated ways of linking modules into models.

```
MODULE END_OF_SERVICE (QUEUE_ID, RESOURCE_ID)
  CALL CHANGE_STATUS (RESOURCE_ID, 'IDLE')
  IF (LENGTH_OF_LIST (QUEUE_ID) >0)
        CALL START_OF_SERVICE (RESOURCE_ID)
  RETURN
  END
MODULE START_OF_SERVICE(RESOURCE_ID)
  CALL CHANGE_STATUS(RESOURCE_ID, 'BUSY')
  RETURN
  END
```

Figure 1.   Single Server Queue Models

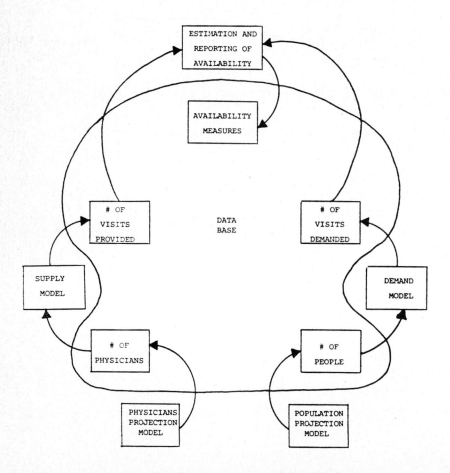

Figure 2.   Example of Individual Module Simulation

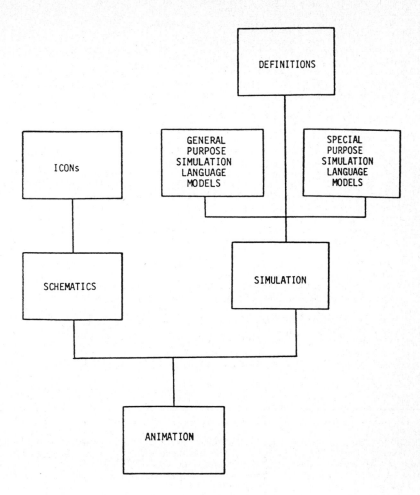

Figure 3. Modeling Formalisms and Their Relationship

5.0 BIBLIOGRAPHY

1. Henriksen, James O. and Robert C. Crain, <u>GPSS/H User's Manual</u>, Wolverine Software, 1985.
2. Ketcham, Michael G., John W. Fowler, Don T. Phillips, "New Directions for the Design of Advanced Simulation Environments", <u>Proceedings of the 1984 Winter Simulation Conference</u>, December 1984, pp. 563-568.
3. Kettenis, D. L. "Combined Simulation with SIMULA '67" in <u>Simulation of Systems</u>, North-Holland, 1979.
4. Law, Averill M. and Christopher S. Larmey, <u>An Introduction to Simulation Using SIMSCRIPT II.5</u>, CACI, 1984.
5. Miner, Robin J. and Laurie J. Rolston, "MAP/1 Tutorial", <u>Proceedings of the 1984 Winter Simulation Conference</u>, pp. 59-62.
6. Nance, Richard E., Ahmed L. Mezaache, C. Michael Overstreet, "Simulation Model Management: Resolving the Technological Gaps", <u>Proceedings of the 1984 Winter Simulation Conference</u>, December 1981, pp. 173-179.
7. Ören, Tuncer and Bernard Zeigler, "Concepts for Advanced Simulation Methodologies", <u>Simulation</u>, Volume 32, No. 3, March 1979, pp. 69-82.
8. Ören, Tuncer, "Computer-Aided Modeling Systems", <u>Progress in Modeling and Simulation</u>, PP. 189-203, ACADEMIC PRESS, 1982.
9. Ören, Tuncer I., "GEST-A Modeling and Simulation Language Based on System Theoretic Concepts," in <u>Simulation and Model-Based Methodologies: An Integrative View</u>, Springer-Verlag, 1984.
10. Ören, Tuncer I., "Architecture of MAGEST: A Knowledge-based Modeling and Simulation System" in <u>Simulation in Research and Development</u>, North Holland, 1985.
11. Pegden, C.Dennis, "Introduction to SIMAN", <u>Proceedings of the 1983 Winter Simulation Conference</u>, December 1983.
12. Pritsker, A. Alan B., <u>Modeling and Analysis User Q-GERT Networks</u>, Halsted Press, 1977.
13. Pritsker, A. Alan B., <u>The GASP IV Simulation Language</u>, John Wiley & Sons, 1974.
14. Pritsker, A. Alan B., <u>Introduction to Simulation and SLAM II</u>, Second Edition, Halsted Press, New York and Systems Publishing Corporation, West Lafayette, Indiana, 1984.
15. Shriber, Thomas J., <u>Simulation Using GPSS</u>, John Wiley & Sons, New York, 1974.
16. Standridge, Charles R. and Susan Marshall, "Enhancing Simulation Analyses of Health Care Delivery Policies Using Database Capabilities", <u>Proceedings of the 1981 Winter Simulation Conference</u>, pp. 163-172.
17. Standridge, Charles R., "The Simulation Data Language: Applications and Examples", <u>Simulation</u>, October 1981.
18. Standridge, Charles R., "Performing Simulation Projects with the Extended Simulation System", <u>Simulation</u>, December 1985.
19. Zeigler, Bernard P., "Concepts and Software for Advanced Simulation Methodologies", <u>Simulation with Discrete Models a State-of-the-Art View</u>, December 1980, pp. 25-33.
20. Zeigler, Bernard P., <u>Multifaceted Modeling and Discrete Event Simulation</u>, Academic Press, 1984.

Modelling and Simulation Methodology
in the Artificial Intelligence Era
M.S. Elzas, T.I. Ören and B.P. Zeigler (Editors)
© Elsevier Science Publishers B.V. (North-Holland), 1986

Chapter II.5

STRUCTURING OF LINEAR OPTIMIZATION PROBLEMS

Ulrike Maschtera, Walter Schneider

J.K.University, Institut für Informatik
Altenbergerstr.69,A-4040 Linz,Austria

The modelling process consists of a series of
abstraction levels deriving a formulation
suitable for the solution process from observations of the real system. By underlying a
relation-oriented view of a linear optimization
model the user can input his system observations
in simple natural language sentences. Suitable
coupling operations, consistency checks and reformulation procedures assist the user in construction and (in)validation of his model.

1. INTRODUCTION

The modelling process consists of a series of abstraction levels
deriving a formulation suitable for the solution process from real
system observations. In case of linear optimization the target
formulation is a set of linear (in-)equalities and one or more
optimization function(s). Therefore supporting (linear) modelling
means assisting the transformation of system observations into (linear)
in/equalities.

Analogously to Zeigler (1982) we distinguish three stages: system
description, model composition and experimentation. However, the
manyfold relationships in (linear) optimization models make strict
hierarchical model construction difficult for an unexperienced user.
Therefore a relational way of system description and suitable
coupling operations were sought. The result is a system_relation_base
and a model_base from which linear optimization models are derived.

The relational view is essential for every part of CALM, our computer-
aided linear modelling support. Therefore we will begin with the
description of its derivation from linear optimization model (LOM-)
formulations and of its connexion to recent LOM-formulating practice.

2. RELATIONAL VIEW OF LOMS

Decomposition of a LOM can be done in at least two steps. The first
decomposition renders k linear optimization functions and m linear
in/equalities (called restrictions) which have to be fulfilled
simultaneously.

Every restriction/optimization function defines a relationship between
a set of n+1 variables. One of those variables is marked representing

the relationship.

ex1: A machine M with limited capacity can produce two products A,B.
     Then the amount of produced objects A and the amount of produced
     objects B are related because of the limited capacity of M.

Therefore a restriction can be decomposed in two ways:
either *object-oriented* by associating the n variables (here products)
       to the set of objects and installing one (1:1)relationship
       between the marked variable (here machine,subject) and the set
       of objects,

       ex: PRODUCES(machine,{products})

or   *relation-oriented* by installing n (1:1)relationships (called
       RATOMs) between the subject and each object. Then the restriction
       can be rebuilt by applying coupling operations to any two
       RATOMs which have the same subject (such RATOMs describe the
       same type of relationship). The result of the coupling operations
       are 'composed RATOMs'. They describe a relation between the
       subject and a 'composed object' which is obtained by aggregating
       the objects involved in the coupling operation.

       ex: PRODUCES(machine,product_A) }→ *PRODUCES(machine,product_AB)*
       *   PRODUCES(machine,product_B)*

In the first case a model is enlarged by adding new members to the set
of objects or by adding a new restriction. In the second case new RATOMs
are added to the set of RATOMs.

As long as all the objects belong to one set (eg. set of products) and
the subjects of all restrictions belong to another set (eg. set of
machines), the advantages of object-orientation are obvious. The result
is a strict hierarchical model decomposition. It can be described by
a tree, whose nodes on the first level are subjects and whose nodes on
the other levels are objects. Then the relationship between a subject
and the set of objects is given by the set of tupels $(object_i, a_{.i})$.
The tupels form the leafs of the tree.

$$model$$

$$subject_1 \quad ..... \quad subject_n$$

$$(object_1, a_{11}) \; .... \; (object_n, a_{1n}) \; ... \; (object_1, a_{m1}) \; .... \; (object_n, a_{mn})$$

The result of relation-oriented decomposition is a *model_R_tree*, whose
leafs are RATOMs and whose nodes are 'composed RATOMs'. In the following
figure aggregation is represented by $\lfloor , \rfloor$.

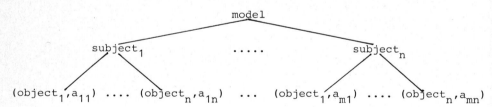

$$\begin{bmatrix} sub_1 \\ ... \\ sub_m \end{bmatrix} : \begin{bmatrix} \lfloor 3obj_1 - 2obj_2 \rfloor \\ .... \\ \lfloor obj_1 + 2obj_2 \rfloor \end{bmatrix} \begin{bmatrix} \leq \\ . \\ \leq \end{bmatrix} \begin{bmatrix} 0h \\ ... \\ 20L \end{bmatrix} ; ADD$$

$$sub_1 : \lfloor 3obj_1 - 2obj_2 \rfloor \leq 0h; EXPAND \qquad sub_m : \lfloor obj_1 + 2obj_2 \rfloor \leq 20L; SHARED$$

$$sub_1 : obj_1 \leq 2h \quad sub_1 : obj_2 \geq 3h \qquad sub_m : obj_1 \leq 20L \quad sub_m : obj_2 \leq 10L$$

However, when de/composing *complex systems* under *varying aspects*, the
partitioning of variables into two disjunctive sets (objects,subjects)
is neither obvious (for a novel user) nor singular (every pivot-
transformation exchanges the roles of one subject and one object) nor
fix (it can depend on the aspect of composition: a machine is subject
in production models (rendering a LOM) and object in investment models
(rendering an integer programming model); both aspects can be combined
in a mixed integer model).

Here relation-orientation shows its advantages
1) because a RATOM is *similar to a simple sentence* in a natural language
   consisting of subject, praedicate, object (limitation and numeral)
2) because the coupling of RATOMs represents a *conjunctive coordination*
   of such sentences and
3) because a RATOM can be represented in both *r-dual* forms (Maschtera
   1984); therefore subject and object can be exchanged easily
   according to the aspect-dependant necessities of composition.
Thus the user is supported in two essential steps in LOMing, namely
in PARTITIONING the variables and SORTING the relations according to
the subjects.

Another advantage of the relational view comes from the fact that in
(linear) mathematical modelling the relationships between entities
are described in form of coefficients (integers and reals). These are
apt to express two aspects, the *direction of influence* (given by the
sign) and the amount of influence (the absolute value). While the
amount of influence will vary over time or from system to system, the
direction of influence is a *generic* characteristic of the system. It
is a *semantic property* of the relations restricting the chooseable ways
of influence (in LOM: enhancing/diminishing/indifferent) to the only
semantically possible one(s).
   *ex2: A bottling machine will always ENHANCE the amount of full bottles
        and DIMINISH the amount of empty bottles, but it will never
        DIMINISH full bottles and ENHANCE empty ones!*

The relation-oriented view and the coupling operations explicitly
DISTINGUISH THE DIRECTION OF INFLUENCE. Therefore CALM is based on
the relation-oriented view and associative aids - which have been
included for the sake of convenience - have been adjusted to this view.
Thus we distinguish the following five types of RATOMs:
   (1) subject:object≤numeral, which is equal to: subject+object=numeral
   (2) subject:object≥numeral, which is equal to: subject-object=numeral
   (3) subject:=numeral
   (4) object:=object+numeral*subject
   (5) object:=object-numeral*subject }→ associative aids ('belong_to')
RATOM_type (1) and (4) are mapped to *ENHANCE* and can be represented
by the diagram of fig1a. RATOM_type (2) and (5) are mapped to
DIMINISH and can be represented by the diagram of fig1b. Thus *ENHANCE*
and *DIMINISH* can be viewed as RATOM_super_types.

numeral > | *subject* | — *object* >   < *numeral* — | *subject* | < *object*

fig1a: *RATOM_type ENHANCE*   fig1b: *RATOM_type DIMINISH*

RATOM_type(3) is used when general identifiers for 'numerals' are
fixed to a value in order to derive a 'concrete model' from a
'general model' (for the definition of 'concrete model' and 'general
model' see Fourer 1983, p.145f,175f).

Three coupling operations are needed to compose a LOM from a set of
RATOMs. They can be subdivided into the two coupling operations

SHARED/EXPAND - which are applied to RATOMs with equal subject - and
into *ADD* - which is applied to RATOMs with different subjects.
SHARED/EXPAND represent the conjunctive 'AND' of a natural language.
They are used to derive 'composed RATOMs' which represent one
restriction. On the other hand *ADD* stands for the logical 'AND' which
combines 'composed RATOMs'(restrictions) to a LOM.

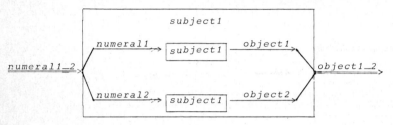

fig2a: coupling operation SHARED (used for identical RATOM_super_types)

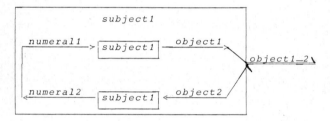

fig2b: coupling operation EXPAND (used for different RATOM_super_types)

The amount of influence can be further decomposed into the absolute
value of influence and its measure. In order to achieve coupling
automatically, CALM adjusts the coefficients such that the in/equalities
are *correct in their measures*. This is done within the coupling
operations with the help of a measure_base, where standard as well as
user defined measures are stored and related to another. Note that
relations between groups, eg. *1 DM³ ≙1L* are inherited by all members.

group: HOUR	group: DM³	group: LITER	user_defined measures:
1 h ≙ 60 min	1 m³ ≙ 1000 dm³	1 L ≙ 10 dL	1 WORKING_DAY≙8 h
1day≙ 24 h			1 BOTTLE ≙0,7 L
⋮	⋮	⋮	

3. NATURAL LANGUAGE INTERFACE - PROTOTYPE

The objective of a natural language interface is to *extract the users'
knowledge* of the problem domain in terms to which they are used and
to *represent* it in a form which is suitable for *automatic model
formulation*.

As mentioned before one variable can be assigned to each restriction.
It is distinguished from the other variables by defining a concrete
relationship between them. In a natural language sentence describing
this relationship it will become the subject, the other variables will

become objects and the relationship between any object and the subject will be expressed by the praedicate. Therefore CALM allows input in the form of such simple sentences, presenting a mask where the user has to fill in his identifiers.

Due to the target formulation LOM the praedicate can be regarded as *synonym* for *ENHANCE* or *DIMINISH*; *IS_INDIFFERENT* is assumed for every relation between entities which is not explicitly stated. *MAXIMAL* or *MINIMAL* define the range of variability of the subject resulting in inequalities ($\leq/\geq$); *EXACTLY* (=) is assumed, whenever neither maximal nor minimal is input. Optimization functions are characterized by their lack of limitation and a praedicate which is a synonym for *GAIN*.

For the sake of convenience another basic type of praedicate - *IS/ARE EXISTENT* - has been included. It describes a relationship where either subject or object is given implicitly. Thus sentences like
ex3:   *'There are maximal 10 t of raw material Arilen existent'*
      or *'Maximal 10 t Arilen are on store'*
      or *'Free_capacity_of_Arilen is maximal 10 t'*
      or *'Maximal 10 t Arilen can be used'*
represent a relation between the subject *free_capacity_of_Arilen* and object *Arilen(_used)* with direction *is_diminished*, limitation *maximal* and numeral *10 t*.

Note that an identifier for the subject is generated by adding *free_capacity_of* to the name of the object. This is the default meaning for limitation $\leq$. The praefix *supplement_of* is used for $\geq$. (These defaults can be redefined by the user.) Note that in case of limitation *EXACTLY* this type of praedicate represents RATOM_type(3).

CALM allocates the direction of influence solely at the praedicate. Once a synonym has been allocated at a praedicate (*eg. ENHANCE to produce*) the same allocation will be tried for every further usage of the praedicate. However, the semantics of identifiers - which can be expressed within their adjectives (ex2,ex4) or by input sentences (ex6) - can transform the meaning of some praedicates. In that case the user can choose one of the following actions:
1) If the former meaning of the praedicate should be preserved, he has to correct the last input sentence and choose another praedicate.
2) If he detectes now, that the former allocation was erroneous, the praedicate has to be allocated afresh.
3) If the praedicate has more than one meaning dependant on the context in which it is used, it can be allocated multiply.
   (For instance, *belong_to* can be mapped to *ENHANCE* and *DIMINISH*. This shows that the set which is currently defined has inhomogeneous semantics.)
Model (in)validation aids are included to make evident such situations and the consequences of the actions chosen by the user. The assumption underlying this simplification is that every person and every problem area have their own style/terms. As a consequence, the vocabulary - once defined - will not change very much. Thus, if an OR-guru has established a model for a problem domain with CALM, the users of the model have the means to do changes in a natural language environment. (Furthermore synonym checking has shown to exert a teaching influence on the user.)
ex4: 'The Arilen producing machine works for 2 hours.'
   is discerned as RATOM
   'Arilen_producing_machine works_for a time_of 2 hours.'
   and shows that RATOMs like the following ones are missing:
   'Arilen_producing_machine produces Arilen.'
   'Arilen is_produced in_time_of 3 minutes.'

(This will be recognized by the structural (in)validation aids).

The decomposition of relations in more than two -jects (where -ject stands for subject or object) is always possible for LOMs and is implemented in the form of a help-function.

ex5: *'Mixture$_k$ contains twice as much of ingredient$_i$ as mixture$_l$.*

Obviously ingredient$_i$ is the reason for the relationship between mixture$_k$ and mixture$_l$. Therefore ingredient$_i$ becomes subject and the mixtures become objects of the RATOMs. Furthermore the fact that the user was 'unable' to input the relations in RATOM_form suggests that the objects are generalized identifiers and have to be specified with respect to the subject:

$$ingredient_i: ingredient_{i\_}of\_mixture_k = 1\ parts_{ik}$$

$$ingredient_i: ingredient_{i\_}of\_mixture_l = 2\ parts_{il}$$

Specification of identifiers can be expressed via relations. Such sentences contain more than two -jects and a praedicate for which synonym checking cannot be completed successfully.

ex6: *'A belongs_to stations'.*
'B belongs_to stations'.
'C belongs_to stations'.
then: *'Cars drive from garage to stations.'*
stands for: *'Cars consist_of cars_from_garage_to_station_A.'*
           'Cars consist_of cars_from_garage_to_station_B.'
           'Cars consist_of cars_from_garage_to_station_C.'

4. MODEL COMPOSITION

The relationships defined by such simple input sentences are stored in a *system_relation_base*. They describe the communication of system elements in relational form.

As pointed out before, one of the abstraction steps in modelling concerns the partitioning of system elements into sub- and objects which is neither obvious nor singular nor fix. Therefore the partitioning is not an individual property of system elements, but an attribute allocated by the modeller. It is up to his knowledge and experience to assure that the partitioning results in a *model formulation which is both feasible and tight*. Therefore support in modelling means support in PARTITIONING, COUPLING and (IN)VALIDATION as well as in MODEL REFORMULATION.

4.1. Partitioning and Coupling

In order to honour the modeller's privilege of partitioning, CALM preserves the roles of the system elements as it is indicated in the input sentences as long as coupling operations can be applied directly. In case input sentences cannot be coupled according to the partitioning chosen by the user, they are put aside
1) either until coupling is possible in the primal form
2) or until coupling is possible in the r-dual form and dualisation is accepted by the user

ex7: primal: *'Product_A is_produced_by machine.'*
     dual: *'Machine produces(ENHANCES) product_A.'*

     primal: *'Cars consist_of cars_from_garage_to_station_A.'*
     dual: *'Cars_from_garage_to_stations belong_to(ENHANCE) cars.'*

3) or until the model (in)validation part detects inconsistencies and input and/or partitioning have to be redone (see ex10).

4.2. Model (in)validation

Model (in)validation can be divided into three groups: definitional model (in)validation, numerical model (in)validation and structural model (in)validation.

DEFINITIONAL model (in)validation should check the similarity of identifiers up to a user defined degree in order to detect typing errors and inconsistencies within the identifiers of system elements.
ex8: Two identifiers are recognized as similar if the strings composed of the first n letters are equal with the exception of m<n letters (these can be different or omitted).
Two identifiers are recognized as similar if any two different strings belong to a previously defined set (eg. relation,realtion).

Numerical and structural model (in)validation represent the third stage of modelling: 'experimentation within modelling'. Thereby experimentation is defined in its widest meaning as 'structured repetitive application of knowledge for the sake of derivation of more knowledge on the observed problem domain'.

'NUMERICAL' model (in)validation should help the user to check the range of the system elements as it is induced by the RATOMs. In case of general models (where the 'numerals' are variables) the user is informed of all the constraints per variable which have been input up till that time.
ex9: For instance consider example 5 (mixing problem). If the user inputs his observations in the following form:

$ingredient_i: mixture_k = 1\ parts$

$ingredient_i: mixture_l = 2\ parts$
$\qquad :$
$\qquad :$
$ingredient_j: mixture_k = 3\ parts$

then the amount of $ingredient_i$ in $mixture_k$ and the amount of $ingredient_j$ in $mixture_k$ are represented by the same variable $mixture_k$, whose value is fixed to 1 parts and 3 parts simultaneously. This is a contradiction. Either the identifiers of the RATOMs have to be specified as before or a distributive coupling of the RATOMs has to be chosen (The latter case results in a mixed integer problem.).

STRUCTURAL model (in)validation checks the integrity of the model with respect to semantics which is implicitly defined as well as with respect to model connectivity. *Semantic model integrity* is tested by using RATOMs and coupling operations as rules for deriving relations which the user has to check on correctness.
ex10: previous input: bottling_machine bottles(DIMINSHES) wine.
wine_type_A belongs_to(ENHANCES) wine.
then: bottling_machine DIMINISHES wine_type_A? YES!

previous input: bottling_machine fills(DIMINSHES) bottles.
full_bottles belong_to(ENHANCE) bottles.
empty_bottles belong_to(ENHANCE) bottles.
then: bottling_machine DIMINISHES empty_bottles? YES!
bottling_machine DIMINISHES full_bottles? NO!!
error: bottles has inhomogeneous semantics within a filling aspect.
correction: full_bottles DIMINISH bottles.

With respect to *model connectivity* there are two deficient situations: loops and unconnected parts of a model. *Loops* usually occur when the user forgets to discern identifiers, eg. identifiers of different periods.

ex11: *'One worker teaches five workers.'*
    Using the dot to abbreviate membership (eg. of set PERIOD)
    the correct input is:
    'One worker.j teaches(ENHANCES) five worker(s).j+1.'

Unconnected parts of the model are easily detected by checking the model structure because there has to exist a connection from every variable to (at least one of) the subject(s) of the optimization function(s) in a valid LOM. Unconnected parts of the model usually occur when element identifications are typed incorrectly or chosen inconsistently (see ex10: *bottles* used for *full_bottles* as well as *empty_bottles* within a filling aspect; ex4: relations expressed within adjectives). Note that inconsistent identification can be the consequence of the default identification of subjects which is necessary in connection with praedicate *IS/ARE EXISTENT*, in case the user does not stick to the suggested defaults. Therefore renaming of identifiers is possible at any stage of CALM.

4.3. Model Reformulation

The quality of a model is judged by its *tightness* with respect to the applied solution process. In order to achieve tightness models must be *reformulated according to their structures*. Therefore reformulation procedures have to be applied after the model composition step. In case of LOMs the number of subjects (using standard simplex) or objects (using the improved algorithm of Schneider(1984)) are crucial for the solution time and have to be as small as possible. This is achieved by substitution of simple input equations.

ex12: *Consider again a mixing problem: ingredients—-> $\boxed{mixing}$ —->mixtures*

    In the standard formulation the subjects are the ingredients (slack variables,input,x_{n+k}), the objects are the target mixtures (output,x_j) and the percentage of ingredient$_i$ used for mixture$_j$ is represented by coefficient a_{ij}. Then the model is:

$$ingredient_i: \Sigma_{j=1}^{n} a_{ij} x_j \leq ingredient_i\_on\_store \quad with\ \Sigma_i a_{ij} = 1.$$

    This formulation is obtained from the following one by substituting the mixing RATOMs (see ex5) into the inequalities which describe the availability of ingredients:

$$ingredient_i: \Sigma_{j=1}^{n} ingredient_i\_of\_mixture_j \leq ingredient_i\_on\_store.$$

    The 'LOM-knowledge' $\Sigma_i a_{ij} = 1$ is obtained eo ipso because CALM's coupling operations adjust the coefficients according to the measures of the component -jects:
    Consider the RATOMs of ex5; if the user relates his measures to each other or to standard measures contained in the measure_base, eg. 3 parts$_{ik} \hat{=} 2L$, 5 parts$_{il} \hat{=} 1L$,

    then the numerals of the transformed RATOMs are $\frac{2}{3} L$ and $\frac{2}{5} L$, respectively. After substitution the mixing equation is:

$$ingredient_i: \frac{2}{5} x_k + \frac{2}{3} x_l \leq \frac{4}{15} L$$

Substitution should be redone before outputting the solution in order to preserve the user's terminology.

5. MODEL BASE

The target formulation determines the appearence of the nodes of the model_R_tree. Therefore the depth and the aspects of composition influence each node. If two models have common submodels, then the respective model_R_subtrees are equal only if the submodels are on the lowest level. Whenever the submodels are on different levels or have different refinement the model_R_tree has to be rebuilt. This implies additional work and hinders the actualisation of models in case of numeric or semantic system changes. Therefore a model base has been inserted between system_relation_base and model_R_tree. Its objective is the same as the objective of the system entity structure in Zeigler (1982), containing 'the current state of the knowledge base' in the hierarchical form which results from the partitioning step. However, in order to simplify updates every (part of a) model is stored only once.(Note that -jects are part of a model.) This results in a base, where a model can be viewed as a 'file of partial models'.

6. EXTENSIONS OF CALM

CALM formulates LOMs from 'simple input sentences' according to a coordinative aspect (AND). Other target formulations can be obtained by extending the types of praedicates and/or the number of -jects which are involved in an input unit (for instance in order to describe a relation dependant on a system status, ex13) and by defining suitable coupling operations.

ex13: Disjunctive coordination of simple input sentences or models results in (mixed) integer models:
      'if RATOM1 then RATOM2 else RATOM3'
      'either RATOM1 or RATOM3'....(see Maschtera/Schneider(1985))

ex14: The nonlinear restriction $x_3 : x_1 x_2^2 \le h$ can be decomposed into four RATOMs: $x_3 : z_1 \le b$ (1);
      $z_1 : x_1 = 1; z_1 : x_2 = 1; z_1 : x_2 = 1;$ (2)
      where RATOMs (2) are coupled multiplicatively before coupling the result and (1) coordinatively.

ex15: Queueing models could have stochastic numerals, subjects of specific process types and coupling operations which assure that the objects are passed on between the subjects (Kohel/ Maschtera(1985), Maschtera(1985)).

Another valuable extension of CALM is a questionaire. It can be implemented by extending the numerical (in)validation aids (by a simplex algorithm) and the natural language interface (to accept questions).

REFERENCES

Fourer, R.(1983): Modelling Languages Versus Matrix Generators for Linear Programming, CACM, Vol 9, nr 2, pp143-183.

Kohel K.,Maschtera U.(1985): Assoziation bei der Modellierung diskreter Simulationssysteme: ein Konzept und Überlegungen zu seiner Implementierung. In: Simulationstechnik, D.P.F.Möller(ed), Bad Münster a.St.-Ebernburg, Germany, pp152-156.

Maschtera U.(1984): <u>Duality Concepts in Discrete Event Simulation.</u>
    In: Applied Informatics, M.H.Hamza(ed), Innsbruck, Austria,pp29-32.

Maschtera U.(1985): Aggregation von Prozessen im Rahmen der konzeptio-
    nellen Modellierung diskreter Simulationssysteme. In: Simulations-
    technik, D.P.F.Möller(ed), Bad Münster a.St.-Ebernburg, Germany,
    pp 157-161.

Maschtera U.,Schneider W. (1985): <u>A Relational View of a Linear
    Optimization Model and Its Consequences For the Modelling
    Process.</u> In: System Modelling and Optimization, A.Prékopa,
    B.Strazicky,J.Szelezsán(ed), Budapest, Hungary.

Schneider W. (1984): <u>Ein Verfahren zur Rechen- und Speicherplatzein-
    sparung beim Simplexalgorithmus.</u> In: Operations Research
    Proceedings, D.Ohse(ed), St.Gallen, Switzerland,pp 440-446.

Zeigler, B.P. (1982): <u>Structures For Model Based Simulation Systems.</u>
    In: Simulation and Model Based Methodologies: An Integrative
    View, T.I.Ören et al.(ed), Ottawa, Canada,pp 185-216.

SECTION III
SYMBOLIC PROCESSING
IN
SIMULATION

Modelling and Simulation Methodology
in the Artificial Intelligence Era
M.S. Elzas, T.I. Ören and B.P. Zeigler (Editors)
© Elsevier Science Publishers B.V. (North-Holland), 1986

Chapter III.1

MODEL COMPONENTS FOR SYMBOLIC PROCESSING BY KNOWLEDGE BASED SYSTEMS: THE STIPS FRAMEWORK

Franz R. Pichler

Institute of Systems Science
Department of Systems Theory and Information Engineering
Johannes Kepler University Linz
Linz, Austria

1. INTRODUCTION

This chapter provides a principal framework for the discussion of problem solving mechanisms which have been established by system-theoretical means. We use a conceptual basis similar to GPS, the General Problem Solver of Newell, Shaw and Simon (1959, 1960). GPS was originally developed as a program for working on problem solving tasks in a general environment of **objects** and **operators**. We use a specific systems theory-instrumented environment. The objects of interest to us are the different possible **systems specifications** which are considered abstract model components. The general operators used in GPS are replaced in our framework by **systems specifications transformations** which serve to relate systems specifications to one another. They represent very often important partial systems problems which are discussed and elaborated upon in (mathematical) systems theory. Macrooperators are realized by algorithms constructed from the basic set of such transformations. We call them **systems specification algorithms.** Every such (meaningful) algorithm computes the solution of a specific **system problem**. The determination of such algorithms can be considered the result of a successful search in a **state space** running a **state machine**. Depending on the kind of search emploed, the AI literature distinguishes beween **blind search** ("BRUTE FORCE" problem solving), **heuristic search** ("RULE OF THUMB" problem solving) and **intelligent search** ("SHORT CUT" problem solving). A graphic representation of the search space and search trajectories can be given by Petri Nets. Whenever the transformations and the knowledge concerning their firing is used to define inference rules the AI concept of an **inference engine** can be used to control the state machine which generates the search trajectories and in consequence to define meaningful specific systems specification algorithms. Then it is also possible to use the whole conceptional frame work of STIPS (= System Theory Instrumented Problem Solving) to construct a related expert system shell STIX.

The following sections provide an introduction to the world of systems specifications and systems specification transformations which we want to use in STIPS. Furthermore, some basic considerations for constructing STIX are included. Finally we try to show how STIPS can be used to implement MIPS, a **finite state machine problem solver**. MIPS is an ongoing research project which will be used for developing problem solving tools to enhance CAD workstations. The latter are intended for use in **Design For Testability** tasks.

To some extent our paper here is a continuation of Pichler (1982) and Pichler (1984).

2. STIPS - A SYSTEMS THEORY INSTRUMENTED PROBLEM SOLVER

2.1. PROBLEM SOLVING

By a **problem solver** we mean a (man/machine) relation PS which accepts as input problems prob from a set PROB, the **problem-space**, and solves them by generating a solution sol ϵ SOL (the **solution-space** of PS). We would like to distinguish between two cases of problem solving: PS is called an **analysis-problem solver** APS if it is an abstraction of a model of a real life situation and prob expresses a certain question about it. We have, on the other hand, a **synthesis problem solver** SPS whenever the problem prob defines as a goal a certain abstraction of a model of a real life situation which has to meet certain constraints.

Let us call an abstract version of a model a **system**. Then, in an APS each problem prob is a question about the property of a system; the related solution sol gives the answer. A SPS, on the other hand, "computes" as a solution a system which has certain desired properties specified in the problem prob.

Certainly the construction of problem solvers PS of the types APS and SPS has always been of considerable interest for science and engineering. **Systems Theory** is a branch of science dedicated to the study of certain methods for problem solving. These methods can be used as tools (instruments) for constructing problem solvers PS which serve a number of different purposes. We intend to show how the framework and theoretical means of Systems Theory can be used for that task. We call this style of constructing the man/machine relation PS **Systems Theory instrumented** and the whole activity is designated by us as **Systems Theory instrumented problem solving** (STIPS). In our further discussion we will outline the STIPS-methodology and we will try to develop fundamental concepts for the knowledge engineering of STIPS. Our ultimate goal is to lay a basis for the construction and implementation of an expert system shell STIX which incorporates the STIPS framework. It is intended to serve as a basis for the construction of special Systems Theory instrumented problem solvers by expert systems. Some examples are
1) a Linear Systems instrumented problem solver expert system (LSIXPS) and
2) a Finite State Machine instrumented problem solver expert system (FSMIXPS).

Any powerful Systems Theory instrumented expert system must have a rather sophisticated knowledge base. Altough in general the overall problem solving strategy of any STIPS-XPS will be of a heuristic nature, the individual steps will depend upon intelligent action which will only be possible when the user has access to the existing knowledge of Systems Theory.

Next in this section we describe the different classes of systems specifications used in STIPS as objects for analysis and synthesis. After that we specify the different possible transformations which relate systems specifications to each other. The following section 3 then developes the concept of a STIPS-algorithm. Every such algorithm computes a Macro-operation needed to realize global state transformations in the state space of the XPS state machine.

2.2. STIPS - SYSTEMS SPECIFICATIONS

The general systems specifications of STIPS are abstract versions of important components found in models of real life situations.
We distinguish five fundamental classes of general systems specifications SPEC

- the class **SPEC-B** of black boxes
- the class **SPEC-G** of generators
- the class **SPEC-D** of dynamics
- the class **SPEC-A** of algorithms
- the class **SPEC-N** of networks

In the following we give a non-mathemaitcal description of these classes. We also point to well-known examples for specific types representing subclasses. Our aim is to familiarize the reader with our classification scheme. However, any implementation as objects in the knowledge base of an XPS-system will ultimately only be possible after a formal mathematical definition has been made. At this time we do not suggest an universal approach for that. It seems to be more efficient to adjust the formal specifications to meet the requirements of the area of problem solving involved. In the last chapter we show how such an adjustment can be performed using the example of Finite State Machine Theory for applications in computer design tasks.

SPEC-B denotes the class of specifications for model components of the behavior type **(black boxes)**. Sets of variables, relations and functions described in set-theoretical terms, I/O time systems (in the sense of Mesarovic and Takahara (1975)) can serve to exemplify members of **SPEC-B**. So can also B.P. Zeigler's specifications of the types IORO or IOFO (Zeigler, 1976).

SPEC-G is the class of **generative systems specification**. Each of its members defines a "generator" consisting of a locally given "next" state function of some kind. Finite State Machines, Differential Equation Systems and Discrete Event Systems are important subclasses of **SPEC-G**. However Petri-Nets, formal grammars, difference equations, recursions or binary relations can also be interpreted as generator specifications.
The class **SPEC-G** is of considerable importance in problem solving. Its members often reflect properties of a model component which are very desirable in problem solving. When specialized towards the application area they frequently constitute the fundamental object for theoretical investigation (e.g. the Maxwell equations in electrodynamics) or computer simulation (e.g. state-space equations for dynamic systems).

The class **SPEC-D** of **dynamic systems specifications** is characterized by the existence of "global" state transformations. Many special classes of dynamic systems specifications in that sense are known in System Theory but also in Applied and Pure Mathematics. Some of them serve as "general constructs" (in the sense of G. de Zeeuw) e.g. the dynamical systems of Birkhoff (1927) or the general dynamical systems of Mesarovic (1975), Pichler (1975) oder Kalman (1969). A natural approach for getting dynamic systems specifications is to "integrate" generative systems specifications ("to run generators") e.g. by integrating (= computing the solutions of) differential equations.

SPEC-A is the class of **algorithms**. Every member of **SPEC-A** is characterized by a set of (basic) operations together with a control structure. The latter describes the sequence of operations for computing output-data from given input-data in a finite number of steps.
Formal specifications of algorithms can be given by grammatically correct strings representing some kind of program for computation (e.g. strings written in "polish notation"). But flow-diagrams and programs written in a higher-programming language which run on a computer are also examples of algorithmic systems specificastions.

The last but not least important class of general systems specifications to be discussed here is the class **SPEC-N** of **networks**. Any member of **SPEC-N** consists of a (usually finite) family $X_1, X_2,...,$ of systems specifications where $X_i \in$ **SPEC-B** $\cup$ **SPEC-G** $\cup$ **SPEC-D** $\cup$ **SPEC-A**, together with a **composition scheme** (coupling scheme) C such that the resulting compound $C(X_1, X_2,...)$ is also a well-defined system specification. Very often the family members X_i are of the same category of systems specifications and in consequence also $C(X_1, X_2,...)$. We see that a network differs from the foregoing specifications in that it does not describe the "function" of a model component but rather its "structure". Network specifications in that sense are of course well known to us and are often used in modelling and problem solving. The idea of a "block diagram", for example, reflects in a very true sense a network specification. Special but very important network specifications are given by hierarchical multilevel systems specifications (e.g. Mesarovic, 1970).

The five classes of general systems specifications which were introduced here are fundamental for describing model components in an abstract way. A similar classification was previously suggested by the work of Klir (1969, 1982, 1985). However the classes introduced by Wymore (1967) and Zeigler (1976, 1984) also fit into our framework.

To be successful with the STIPS framework in implementing an XPS it is necessary that there be enough knowledge for generalizing and specializing a given systems specification. Such operations even have to be available as primitives in the knowledge base to be wired into the PS state machine. The reader may take as an example the special systems specification of a Finite State Machine FSM to embed it into a classification tree consisting of generalisations and specializations.

2.3. STIPS-TRANSFORMATIONS

STIPS has to provide all kinds of transformations which translate the different known systems specifications into each other. Figure 1 represents a complete directed graph showing all possible classes of such transformations for the five classes of general systems specifications introduced earlier.

An individual transformation T translates a given system specification $S \in$ **SPEC-S** into a system specification $S' \in SPEC-S'$; $T_{SS'}(S) = S'$. The following interpretation of STIPS-transformations T is possible in the context of problem solving: In case of an **analysis problem** the resulting system specification $S' = T(S)$ often enables a given problem to be more easily solved. A typical example is a system of linear equations S which can be solved by transforming S into a triangular (or - even better - into a diagonal) form S'.

In a **synthesis problem** (design problem) a system specification S is given by the goal as stated in the problem definition. The synthesis task is to find an alternative system specification $S' = T(S)$ which meets certain realization constraints. Any engineering synthesis problem (e.g. a digital filter synthesis problem in information engineering or the synthesis of a VLSI circuit with specified I/O behavior) can serve as example.

Let us now individually discuss the nature of the general STIPS-transformations shown in Figure 1. For that purposes we shall let $T_{SS'}$ denote the class of transformations which map systems specifications $S \in$ **SPEC-S** into systems specifications $S' \in$ **SPEC-S'**.

T_{BG} consists of STIPS-transformations which translate a "black box" B into a "generator" G. In engineering-oriented System Theory such transformations are usually called **realization-transformations**; powerful methods are available to compute from a given (specialized) black box a related generator (for example the well-known realization algorithm of Ho and Kalman which computes for a given causal I/O map a related linear constant system (F,G,H)).

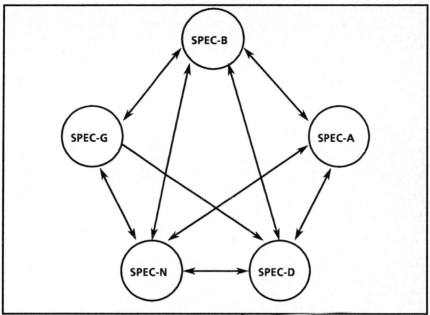

Figure 1: STIPS-Transformations

T_{BA} is the class of STIPS-transformations which map a given "black box" B to an "algorithm" A. There are of course many examples in problem solving which make use of a transformation of this kind. We can mention as an example the task of relating a given I/O table (to describe multiplication of integers for example) to a realizing algorithm (e.g. a multiplication algorithm).

With T_{XN} we denote the set of STIPS transformations which have "networks" as images. Any transformation which "structures" a system specification in one or the other way belongs to that set. A very important subclass of T_{XN} is given by **decomposition-transformation**. For a decomposition transformation T_{XN} with $N = T_{XN}(X)$ an "inverse" transformation T_{XN} has to exist such that $X' = T_{NX}(N)$ simulates X. Therefore the result $N = T_{XN}(X)$ of a decomposition transformation is essentially a refinement (or a structured version) of X. It is evident that this category of STIPS transformations is especially important.

The previously described examples from the complete set of classes of general STIPS transformations should suffice to familiarize the reader with the concept: It is rather easy to provide examples for specific transformations which serve as important tools for STIPS. Exceptionally rich sources are provided by Finite State Machine Theory and by Linear System Theory. Both theories are of traditional importance for information- and computer engineering. However many examples of STIPS-transformations can also be found in Applied and Pure Mathematics.

3. STIPS - STATE MACHINE CONSTRUCTION

We have in the previous chapters introduced the objects and the basic transformations which will be used in STIPS. In this chapter we will direct our attention to the construction of algorithms which receive STIPS-systems specifications as data and use STIPS-transformations as operations. We will call such an algorithm a STIPS-**algorithm**. In the following section we shall begin by discussing the concept for generating STIPS algorithms.

3.1. STIPS-STATE MACHINE

Let **I** denote a set of STIPS-transformations $T_{SS'}$ with S, S'ϵ{B,G,D,A,N}; with **Q** we denote a set of STIPS-transformations. We define the partial state machine **M** by the triple $M = (I,Q,\Delta)$ where Δ is the partial state transition function $\Delta: Q \times I \to Q$. A pair **(q,i)** consisting of a STIPS-systems specification q = S and a STIPS-transformation i = $T_{SS'}$ is mapped by Δ to the STIPS-system specification **q'** = S' = $T_{SS'}(S)$.
We call **M** a STIPS **state machine**.
Let a well-chosen inputword $w = i_0 i_1 i_2 ... i_{n-1} = T_0 T_1 ... T_{n-1}$ be given; the state machine **M** then computes for the initial state S_0 the state-trajectory $S_0 S_1 ... S_n \epsilon Q^*$. The reached system specification S_n is the result of the computation derived in **M** by the STIPS algorithm $T_0 T_1 ... T_{n-1}$ starting from the initial system specification S_0; $S_n = \Delta^*(S_0, T_0 T_1 ... T_{n-1})$. We see that the concept of the STIPS state machine **M** is a convenient mean for describing the algorithmic realization of a STIPS transformation T which is the composition of certain (usually more primitive) transformations $T_0, T_1, ..., T_{n-1}$; $T = T_0 \circ T_1 \circ ... \circ T_{n-1}$.

3.2. STIPS-STATE MACHINE DYNAMICS

In the following section we will elaborate some concepts which will later be needed to discuss the implementation requirements and the use of the STIPS-state machine for the conceptualization of STIPS-expert systems.

Let us assume that an initial state $S_0 \epsilon Q$ is given. We are then interested in computing the directed graph strat $S_0 = (Q(S_0), I(S_0))$ consisting of the set $Q(S_0)$ of all states which are reached in **M** from S_0 (= the set of nodes in strat S_0) together with the set $I(S_0)$ of all admissible STIPS-transformations T (= the arrows of strat S_0) which have been applied to compute $Q(S_0)$. In STIPS-terminology strat S_0 is called the **stratification graph** of S_0. In automata-theoretic terms strat S_0 describes the partial dynamics of **M** which is generated from S_0. In our context every path of length n in strat S_0 determines by its concatenated arrows a STIPS-algorithm $T_0 T_1 ... T_{n-1}$. Depending on its nature such an algorithm can be of use in contributing to the solution of an analysis or a synthesis problem. In Figure 2 a simple example is elucidated; an abstract STIPS-state machine **M** is accompanied by a related stratification graph.

Let us now assume that a stratification graph strat S_0 of **M** contains an algorithm $T_0 T_1 ... T_{n-1}$ which computes a decomposition $S = \Delta^*(S_0, T_0 T_1 ... T_{n-1})$ of S_0. Furthermore we shall assume that **M** is of a completeness such that the components S_i of S (S = $C(S_1, S_2, ...)$) are also nodes in strat S_0. Then strat S_0 contains a tree decomp S_0 with root S_0 and leaves $S_1, S_2, ...$ (the component systems specifications of the decomposition). We call decomp S_0 a **decomposition tree** of S_0. Knowing how to generate decomposition trees by **M** is certainly of important practical value. The set of all decomposition trees of S_0 has been called by Zeigler (1984) the **systems entity structure** of S_0. We designate it with the symbol ent S_0. A human problem solver who is able to compute the system entity structure ent S_0

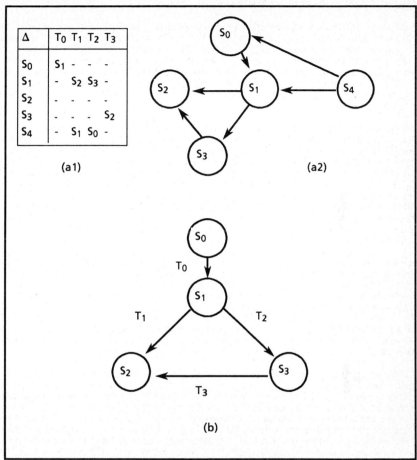

Δ	T_0	T_1	T_2	T_3
S_0	S_1	-	-	-
S_1	-	S_2	S_3	-
S_2	-	-	-	-
S_3	-	-	-	S_2
S_4	-	S_1	S_0	-

(a1)   (a2)

(b)

Figure 2: (a1) Δ-table of **M**
(a2) Δ-graph of **M**
(b) stratification graph strat S_0 of S_0

for some important types of systems specifications S_0 undoubtly has an important tool at his disposal. He can take into consideration the different possible internal structural specifications and select an appropriate one to continue his investigation. Therefore a STI enhanced workstation depends in its value strongly on the degree of availability of computing power for systems entity structure computation. For this reason we will later devote some attention to this subject when we discuss the special candidates which can be used for implementing the STIPS methodology.

3.3. On STIPS-STATE MACHINE IMPLEMENTATION

So far our discussion has remained very general. This has not allowed us to consider details of the features of the "state language" or the "process language" (Newell, Simon, 1972) which can be implemented on **M**. It seems that historically the emphasis has often been on a general discussion of problem solving by state-space search techniques (we refer here to the fundamental work on GPS (e.g. Newell, Shaw and Simon 1959). However also special domains of problem solving (e.g.the famous Logic Theory Machine of Newell, Shaw, Simon (1957) have often been studied.

Today, by the availability of cheap computer power work is leading to the development of expert systems which know special results of Systems Theory. Examples are the work of G. Klir to implement the General Systems Problem Solver GSPS (Klir 1982) and the fundamental contributions of B.P. Zeigler and his group to create tools for knowledge-based modelling and simulation (Zeigler 1984). Our future work to construct the STIPS expert system shell STIX will remain also within the traditional framework of Systems Science and Artificial Intelligence. An important task will be to construct an appropiate modelling and simulation language for the implementation of the STIPS state machine. The pioneering work of Tuncer I. Ören (compare for example with Ören (1982)) on the modelling and simulation language GEST can be an important guideline for it.

However it will be necessary to carefully consider the special symbol structures for object and operation representation which are required in STIX in order to have a broad basis for the final implementation of special STIPS expert systems. Therefore an important task for our future work will be to find an appropriate language to implement the states and state-transformations of the STIPS state machine **M** but also for the control-mechanisms which are realized by the STIX inference engine. Petri-Nets have proven a valuable tool for similar tasks (Rammig 1984, Starke 1985). They seem also to be promising candidates for our purposes.

4. MIPS: A FINITE STATE MACHINE PROBLEM SOLVER

MIPS is derived from STIPS by specializing the category of systems specifications to that of Finite State Machines (FSM). Any such machine FSM is characterized by the existence of a finite number of states q which form the **state set** Q, a finite **input-alphabet** I, a finite **output-alphabet** O and two functions δ and λ; these functions go from Q x I to Q and from Q x I to O, respectively. δ is the **next-state function** , λ the **output function**. Symbolically we write FSM: $= (I,O,Q,\delta,\lambda)$. Finite State Machines in that sense are well known and a well developed Systems Theory is available to solve all kinds of problems related with FSM's (for textbooks we refer to the "classics" of Arbib (1969), Kohavi (1970) or Hartmanis-Stearns (1966)). In STIPS classification a FSM is a special type of generator (finite, discrete time, time-constant).
From a mathematical point of view a FSM could be classified as a nonautonomous ordinary difference equation on finite sets (determined by the next state function δ) together with an output function λ.

Besides Systems specifications of FSM type, MIPS has to contain all kinds of special systems specifications derivable by certain operations which are considered of importance for FSM problem solving.

Examples are:
1) generalizations of FSM's (e.g. FUZZY State Machines, Nondeterministic State Machines, Turing Machines and others)

2) specifications of FSM's (e.g. Binary Finite State Machines, Linear State Machines, Feedbackshiftregisters and others) or

3) such important systems specifications as Petri-Nets, Directed Graphs, Lattices, Semigrioups, Memory Machines and others.

It is only natural that functions, relations, special algorithms at different levels of refinement should also be contained in MIPS.

To facilitate the construction of special sections of MIPS it seems advisable to develop an appropriate FSM expertsystem shell MIX. It should be developed on the basis of the expert systems shell STIX.

The applications of MIPS and in consequence of MIX enhance current design and analysis procedures in different areas of computer- and information engineering. Examples in which we are interested in our research are:
1) the problem areas "Design for Testability" (DFT) to improve current workstations for electronic hardware design with respect to testability features and
2) applications in cryptography.

5. CONCLUSIONS

System Theory is concerned with the construction (design) and investigation (analysis) of abstract models which can be used for problem solving. Current advances in high technology allow the implementation of the methods established by Systems Theory on computerized workstations. It would be desirable to have the Systems Theory knowledge engineered on an expert system (STIXPS). We have tried to describe in a general way the model components (in form of the STIPS-systems specifications) and the related operations (STIPS transformations) for the symbolic processing of such components. The key concept developed by us is given by the STIPS-algorithm. Such an algorithm is considered to be "nice" when the systems transformation T which it realizes solves an important systems problem. The "source" for deriving "nice" algorithms for a given system specification S_0 is given by the stratificatuion graph strat S_0 of S_0. Of special importance is the subgraph which describes the entity structure ent S_0. This entity structure is the union of all possible decomposition trees decomp S_0 of S_0.
However, the selection of STIPS algorithms which are in a certain sense "nice", has to be based on heuristic search in the stratification graph strat S_0 of the system specification S_0.

The power of the framework discussed here depends on the existence of a knowledge-base KB which is rich enough for the generation of powerful algorithms by the STIPS state machine which is controlled by the STIX inference engine.

We can not claim that the ideas which we present here are entirely new. After some own study we found out that our ideas are quite in line with the GPS philosophy. This philosophy was developed very early in AI by Newell and Simon. Therefore we are able to use all the results of GPS to build the basic framework. To further investigate what a state language, a process language and a control language for STIPS and STIX should look like seems to be an important research topic. Further efforts will be devoted to MIPS and MIX. As we pointed out earlier the intention is to construct a tool which can be applied in special design tasks, such as "Design for Testability" (DFT) of "Cryptography".

This work has been partially supported by SIEMENS AG, Bereich ZTI, Munich, West Germany, under Project STI-DFT.

6. REFERENCES

Arbib, M.A. (1969): Theories of Abstract Automata
     Prentice Hall, Englewood Cliffs, N.J.

Birkhoff, G.D. (1927): Dynamical Systems
     Amer.Math.Soc.Coll.Publ., Vol.9, New York

Hartmanis, J., R.E.Stearns (1966): Algebraic Structure Theory of Sequential
     Machines
     Prentice Hall, Englewood Cliffs, N.J.

Kalman, R.E., P.L. Falb, M.A. Arbib (1969): Topics in Mathematical Systems Theory
     Mc Graw Hill Book Comp., New York

Klir, G.J. (1969): An Approach to General Systems Theory
     Van Nostrand Reinhold, New York

Klir, G.J. (1982): General Systems Framework for Inductive Modelling
     in: Simulation and Model-Based Methodologies: An
     Integrative View, T.I. Ören, B.P. Zeigler and M.S.Elzas (eds.),
     Springer Verlag Berlin, 1984, pp.69-90

Klir, G.J. (1985): The Architecture of Problem Solving
     Plenum Publishing Corporation, 233 Spring Street, New
     York 10013

Kohavi, Z. (1970): Switching and Finite Automata Theory
     Mc Graw Hill, New York

Mesarovic, M.D., D. Macko and Y. Takahara (1970): Theory of Hierarchical,
     Multilevel Systems
     Academic Press, New York

Mesarovic, M.D., and Y. Takahara (1975): General Systems Theory: Mathematical
     Foundations
     Academic Press, New York

Newell, A., J.C.Shaw, H. Simon (1957): Empirical explorations with the Logic
     Theory Machine
     in: E.A.Feigenbaum and J. Feldman, Computers and
     Thought, Mc Graw Hill Book Company, New York 1963, pp
     109-133

Newell, A.. H.A. Simon (1959): GPS, a program that simulates human thought
     in: Computers and Thought, E.A. Feigenbaum and J.
     Feldman (eds.), Mc Graw Hill Book Company, New York
     1963, pp. 279-293

Newell, A., J.C. Shaw, H.A.Simon (1960): A Variety of Intelligent Learning in a
General Problem Solver
in: Self-Organizing Systems, M.C. Yovits, S. Cameron (eds.),
Pergamon Press, New York, pp. 153-189

Newell, A., H.A. Simon (1972): Human Problem Solving
Prentice Hall, Englewood Cliffs, N.J.

Pichler, F. (1975): Mathematische Systemtheorie, Dynamische Konstruktionen
Walter de Gruyter, Berlin

Pichler, F. (1982): Symbolic Manipultion of Systems Models
in: Simulation and Model-Based Methdologies: An
Integrative View, T.I. Ören, B.P. Zeigler, M.S.Elzas (eds.),
Springer Verlag Berlin, 1984, pp. 217-234

Pichler, F. (1984): General Systems Algorithms for Mathematical Systems Theory
in: Cybernetics and Systems Research 2, R.Trappl (ed.),
Proceedings of EMCSR 84, Vienna, Austria, North Holland,
Amsterdam, 1984, pp.161-164

Rammig, F.J. (1984): Design Aids for Highly Distributed Hardware
Proceedings of the IFIP WG 105, Workshop on Hardware
Supported Implementation of Concurrent Languages in
Distributed Systems, Bristol, U.K., March, 26-28, 1984

Starke, P.H. (1985): Petri-Netz-Maschine: A software tool for analysis and
validation of Petri nets
in: Systems Analysis and Simulations 1985, Vol.I, A.Sydow
(ed.), Proceedings of the International Symposium, Berlin
(GRD), 1985, Akademie Verlag Berlin, pp. 474-475

Wymore, A.W. (1967): A Mathematical Theory of Systems Engineering: The
Elements
Wiley, New York
(out of print; New orders can be made at: Robert E.
Krieger, P.O.Box 542, Huntington, N.Y. 11743)

Zeigler, B.P. (1976): Theory of Modelling and Simulation
Wiley, New York

Zeigler, B.P. (1984): Multifacetted Modelling and Discrete Event Simulation
Academic Press, London

Modelling and Simulation Methodology
in the Artificial Intelligence Era
M.S. Elzas, T.I. Ören and B.P. Zeigler (Editors)
© Elsevier Science Publishers B.V. (North-Holland), 1986

Chapter III.2

POSSIBILITIES FOR EXPERT AIDS IN SYSTEM SIMULATION

Alfred W. Jones

Computer Systems Department
Florida Atlantic University
Boca Raton, Florida   33431
U.S.A.

Seven elements in the simulation process are identified,
three involved in model construction, three in the
planning of the experiments to be performed with the
model, and a seventh element consisting of the monitoring of simulation runs.   Possible expert aids are
examined for each element. Particular attention is paid
to the model simplification and run monitoring elements.
Existing expert systems developed for semigroups are
directly applicable to the monoid associated with the
mathematical structures defined by us and identified as
stochastic simulation machines.

1.   ELEMENTS OF THE SIMULATION PROCESS

We shall first review the anatomy of the simulation process as described by
Oren and Zeigler (1979).   They identify six elements which we have encapsu-
lated in the memnonic soibean; that is, the letters s, o, i, and b, e, and an.
Briefly, their meanings are:

s: structure creation for the simulation model

o: output identification (in a performance evaluation model, this would be
     the measures of system performance)

i: input needed to produce the desired output

The above three steps all have to do with model construction, and the next
three with construction of the "experimental frame," to use Oren and
Zeigler's term.

b: the beginning or initial conditions governing the conduct of the
     experiment

e: the rules by which the experiment will come to an end

an: the analysis of the results of the simulation runs

To these six elements of the simulation process, we have added a seventh.

rim: run time interactive monitoring; this includes debugging, and much more

Before discussing the expert aids we feel are relevant to each step, we shall
describe what we mean by a stochastic simulation machine so that these aids
may be described in terms of the machine.

2.   STOCHASTIC SEQUENTIAL MACHINES

Carlyle (1963) defined <u>stochastic sequential machines</u> as specified by three finite sets, X, Y, and S, and a conditional probability function p (y,s'|s,x) defined for all s and s' in S, x in X, and y in Y.   He further defined a stochastic finite-state system as consisting of a machine M and a probability distribution pi(s) which gives the initial probabilities of the machine associated with its possible states s (s   an element of S).   He developed theorems for studying the equivalence of such systems, similar to the familiar theorems associated with finite automata.   One may recall that the problems of equivalence and of minimum state finite automata are related.   Traditionally, there is an iteration process applied to creating equivalence classes for states whose outputs agree when the same sequence of inputs is applied.

We have a theorem which shows this process to be equivalent to finding the symmetry group of the monoid of the conditional probability functions, where the monoid operator is defined as the application of one transition followed by another.   The advantage of the theorem is that it frees one from the necessity of assuming finiteness of the stochastic sequential machine (Jones 1984, p.259).

For this reason, and for convenience in using the stochastic machine concept for building simulations of the combined discrete type, we offer the generalization below. It is similar in some ways to the models described by Zeigler (1976, Chapters 5 and 9).

One of the key features in the model is the coordinatization of the states of the model, which is particularly useful when using such general simulation languages as GASP IV, SLAM, and SIMAN.

<u>Definition</u>: a stochastic simulation machine is a quadruple SM = (X,Y,Q,P) where:

X	is a finite set: the set of inputs (event subroutines or procedures)
Y	is a finite dimensional set: the set of output vectors y
Q	is a partitioned finite dimensional set: the set of states q
P (y,q'/x,q)	is a partitioned next state-output function: some of its elements may be conditional probabilities, others conditional probability densities, and still others simply deterministic

Notice that, although X is restricted to be a finite set, a given input may follow another in an arbitrarily small amount of time.   In the case where the input has an associated event subroutine defined in terms of a set of differential equations, this small amount of time would be specified as the integration step size.   This means that stochastic simulation machines are appropriately defined to include combined continuous and discrete models.

Included in the set X is the "identity" input, the input which changes no state.   Thus, the finite set X is a set of generators for a monoid of transformations taking the set (Q,Y) into itself.

A frequently practical coordinatization for Q is Q=(T,E,F,S), where T is simulation clock time, E is the input queue, F is a set of files (frequently queues), and S is a finite set of elements.   Each of these coordinates is a macro coordinate and will, in general, be further coordinatized.

The coordinate S includes "status indicators" which may be used to identify certain "break-point" conditions, such as when one set of differential equations is to be replaced by another.   For example, when modeling the trajectory of a pilot using an ejection set, the status of his trajectory changes when his back is no longer constrained by the chair he was sitting in, and so the governing set of differential equations is changed. From knowing the present state s of S, it will be known what section of sectionally defined analytic functions are to be used.

All or part of S may be a homomorphic image of (T,E,F). The advantage of creating S in this way, even though it may involve redundancy, lies in the way the event subroutines representing the next state function can be simplified. Stated abstractly, $p(y,q'/x,q)$ can, for certain of its components, be written as $p(y,q'/x,s)$, thus greatly simplifying the logic needed in the procedures constituting the corresponding event subroutine. For example, the state transition brought about by the arrival of a customer to a bunch of servers is conditional upon the busy status of the servers and not upon the details of where the other customers are.

The existence of the input queue E in the coordinatization of Q is evidence that the stochastic simulation machine is conceived of as autonomous, with the input queue being part of the state description. This corresponds to the world view adapted by many general purpose simulation languages. It enables a simulation run to be executed without presenting the model with an exogenous stream of inputs. The initial input is supplied, and then bootstrapping operations generate subsequent inputs by means of the input queue E, or "event calendar," an equivalent term. The elements of E are sometimes called event notices. In entity driven simulations, an entity is associated with each such notice, together with the element x of the input set and the time t when the event is to take place (the element x is to be applied).

$P(y,q'/x,q)$, the next state-output function, replaces the value t indicating present clock time into the value $\underline{t'}$, the input time of the next element of the event calendar. It effects the removal of this element from E and also the placement of other event notices onto E. It performs file manipulations on the elements of F and a change from s to some other element s' chosen from the finite set S.

The component of P making changes in the state component in S can be represented as a conditional probability function with the markov matrices $M(y/x)$ completely describing the passage from one state to the probability distribution of the succeeding state. The matrix representation is possible because of the finiteness of S. The concept is generalizable to describing the running of a stochastic simulation machine as the realization of an embedded markov process.

For straightforward simulations, the execution of a subroutine (procedure) representing the action of an element of P, as far as E is concerned, involves the removal of only one element from E, and this element effects the next state transition. But the removal and destruction of other elements of E is also possible. This amounts to the cancellation of a future event and its possible replacement of another event. This is particularly useful for realizing variable step integration when the exact timing of a change in the state s is not known in advance.

For the full generality of P, we have written it in Shannon transition form, where the output value and the next state value are not necessarily statistically independent. If they are, the Mealy transition form can be used, or even the simpler Moore form. For the finite state case, the last two forms are well known to be equivalent.

2.1   An example of an SSM (stochastic simulation machine)

We have presented elsewhere and in detail three examples of an SSM (Jones 1984). We shall sketch the third and simplest of those examples here in order to illustrate some of the general concepts presented above.

Two telephone customer lines share three outgoing trunks to a central office by means of a limited access arrangement known as a graded multiple. The simplest such multiple is one in which the first line has access to trunks 1 and 3, while the second line has access to trunks 2 and 3. Trunk 3 is known as the overflow trunk. The state space of the multiple can be represented by the vectors (i,j,k) where i has the value 0 if trunk 1 is idle and the value 1 otherwise. Similarly for j. k has three values, namely 0 if the trunk is idle, 1 if the first line is using it, and 2 if the second line is using it.

We observe that this state space is finite and contains 12 elements. The input set X is generated by the 12 x 12 identity matrix, the arrival event matrix, and the departure event matrix. Each column of each of these two matrices gives the probabilities the new state will be that indicated by the corresponding row entry. To each of these 12 x 12 matrices we add another column which will give the values of the output function.

If the traffic demands of each line have the same characteristics, then the state space is symmetric with regard to the interchange of these two lines. This symmetry can be expressed in terms of a permutation matrix T. Denoting arrival matrix by A and the departure matrix by B, and the inverse of T by T', then T'AT=A and T'BT=B. That is to say, T transforms the semigroup of inputs associated with SSM into itself. The sum of symmetric states remains invariant under the transformation and so forms a macro state. The new macro states form a new state space which is homomorphic to the original. The monoid generated by the identity and A and B will indeed produce exactly the same outputs as the new reduced monoid transforming the space of macro states when the behavior of line 1 is to be considered as identical to the behavior of line 2 in a statistical sense. Without too much work in this simple case, one can see that the new state space contains only 6 elements instead of the original 12.

This illustrates the mechanism whereby simplification is obtained when it is possible to "lump" the outputs into equivalence classes due to symmetry. The procedure is exactly analogous to what one can do with finite state machines. The minimum state space machine is obtained by creating r-equivalence sets of states. When outputs are themselves lumped into equivalent sets, then r-equivalence under the new identification of equivalent outputs results in larger equivalence sets of states. The result is a smaller minimum state machine.

3.   USING EXPERT AIDS FOR MODEL CONSTRUCTION

In order to get started in model construction, it is necessary to translate the systems description and problem statement into abstract model terms. Oren (1979) describes a language, MAGEST, expert systems advisor, for doing this. The value of using a systems model should be clear from the writings of Zeigler, Elzas, and Oren.

We note that there has been a tendency of late to particularize models, using domain specific knowledge in order to present simulationists with pictures and icons suitable for a particular field. Our feeling is that we may be misusing the richness of computer graphics and other technical advances

in doing this. There is at least one class of simulationists whose expertise
lies in certain familiarity with certain standard abstract models such as
queuing nets, service systems, and processing systems. Interacting with such
a model base at this point will lessen the enormous duplication of effort we
notice at the present time.

Suppose now that, by means of this MAGEST type dialogue, a feasible
working SSM has been created.

The next stage will be to exploit the symmetry of the model structure
created. The sheer dimensionality of this structure makes human simplification a formidable task. It is at this point that we shall call on the expert
simplification aid provided us by the work of Vos (1981) and possibly of
Cannon (1982). To be more specific, Vos and his associates have succeeded
in solving some outstanding problems in semigroup theory by writing an
expert system in PL1 to serve this purpose. Cannon, in turn, has created
his own language for doing group theory. This means that the structure of
monoids, which are simply semigroups with an identity, can be deduced.
Associated with all possible homomorphic images of such an algebraic system
are the "normal subsystems" and corresponding quotient systems, which are
indeed the homomorphic images.

Having used these expert aids to simplify the structure as much as possible,
we shall turn to the problem of simplification of the output requirements.

We shall next invoke the aid of an expert system to discover the symmetry
of the outputs. Their redundancy should also be examined. For example, if
one knows the distribution of the length of service queues, it is usually
possible to deduce the distribution of waiting times, so that the latter
information need not be collected separately.

After the maximum reduction of the output set has been achieved, then a
return must be made to the model structure so that it can be correspon-
dingly reduced by means of the new symmetry exploited for the outputs.

The third aspect of model construction, namely the pruning of the input set,
is more complicated and needs a more detailed discussion.

3.1   The imbedded chain concept

As previously stated in our article, we identify the next-state-output
function with input element x from X and with the corresponding subroutine
which effects the changes. The input to the subroutine includes the present
state of the system. It is natural to refer to this subroutine as event
subroutine x, and we shall now do so.

The input alphabet is given by the elements x of the finite set X. Model
simplification is effected when the size of this alphabet, i.e., the number of
subroutines, is as small as possible. For both discrete event models and
continuous models, as constructed for such languages as GASP IV, SLAM,
and SIMAN, model execution involves advancing the simulation clock an
increment after each application of event subroutine x.

By a device which we have called time anticipation, it is possible to
construct the required event subroutines in such a way that already determined events can be recorded without moving the simulation clock. That is,
the actual points in time where a subroutine is applied is a subset of all the
points in time where a change takes place. This saves a great deal of
computation for both continuous and discrete models. The result is that the
sequence of points where the subroutines are applied form an embedded
chain in the entire state trajectory.

To illustrate this, we refer to the simulation of the operation of a bank of elevators in an office building, an example which is described in some detail in a previous paper (Jones, 1984). Here, it is possible to use one subroutine for describing the entrance of passengers already waiting for an elevator, even though they step into the elevator at times later than the indicated value of the simulate clock while the subroutine is being applied. There is no loss in statistical output analysis brought about by using this device. The subroutine has to be reapplied in an iterative way, with a clock time change after the batch of customers waiting have all been accommodated, since new arrivals may have appeared in the interim.

Another illustration shows how this can be applied to continuous models. An example in Pritsker (1974, p. 201 ff) gives a combined discrete event / continuous event simulation model of oil tankers plying their way between Alaska and the state of Washington. At the unloading dock, differential equations describe the unloading act which will be interfered with when the dock shuts down at night or when the storage tank has reached capacity. The equations are capable of an analytic solution, so the incremental change of time introduced to describe their behavior is unnecessary. The subroutine "state" which describes this continuous change of state, can be replaced by an event subroutine where analytical solutions determine when the next event subroutine x should be applied.

4.   USING EXPERT AIDS TO DESIGN EXPERIMENTS TO BE PERFORMED ON THE MODEL

Statistical aids are the ones most needed for determining how the simulation run should begin and how it should end. Much is already known about the best way to handle processes having certain distinguishing characteristics. For example, when modeling an inventory system with batch replacement, recognition that it is a regenerative process with regeneration points being defined by the arrival of replenishments leads to aggregating statistics for each cycle. This greatly reduces the variance which would be obtained by using the steady state approach.

Rules for ending the model experiment will profit by expert aids. Such aids should provide rules for simulation termination as a function of the ongoing results obtained during the simulation execution. This is necessary, since it is seldom known ahead of time how long a run should be performed in order to obtain results accurate to a desired degree of precision.

One language, SIMAN, already has a collection of statistical subroutines for aiding in the analysis phase of the simulation. This seems to be in exactly the right direction since, by creating a separate output file for each simulation run, the expert statistical analysis package can perform analyses and experiments on the output by itself. This eliminates the necessity of having to perform another simulation run simply because one was not able to foresee the way the ongoing output data should be analyzed. What remains is to add some advisory functions to such a package which will make use of the appropriate subroutines. Since many simulationists find statistics rather irksome, assistance at this level should eliminate a good deal of the drudgery now associated with it.

5.   EXPERT AIDS FOR THE EXECUTION OF THE MODEL EXPERIMENT

Compilers used to realize the model of the system to be simulated can be relied upon to detect syntax errors upon compilation and other errors during

run time.   They do not do anything about logical errors, an admittedly
difficult problem which continues to occupy the attention of the professional
computer science community.

Some languages such as GPSS, SLAM, and SIMAN have a trace element
which has been known to overwhelm the simulationist with too much detail.
GPSS H can present some of the results in graphical form, thus revealing
some blatant model misassumptions such as permitting automobiles on a
highway to be at the same place at the same time.

The SIMAN interactive debugger (Pegden, 1985) permits the simulationist
greater run time freedom in seeing what he wants to during the simulation
run.   Again, the choices are enormous and their proper exercise would be
greatly facilitated by an expert advisor who would display state changes in
an appropriate fashion.

An expert monitoring system would be able to make run time decisions as to
data collection.   For example, it is not known beforehand in the statistical
analysis of a system which achieves steady state conditions <u>when</u> that system
has actually achieved a steady state.   The expert monitor can continually
measure the difference between input and output rates of entities processed
by the system, thus directing data collection when these rates are sufficiently close to each other.

The expert monitoring system could also abort an unproductive simulation,
giving a report on the reasons for the abort decisions and recommendations
for change.

6.   SUMMARY

We have presented a structure for introducing expert aids to the simulation
process, using the stages identification made by Oren and Zeigler, and basing
the actual implementations upon the use of SSM's (stochastic simulation
machines).   This leads to simplification at each of the stages.   Particular
attention was paid to systematic reduction in:

. the model input alphabet
. output requirements
. dimensionality and the number of states in the model representation
   space
. initial conditions
. procedures for simulation termination
. minimal embedded chain creation.

Existing expert systems created for determining the anatomy of monoids
already exist. Thus, some of the suggestions given in the paper are already
implementable.   Other aids in existence should profit in their utility by
adapting the SSM model or some other general systems model such as those
due to Zeigler, Oren, and Elzas.

ACKNOWLEDGMENT

We express appreciation for the many suggestions made by Zeigler and Oren,
resulting in a clarification of the main ideas herein presented.

REFERENCES

Cannon, J.J. (1982). A language for group theory, Department of Pure
Mathematics, University of Sydney, Australia, 365 p.

Carlyle, J.W. (1963). Reduced forms for stochastic sequential machines.
Journal Math. Anal. Appl., Vol 7, pp. 167-175.

Jones, A.W. (1984). Minimizing system models for efficient simulation.
Proceedings, 17th Annual Simulation Symposium. (IEEE) pp. 235-260.

Oren, T.I., and Zeigler, B.P. (1979). Concepts for advanced simulation
methodology, Vol 32, nr. 2, pp. 69-82.

Pritsker, A.A.B. (1974). The GASP IV simulation language. John Wiley,
Chapter 7.

Winker, S., Wos, L., and Lusk, E. (1981). Semigroups, antiautomorphisms,
and involutions: a computer solution to an open problem. Mathematics
of computation, Vol 37., nr. 156.

Zeigler, B.P. (1976). Theory of modeling and simulation. John Wiley, p. 188.

Zeigler, B.P., Elzas, M.S., Klir, G.J., Oren,T.I. (Eds.) (1979). Methodology in
systems modeling and simulation. North-Holland Publishing. Chapter 2.

Modelling and Simulation Methodology
in the Artificial Intelligence Era
M.S. Elzas, T.I. Ören and B.P. Zeigler (Editors)
© Elsevier Science Publishers B.V. (North-Holland), 1986   153

Chapter III.3

APPLICATIONS OF EXPERT SYSTEMS CONCEPTS TO ADAPTIVE
EXPERIMENTATION WITH MODELS

A. Jávor

Central Research Institute for Physics
of the Hungarian Academy of Sciences
H-1525 Budapest, P.O.Box 49.
HUNGARY

After a brief description of the problems of effectiveness in classical "manually controlled"
simulation experiments, the possibility of applying the concepts of Expert Systems to the adaptive
control, using an Expert Simulation System (ESS)
is shown. Adaptive control of the experiment via
a model base and the experimental frame using an
inference engine is shown. The ESS structure with
regard to both up-to-date and future hardware as
well as the fields of applications are discussed.

1. INTRODUCTION

Both Expert Systems and Simulation Systems are intended as aids to
acquire knowledge about certain existing or anticipated aspects of
the world and thereby to improve our understanding and make decisions
based on it. Hamming's statement that "The purpose of computing is
insight, not numbers" (Hamming 1962) applies to these fields extremely well.

Simulation - aimed at the building of models and conducting experiments with them to investigate existing or hypothetical dynamic systems - is used in two wide areas:
(a) investigation of their nature and getting a better understanding
    of their qualitative and quantitative behaviour;
(b) promoting the construction of new systems for given purposes (i.e.
    Computer Aided Design). In both cases some a priori knowledge
    about the behaviour (specification) and structure of the systems
    to be modelled is available and the aim is to get a more detailed
    and/or substantiated picture about the structure/behaviour of
    them.

Powerful tools for the simulation of highly complex systems are available in many fields. These simulation models provide highly sophisticated representation of the subject investigated. For the solution
of modelling as a whole (Zeigler 1984, Spriet, Vansteenkiste 1982)
however there is a need for numerous auxiliary programs. The effectiveness of modelling is significantly diminished if the evaluation, model manipulation and experiment control is undertaken by
comperatively ineffective manual methods.

Expert systems on the other hand suggest methods which may be applied
to evaluation, decision making and incorporation of newly acquired

knowledge into the system by learning process. It seems plausible
that unifying these two procedures having complementary virtues can
improve the effectiveness of modelling considerably.

In the present paper an outline of the application of expert system
concepts to the adaptive experimentation with models is given.

2. GENERAL SYSTEM STRUCTURES

System structures can be studied as in Figure 1.

In Figure 1/a a conventional simulation system structure is depicted.
It is important to note the connection drawn with a dotted line.
This indicates that the modification of the experimental conditions
and the model itself is controlled by the experimenter and is not
incorporated into the system as an automatic computerized feature.
The management of the database is performed in a similar way.

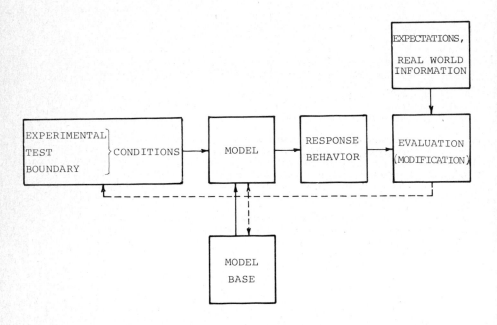

Figure 1/a
Conventional Simulation System Structure

Figure 1/b depicts the block scheme of an Expert System. A very important feature of such systems is their capability of acquiring new
information and updating their *knowledge base* through a *learning
process*. The knowledge base itself consists generally of a very large
number of relatively simple rules.

Now let us consider how the performance of high level system repre-

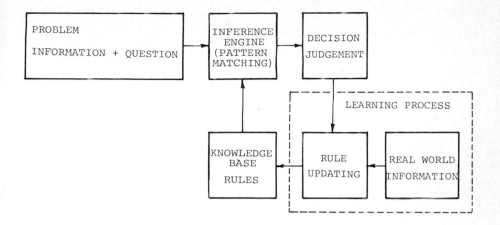

Figure 1/b
Expert System Structure

sentation by simulation models can be augmented by adaptivity and
intelligent control using knowledge based methods.

The structure of an *Expert Simulation System (ESS)* enabling goal
oriented intelligent control of simulation experimentation is suggested in Figure 1/c.

Comparing the two previous schemes with the suggested one, brings
out the following important points:

(i) An automated decision feedback from the output of simulation runs
     to the adjustment of the model and experimental conditions can
     be realized with the following results.

     - In CAD the specification of the system to be designed - in form
        of expected behavior patterns - is matched against the behavior
        of the actual model and with the help of the model base the
        structure and building blocks of the model are recursively
        modified. This results in achieving synthesis using analysis;
        realizing real Design Automation instead of CAD. In this case
        the model base contains a library of building elements and some
        connection patterns. The knowledge base has to contain certain
        behavioral specifications with regard to the library of model
        elements and input segments; and the model is modified using
        the model base.

     - Another area where simulation is used may be summarized as sys-
        tem identification. This may refer to a large number of subject
        matters where we intend to increase our knowledge about the
        real world making black box type models more "gray" or possibly
        "white". Such fields may be; brain or neuron network models,
        economic models on a world or national scale etc.

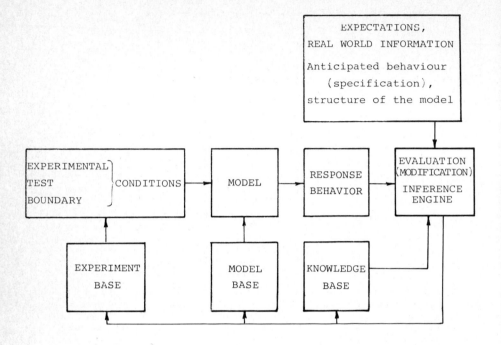

Figure 1/c
Expert Simulation System (ESS) Structure

(ii) The modification of models in the feedback loop via the inference mechanism evaluating the results of simulation is undertaken through the model base where the primitives or building
blocks - of which models can be assembled - are stored. Simultaneously the knowledge base containing also the information
gained about the behavior of the present model is updated.

(iii) The matching of model behavior to some expected pattern is
based on simulation. The effectivity of the process can be enhanced by the appropriate choice of experimental or test input
sequences. If the dynamic behavior of the model meets the expectations then additional test sequences may be chosen to
investigate the model further; perhaps from other sides. On the
other hand if deviations from the expectations are detected,
the continuation of model testing may be directed towards the
determination of possible causes in the model structure. For
these purposes the *experiment base* of the system has to consist
of a library of experimental input segments which may be chosen
consecutively by the inference process in accordance with the
results obtained during simulation run. The results during
dynamic simulation are continuously compared with the "expectations" and using the knowledge base the inference engine of the

system controls the continuation of the input of the model and thereby the simulation run.

The experimental segments are stored in the *experiment base* and have to be
(a) defined in relative time; getting their absolute time values at their activation,
(b) reentrant,
(c) composed of a sequence of events together with conditions and branching points.

The chaining of such segments or sequences during simulation run is illustrated in Figure 2.

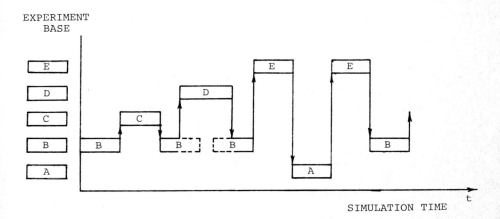

Figure 2
Conditional Linking of Input Segments

The input segments stored in the experiment base are labelled A through E. The activation of these segments during simulation run is indicated along the simulation time axis. The transfers from one segment to another are indicated by arrows and are dynamically controlled by the inference engine using the results of the simulation and the knowledge base. As can be seen, the segments may be used repeatedly as in the cases of segments B and E. On the other hand the transfer may take place at the end of the segments or in some intermediate place during their execution, controlled by a built in condition test. In the latter case - after the execution of the input segment(s) to which transfer took place - control is returned to the previous input segment and the experiment is continued from the same place in the body of the segment from which the transfer was made as in the case of the second transfer from segment B in Figure 2.

To conduct such experiments the experimenter has to be able to describe - using an appropriate language - the segments for the

experiment and the knowledge base. Some of the main points
thereby are
- the specification of external and observational variables by
  means of identifiers,
- declaring timing delays and provide initial setting of the
  model,
- declaring input sequences, scheduled state changes and pre-
  scribing scheduled tests,
- controlling conditional transfer upon testing variables inside the segments or transfer to other segments,
- definition of segments with conditional branching and relative
  timing,
- linking segments to each other conditionally or unconditionally.

The adaptive input sequence generators based on continuous evaluation of simulation results and inference can be implemented
easily. Using a block oriented nonprocedural model structure
the generator in a DEVS formalism (Zeigler 1984) can be implemented as a special building block of the model as can be seen
in Figure 3.

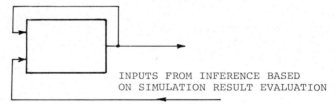

RESCHEDULING OF NEXT EVENT

INPUTS FROM INFERENCE BASED
ON SIMULATION RESULT EVALUATION

Figure 3
Adaptive Input Generator Controlled by Inference Based
on Current Simulation Results

A simple input event generator routine in such an environment
is defined as follows

<generator> ::= <generate input event; set time for next event
                in time scheduling structure>

Our special element extends the rescheduling by a further
- conditional - input through which control can be applied.
Here the scheduling of the next input event is controlled in
an adaptive way as a function of the simulation result trajectory with a conditional control driven by the inference engine.

These principles have already been implemented and tested in a
special field i.e. the simulation of digital logic (Jávor, Révész, Tóbiás 1982a).

(iv) The adjustment of the model and the control of the simulation
     run is mediated by the knowledge base, which contains complex
     behavioral descriptions of model segments.

The *production rules* having the general form

    if (condition) then (actions)

may have highly complex nature both in case of model modification as in experiment control through the experiment base.

During the development of a programming system - in our case the ESS - it has always to be kept in mind that it is not an abstract theoretical object but a practically applicable tool that has to take into account the implementation as well as the demands of the perspective users. There are two important questions in this respect that we have to deal with.

- The Hardware Aspect
- The Scope of Applications

3. THE HARDWARE ASPECT

Although it is not the purpose of this paper to go into the details of hardware; such considerations cannot be omitted since they will have rapidly increasing influence on simulation as well. The reason for this is twofold. On the one hand the complexity of the integrated circuits and the possibilities provided by them grow exponentially in accordance with Moore's prediction (Moore 1979). On the other hand the solution of problems by simulation represents an actual need for the application of parallel processing hardware. It is also important that the natural representation of simulation models suggest the configuration of a network of processing elements (Concepcion, Zeigler 1985).

Beyond the research of multiprocessing structures for simulation (Concepcion, Zeigler 1985, Ameling 1985, Dekker 1985) there is already urgent practical need for simulating very large scale systems where due to the size of the model parallel processing is unavoidable. For the simulation of VLSI digital logic circuits adaptive array processors with 65536 processing elements and the development of such containing 1 million processing elements have been reported (Tsuneta Sudo, Takyoshi Nakashima, Makato Aoki, Toshio Kondo 1982). For the fifth generation (Moto-oka 1982) beside the high throughput of parallel processing based on VLSI technology, hardware implemented inference engines as LISP or PROLOG machines will be available. The main factor however seems to be the *reconfigurable network of processors* as a modelling tool.

On the one hand simulation applications in the future can be expected to be concentrated on very large supercomputers providing the facilities of fifth generation technology and architecture. This holds for the extremely large models where extreme computing power is necessary. The other hardware tool that will play an increased role in simulation will be the personal computer with highly increased capabilities. Here interactivity and graphic man-machine communications have to be stressed.

The architecture of future ESS systems thus have to be easily transferable to these hardware structures otherwise the inevitable and fundamental change in hardware architecture will unavoidably outdate the systems developed.

Some of the important points are as follows.

- Using *non-procedural* model description philosophy that can easily
  be mapped into the multiprocessing structures. This way by making
  a 1:1 correspondence between the block element describing procedures and respective processing elements preserve the structure
  and also reconfiguration by the inference part of the ESS can easily be attained in both cases.

- Developing scheduling procedures that are effective in multiprocessing environment.

- Race conditions, feedback loop handling have to be taken care of to
  provide a realistic representation of reality by the model (Jávor
  1975, Jávor 1983, Jávor 1985). These problems have already been
  treated in case of quasiparallel simulation using conventional sequential machines. For models consisting of a network of building
  block elements where the interconnection between them is realized
  by connections of their outputs to the inputs of the others and
  where the state description is such that the output value of an
  element is unconditionally fed to the inputs of the elements
  coupled to it, i.e. so called "level type" systems (like, say digital logic networks), feedback loops may cause the problems (such
  are "significant hazards" in a flip-flop where due to certain input combinations the next state may be undetermined). In these
  cases the Quasideterministic State Description (Jávor 1975) can
  solve the problem. Here the identification of the feedback loops
  in model network topology is undertaken and if such a situation occurs during the dynamic simulation run the model assumes one possible state and gives a simultaneous warning signal. In case of
  "entity-type" systems where the operation in a model is described
  by the movement of "entities" in the model network, similar problems may arise supposing, for example that a storage facility is
  near its empty state in which case simultaneously arriving demand
  and refilling can result either in
  (i) the fulfillment of the demand if the subroutine of "filling"
      is the first to be called or otherwise the demand cannot be
      fulfilled, or
  (ii) a case where a single resource is requested simultaneously by
      two users.
  Such conditions can be handled by a transformation of such systems
  into their "level type" equivalent - based on the concept of the
  duality of events (Jávor 1983). The solutions however have to be
  adapted to parallel simulation so that a possibly 1:1 correspond-
  dence between the behavior of the modelled system and the multi-
  processor network should be attained, with simultaneous detection
  of the hazards.

- The interactive control and evaluation of model building and the
  simulation run using graphic display possibilities has to be ar-
  tanged. Here two main points should be mentioned.

  (i) The building of the model - using the *model base* - as well as
      the description of the experiment - utilizing the elements of
      the *experimental frame* - has to be assisted by graphic repre-
      sentation of both the model elements and their interconnections
      as well as that of the experiment description. The display of
      menus and the results of model consistency checking enhance
      the modelling effectiveness as a whole.

  (ii) The other - possibly even more important - aspect is the ac-
      cess to the results of the simulation run. When the complexity
      of the model under investigation is high it is often the case

that it cannot be fixed in advance what information and in
which form it will be needed after the simulation. Frequently
the first results may give a hint about further inquiries.
To supply every result would be practically impossible for
the system due to economic reasons and, moreover, instead of
of helping the experimenter it would make his situation more
difficult by the overflow of information. An example showing
the advantage of this approach is the simulation of a digital
logic network where the possibility to access interactively
and display the waveforms on different parts of the circuit
provides the same possibilities to the investigator of the
model as a multitrace measuring oscilloscope did in times of
discrete component physical modelling. The method has been
applied and widely tested in practice (Jávor, Révész, Tóbiás
1982b). Lastly the graphical monitoring of the simulation experiment during the run with the possibility of interaction
provides a facility for quick surveying and possibly inter-
vening in the experiment.

- Postprocessing for data compression and visual display of the output as well as backtracking of the simulation run (also allowing
the restarting of simulation from arbitrary earlier time value)
can be realized by the cheap availability of very large memories.

4. THE SCOPE OF APPLICATIONS

It is always desirable to make tools as universally applicable as
possible. On the other hand it is obvious that tools tailored to a
given purpose can more conveniently and effectively be used in their
specific application domain. The users, i.e. people concerned with
modelling, are experts in some specific section of the domain to
which the model belongs. They are not interested in the theoretical
aspects of modelling methodology which is the concern of the system
designers. For the resolution of this conflict between universality
and efficiency the solution of a single universal internal core of
the system with specific outer language interface layers has already
been proposed and shown that an optimal solution can thereby be a-
chieved (Jávor 1982).

The requirement for specific subject oriented and user friendly man-
machine communication interface with the system is even more stressed
in case of Expert Systems and this applies to our case of ESS as well.
Here the setting of objectives sometimes are not restricted to use a
terminology and description style of the subject matter but also to
use a language close to natural languages. This is an ambitious approach but the ambiguities in problem description as well as the
large efforts needed for implementation suggest that a problem oriented description with certain restrictions to the language structure
may be preferred. This experience has been substantiated by expert
system development and practice (Amstutz 1984).

In model description non-procedural language is to be advocated (Jávor 1982, Jávor, Benkő, Tarnay 1985) as a means of revealing the model structure well and facilitating its hierarchical decomposition.
The knowledge based simulation system MAGEST developed by the pioneering work of Ören and his associates (Ören, Aytac 1985) uses this
approach as well.

For the intermediate language in which the ESS should be written the

portability i.e. availability of the language on numerous computers
including possibly future advanced personal computers has to be considered as highly important.

5. CONCLUSIONS

In recent years the more and more widespread application of simulation in several fields has shown that for solving problems by modelling an effective similation system is insufficient and several
means for model manipulation, experiment control and result evaluation are needed. To counteract the tendency that the bottleneck in
problem solving should be in this area the inclusion of knowledge
based expert systems is required.

Concentrating on the main points originating from practice, outlines
of the trends in incorporating and using a knowledge base and an inference procedure to achieve more effective problem solving with
modelling by the development of future Expert Simulation Systems has
been given.

REFERENCES

Ameling, W. (1985). Simulation Using Parallelism in Computer Archi-
    tecture. In: Simulation in Research and Development, Jávor, A.
    (ed). North-Holland, Amsterdam, pp. 3-15.

Amstutz, A.E. (1984). Automated Computer Application Generation and
    Maintenance. In: Productivity - Expert Systems - Simulation 2nd
    International Symposium & Exhibit' 84, Paris, France.

Concepcion, A.I., Zeigler, B.P. (1985). Distributed Simulation of
    Cellular Discrete Time Models. In: Simulation in Research and
    Development, Jávor, A. (ed). North-Holland, Amsterdam, pp. 25-30.

Dekker, L. (1985). Parallel Simulation in Research and Development.
    In: Simulation in Research and Development, Jávor, A. (ed).
    North-Holland, Amsterdam, pp. 17-23.

Hamming, R.W. (1962). Numerical Methods for Scientists and Engineers,
    McGraw-Hill Book Company, Inc.

Jávor, A. (1975). An Approach to the Modelling of Uncertainties in
    the Simulation of Quasideterministic Discrete Event Systems,
    Problems of Control and Information Theory, Vol 4, nr. 3, pp.
    219-229.

Jávor, A. (1982). Proposals on the Structure of Simulation Systems.
    In: Discrete Simulation and Related Fields, Jávor, A. (ed).
    North-Holland, Amsterdam, pp. 9-18.

Jávor, A. (1983). Dual Nature of Events in Discrete Simulation,
    Mathematics and Computers in Simulation, Vol XXV, nr. 1, North-
    Holland, Amsterdam, pp. 66-69.

Jávor, A. (1985). Handling Indeterminacies in Discrete Simulation for
    Performance Analysis. In: Digital Techniques in Simulation, Com-
    munication and Control, Tzafestas, S.G. (ed). Elsevier Science
    Publishers B.V. North-Holland, pp. 73-78.

Jávor, A., Benkő, M., Tarnay, K. (1985). Multimode Simulation Concepts. In: Simulation in Research and Development, Jávor, A. (ed). North-Holland, Amsterdam, pp. 135-138.

Jávor, A., Révész, Á., Tóbiás, P. (1982a). A Closed-Loop Feedback Controlled Simulation System. In: Discrete Simulation and Related Fields, Jávor, A. (ed). North-Holland, Amsterdam, pp. 87-96.

Jávor, A., Révész, Á., Tóbiás, P. (1982b). Simulation System with a Single Core and Several Outer Layers. In: Discrete Simulation and Related Fields, Jávor, A. (ed). North-Holland, Amsterdam, pp. 65-85.

Moore, G. (1979). VLSI: Some Fundamental Challenges, IEEE Spectrum, Vol 16, nr. 4, pp. 30-37.

Moto-oka, T. (ed) (1982). Fifth Generation Computer Systems, North-Holland, Amsterdam.

Ören, T.I., Aytac, K.Z. (1985). Architecture of MAGEST: A Knowledge-Based Modelling and Simulation System. In: Simulation in Research and Development, Jávor, A. (ed). North-Holland, Amsterdam, pp. 99-109.

Spriet, J.A., Vansteenkiste, G.C. (1982). Trends in the Role of Modelling and Simulation. In: Discrete Simulation and Related Fields, Jávor, A. (ed). North-Holland, Amsterdam, pp. 3-8.

Tsuneta Sudo, Takyoshi Nakashima, Makato Aoki, Toshio Kondo (1982). An Adaptive Array Processor, IEEE International Solid State Conf. pp. 122-124.

Zeigler, B.P. (1984). Multifacetted Modelling and Discrete Event Simulation, Academic Press.

Modelling and Simulation Methodology
in the Artificial Intelligence Era
M.S. Elzas, T.I. Ören and B.P. Zeigler (Editors)
© Elsevier Science Publishers B.V. (North-Holland), 1986

Chapter III.4

WORLD VIEW BASED
DISCRETE EVENT MODEL
SIMPLIFICATION

C. Michael Overstreet

Department of Computer Science
Old Dominion University
Norfolk, VA 23508 USA

Richard E. Nance

Systems Research Center
Virginia Tech
Blacksburg, VA 24061 USA

The discrete event world views of event scheduling, activity scanning, and process interaction
all assist modelers in the formulation of discrete
event models. Starting with model specification
in a more primitive form, called a Condition
Specification, transformations into each world
view are presented. The "quality" of such
transformations is indicated in part by the degree
to which they take advantage of the simplification
possible with each target world view.

This research was supported in part by the U.S. Navy under contract
N60921-83-A165 through the Systems Research Center at Virginia Tech.

1. INTRODUCTION

The now classical discrete event world views of event scheduling, activity scanning, and process interaction all effectively assist
modelers in the formulation and specification of discrete event
models. This assistance takes several forms. Each world view provides a technique for decomposing a model into a collection of smaller
pieces which can be described individually (a basic principle in problem solving) and provides a collection of concepts and a vocabulary
for describing the decompositions. Each world view is also supported
by one or more programming languages to assist in creating an implementation. Each world view may also simplify the modeler's task of
specifying model behavior by allowing the modeler to use "implicit
knowledge" (discussed below) about the state of the model as he or she
creates a model specification.

To better understand the relationships among these world views and how
each can use "implicit knowledge," we present an informal (i.e., non-
mathematical) characterization of each. Then, based on a more primitive form for model specification called a Condition Specification
(CS), we present transformations from this primitive form into each of

the three world views.

This transformation process is enlightening, revealing how "implicit knowledge" about the state of a model can be used to simplify the resulting specification and likely to improve the run time efficiency of an implementation based on the transformed specification.

We give a brief description of a CS, the basis for the transformations we discuss. The CS approach is illustrated by an example which is also used to illustrate the transformations into the different world views.

2.   CONDITION SPECIFICATIONS AND GRAPHICAL REPRESENTATIONS

The purpose in using a CS for model description is to explicitly state many logical dependencies which may be implicit (and difficult to discover) if a model is described in a language using any of the three standard world views. This results in an additional effort in creating the initial model specification. But because of the form of the specification, a significant amount of static analysis can be performed prior to model implementation to detect some types of potential errors in the specification.

To forewarn the reader, a word about the terminology chosen for use in CSs may be useful. What are here called "objects" and "attributes" are similar to Zeigler's "entities" and "variables" (Zeigler 1984, p. 194 ff.) Our terms are consistent with previous work (Nance 1981, Nance, Overstreet 1984, Overstreet, Nance 1985) which is based on the object oriented paradigm exemplified in languages such as Smalltalk (Goldberg, Robson 1984).

In a CS, a model is a collection of Objects and a collection of Action Clusters (ACs). Each object is composed of attributes and possibly additional objects. The attributes record part of the state of the object. The additional objects, if any, complete the state definition for the composite object. The model itself is such an object.

The collection of ACs defines the dynamic behavior of the model. Each AC consists of a Boolean expression and a collection of actions. The actions of an AC are to occur whenever the AC's Boolean expression, also called its condition, is TRUE. Thus the form of a CS is similar to the production rule approach to knowledge representation (Newell, Simon 1972, pp. 23-33). The CS approach has been described elsewhere (Overstreet, Nance 1985, Zeigler 1984, pp. 353-358) and while our treatment is brief, it should be sufficient to follow the development. Some additional specifics of CSs are illustrated in the example of Section 2.1.

Zeigler discusses constructing a model specification by describing its "entity structure" (Zeigler 1984). The approach taken here is influenced by Zeigler's work, although exhibiting a major departure. The objects in a CS do not provide a "partitioning" (in the mathematical sense) of the model; Zeigler's entity structure does. We find the idea of the objects providing a partition of the model into "disjoint submodels" (whatever that may mean) very appealing and abandon this idea with reluctance. However, we find it necessary to do so when considering models with objects that participate in joint activities. To automatically generate an acceptable specification in the "process interaction" world view, the activities (and the state variables

necessary to control the activities) must be associated with each of
the objects participating in the activity. Thus no partition results.

2.1 Example

We use the classical Machine Repairman model to illustrate different
world view representations. This model is from (Palm 1947) and (Cox
1961).

Informal Description: A single repairman services a group of n identical semiautomatic machines. Each machine requires service randomly
based on a time between failure which is a negative exponential random
variable with parameter "mean_uptime." The repairman starts in an idle
location and, when one or more machines requires service, the repairman travels to the closest failed machine. Service time for a machine
follows a negative exponential distribution with parameter
"mean_repairtime." After completing service for a machine, the repairman travels to the closest machine needing service or to the idle location to await the next service request. The closest machine is
determined by the shortest travel time. Travel time between any two
machines or between the idle location and a machine is determined by a
function evaluation.

An object specification for this model is provided in Figure 1.

Object	Attribute	Attribute Type
environment	system_time	nonnegative real
	n	positive integer constant
	max_repairs	positive integer constant
	mean_uptime	positive real constant
	mean_repairtime	positive real constant
	initialization	time-based signal
machine[1..n]	n	positive integer constant
	max_repairs	positive integer constant
	mean_uptime	positive real constant
	mean_repairtime	positive real constant
	mach[1..n]	1..n constant
	failure	time-based signal
	arr_mach	time-based signal
	end_repair	time-based signal
	num_repairs	nonnegative integer
	failed[1.. n]	Boolean
repairman	max_repairs	positive integer constant
	mean_repairtime	positive real constant
	status	{ avail, travel, busy }
	location	{ idle, 1..n }
	end_repair	time-based signal
	arr_mach	time-based signal
	num_repairs	nonnegative integer
	arr_idle	time-based signal

Figure 1: Machine Repairman Object Specification

Note that each attribute is associated with at least one model object;
some are associated with multiple objects. This multiple attribute
object association is useful for transformation into a process in-

teraction world view. (For this paper, the object-attribute association is used only for transformation into a process interaction world
view.) The attribute types are Pascal's with the significant addition
of a "time-based signal." A time-based signal is a Boolean, with its
value changing from FALSE to TRUE due to the passage of simulation
time. See the discussion of the "SET_ALARM" primitive below.

```
+----------------------------+---------------------------------------+
| Action Cluster Id:         |                                       |
|   Condition                |                 Actions               |
+----------------------------+---------------------------------------+
| initialization:            | READ( n, max_repairs, mean_uptime,    |
|   initialization           |    mean_repairtime )                  |
|                            | CREATE( repairman )                   |
|                            | FOR i := 1 TO n DO                     |
|                            |    CREATE( machine[ i ] )             |
|                            |    mach[ i ] := i                     |
|                            |    failed[ i ] := FALSE               |
|                            |    SET_ALARM( failure( i ),           |
|                            |       neg_exp( mean_uptime ) )        |
|                            |    END FOR                            |
|                            | num_repairs := 0                      |
|                            | location := idle                      |
|                            | status := avail                       |
+----------------------------+---------------------------------------+
| termination:               | STOP                                  |
|   num_repairs >            |                                       |
|     max_repairs            |                                       |
+----------------------------+---------------------------------------+
| failure( i: 1..n ):        | failed[ i ] := TRUE                   |
|   failure                  |                                       |
+----------------------------+---------------------------------------+
| begin repair( i: 1..n ):   | SET_ALARM( end_repair,                |
|   arr_mach                 |    neg_exp( mean_repairtime ) )       |
|                            | status := busy                        |
|                            | location := mach[ i ]                 |
+----------------------------+---------------------------------------+
| end repair( i: 1..n ):     | SET_ALARM( failure( i ),              |
|   end_repair               |    neg_exp( mean_uptime ) )           |
|   end_repair               | failed[ i ] := FALSE                  |
|                            | status := avail                       |
|                            | num_repairs := num_repairs + 1        |
+----------------------------+---------------------------------------+
| travel to idle:            | SET_ALARM( arr_idle,                  |
|   ( FOR ALL i IN 1..n,     |    traveltime( location, idle ) )     |
|     NOT failed[ i ] )AND   | status := travel                      |
|     status = avail AND     |                                       |
|     location ≠ idle        |                                       |
+----------------------------+---------------------------------------+
| arrive idle:               | status := avail                       |
|   arr_idle                 | location := idle                      |
+----------------------------+---------------------------------------+
| travel to mach:            | VAR i: 1..n                           |
|   status = avail AND       | i := closest_failed_mach( failed,     |
|     (FOR SOME i IN 1..n,   |    location )                         |
|     failed[ i ] )          | SET_ALARM( arr_mach,                  |
|                            |    traveltime( location, mach[i] ) )  |
|                            | status := travel                      |
+----------------------------+---------------------------------------+
```

Figure 2: Machine Repairman Action Clusters

Figure 2 is the ACs for this model. A Pascal-like syntax is used in the action descriptions. Time sequencing is handled by a "SET_ALARM" primitive. The effect of this primitive is to change the value of a Boolean attribute, a parameter, from FALSE to TRUE at a specified instant. The SET_ALARM arguments are the attribute whose value is to be changed (along with optional values to be passed forward in time) and the length of the time delay until the instant the attribute is to take on the value TRUE. With this approach, all conditions of ACs are Boolean expressions, although some are strictly time-based (that is, once an alarm has been set, the value of the condition depends entirely on simulation time). The special condition "initialization" is true only at the instant model execution is started.

We omit the trivial definitions of the functions "closest_failed_mach" which identifies the closest failed machine to the repairman's current location and the function "traveltime" which determines the travel time from the repairman's current location to a particular machine or the idle location.

One advantage of a CS is that potential interactions among components of a specification can be analytically deduced. One representation permitting deductive analysis is an <u>Action Cluster Interaction Graph</u> (<u>ACIG</u>). In this graph, the nodes represent ACs and the edges the ability of one AC to directly influence (by way of shared attributes) another AC. In an ACIG, an edge leads from AC 1 to AC 2 if the actions of AC 1 can cause the condition of AC 2 to become true either at the same instant AC 1 is activated or at a future instant (through a change to an attribute value resulting from a SET_ALARM action).

Figure 3 is the ACIG for the Machine Repairman example. In this figure, an AC which can cause another AC to occur in the same instant (that is, with no advance in simulation time) is connected to it by a dashed line. If an AC can cause another AC to occur at a future time (through a SET_ALARM action), the ACs are connected by a dotted line.

We do not discuss how this graph is derived here. See (Overstreet, Nance 1984) for a discussion of how this graph can be automatically generated from a CS and some of the interesting problems involved in this process. The graph is introduced here since a representation in each of the three world views can be generated directly from it (see Section 4).

2.2 <u>Petri Net Graphs</u>

Several other interesting graphs can be algorithmicly generated directly from a CS. In one of these, if one type of node is used for conditions (column one of Figure 2) and another for actions (column two), then we have generated something very similar to a Petri net representation of the model specification. See (Peterson 1977) for a discussion of Petri Nets. The condition nodes form the <u>transitions</u> of the Petri net; the action nodes the <u>places</u>. The Petri net has an edge from condition i to action j if condition i controls action j. Likewise the Petri net has an edge from action j to condition i if action j can cause condition i to be satisfied.

Since Petri nets can explicitly represent the conjunction of conditions, but not disjunction or negation, a graph much closer to a Petri net representation can be generated if the conditions are decomposed into those subexpressions which can be combined by logical ANDs to reform the original condition. Subexpressions from this process are used to construct a set of subexpressions (a set since this eliminates repetition of identical subexpressions). This set becomes the transitions for a Petri net. If an edge leads from both subexpression one and subexpression two to an action node, then both subexpressions must be satisfied for the action to occur.

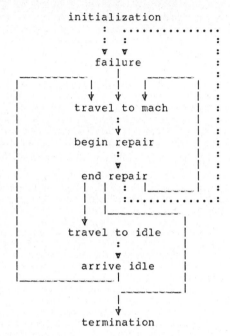

Code: '----' Head AC can cause tail AC to occur in the same instant.
    '....' Head AC can cause tail AC to occur, but after time delay.

Figure 3: Machine Repairman Action Cluster Incident Graph

3. WORLD VIEW CHARACTERIZATIONS

We do not attempt a formal characterization of the three world views (see (Zeigler 1976, Chapter 9) for a more formal approach). The objective is to provide an algorithmic transformation into each of the three world views with the significant constraint that each transformed specification should take advantage of the features provided by the target world view.

The characterization of each world view is based on an interpretation of the fundamental concept found in SIMSCRIPT (Dimsdale, Markowitz 1964) for the event scheduling world view, in CSL (Buxton, Laski 1963) for the activity scanning world view, and in SIMULA (Dahl, Nygaard 1966) for the process interaction world view.

Locality is defined by Weinberg as "that property when all relevant parts of a program are found in the same place" (Weinberg 1971, p. 229). Locality is regarded as a positive attribute by the software

engineering community since software is probably more easily understood and maintained if all the parts of a program which effect certain behavior are contiguous.

Unfortunately, the "relevant parts of a program" change depending on
the issue of interest. Thus it is impossible for one arrangement of
the source text of a program to exhibit locality for all possible
questions that the source text might be accessed to answer.

Each world view characterizes a different kind of locality.

> Event scheduling provides locality of time: each event routine
> in a model specification describes related actions that may all
> occur in one instant.

> Activity scanning provides locality of state: each activity rou-
> tine in a model specification describes all actions that must oc-
> cur due to the model assuming a particular state (that is, due to
> a particular condition becoming true.)

> Process interaction provides locality of object: each process
> routine in a model specification describes the action sequence of
> a particular model object.

These approaches are illustrated by the transformations of the next
section.

4. WORLD VIEW TRANSFORMATIONS

Transformations into each of the three world views can be viewed as a
two step process. First, appropriate subgraphs are generated from an
ACIG, with different types of subgraphs for each world view. This can
be done entirely algorithmicly as described below. The second step
simplifies each specification by use of precondition/postcondition
analysis. This more complex step is also discussed below.

A CS contains three types of ACs: (1) determined if the attributes in
the condition expression are all time-based signals, (2) contingent if
the condition expression contains no attributes which are time-based
signals, and (3) mixed if the conditions contains both time-based signal and non-time-based signal attributes. Thus the condition value
for a determined AC depends only on the value of simulation time (at
least, after the signal has been scheduled).

The simple transformation of a CS with mixed ACs into an equivalent
specification with no mixed ACs is accomplished by the addition of attributes (Overstreet 1982). For the development that follows, it is
convenient to assume that the specification contains no mixed ACs.

Each Condition Specification contains one special attribute, "initialization." The transformation algorithms discussed below are based, in
part, on identifying those attributes that are time-based signals.
For these algorithms, it is useful to treat the "initialization" attribute as both time-based (for event scheduling) and non-time-based
(for activity scanning). This dual treatment is not unreasonable because it seems equally correct to regard initialization as occurring
when system time is zero (it is a determined or time-based action) or
as occurring because the model execution is initiated (a contingent
action, the model should be initialized every time it is started).

4.1 Event Scheduling

We assert that the adoption of an event scheduling world view requires the programmer first to identify all determined (i.e., time-based) model actions. The programmer then identifies, for each determined action, all contingent actions which can occur as a result of the determined action and in the same instant. Each event specification then consists of one determined AC and a collection of contingent ACs related to it.

Given an ACIG for a model specification, determined actions are identified by those nodes with dotted input edges (using the notation of Figure 3). The contingent actions which can occur in the same instant as each determined action and which are caused by the determined action are identified by the dashed edges leading from the determined node. These subgraphs, called event subgraphs, are easily generated. Each subgraph represents the sequence of actions of one event specification. Figure 4 depicts the five event subgraphs for the Machine Repairman model.

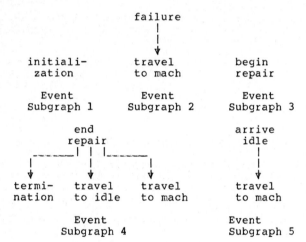

Figure 4: Machine Repairman Event Subgraphs

For the five event subgraphs, subgraph 1 contains the single action cluster "initialization." Subgraph 2 starts with the AC "failure," and, since a "failure" can cause a "travel to mach" to occur in the same instant, it also contains the AC "travel to mach." The "begin repair" can cause no other actions to occur in the same instant so the graph contains this single AC, but the "end repair" AC can cause either a "termination," a "travel to idle," or a "travel to mach" to occur in the same instant, so the subgraph contains all four ACs. As depicted in subgraph 5, the "arrive idle" AC can cause a "travel to mach."

4.2 Activity Scanning

We assert that the employment of an activity scan world view requires the programmer first to identify all conditions to which the model must respond (other than those dependent strictly on the passage of simulation time). After this, the programmer identifies, for each condition, all actions which should occur unconditionally including

those which should occur at a known time in the future. Each activity
specification consists of one condition and a collection of actions
which must occur when that condition becomes TRUE.

Given an ACIG for a model specification, contingent actions are identified by those nodes with dashed input edges (using the notation of
Figure 3). The determined actions which can occur as a direct result
of each contingent action are identified by the dotted edges leading
from the contingent node. Thus subgraphs, called activity subgraphs,
of the ACIG are easily generated in which each subgraph represents the
sequence of actions for one activity specification. Figure 5 depicts
the activity subgraphs for the Machine Repairman model.

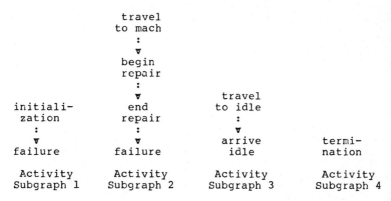

```
                        travel
                        to mach
                          :
                          ▿
                        begin
                        repair
                          :
                          ▿              travel
     initiali-           end            to idle
      zation            repair            :
        :                 :               ▿
        ▿                 ▿             arrive          termi-
     failure           failure          idle           nation

     Activity          Activity        Activity        Activity
    Subgraph 1        Subgraph 2      Subgraph 3      Subgraph 4
```

Figure 5:   Machine Repairman Activity Subgraphs

Activity subgraph 1 indicates that, once an "initialization" has occurred, a "failure" must necessarily occur. Likewise, activity subgraph 2 indicates that once a "travel to mach" has occurred, a "begin
repair," an "end repair," and a "failure" must necessarily occur (unless the simulation is terminated). From subgraph 3, the "travel to
idle" results in an "arrive idle," and a "termination" results in no
other actions.

4.3 Process Interaction

We assert that a process interaction world view requires the programmer first to identify all model objects whose action sequences must be
defined. Subsequently, the programmer specifies the action sequence
for each object.

The object specification, illustrated in Section 2, associates each
attribute with one or more objects, from which each AC can be associated with one or more model objects. Each AC is associated with each
model object if the object contains an attribute (1) which occurs in
the AC condition, or (2) which the AC alters.

After this association of objects and ACs is complete, subgraphs are
generated to represent the action sequences of each object. Each process subgraph contains all nodes which represent the ACs associated
with that object and all edges connecting any of those nodes. These
subgraphs, called process subgraphs, also provide sequencing of the
object actions. Figure 6 depicts the process subgraphs for the
Machine Repairman model.

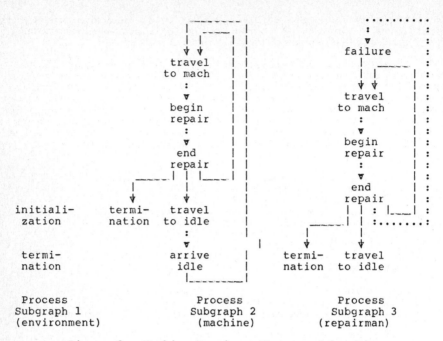

Figure 6:   Machine Repairman Process Subgraphs

This model has three process subgraphs. Although each process subgraph normally depicts the sequence of possible actions for some model
object, complete sequencing of actions may not be provided. For example, for this model, the process subgraph for the environment, subgraph 1, consists of two ACs, "initialization" and "termination" and
the graph is not connected. This is not unusual for an environment
object (which often contains only initialization and termination ACs),
but unconnected process subgraphs can also occur for other model objects. The other two subgraphs for the machine and repairman objects
do depict action sequences for the objects and nicely reveal the cycl-
ical behavior of each.

For each of these transformations, the union of the set of nodes in
the subgraphs may not be the complete set of nodes in the original
ACIG since some nodes may appear in no generated subgraph. Surpris-
ingly, this is not a problem since for each of the three world view
transformations, any node not included in any of the world view subgraphs cannot occur in any execution based on the CS (Overstreet
1982). Thus the action cluster associated with any unincluded node
can be deleted from the specification without affecting model behavior
although this likely indicates an error in the specification.

5.   WORLD VIEW BASED SIMPLIFICATION

Each individual event, activity, and process specification resulting
from the above graphs can potentially be simplified by removal of unnecessary tests or actions and simplification of some control struc-

tures. This is an important part of the transformation process, for
it allows the resulting specifications to take additional advantage of
the representation power of the target world view.

All simplification illustrated here is the result of a pre/post condition analysis for sequences of model actions. The condition expressions for each AC should define a minimal precondition for the actions
of that cluster. Each subgraph, whether event, activity, or process,
defines a sequence of model actions. Analysis of the actions of each
sequence allows formulation of postconditions for each AC. Comparison
of the postcondition of an AC with the precondition of each of its
successors (as identified by the appropriate subgraph) provides the
basis for simplification of the specification.

Several types of simplifications possible are illustrated with an example. Consider a specification of the End Repair event following an
event scheduling world view. A direct transformation (without any
simplification) of the ACs into an event specification is presented in
Figure 7. Lines 1 through 4 are from the End Repair AC, lines 5 and 6
from "termination," lines 7 through 9 from "travel to idle," and lines
10 through 13 from "travel to mach."

```
        end repair( i: 1..n )

 1:        SET_ALARM( failure( i ), neg_exp( mean_uptime ) )
 2:        failed[ i ] := FALSE
 3:        status := avail
 4:        num_repairs := num_repairs + 1

 5:        WHILE( num_repairs > max_repairs )
 6:           STOP
           END WHILE

 7:        WHILE( ( FOR ALL i IN 1..n, NOT failed[ i ] ) AND
              status = avail AND location ≠ idle )
 8:        SET_ALARM( arr_idle, traveltime( location, idle ) )
 9:        status := travel
           END WHILE

10:        WHILE( status = avail AND
              ( FOR SOME i IN 1..n, failed[ i ] ) )
              VAR j: 1..n
11:        j := closest_failed_mach( failed, location )
12:        SET_ALARM( arr_mach, traveltime( location,
              mach[ j ] ) )
13:        status := travel
           END WHILE
```

Figure 7:   End Repair Event Specification -- Unsimplified

Note that the condition of each contingent AC becomes the condition
for a "while" construct. A "while" is required rather than an "if"
since the actions of the AC should be repeated as long as its condition is satisfied.

Several types of simplification of this specification are possible.
For this event specification, all WHILE constructs have been replaced
with noniterative constructs (the simplified specification is presented in Figure 8). For the "travel to idle" and "travel to mach" ACs,
this can be done since an action of each changes the value of the condition to FALSE. For example, in Figure 7, the condition of line 7

specifies that status must have the value "avail," but line 9 sets its
value to "travel." In the case of the "termination" AC, lines 5 and 6
of Figure 7, the STOP action of line 6 implies that the condition of
the AC is not to be reevaluated.   Thus a postcondition of these ACs
implies that their precondition is not satisfied without some further
model action.

Another obvious simplification is possible when an action of a preceding AC eliminates the necessity of testing the value of an attribute
in the condition of a successor AC. This happens several times in
this event specification. In line 3 of Figure 7, status is set to
"avail." Thus, its value need not be explicitly tested in the conditions of 7 and 10.

The validity of eliminating the test of the value of location of line
7 is more difficult to justify, but still results from a postcondition
of the End Repair AC. A partial analysis, to illustrate the process,
follows. Unlike the simplifications of the test for status in lines 7
and 10, the value of location is not altered by the End Repair AC.
But a precondition for the occurrence of End Repair is that location
not have the value "idle." This condition is satisfied since (1) the
value of location is only altered by the Begin Repair and Arrive Idle
ACs, (2) an End Repair can only occur after a Begin Repair (since this
is the only place the end_repair alarm is set), (3) the value of location is not "idle" after the Begin Repair action, and (4) an Arrive
Idle cannot occur between a Begin Repair and End Repair (so that the
value of location cannot be altered before the End Repair occurs).

```
         EVENT end repair( i: 1..n )

 1:          SCHEDULE( failure( i ), neg_exp( mean_uptime ) )
 2:          failed( i ) := FALSE
 3:          num_repairs := num_repairs + 1

 4:          IF num_repairs > max_repairs
 5:            STOP
             END IF

 6:          IF FOR ALL i IN 1..n NOT failed[ i ]
 7:            SCHEDULE( arr_idle, traveltime( location, idle ) )
             ELSE
               VAR j: 1..n
 8:            j := closest_failed_mach( failed, location )
 9:            SCHEDULE( arr_mach, traveltime( location,
               mach[ j ] ) )
             END ELSE

10:          status := travel
             END EVENT
```

Figure 8:   End Repair Event Specification -- Simplified

Two other simplifications are made in producing Figure 8. First, the
two conditions in lines 7 and 10 are such that if one is true, the
other is false. So the two WHILEs become an IF-THEN-ELSE construct.
Secondly, the action of line 3 of Figure 7 has been eliminated. This
is valid since, if the model execution does not terminate, the value
of status will be changed to "travel" either in lines 9 or 13 since
these two alternatives are part of an IF-THEN-ELSE action. So there
is no point is setting it to "avail" in line 3.

The result of these simplifications is presented in Figure 8.
SET_ALARMs are replaced with SCHEDULEs so that the syntax follows that
of event scheduling languages.

Because of space constraints, the additional simplifications to complete the event scheduling specification are omitted. The process for
each of the three world views is similar and consists of deriving
postconditions of sequences of ACs and comparing them with preconditions of other ACs. The simplifications are dependent on the different groupings of ACs provided by each world view, since each re-
grouping changes postconditions.

The simplifications performed are necessary if the resulting specification is to take more complete advantage of the target world view.
While some simplifications are easily automated, others appear complex. Our experience in this area indicates that the automated
discovery of some simplifications requires a robust theorem proving
system. (The simplification of line 7 of Figure 7 provides an example. The proof that it is not necessary to consider the value of "location" is not trivially derived.) The purpose of the pre/post condition analysis is to prove a collection of theorems about the specification. For example, some simplifications occur because we can prove
that after one action has occurred, one subexpression of the logical
conjunction comprising the precondition for another action must be
true. So it is unnecessary to test its value when evaluating the condition after the first action has occurred. Proving any of these
"theorems" can be exceedingly complex; no a priori bound for the complexity can be established.

We are convinced that modelers intuitively use a pre/post condition
analysis when writing programs. If they are "good programmers," they
eliminate many model actions, explicit tests for parts of preconditions (or in some situations, entire preconditions) whenever the tests
or actions are unnecessary. Each eliminated test or action becomes
"implicit" in the resulting program. But in another world view, this
implicit test or action may require explicit representation in the
model specification. This implies that creation of a general algorithm capable of translating any model specification in one world view
into an equivalent specification in another world view requires the
ability to algorithmicly "rediscover" these "implicit" tests and actions.

Each of the transformations we presented involves reorganizing aggregates into different groupings, with elimination of redundancy in each
grouping. The inverse transformation requires rediscovery of what has
been eliminated from these new groupings. This poses a formidable
problem; we suspect that general inverse transformations cannot be
constructed.

6. SUMMARY

In other places (Overstreet, Nance 1984), we have discussed augmenting
the model specification process by providing analysis tools to evaluate a model specification during development. The traditional world
views produce model specifications with embedded "implicit knowledge"
which can simplify the specification process but at the price of inhi-
biting or preventing assistance through analysis. The benefits of
model analysis may discourage the direct use of current world view
representation forms.

The characterization of each world view as providing a different type
of locality reflects our view that no single world view is necessarily
superior to any other for all types of models. This lack of superiority is due to the significant variation in model simplification possible with each world view. The choice of the "proper" world view for a
particular model can impressively reduce the task of specifying model
behavior due to the variation in "implicit" actions and conditions
possible within each world view.

The ability of each world view to simplify the specification process
(at least in terms of how much must be specified) depends on omission
of "implicit" actions and conditions. Since what can be implicit
versus explicit varies among the world views, direct translation among
the various world views appears impossible. However, translation from
a more primitive form, a Condition Specification, into representations
which take advantage of each of the three world views is possible.
The translation process is instructive in understanding relationships
among the three world views.

REFERENCES

Buxton, J. N. and J. G. Laski (1963). Control and Simulation
    Language, The Computer Journal, vol 5, pp. 194-199.

Cox, D. R. and W. L. Smith (1961). Queues, Methuen and Company, Inc.

Dahl, O. and Kristen Nygaard (1966). SIMULA -- An ALGOL-Based Simula-
    tion Language, Communications of the ACM, vol 9, nr. 9, pp. 349-
    395.

Dimsdale, B. and H. M. Markowitz (1964). A Description of the SIM-
    SCRIPT Language, IBM Systems Journal, vol 3, nr. 1, pp. 57-67.

Goldberg, Adele and David Robson (1984). Smalltalk-80: The Language
    and its Implementation, Addison-Wesley, Reading, Mass.

Nance, Richard E. (1981). The Time and State Relationships in Simula-
    tion Modeling, Communications of the ACM, 24, nr. 3, pp. 173-179.

Nance, Richard E. and C. Michael Overstreet (1984). Graph-Based
    Analysis of Discrete Event Simulation Model Specifications,
    Technical Report CS83028-R, Department of Computer Science, Vir-
    ginia Tech, Blacksburg, 24061.

Newell, Allen and Herbert A. Simon (1972). Human Problem Solving,
    Prentice-Hall, Inc., Inglewood Cliffs, NY.

Overstreet, C. Michael (1982). Model Specification and Analysis for
    Discrete Event Simulation, PhD Dissertation, Department of Com-
    puter Science, Virginia Tech, Blacksburg, 24061.

Overstreet, C. Michael and Richard E. Nance (1985). A Specification
    Language to Assist in Analysis of Discrete Event Simulation
    Models, Communications of the ACM, vol 28, nr. 2, pp. 190-201.

Palm, D. C. (1947). The Distribution of Repairmen in Servicing Au-
    tomatic Machines, Industritidningen Norden, vol 175, p. 75,
    (Swedish).

Peterson, James L. (1977). Petri Nets, Computing Surveys, vol 9, nr.
    3, pp. 223-252.

Weinberg, Gerald M. (1971). The Psychology of Computer Programming, Van Nostrand Reinhold, New York.

Zeigler, Bernard P. (1976). Theory of Modelling and Simulation, John Wiley & Sons, New York.

Zeigler, Bernard P. (1984). Multifacetted Modelling and Discrete Event Simulation, Academic Press, London, 372 pp.

Modelling and Simulation Methodology
in the Artificial Intelligence Era
M.S. Elzas, T.I. Ören and B.P. Zeigler (Editors)
© Elsevier Science Publishers B.V. (North-Holland), 1986

Chapter III.5

TRANSFORMING A DISCRETE-EVENT SYSTEM INTO A LOGIC PROGRAMMING FORMALISM

Walter A. Zajicek

Institute of Systems Sciences
Department of Systems Theory
Johannes Kepler University Linz
AUSTRIA

Using a small example this paper shows the way how to get a LOgic Programming Specification using a Discrete-EVent System Specification. An introduction into these two specification types is given. The idea how to construct the corresponding LOPS model using the detailed DEVS description is given. In order to make the concept of the LOPS modelling process more explicit some examples will be reviewed. A comparison between the DEVS and LOPS specification types terminates this work.

1. INTRODUCTION

1.1 Discrete-Event System Formalism

The Discrete-EVent System (DEVS) formalism introduced by Zeigler (Zeigler 1976, 1984, Pichler 1975) provides a formal basis for specifying models expressable within discrete event simulation languages. Focussing on the transition system, omitting the output portion, a DEVS specification is a structure $M = < X, S, \delta, ta>$ where
  X is a set, the names of external event types
  S is a set, the sequential states
  δ is a function consisting of two parts:
  $\delta_0: S ---> S$ the internal transition function
  $\delta_{ex}:QxX ---> S$ the external transition function
  $Q:= \{ (s,e) / s \in S, 0 <= e <= ta(s) \}$ is the total state set
  ta: $S ---> R_{+,0,\infty}$ is called time advance function.

The modular form of a multicomponent DEVS specification DEVN will be taken up now. In this formalism, each component system is specified as a DEVS and these DEVS are coupled by some output-translation functions $Z_{i,j}$. In case of more than one event at the same time a SELECT function provides the tie-breaking selector.
A multicomponent DEVS in modular form (DEVS network (DEVN)) is a structure $DN = < D, \{M_i\}, \{I_i\}, \{Z_{i,j}\}, SELECT >$ where
  D is a set, the component names $(D:= \{1,2,...,n\})$
    for each i in D
  M_i is a component $M_i = < X_i, S_i, \delta_i, ta_i >$
  I_i is a set, the influencees of i (I_i is a subset of D)
    and for each j in I_i
  $Z_{i,j} : S_i ---> X_j$ is a function, the i-to-j output-translation
  SELECT:subsets of D ---> D is the tie-breaking selector such that for any non-empty subset E of D SELECT(E) is a member of E.
An example of a multicomponent DEVN will be given in section 2.

1.2 Logic Programming Specification

The underlying concept to Logic Programming is that of symbolic
logic, that can directely be used as a programming language
(Buchberger, Lichtenberger 1980, Hofstadter 1979, Hogger 1984,
Kowalski 1979, Manna 1985). The LOgic Programming Specification
(LOPS) itself can directely be interpreted by modern computers. In
the following I shall focus on a PROLOG-like (PROgramming in LOGic)
specification style that is a special type of a LOPS.

Facts, Rules and Goals

Facts (assertions) are stated using predicates. The fact
HUMAN(socrates) declares the following three things:
   - HUMAN is a predicate name
   - "socrates" is a constant (individual)
   - the truth-value of HUMAN(socrates) is true (t).
Rules or implications have the form
$$A \longleftarrow B_1 \text{ and } B_2 \text{ and } \ldots \text{ and } B_m$$
where $A, B_1, B_2, \ldots, B_m$ are predicates. This implication simply means
if B_1 and B_2 and ... and B_m are all true then A is true. In an
implication the predicate on the left of the $\longleftarrow$ is called the
consequent; those predicates on the right of the $\longleftarrow$ are called
the antecedents.
Goals are usually marked with a "?" at the beginning of the goal
string. Using the predicate plus(x,y,z) to express x+y=z one
possible goal is "?plus(x,1,3)". If the domain of discourse, which
is a non-empty set D of individuals, is given by D:= {0,1,2,3}, one
possible set of describing the plus-relation is:
      P1: plus(0,z,z)   P2: plus(z,0,z)   P3: plus(1,1,2)
      P4: plus(1,2,3)   P5: plus(2,1,3)
In the course of execution, the interpreter activates the goal
"?plus(x,1,3)" and then scans sequentially through P1 - P5 seeking
the first responding procedure, which is P5. By invoking P5 it
assigns 2 to x and therefore the answer is: x = 2 .

Logical Inference

Logical inference is the process of deriving a sentence s from a
set S of sentences by applying one or more inference rules (Hogger
1984). A very simple method of derivation makes use of just one
inference rule called resolution. Each application of the rule is
called an inference step and deals with sentences of just three
kinds:
      denial: $not(A_1, A_2, \ldots, A_n)$
      assertion: A
      implication: $A \longleftarrow B_1, B_2, \ldots, B_m$
One of the simplest form of resolution is:
      assuming (not A and A $\longleftarrow$ B) infer   (not B)
The process of deriving a sentence s using logical inference is
very similar to generating a proof for some expression within a
formal system (Hofstadter 1979). Every formal system utilizes
letters or symbols, it has axioms and symbol-shunting rules, that
are either called rules of production or rules of inference.
Starting with an axiom and then using some rules one receives
strings that are producible by the rules, these strings are then
called theorems. The logical inference mechanism used in PROLOG is
an automatic backtracking mechanism. It is used to get a l l the
solutions for a variable in a goal string. PROLOG executes
programmes by matching patterns. PROLOG first selects one matching
fact and, if later eventually execution fails, backtracks and
selects another matching fact.

2.   EXAMPLE OF A MULTICOMPONENT DEVS IN MODULAR FORM

2.1   Nand Module

The Nand Module described as a DEVS $M_{NAND} = < X, S, \delta, ta >$ is
defined in the following way:

X :=   (0,1)   x   (1,2)   (typical element of X is (x,p))
S :=   (0,1) 3   (typical element of S is (s_1,s_2,s_3))

the function δ consits of two parts:

$\delta_0(s_1,s_2,s_3) := (s_1,s_2,nand(s_1,s_2))$

$\delta_{ex}((s_1,s_2,s_3),(x,p)) :=$
$$(x,s_2,s_3) \quad if \ p = 1$$
$$(s_1,x,s_3) \quad if \ p = 2$$

the time advance function ta: S ---> R_0+

$$ta(s_1,s_2,s_3) := \begin{array}{ll} 00 & if \quad s_3 = nand(s_1,s_2) \\ dt & if \quad s_3 \neq nand(s_1,s_2) \end{array}$$

Figure 1 will certainly make the given concept clear.

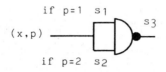

if p=1 s_1

(x,p)

s_3

if p=2 s_2

Figure 1
DEVS   Nand Module

2.2   The Flip-Flop-Element

To store a signal one may use simply a Flip-Flop-Element (FFE).
This element has two inputs S(set) and R(reset) and the stored
signal output Q. Figure 2 shows a S',R' Flip-Flop realised with two
nand gates. (S' is the complement of S).

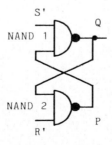

S'

Q

NAND 1

NAND 2

P

R'

Figure 2
DEVN Flip-Flop-Element

The truth-table of this FFE is given in figure 3.

Input		Output			
S R	S'R'	Q P	Q" P"		
1 0	0 1	0 0	1 1		
1 0	0 1	1 1	1 0		
0 0	1 1	1 0	1 0		
0 1	1 0	1 0	1 1		
0 1	1 0	1 1	0 1		
0 0	1 1	0 1	0 1		

Figure 3
Truth table of FFE in figure 2

The multicomponent DEVS of this FFE with two nand modules is the following structure

$$DN_{FFE} = < D, \{M_1, M_2\}, \{I_1, I_2\}, \{Z_{12}, Z_{21}\}, SELECT >$$

where

$D := \{1,2\}$ (component names)
$M_1 := M_2 := M_{NAND}$ (the component DEVS, see 2.1)
$I_1 := \{2\}$, $I_2 := \{1\}$ (influencees)
$Z_{12}(s_1, s_2, s_3) := (s_3, 1)$ $Z_{21}(s_1, s_2, s_3) := (s_3, 2)$ (outputtranslation)
$SELECT(\{1,2\}) := 1$ $SELECT(\{i\}) := i$ (tie-breaking selector)

With this DEVN specification   it is using the   DEVN language (Zeigler 1984, p. 137)   very easy to build the corresponding FFE simulator, which is illustrated in figure 4 in detail.

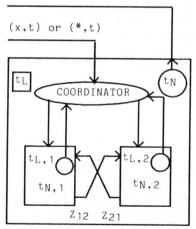

Simulator of M_1 Simulator of M_2

Figure 4
Simulator of DN_{FFE}

3.   THE TRANSFORMATION FROM DEVS TO LOPS

The problem here is to find a general way to extract from a
structure   M = < X, S, δ, ta >   the   f a c t s   and
r u l e s   that will fully specify the LOPS in terms of logic.
As the   facts or assertions deal only with the special input and
the initial state the emphasis lies upon finding the rules or
implications. A certain way to extract the implications from the
structure M is the following one:

Internal state transition rule:

STATE(δ_0(s),t) <--- STATE(s,t') and EQUAL(t,t'+ta(s)) and
                   NOINPUT(t',t) and NOT(INPUT(x,t))

No input rule:

NOINPUT(t',t) <--- NOT (INPUT(x,t")) and LESS(t',t") and
                   LESS(t",t)

External state transition rule:

STATE(δ_{ex}(s,x), t) <--- STATE(s,t') and INPUT(x,t) and
                   NOINPUT(t',t) and LESSOREQUAL(t,t'+ta(s))

The corresponding situations to the internal and external state
transition are illustrated in figure 5.

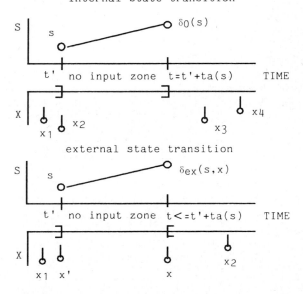

Figure 5
Internal and external state transition situations

The following list gives an explanation of the above used
predicates:
STATE(s,t) means that the system M is in state s at time t.
INPUT(x,t) means that the input at time t is x.
EQUAL(t,t') is true if and only if (iff) t equals t'.
LESSOREQUAL(t,t') is true iff t is less or equal t'.
NOT(predicatename(.,.....,.)) is true iff predicatename(.,.....,.) has
assigned the truth-value false.

One has to put the component names into account in case of the
multicomponent DEVS (DN=<D, $\{M_i\}$, $\{I_i\}$, $\{Z_{i,j}\}$, SELECT>) in modular
form.
STATE(i,s,t) means the component DEVS M_i is in state s at time t.
INPUT(i,j,x,t) means that M_j receives an input x at time t from M_i.
Now it is possible that at a given time t more than one input
arrives at a component. To solve this problem a predicate must be
defined to distinguish more and less recent states of a component
at the given time t. With the help of the tie-breaking function
SELECT the less recent states can be recognized, saved and not be
used in the continuing deriving process.

4.   EXAMPLES OF LOGIC PROGRAMMING SPECIFICATIONS

4.1 Transforming the Nand Module

The nand module of 2.1 will now be transformed and it is described
by the following facts and rules:

    The facts:
STATE((s_{01},s_{02},s_{03}), 0)
INPUT((x_0,p_0), t_0), INPUT((x_1,p_1), t_1), ..., INPUT((x_n,p_n), t_n)

    The rules:
    Internal state transition rule:
STATE((s_1, s_2, nand(s_1,s_2)), t) <---
    STATE((s_1,s_2,s_3), t') and EQUAL(t, t'+dt) and
    NOT(EQUAL(s_3,nand(s_1,s_2))) and NOINPUT (t', t) and
    NOT(INPUT((x,p), t))

    No input rule:
NOINPUT(t', t) <--- NOT (INPUT((x,p), t")) and LESS(t',t") and
                    LESS(t",t)

    External state transition rules:
STATE((x,s_2,s_3), t) <---
    STATE((s_1,s_2,s_3),t') and NOT(EQUAL(s_3,nand(s_1,s_2))) and
    LESSOREQUAL(t,t'+dt) and INPUT((x,p),t) and EQUAL(p,1) and
    NOINPUT (t',t)
STATE((x,s_2,s_3),t) <---
    STATE((s_1,s_2,s_3),t') and EQUAL(s_3,nand(s_1,s_2)) and
    INPUT((x,p),t)) and EQUAL(p,1) and NOINPUT (t',t)
STATE((s_1,x,s_3),t) <---
    STATE((s_1,s_2,s_3),t') and NOT(EQUAL(s_3,nand(s_1,s_2))) and
    LESSOREQUAL(t,t'+dt) and INPUT((x,p),t) and EQUAL(p,2) and
    NOINPUT (t',t)
STATE((s_1,x,s_3),t) <---
    STATE((s_1,s_2,s_3),t') and EQUAL(s_3,nand(s_1,s_2)) and
    INPUT((x,p),t)) and EQUAL(p,2) and NOINPUT (t',t)

4.2 LOPS for Hardware Design Specification

Using the LOPS technique a hardware or logic circuit designer has a powerful tool to work with. The logic circuit designer usually specifies three things in order to test if the actual design is correct:
- the gate elements (nand, nor, not,..)
- how these gate elements are linked to each other
- the input to the logic circuit.

The following description of the gate elements is not only functional but includes also the switching delay , what is an essential feature in the hardware design process. In this example the other direction of the transformation from LOPS to DEVS, that is still to be investigated, can be applied.

Description of NAND and NOT elements:

The NAND gate has two input pins (pin 1, pin 2) and one output pin (pin 3). The output pin takes the value 0 iff both input pins have the value 1. The predicate NAND(elementname,pin 3, (x, t_1-t_2)) declares that using the NAND rule the gate element with name "elementname" takes the value x at pin 3 from time t_1 until time t_2. To make sure that only the right elements use the NAND rule the following convention is necessary:

An element that uses the NAND rule must have an elementname beginning with "NAND"; NAND1 is therefore a valid name for the NAND rule:

NAND(elementname, pin 3, (z, t_5-t_6)) <---
    D(elementname, pin 1, (x, t_1-t_2)) and LESS(t_1, t_2) and
    D(elementname, pin 2, (y, t_3-t_4)) and LESS(t_3, t_4) and
    LESS(t_3, t_2) and LESS(t_1, t_4) and
    ((x=0, y=0, z=1, $t_5=min(t_1,t_3)+dt$, $t_6=max(t_2,t_4)+dt$) or
     (x=0, y=1, z=1, $t_5=t_1+dt$, $t_6=t_2+dt$) or
     (x=1, y=0, z=1, $t_5=t_3+dt$, $t_6=t_4+dt$) or
     (x=1, y=1, z=0, $t_5=max(t_1,t_3)+dt$, $t_6=min(t_2,t_4)+dt$))

The predicate D(elementname, pin 1, (x,t_1-t_2)) says that the gate element "elementname" has at its pin 1 the already defined state x from time t_1 to time t_2.
Similar to the NAND rule the NOT rule is defined now.
    NOT rule:
NOT(elementname, pin 2, (y, t_3-t_4)) <---
    D(elementname, pin 1, (x, t_1-t_2)) and LESS(t_1, t_2) and
    ((x=0,y=1, $t_3=t_1+dt$, $t_4=t_2+dt$) or (x=1,y=0, $t_3=t_1+dt$, $t_4=t_2+dt$))

The Connection of gate elements and some other rules:

    The connection rule:
D(elementname 1, pin i, (x, t_1-t_2)) <---
    CON(elementname 2, pin j, elementname 1, pin i) and
    D(elementname 2, pin j, (x, t_1-t_2))
where
    CON(elementname 2, pin j, elementname 1, pin i)
tells the LOPS that pin j of gate element "elementname 2" is connected with pin i of gate element "elementname 1".
    The simplification rule:
D(elementname, pin i, (x, t_1-t_2)) <---
    D(elementname,pin i,(x,t_3-t_4)) and D(elementname,pin i,(x,t_5-t_6))
    and LESS(t_5, t_4) and LESS(t_3, t_6) and
    ($t_1=min(t_3, t_5)$, $t_2=max(t_4, t_6)$)
    New value definition rules:
D(elemname,pin 3,(x,t_1-t_2)) <--- NAND(elemname,pin 3,(x,t_1-t_2))
D(elemname,pin 2,(x,t_1-t_2)) <--- NOT(elemname,pin 2,(x,t_1-t_2))

Definition of the input and the initial state:
An input example is D(INPUT, pin 3, (1, 0-15)). An initial state
assignment to pin 2 of NOT 7 is D(NOT 7, pin 2, (0, 0-dt)).

4.3   The Flip-Flop-Element

For an illustration of this FFE see figure 6. In this example the
question is what output will occur at the output pin 1 (forward
reasoning). But one can also ask for the input while the output is
given (backward reasoning). Van E. Kelly and Louis I. Steinberg
(1982) developed a system, called CRITTER, that is a system for
"critiquing" digital circuits. The major difference to the LOPS
example is that in CRITTER each element is characterized by a set
of features, such as its TYPE, VALUE, START-TIME, and DURATION,
while in the LOPS example the elements are only gate elements
(nand, nor, not) that are already characterized for the user (NAND
rule, NOT rule,..).

FLIP-FLOP-ELEMENT

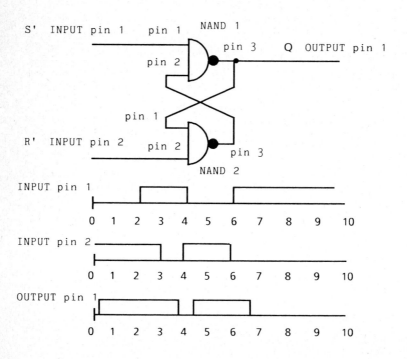

Figure 6
Illustration to the LOPS FFE Example

The facts:
D(INPUT, pin 1, (0, 0-2))   D(INPUT, pin 2, (1, 0-3))
D(INPUT, pin 1, (1, 2-4))   D(INPUT, pin 2, (0, 3-4))
D(INPUT, pin 1, (0, 4-6))   D(INPUT, pin 2, (1, 4-6))
D(INPUT, pin 1, (1, 6-10))   D(INPUT, pin 2, (0, 6-10))
D(NAND 1, pin 2, (0, 0-dt))   D(NAND 2, pin 1, (0, 0-dt))
CON(INPUT, pin 1, NAND 1, pin 1)   CON(INPUT, pin 2, NAND 2, pin 2)
CON(NAND 1, pin 3, NAND 2, pin 1)   CON(NAND 2, pin 3, NAND 1, pin 2)
CON(NAND 1, pin 3, OUTPUT, pin 1)

The rules: (see 4.2)
The NAND rule, the connection rule, the simplification rule and the
new value definition rule for the NAND elements.

The question:
 Which (x, t_1-t_2) will satisfy the goal
     ? D(OUTPUT, pin 1, (x, t_1-t_2))
The LOPS comes out with the desired answer:

The answer(s):
D(OUTPUT, pin 1, (0,0-dt))
D(OUTPUT, pin 1, (1, dt-(3+2dt)))
D(OUTPUT, pin 1, (0,(3+2dt)-(4+dt)))
D(OUTPUT, pin 1, (1, (4+dt)-(6+2dt)))
D(OUTPUT, pin 1, (0,(6+2dt) -10))

4.4   The Clockgenerator

Examples of this kind can be used as a basis for troubleshooting.
That subject, too sizable to deal with in any detail here, is
covered elsewhere (Davis, Shrobe 1983). Roughly speaking
troubleshooting means to investigate a circuit if somewhere in the
circuit is a critical value that is to explore further in order to
recognize a discrepancy at some spot. This discrepancy permits the
detection of a faulty gate. For an illustration see figure 7.

The facts:
D(INPUT, pin 1, (0, 0-1))   D(INPUT, pin 1, (1, 1-10))
D(NAND, pin 1, (1, 0-dt))   D(NAND, pin 3, (1, 0-dt))
D(NOT1, pin 1, (1, 0-dt))   D(NOT1, pin 2, (0, 0-dt))
D(NOT2, pin 1, (0, 0-dt))   D(NOT2, pin 2, (1, 0-dt))
CON(INPUT, pin 1, NAND , pin 2)   CON(NAND , pin 3, NOT 1, pin 1)
CON(NOT 1, pin 2, NOT 2 , pin 1)   CON(NOT 2 , pin 2, NAND, pin 1)
CON(NOT 2 , pin 2, OUTPUT, pin 1)

The rules: (see 4.2)
The NAND rule, the NOT rule, the connection rule, the
simplification rule and the new value definition rules .

The question:
 Which (x, t_1-t_2) will satisfy the goal
     ? D(OUTPUT, pin 1, (x, t_1-t_2))
The LOPS comes out with the desired answer:

The answer(s): (dt=1/3)
D(OUTPUT, pin 1, (1,0-2))   D(OUTPUT, pin 1, (0, 2-3))
D(OUTPUT, pin 1, (1,3-4))   D(OUTPUT, pin 1, (0, 4-5))
D(OUTPUT, pin 1, (1,5-6))   D(OUTPUT, pin 1, (0, 6-7))
D(OUTPUT, pin 1, (1,7-8))   D(OUTPUT, pin 1, (0, 8-9))
D(OUTPUT, pin 1, (1,9-10))

CLOCKGENERATOR

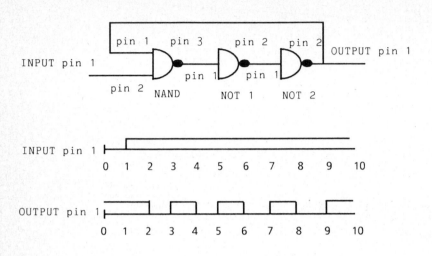

Figure 7
Illustration to the LOPS Clockgenerator Example

Other techniques for reasoning about Hardware are Temporal Logic (Moszkowski 1985) and Concurrent Prolog (Suzuki 1985). Temporal Logic, a generalization of Predicate Logic, augments the syntax of Predicate Logic to include time-dependent formulas such as "always" w and "sometimes" w, where w is itself a formula. Concurrent Prolog is a logic programming language and is very similar to Prolog, but Concurrent Prolog also has multiprocessing features and can be used to describe highly concurrent circuits. In the excellent book Computer Engineering by Gordon Bell and his colleagues the ISPS (Instruction Set Processor Specification) and PMS (Processor-Memory-Switch) notation are described in appendix 1 and 2 (Bell, Mudge, McNamara 1978). Compared with the presented hardware design specification technique these notations are higher level system description methods for defining the Instruction Set Processor (ISP) of a computer, the operations, instructions, data-types and interpretation rules used in the machine and for providing a structural representation of a computer system as a graph.

5. DEVS VERSUS LOPS

The DEVS is specified using mathematical standard notation (sets, functions,...) while in LOPS the predicates play the central role. The major difference between a DEVS and a LOPS is that DEVS simulators are constructed using a conventional programming language (FORTRAN,PASCAL,...). The LOPS simulator does not contain anything about the control of the simulation algorithm, one need only specify the logic part of the algorithm. This is an outstanding advantage for the LOPS seen from the point of view of the designer, it is today still a disadvantage when one puts the emphasis upon the program execution time.

ACKNOWLEDGEMENT

Thanks are due to Professor B.P. Zeigler, R. Mittelmann and H. Hofbauer for providing insightful comments and suggestions. I am especially indepted to Professor F. Pichler for the encouragement that made it possible to write this paper.

REFERENCES

Bell, G.C., J.C. Mudge, J.E. McNamara (1978).
  COMPUTER ENGINEERING A DEC View of Hardware Systems Design,
  Digital Press, Bedford, Massachusetts, 585 p.

Buchberger, B., F. Lichtenberger (1980).
  Mathematik für Informatiker I Die Methode der Mathematik,
  Springer Verlag, Berlin, 315 p.

Davis, R., H. Shrobe (1983).
  Representing Structure and Behavior of Digital Hardware,
  IEEE, COMPUTER, October 1983, pp. 75-82.

Hofstadter, D.R. (1979).
  Gödel, Escher, Bach: an Eternal Golden Braid,
  Basic Books, New York, 777 p.

Hogger, Ch.J. (1984).
  Introduction to Logic Programming,
  Academic Press, London, 280 p.

Kelly, V.E., L.I. Steinberg (1982).
  The CRITTER System: Analyzing Digital Curcuits by Propagating
  Behaviors and Specifications,
  Proc. AAAI Conf., Aug. 1982, pp. 284-289.

Kowalski, R.A. (1979).
  Logic for Problem Solving, North-Holland, New York, 287 p.

Manna, Z., R. Waldinger (1985).
  The Logical Basis for Computer Programming
  Vol.I: Deductive Reasoning,
  Addison Wesley, London, 618 p.

Moszkowski, B. (1985).
    A Temporal Logic for Multilevel Reasoning About Hardware,
    IEEE, COMPUTER, Febuary 1985, pp. 10-19.

Pichler, F. (1975).
    Mathematische Systemtheorie, De Gruyter, Berlin, 287 p.

Suzuki, N. (1985).
    Concurrent Prolog as an Efficient VLSI Design Language,
    IEEE, COMPUTER, Febuary 1985, pp. 33-41.

Zeigler, B.P. (1976).
    Theory of Modelling and Simulation,
    John Wiley & Sons, New York, 435 p.

Zeigler, B.P. (1984).
    Multifacetted Modelling and Discrete Event Simulation,
    Academic Press, London, 372 p.

SECTION IV
VARIABLE
STRUCTURE- AND LEARNING-MODELS

Modelling and Simulation Methodology
in the Artificial Intelligence Era
M.S. Elzas, T.I. Ören and B.P. Zeigler (Editors)
© Elsevier Science Publishers B.V. (North-Holland), 1986

Chapter IV.1

TOWARD A SIMULATION METHODOLOGY *
FOR VARIABLE STRUCTURE MODELLING

Bernard P. Zeigler

Department of Electrical and Computer Engineering
The University of Arizona
Tucson, Arizona 85721

Recent advances in simulation environments have laid
the basis for yet more challenging support of the
simulation modelling enterprise. This paper explores
one potential area of support that has been made
possible by the development of hierarchical, modular
model specification languages. We suggest that such
languages could be extended to support variable
structure models, in which the hierarchical, modular
structure may experience change over time. Applying
concepts of multifaceted modelling, we move toward a
methodology for support of variable structure modelling. Simulation of variable structure adaptive system
models serves to illustrate the discussion.

1. INTRODUCTION

Advances in simulation environments toward support of hierarchical,
modular model construction are typified by MAGEST (Oren, 1983;
Aytac and Oren, this volume) and BORRIS (Decker, 1980). Such environments facilitate synthesis of complex models by hierarchial
assembly of modular blocks to form yet higher level building
blocks. They have laid the basis for yet more challenging support
of the simulation modelling enterprise. It therefore is appropriate
to explore the possibilities for support of variable structure
models in which the hierarchical, modular structure may experience
change over time in a manner linked to ongoing behavior. Such
models may more realistically portray the behavior of a wide
variety of real systems. We shall focus on examples of adaptive
systems, including an adaptive computer architecture, for which
questions concerning performance of adaptive policies appear to
require models with variable hierarchical, modular structure.
Other kinds of situations in which structural change may be inex-
tricably linked to ongoing behavior include simulation of fault
prone systems with such objectives as establishing trouble
shooting paradigms, designing self testing add-ons, or increasing
fault tolerances; evolution of socio-cultural systems subject to
intermittent changes of governmental regimes; economic studies
taking to account discontinuous changes in monetary, fiscal and
social policies.

In this paper, we shall attempt to provide a definition of "non-
trivial" variable structure model in order to concentrate the
discussion on a class of models truly requiring advances in computerized support. Concepts of multifaceted modelling methodology

* Footnote: This work was supported by the National Science
          Foundation under grant DCR 8407230.

(Zeigler, 1984) are then employed to lay a basis for a simulation methodology of variable structure modelling. Two examples of adaptive systems, a workload-adaptive computer architecture, and an adaptive expert system, are given to illustrate the concepts introduced. The paper closes with suggestions for future research and development in the design of simulation environments supporting variable structure modelling.

2.   NON-TRIVIAL VARIABLE STRUCTURE MODELS

In an early paper (Oren, 1975), and more recently in a taxonomy of models (Oren, 1979, 1985), Tuncer Oren introduced the term "variable structure model" in the sense in which we shall use it here. However, we shall be interested in formulating a "non-trivial" notion of variable structure model that focuses attention on models which cannot be treated with conventional simulation language concepts. To designate this restricted class precisely, we refer to the hierarchy of levels of dynamical system specification formalized by Zeigler (1975) and Klir (1979). Recall that a modelling formalism may specify a system at the "network" or "coupling of systems" level. In such a model, the structure - the component models and the scheme which couples them together - is fixed. In other words, once the model has been defined, such a structure does not change during a simulation run. Although the structure may be altered between runs, for example, within an optimization loop, such modifications result in different models. On the other hand, a variable structure model is one which contains within its own definition, rules for altering the structure just referred to. Thus, in a simulation run, such a model may exhibit both changes in the values of its variables (ordinary behavior) as well as changes in its constitutive components and their interconnection (structural behavior). To accommodate such models, we must introduce a higher level of system specification, corresponding to Klir's (1979) meta-system level.

The subclass of variable structure models that we wish to designate as non-trivial, has the following additional characteristics: 1) the structure varies in a discrete rather than a continuous manner, so that discrete structure states (configurations of components and couplings) can be distinguished, and 2) the model has a specification for the manner in which transitions between such structure states are realized over time (more will be said about this in sequel).

This definition of non-trivial variable structure model certainly designates a restricted subclass of variable structure models, disqualifying other kinds of models which may exhibit a modicum of structural variation. For example, classical models such as neural nets in which the neuron connection strengths may vary (Barto et.al., 1983) are excluded because such variation is continuous, there are no distinct structural states (all configurations are parametric variations of each other) and, necessarily, there is no provision for the time behavior involved in structure transitions. Cellular models (Zeleny, 1985) such as plant growth models (Hogeweg, 1980) which portray only evolution of form are excluded as they do not include an account of the behavior of the plant at each growth stage, not to speak of the transition from one stage to its successor. Our motivation is that, at this point, treatment of the excluded cases does not urgently require the methodological advances we wish to explore, although they too might benefit from facilities developed for the more demanding non-trivial variable structure models.

Figure 1 depicts the situation with regard to structural change in non-trivial variable structure models. Nodes in the graph represent structure states with directed arcs representing structure state transitions. Since each structure state represents a model structure, it has associate with it a behavior state (the values assigned to its state variables) at each time instant during its existence. In making the transition from a structural state to its successor, the model must tell how to relate the final behavior state of the former to the initial behavior state of the latter. In general an adequate model of reality will depict this adjustment of behavior states as consuming a non-zero interval of time. We say that the model is in the <u>changing mode</u> during such an interval, and that it is in <u>normal mode</u> otherwise, i.e., while in a structure state. Only in special cases typified by the neural net connection strength variation, does the changing mode degenerate to a trivial identity mapping between initial and final behavior states.

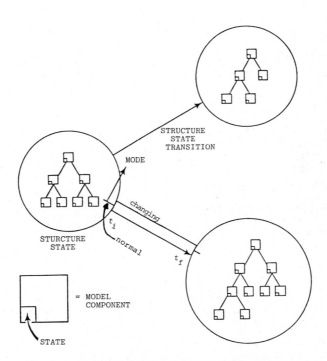

FIGURE 1.   STRUCTURE STATE TRANSITIONS IN NON-TRIVIAL VARIABLE
STRUCTURE MODELS.   NOTE THAT SUCH A TRANSITION MAY
TAKE PLACE OVER A NONZERO INTERVAL $[t_i, t_f]$ AND INVOLVES
ENTERING THE CHANGING MODE IN WHICH THE COMPONENT
STATES AT t_i ARE TRANSFORMED INTO SUCCESSORS AT t_f.

To summarize, a non trivial variable structure model displays two
types of behavior: <u>structure</u> behavior, in which successive structure
states viewed over time, and <u>ordinary</u> behavior, in which state
variable values are time indexed. These types of behavior are interlinked during the changing mode.

3. MULTIFACETED MODELLING METHODOLOGY: BASIS FOR VARIABLE STRUCTURE
    MODEL SPECIFICATION

A basis for a simulation methodology of variable structure models is
found in the paradigm for model construction within multifaceted
modelling methodology (Zeigler, 1984). As outlined in Figure 2, in
the later methodology, the system entity structure organizes the
family of models residing in a model base. To accomplish a given
modelling objective a user prunes the entity structure to extract an
appropriate model static structure. Pruning involves choice of decomposition, components, their descriptive variables and coupling
relations. A pruned entity structure provides the template for
synthesis of a simulation model.

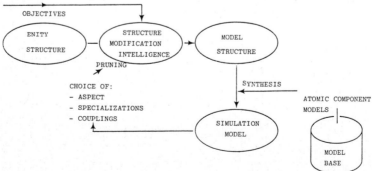

FIGURE 2. TRANSFORMATION OF METHODOLOGIES: MULTIFACETTED MODELLING TO VARIABLE
           STRUCTURE

In variable structure modeling methodology, the user can be thought
of as replaced by intelligence, embedded within the model itself,
which prunes the entity structure to specify a successor model. Thus
we have a feedback loop in which the model responds to incoming
objectives by suitably transforming its structure. In this case, the
model structure is obviously no longer static. Normally, we would
expect successive model structures to be somewhat related, i.e., to
differ in only addition, deletion or modification of a few components,
variables, or coupling relations. Although we would not necessarily
expect to find an entity structure literally represented within the
model, the entity structure formalism provides a convenient means of
explicitly specifying the set of possible structures that the model
can assume. An example of a non-trivial variable structure model,
described with the help of entity structure concepts, may clarify
these ideas.

4.   EXAMPLE: WORK-LOAD ADAPTIVE COMPUTER ARCHITECTURE

The notion of non-trivial variable structure model discussed above
will be illustrated by a simulation study of a work-load adaptive
architecture. The motivation for designing such an architecture,
and the fundamentals of the approach, have been reported elsewhere
(Zeigler and Reynolds, 1985). Here we shall focus on the points
which are of interest from the modelling methodology point of view.
The basic unit of the architecture is the flexible process, FP, which
has the capability of either performing as a problem solver or as a
co-ordinator of other problem solvers. The architecture is a scheme
by which such processors form a hierarchy, whose size and other
characteristics adapt to changes in incoming workload. The goal of
adaptation is to maintain good performance while minimizing the
number of employed processors. The scheme is called "hire/fire" in
analogy with the manner in which a business organization adjusts its
personnel size in the face of variations in product demand. A
simulation model of such an architecture, sufficiently detailed to be
employed in its design, is most naturally formulated as a non-trivial
variable structure model as defined above.

4.1. Entity Structure Representation of Model

An entity structure describing the family of model structures is
shown in Figure 3. The system consists of a variable number of flexible processors (FPs) all having the same capabilities. Each FP is a
fixed interconnection of EXECUTIVE, BUFFER, SUPERVISORY, and F-
COMPUTER (functional computer) modules. In outline, the EXECUTIVE
deals with the adaptive level involving communication, and
acceptance/rejection, of hire/fire commands. The BUFFER deals with
the operational level, putting the hire/fire commands into effect and
reconciling them with the ongoing processing of problems. The
SUPERVISORY component comes into play when the FP is acting as a co-
ordinator of lower level problem solvers. The F-COMPUTER is called
upon when the FP is functioning directly as problem solver itself.

When the FP is acting as a co-ordinator, the BUFFER sends problem-
bearing packets to the SUPERVISORY component. As shown in Figure 3,
the latter is itself a composition of a SUPERVISOR and a CO-ORDINATOR.
The SUPERVISOR channels packets bearing new problems from the higher
level, and solutions from the lower level, to the CO-ORDINATOR which
may be one of three different types: the multiserver, MS (a complete
problem is sent to a subordinate with the smallest queue size),

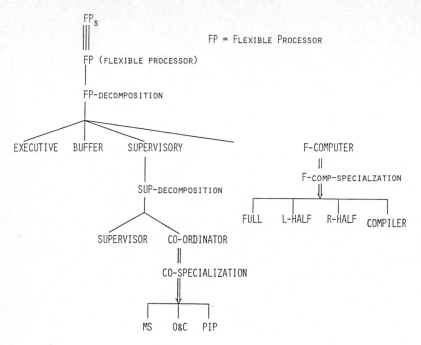

FIGURE 3. SYSTEM ENTITY STRUCTURE FOR FLEXIBLE ADAPTIVE COMPUTER
ARCHITECTURE

divide & conquer, D&C (partial problems are sent concurrently to subordinates and partial solutions are channeled to a special
subordinate
for final compilation), and the pipeline, PL (problems pass through a
sequence of partial operations performed by subordinates). Operation
of the FP as a lowest level problem solver is realized by having the
BUFFER send problem packets directly to the F-COMPUTER for solution.
The F-COMPUTER may take one of several forms depending on the role it
is playing in the co-ordination scheme that it is working under.

Recall that in the entity structure, entities (representing components) alternate with aspects (decompositions) and specializations
(variants). Associated with aspects are coupling constraints. These
govern the manner in which the entities belonging to an aspect can be
coupled together to form the entity dominating the aspect. In the
variable structure context, these elements can be fixed or variable,
depending on whether or not they specify structural features which
can change during a simulation run.

For example, at any time, the FPs are coupled through a hierarchical
scheme illustrated in Figure 4. However, the actual set of FPs con-
stituing the model may vary, and indeed, is governed by the hire/fire
adaptive strategy. Also, an FP can change its style of problem processing between that of direct solution to that of co-ordination.
However, the particular type of co-ordination (the variant of CO-
ORDINATOR of F-COMPUTER) is determined at the time of the change over
and cannot subsequently be altered.

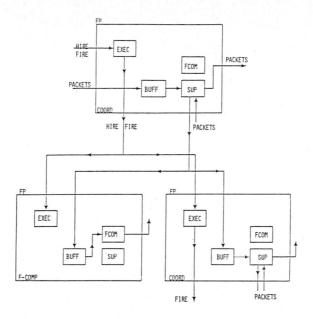

FIGURE 4. ADAPTIVE COMPUTER HIERARCHICAL ORGANIZATION.

4.2   Structure State Transitions: Changing Mode

Our interest is in the manner in which the adaptive architecture
model handles the alternation between normal and changing modes
asserted to be a distinguishing feature of non-trivial variable
structure models.   Referring to Figure 5, we see that there are three
situations that must be handled in the changing mode:

1.   An FP is hiring: this can only occur when the FP is functioning
     as a F-COMPUTER and intends to become a CO-ORDINATOR.

2.   An FP is firing: there are two subcases here.

     a) the FP is an F-PARENT (a CO-ORDINATOR whose children (sub-
        ordinates) are both F-COMPUTERs) which is in the process of
        firing its children.
     b) the FP is an F-COMPUTER and is being fired by its F-PARENT.

We remark that the number of situations in which hiring or firing can
take place has been purposely limited so as to remain within our
abilities to manage the logic unaided by the methodological support
that we are now proposing.

The point we wish to make is that in the changing mode, the processes
of structural change must be correctly interdigitated with those of
ongoing function.   Specifically, the integrity of problem packet
processing must be preserved while the change in structure is put
into effect.   Consider for example, case 1 above.

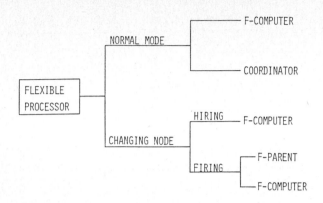

FIGURE 5. TAXONOMY OF FLEXIBLE PROCESSOR'S STATES

Let us start with the EXECUTIVE of an FP currently functioning as an
F-COMPUTER as it accepts a hire command. If there is a packet being
processed by the F-COMPUTER module, then the changing mode is entered.
While in the changing mode, all packets received from above are
placed into the packet queue maintained by the BUFFER. The trigger
to end the changing mode is the receipt of a "done" signal from the
F-COMPUTER module, signaling that it has finished processing the
current packet. The BUFFER then proceeds to send all the packets
which have accumulated in the queue over to the SUPERVISORY module
for distribution down to the children that have been hired in the
meantime. In the current model, hiring of children is handled by
creating new FPs of the specified F-COMPUTER types and consumes zero
model time. In a more realistic model, the recruitment process might
be more time-consuming and the changing mode would remain in effect
at least until this process has been completed.

To complete the picture let us consider case 2 above. We start with
the F-PARENT accepting a fire command and entering the changing mode.
As before, all new packets received from above are stored in the
BUFFER's queue. Fire commands sent to the children, cause them to be
placed in the changing mode as well. In this case, however, the
children F-COMPUTERs continue to work on the packets residing in
their queues until all have been sent upward to the parent SUPERVISOR
(which continues to play this role until the changing mode is completed). When the BUFFER of a child detects the completion of work,
it sends a "flushed" signal to the BUFFER of the parent. When the
latter has received flushed signals from all children, it initiates
normal operation by releasing the first packet in the queue, if any,
to the F-COMPUTER. (A different protocol, specifying a sequence of
fire and flushed messages, is required for each co-ordination scheme
to disengage its components).

4.3   Implementation of the Model

The model of the adaptive architecture was specified in the hierarchical, modular DEVS (Discrete Event System Specification) formalism
and coded in SIMSCRIPT following the methods given by Zeigler (1984).
(See Linos (1985) for details). This facilitated a bottom up approach
to model construction based on the entity structure hierarchy: the
F-COMPUTER and CO-ORDINATORs were synthesized first, followed by the

BUFFER (forming a BUFFER, F-COMPUTER composite for testing), continuing to build up the FP module itself, and finally the hierarchical
coupling of FPs. We found that in debugging successive levels of the
model, it was essential to have attained complete confidence in the
lower level building blocks. Help in specifying structure transitions, advocated in Section 6 of the paper, might have considerably
eased this design and verification process. We rejected the top-down
approach to synthesis because it would have been too difficult to
design stubs for the modules, given that the behavior needed to test
the interfaces is rather complex.

4.4 Adaptive Policy Components

The simulation program was designed as a test bed for exploring adaptive strategies in a convenient way. Shown in Figure 6 are the six
policy components that constitute an adaptive strategy. To discuss
these we refer to Figure 7 which depicts a particular structure state
of the model. The hire generation policy dictates the origin of hire

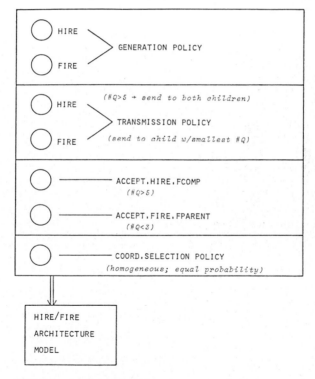

FIGURE 6. POLICY COMPONENTS OF ADAPTIVE STRATEGY. ITALICS
INDICATES POLICIES EMPLOYED IN CURRENT STUDY.

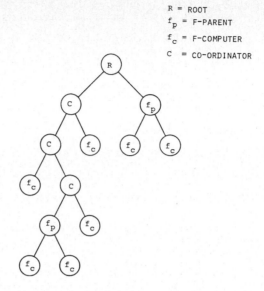

R = ROOT
f_p = F-PARENT
f_c = F-COMPUTER
C = CO-ORDINATOR

FIGURE 7   A) PORTRAYAL OF STRUCTURE STATE OF ADAPTIVE
                 ARCHITECTURE.
           B)&C) HIRE/FIRE GENERATION POLICY ALTERNATIVES

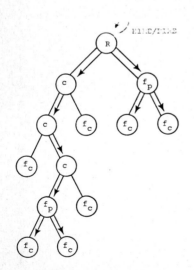

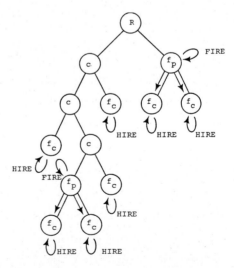

B) CENTRALIZED DIRECTIVES:
   ROOT ORIGINATES HIRE/HIRE
   COMMANDS
   (SHARED DECISION MAKING)

C) DECENTRALIZED DECISION
   MAKING:
   F-COMPUTER ORIGINATES
   HIRE

commands. Two versions were tried; hire commands generated from the
root CO-ORDINATOR only or from the leaf F-COMPUTERS only. Similarly,
the fire generation policy specifies the origin of the fire commands
- from the root or from the F-PARENTs. To implement these policies,
FPs are given hire/fire capabilities-self recurring processes that
generate such commands periodically. The model must specify when such
capabilities are relinquished and when they are acquired (a tricky
case to debug was that in which the F-PARENT has fire generation
ability and in firing its children reverts to an F-COMPUTER: it must
pass up the fire generation ability to its parent).

Hire or fire transmission policies determine whether, and to whom,
descending hire or fire commands are to be transmitted. We experimented with versions in which commands are unconditionally transmitted downward as well as those in which the CO-ORDINATOR passes on
a command if the size of its queue (representing all problems
awaiting partial solutions by its sub-ordinates) is sufficiently
large. In this case, the child with the largest queue size receives
the hire command.

The hire acceptance policy dictates the decision made by an F-
COMPUTER concerning whether to actually initiate the hiring process
upon receiving the go-ahead (hire command). Such hiring may be based
on the granularity of the problems in the module's queue (hire only
when problem is large enough to decompose) as well as on the queue
size (hire only if sufficiently large). Thus, information from both
global sources (originating from higher level transmission decisions)
and local sources may be combined to determine a hiring decision.
Similarly, the fire acceptance policy dictates the corresponding
decision, this time of F-PARENTs, concerning firing of subordinates.
Finally, the co-ordinator selection policy determines the type of
co-ordinator to be hired. We experimented with homogeneous policies
(in which only a single type of co-ordinator was used) as well as
random selection with equal probabilities per type.

4.5 Representative Experiments and Results

Several simulation experiments were performed in which the performance was measured of architecture models specified by various policy
assignments and subjected to various workload conditions. The parameterized architectures generally displayed the adaptive ability
that we expected. Comparing the four co-ordinator selection policies
showed that the homogeneous divide & conquer was markedly superior in
maintaining low average turnaround time in the face of changes in
problem arrival rate. However, under slow problem arrival rates, the
divide & conquer hierarchy size showed wide fluctuations compared to
other policies, a phenomenon which may not be desirable in application. The uniform random selection policy, was generally not too far
behind in performance, and not displaying oscillation tendencies, may
be a better choice in practice. It is interesting that although
turn-around time varied considerably with the various policies,
throughput did not.

Significantly, the simulation revealed that the homogeneous pipeline
co-ordination scheme did not lend itself to good adaptive performance.
Inspection of the structural behavior revealed why: the processor
hierarchy always takes a degenerate linear form. It appears that due
to the linear flow, there was at most one bottleneck at every level
(at the stage with the longest processing time); hiring occured only

at this bottleneck, hence the balanced growth needed to bring sufficient processors into play did not result.

With regard to hire/fire generation policies, under fast arrival rate, a mixed policy-- leaf (F-COMPUTER) hiring/root firing-- was distinctly superior to the three alternate combinations. Under slow arrival rates, the policies did not markedly differ.

Future study of such architectures must be concerned with capturing more realistic constraints. Problems employed in the foregoing experiments had the property of being arbitrarily decomposable into parallel or sequential forms so that pipeline or divide & conquer co-ordination schemes could be freely employed. Clearly, decomposition properties of a problem domain will restrict the co-ordinator choices. Other factors that may prove significant are bounds on the number of processors (requiring contention resolution policies) and time delays in message communication. Nevertheless, the simulation test bed has yielded results which establish the workability of the adaptive scheme and provide best case boundaries for performance. The extensibility achieved in the simulator design will facilitate the more detailed follow-on studies.

4.6   Significance for Variable Structure Methodology

The foregoing example has demonstrated the utility of several concepts. Formulation as a non-trivial variable structure model, fostered understanding of the interlinked state and structural behavior in a manner not possible otherwise. The entity structure description furthered the ability to separate fixed and variable features of model structure. The structure state transitions and changing mode concepts aided in model conceptualization.

5.   ECONOMIC TRANSACTION MEDIA FOR ADAPTIVE SYSTEM MODELS

A fruitful application of variable structure modelling methodology might be to adaptive systems where the adaptation is mediated by means of economic transactions among model components and the environment. We will outline an "economic transaction medium" which could exist on top of a variable structure simulation shell and simulate the economically based adaptive (learning, self-organizing) behavior of the model.

A relatively simple economic paradigm based on Holland's (1984) adaptive systems theory is illustrated in Figure 8. The model is specified as a coupling of agents models as previously discussed. To emphasize the economic underpinning of a component's behavior, the term "agent" may be employed for it. Variable structure comes about from the fact that intermittently some components may be removed and new ones integrated into the model. This process for generating new components and replacing old ones uses the results of an evaluation process which assesses the performance of components within the context of the overall model behavior.

The strategy is to remove poor performers and replace them with ones that are derived from good performers so that overall functioning is continually improved.

A particular scheme, based on an architecture for adaptive expert systems (Zeigler, in preparation) has the following description.

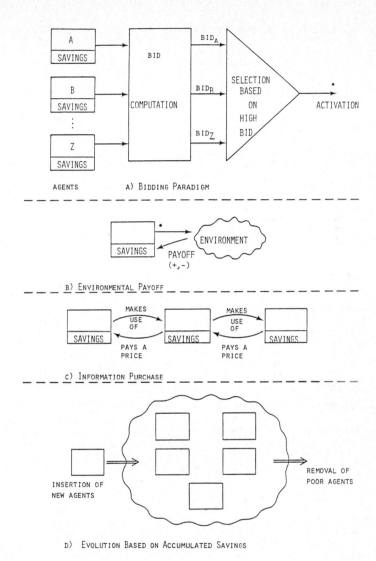

A) BIDDING PARADIGM

B) ENVIRONMENTAL PAYOFF

C) INFORMATION PURCHASE

D) EVOLUTION BASED ON ACCUMULATED SAVINGS

FIGURE 8. ECONOMIC TRANSACTION MEDIUM UNDERLYING ADAPTIVE EXPERT SYSTEM

Each agent (embodying a production rule, in the expert system interpretation) has a variable called its "savings" which reflects its
performance in monetary terms. If the agent engages in some direct

interaction with the environment then it receives "payoff" which is added to its savings. Such payoff may be positive or negative depending on whether the interaction represented a success or failure (e.g., reward for successful solution of a problem, punishment for reaching a dead end). Such direct environmental feedback information must be distributed among the agents that participated indirectly in producing the payoff.

To this end, a system of "information purchase" is maintained by the economic transaction medium. When one agent makes use of information originating from the action of another, it obligates itself to pay for this use by transferring a portion of its savings to those of the second. The actual transfer is performed when the final payoff has been received and is proportional (with the same sign) to the latter. (The proportionality factor may be a constant, or reflect the quantity of information, depending on the apriori knowledge and complexity overhead that can be tolerated by the system). The idea is that agents act as middlemen which tend to acquire savings reflective of their contribution to the ultimate success of the over-all system. Agents with little or no money in the bank are prime candidates for replacement by new agents generated from those with hefty savings accounts. (Holland's 1984 scheme, called the bucket brigade algorithm, differs from the above in that the payment for use of information is always positive and is effected immediately with the transaction).

Success, measured by accumulated savings, can also be used as a basis for selectively activating competitors by means of a bidding scheme. In the adaptive expert system for example, production rules that are triggered in the current working state present bids for activation which are proportional to their savings, among other factors. The conflict resolution mechanism selects the rule with the highest bid to be activated and carry out its transformation of working state. (Parallelism may also permit activation of more than one of the high bidders). "Use of information" in this case is determined by enable-ment, that is, an activated rule expects to receive payment from any subsequently activated rule whose activation condition became enabled as a direct consequence of its transformation of the state.

Generation of successive population of components is done in Holland's (1975) scheme via the "genetic algorithm", a model of genetic evolu-tion. For example, new production rules may be generated as "cross-over" combinations of paired high performers. Some savings from parents can be transferred to the progeny both to enable them to participate in bidding as well as to inhibit takeover of the popula-tion by a few "rich" families and so to avert premature loss of genetic variance which has been found to be a problem in such genetic systems (Brindle, 1981).

6. CONCLUSIONS: SUGGESTIONS FOR SUPPORT OF VARIABLE STRUCTURE MODELLING

Two novel kinds of general properties which can be supported by variable structure simulation environments were pointed out: 1) the existence of the changing mode in non-trivial variable structure models, 2) the mediation of an economic transaction layer in variable structure models of adaptation. We shall briefly discuss some considerations involved in designing such environments.

6.1 Changing Mode

Recall the changing mode is entered whenever a transition from one
structure state to a successor is initiated. A simulation environment supporting the construction of variable structure models could
help the modeller by providing language constructs to separate the
model specification into normal and changing mode sections. Means
might also be provided to help the user with the tricky logic
involved in getting the model to move correctly between normal and
changing modes. To this end, knowledge of the properties of variable
structure models could be embedded in the environment in a manner
similar to that employed by Aytac and Oren (this volume). For example,
the system would know that every transition between structure states
requires entering the changing mode and the latter always terminates
in a normal mode. In increasing degrees of difficulty, it might: 1)
remind the user of these requirements whenever appropriate, 2)
display behavior and structure states which the user wishes to have
trigger the transitions between normal and changing modes, 3) where
feasible, check for satisfaction of the requirements (consistency
with the formalism).

6.2 Economic Transaction Layer

The economic transaction layer underlying the class of adaptive
models discussed above involves a significant computational overhead
relative to the normal functioning of the non-adaptive model layer.
This overhead must be reduced to acceptable levels in order to
facilitate the exploration of adaptive models. Viewed from the adaptive systems design perspective, computer architectures could be
designed in which the monetary transactions and information accounting
would be realized in hardware primitives. Viewed from the modelling
methodology perspective, simulation environments could be developed
with high level language constructs that facilitate the specification
of economic transactions primitives and offer a flexible menu of
choices to try out in the context of a particular model application.

In addition, several features of variable structure modelling
methodology that require extending conventional simulation support
were mentioned. Entity structure support (available independently
(Belogus, 1985; Zeigler, 1984)) could be integrated into simulation
environments. Facilities should also be provided for convenient
presentation of structural behavior in addition to ordinary state
behavior.

Such advanced hardware and software environments for dealing with
complex system models offer suitable implementation challenges to
exploit powerful computing power visible on the horizon.

7. REFERENCES

Aytac, Z. K. and Oren, T. I. (1985) MAGEST: A Model-Based Advisor and
Certifier for GEST Programs (Chapter 5.3, this volume).

Barto, A. G., R. S. Sutton & C. W. Anderson, "Neuronlike Adaptive
Elements That Can Solve Difficult Learning Control Problems," IEEE
Trans. on Sys. Man & Cyber, Vol. SMC-13, No. 5, pp. 835-846.

Belogus, D. (1985(, Multifaceted Modelling and Simulation: A Software
Engineering Implementation, Doctoral Dissertation, Weizmann Institute
of Science, Rehevot, Israel.

Brindle, A. (1981), Genetic Algorithms for Function Optimization, Doctoral Dissertation, Dept. of Computing Science, University of Alberta, Edmonton, Canada.

Decker, M. (1980), "A New General Purpose Interactive Simulator for Hierarchical Modelling of Discrete Systems", Proc. of Summer Computer Simulation Conference, Seattle, WA.

Hogeweg, P. H. (1980), "Locally Synchronized Developmental Systems", Int. J. Generla Systems, Vol. 6, pp. 57-73.

Holland, J. H. (1975), Adaptation in Natural and Artificial Systems, University of Michigan Press, Ann Arbor, MI.

Holland, J. H. (1984), Escaping Brittleness in Expert Systems, In: Machine Learning, Vol. 4, Eds. R. S. Michalski and T. M. Mitchel.

Kampfner, R. and M. Conrad (1983), "Computational Modelling of Evolutionary Learning Processes in the Brain", Null. Math. Biology, Vol. 45, pp. 931-968.

Klir, G. J. (1979), "General Systems Problem Solving Methodology", In: Methodology in Systems Modelling and Simulation, Eds: B.P. Zeigler et.al., North Holland Press, Amsterdam.

Linos, P. (1985), Simulation of a Modular Hierarchically Co-ordinated Adaptive Architecture, Masters Thesis, Department of Computer Science, Wayne State University, MI 48202.

Oren, T. I. (1975), "Simulation of Time Varying Systems", Proc. Int. Cong. of Cybernetics and Systems, Gordon and Breach, Oxford, pp. 1229-1238.

Oren, T. I. (1979), "Concepts for Advanced Computer Assisted Modelling", In: Methodology in Systems Modeling and Simulation, Eds: B.P. Zeigler et.al., North Holland Press, Amsterdam.

Oren, T. I. (1983), "GEST-A Modelling and Simulation Language Based on System Theoretic Concepts", In: Simulation and Model-Based Methodology: An Integrated Perspective, Eds: T. I. Oren et.al., Springer-Verlag, NY.

Oren, T. I. (1985), "Simulation: Taxonomy", In: Encyclopedia of Systems and Control, Pergamon Press, Oxford (in press).

Zeigler, B. P. (1984), Multifaceted Modelling and Discrete Event Simulation, Academic Press, London,

Zeigler, B. P. (1976), Theory of Modelling and Simulation, Wiley, NY.

Zeigler, B. P. and R. G. Reynolds (1985), "Towards a Theory of Adaptive Computer Architecture", Proc. Int. Conf. Distributed Systems, Denver, pp. .

Zeigler, B. P. (in preparation), Expert System: A Modelling Framework.

Zeleny, M. (1985) Simulation Models of Autopiesis: Variable Structure, In: Encyclopedia of Systems and Control, Pergamon Press, Oxford (in press).

Modelling and Simulation Methodology
in the Artificial Intelligence Era
M.S. Elzas, T.I. Ören and B.P. Zeigler (Editors)
© Elsevier Science Publishers B.V. (North-Holland), 1986

Chapter IV.2

RECENT DEVELOPMENTS IN LEARNING AUTOMATA THEORY
AND THEIR APPLICATIONS

NORIO BABA

INFORMATION SCIENCE AND SYSTEMS ENGINEERING
FACULTY OF ENGINEERING
TOKUSHIMA UNIVERSITY
TOKUSHIMA CITY, 770
JAPAN

Variable-structure stochastic automaton operating in an unknown
environment is one of the most important models that simulate
an intelligent behavior of living beings. In this paper, we
discuss the recent developments of the studies concerning learning behaviors of stochastic automaton operating in the general
multi-teacher environment. Further, we discuss briefly how the
learning automata theory could contribute in the coming artificial intelligence era.

1. INTRODUCTION

The concept of learning automata operating in an unknown random environment was
first introduced by Tsetlin (1961). He studied the learning behaviors of deterministic automata and showed that they are asymptotically optimal under some conditions. Later, Varshavskii and Vorontsova (1963) found that stochastic automata
also have learning properties. Since then, the learning behaviors of stochastic
automata have been studied extensively by many researchers. Chandrasekaran and
Shen (1968), Norman (1968a,1972), Lakshmivarahan and Thathachar (1973) and others
have contributed fruitful results to the literature of learning automata. Survey
papers written by Narendra and Thathachar (1974) and Narendra (1983) contain most
of the important recent works along with the valuable comments for future research.

Despite active research in this field, almost all research so far has dealt with
learning behaviors of a single automaton operating in a stationary single teacher
environment. (Koditschek and Narendra (1977) considered the learning behaviors of
fixed-structure automata operating in a stationary multi-teacher environment. Baba
and Sawaragi (1975) and Srikantakumar and Narendra (1982) studied the learning behaviors of stochastic automata under nonstationary random environments with some
special characteristics.) These researches should be extended in order to be applied to the problems (which we encounter considerably often) where one action
elicits multi-responses from unknown multi-teacher environment.

In this paper, we consider the learning behaviors of variable-structure stochastic
automaton operating in the general n-teacher environment. In the first section,
brief explanations about the stochastic automaton operating in the general n-teacher
environment are given. In the second section, basic norms of the learning behaviors
of stochastic automaton operating in the general n-teacher environment are introduced. In the third section, a class of nonlinear reinforcement scheme in the general n-teacher environment is proposed. It will be shown to be absolutely expedient
and ε-optimal. In the fourth section, learning behaviors of stochastic automaton
operating in a nonstationary multi-teacher environment are considered. In the fifth
section, learning behaviors of the hierarchical structure stochastic automata system
operating in the general unknown multi-teacher environment are considered. In the
final section, future perspectives concerning the applications of the learning automata theory are briefly discussed.

2. BASIC MODEL OF STOCHASTIC AUTOMATON OPERATING IN THE GENERAL N-TEACHER ENVIRONMENT

The learning behaviors of a variable-structure stochastic automaton operating in an unknown random environment have been extensively discussed under the model shown in Figure 1.

In this section, we generalize this model and discuss the learning behaviors of the variable-structure stochastic automaton B in the general n-teacher environment as illustrated in Figure 2.

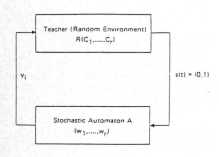

Figure 1
Basic Model of a Stochastic Automaton
Operating in an Unknown Teacher
Environment

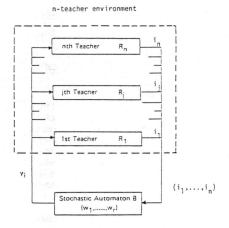

Figure 2
Stochastic Automaton B Operating in
the General n-Teacher Environment

The stochastic automaton B is defined by the set $\{S,Y,W,g,P(t),T\}$. S denotes the set of inputs $(i_1,i_2,\ldots,i_n)$ where i_j $(j=1,\ldots,n)$ is the response from the jth teacher $R_j(C_j^1,\ldots,C_j^r)$ and has binary values 0 and 1. 0 indicates the reward (nonpenalty) response from R_j, and 1 indicates the penalty response from R_j. Y denotes the set of r outputs $(y_1,\ldots,y_r)$. W denotes the set of r internal states $(w_1,\ldots,w_r)$. g denotes the output function $y(t) = g(w(t))$, that is, one to one deterministic mapping. P(t) denotes the probability vector ($P(t) = (p_1(t),\ldots,p_r(t))'$) at time t which governs the choice of the state. T denotes the reinforcement scheme which generates $P(t+1)$ from $P(t)$. The state w_k $(k=1,\ldots,r)$ is chosen at time t with probability $p_k(t)$, where

$$p_1(0) = \ldots = p_r(0) = 1/r, \qquad \sum_{i=1}^{r} p_i(t) = 1.$$

Assume now that the kth state w_k is chosen at time t $(k=1,\ldots,r)$. Then, the stochastic automaton B performs action y_k on the n-teacher environment. In response to action y_k, the jth teacher R_j emits output $s(t) = 1$ (penalty) with probability c_j^k and $s(t) = 0$ (reward) with probability $1 - c_j^k$ $(j=1,\ldots,n)$. Depending upon the action of the stochastic automaton B and the n responses from the n-teacher environment, the reinforcement scheme T changes the probability vector from P(t) to P(t+1). The objective of the design is to choose reinforcement scheme T in such a way that the stochastic automaton B improves its learning performance.

Remark 2.1   In the above model, the input set into stochastic automaton B is binary (0,1). In this case, the environment is said to be a P-model. If the input set into B consists of a finite number of values in the closed line segment [0,1], it is called a Q-model. S-model is one in which the input into B can take an arbitrary value in the closed interval [0,1]. In this section, we only deal with P-model. The results that will be obtained in this paper could be easily extended to the Q- and S-model. (In section 5, we deal with learning behaviors of stochastic automaton under a nonstationary multi-teacher environment of S-model.)

Remark 2.2   Untill section 4, we consider the stationary multi-teacher environment in which the penalty probabilities c_j^k (k=1,...,r ; j=1,...,n) are all constant.

3. BASIC NORMS OF THE LEARNING BEHAVIORS OF THE STOCHASTIC AUTOMATON B IN THE GENERAL N-TEACHER ENVIRONMENT

The concept of the average penalty has been used almost exclusively in the literature in order to judge the effectiveness of a stochastic automaton operating in a single-teacher environment. This concept must be modified when we consider the learning behaviors of a stochastic automaton operating in the general n-teacher environment. It would be reasonable to give a definition in the following way. "When more teachers agree with the action of stochastic automaton B, B receives greater rewards from the n-teacher environment." From such a point of view, we arrive at the following definition of "the average weighted reward in the multi-teacher environment".

Definition 3.1   The average weighted reward in the n-teacher environment is defined as follows:

$$W(t) = \sum_{i=1}^{r} [p_i(t) \{ \sum_{j=1}^{n} j D_{n,j}^i \}] \tag{1}$$

where $D_{n,j}^i$ means the probability that j teachers approve of the ith action y_i of the stochastic automaton B. (j=1,...,n) $D_{n,j}^i$ can be described as follows:

$$D_{n,j}^i = \{(1-c_1^i)\ldots(1-c_j^i)\}\{c_{j+1}^i\ldots c_n^i\} + \ldots + \{c_1^i\ldots c_{n-j}^i\}\{(1-c_{n-j+1}^i)\ldots(1-c_n^i)\} \tag{2}$$

Remark 3.1   The average penalty in a single-teacher environment was defined as

$M(t) = \sum_{i=1}^{r} p_i(t)C_i.$ The definition (1) is a natural generalization of this definition.

Using the definition of the average weighted reward, we can get the several basic definitions concerning learning performances of the stochastic automaton B operating in the n-teacher environment.

Definition 3.2   The stochastic automaton B is said to be "absolutely expedient in the general n-teacher environment", if

$E\{W(t+1)/P(t)\} > W(t)$ for all t, all $p_i(t) \in (0,1)$, i=1,...,r, and all $c_k^i \in (0,1)$

$$, i=1,\ldots,r; \ k=1,\ldots,n. \tag{3}$$

Remark 3.2   The above inequality indicates that the stochastic process $\{W(t), t \in T\}$ is a Semi-Martingale. Taking the mathematical expectation in both sides, we can get

$$E\{W(t+1)\} > E\{W(t)\} \quad \text{for all } t. \tag{4}$$

Definition 3.3   The stochastic automaton B is said to be "expedient in the general n-teacher environment", if

$$\lim_{t\to\infty} E\{W(t)\} > W_0 \quad \text{where} \quad W_0 = \sum_{i=1}^{r} \frac{1}{r}\{\sum_{j=1}^{n} jD_{n,j}^{i}\} \tag{5}$$

Assume now that there exists a βth state w_β such that

$$c_1^\beta + \ldots + c_n^\beta < c_1^i + \ldots + c_n^i \quad \text{for all } 1 \le i \le r \ (\ i \ne \beta\ )$$

$$\tag{6}$$

The above relation means that the action y_β of stochastic automaton B is the most appropriate one. Therefore, we can give the following definition of optimality and ε-optimality.

Definition 3.4   The stochastic automaton B is said to be "optimal in the general n-teacher environment", if

$$\lim_{t\to\infty} E\{p_\beta(t)\} = 1 \tag{7}$$

Definition 3.5   The stochastic automaton B is said to be "ε-optimal in the general n-teacher environment", if the parameters of the reinforcement scheme can be chosen so that

$$\lim_{t\to\infty} E\{p_\beta(t)\} \ge 1 - \varepsilon \quad \text{for any } \varepsilon > 0 \tag{8}$$

Remark 3.3   The above definitions of optimality and ε-optimality could also be given by using the average weighted reward W(t). For an example, the definition of optimality can also be given as

$$\lim_{t\to\infty} E\{W(t)\} = W_\beta, \ \text{where} \quad W_\beta = \sum_{j=1}^{n} jD_{n,j}^{\beta} \tag{9}$$

Remark 3.4   The condition (6) is very general. Even in the singular case that

$$c_1^{\alpha_1}+\ldots+c_n^{\alpha_1} = \ldots = c_1^{\alpha_q}+\ldots+c_n^{\alpha_q} < c_1^i+\ldots+c_n^i \ , \ \text{for all } i \ (\ 1 \le i \le r; \ i \ne \alpha_1,$$

$,\ldots, i \ne \alpha_q$), let us consider the state w_γ that unifies the states $w_{\alpha_1},\ldots,$ and w_{α_q}. Then, we can derive the same results as will be obtained in the next section.

4. ABSOLUTELY EXPEDIENT NONLINEAR REINFORCEMENT SCHEMES IN THE GENERAL N-TEACHER ENVIRONMENT

In this section, we introduce the GAE reinforcement scheme having the nice learning properties as will be explained later.

GAE Scheme

Assume that $y(t) = y_i$ and the responses from the n-teacher environment are m rewards and $(n - m)$ penalties. Then,

$$p_i(t+1) = p_i(t) + (1 - \frac{m}{n})\{\sum_{\substack{j \neq i \\ j=1}}^{r} \phi_j(P(t))\} - \frac{m}{n}\{\sum_{\substack{j \neq i \\ j=1}}^{r} \psi_j(P(t))\} \qquad (10)$$

$$p_j(t+1) = p_j(t) - (1 - \frac{m}{n})\phi_j(P(t)) + \frac{m}{n}\psi_j(P(t)) \qquad (1 \leq j \leq r; j \neq i) \quad (11)$$

where

$$\frac{\phi_1(P(t))}{p_1(t)} = \frac{\phi_2(P(t))}{p_2(t)} = \ldots = \frac{\phi_r(P(t))}{p_r(t)} = \lambda(P(t)) \qquad (12)$$

$$\frac{\psi_1(P(t))}{p_1(t)} = \frac{\psi_2(P(t))}{p_2(t)} = \ldots = \frac{\psi_r(P(t))}{p_r(t)} = \mu(P(t)) \qquad (13)$$

$$p_j(t) + \psi_j(P(t)) > 0, \qquad p_i(t) + \sum_{\substack{j \neq i \\ j=1}}^{r} \phi_j(P(t)) > 0,$$

$$p_j(t) - \phi_j(P(t)) < 1 \qquad (j = 1,\ldots,r ; i = 1,\ldots,r) \qquad (14)$$

The GAE reinforcement scheme ensures absolute expediency and ε-optimality in the general n-teacher environment.

Theorem 4.1   Assume that $\lambda(P(t)) \leq 0$ (15),

$$\mu(P(t)) \leq 0 \qquad (16),$$

and $\lambda(P(t)) + \mu(P(t)) < 0$ for all t and P(t). (17)

Then, the stochastic automaton B with the GAE reinforcement scheme is absolutely expedient in the general n-teacher environment.

Theorem 4.2   Assume that $\lambda(P(t)) = \theta(\overline{\lambda}(P(t)))$ $(\theta > 0)$ (18)

$$\text{and} \qquad \mu(P(t)) = \theta(\overline{\mu}(P(t))) \qquad (19),$$

where $\overline{\lambda}(P(t))$ and $\overline{\mu}(P(t))$ are bounded functions which satisfy the conditions (15) and (16).
Further, suppose that $\overline{\lambda}(P(t)) + \overline{\mu}(P(t)) < -\tilde{\varepsilon}$ for some positive number $\tilde{\varepsilon}$.

Then, the stochastic automaton B with the GAE reinforcement scheme is ε-optimal in the general n-teacher environment.

Since the proofs of the above two theorems are rather lengthy, we will omit them. Interested readers could consult the paper written by the author. (Baba (1983a))

Remark 4.1   The GAE reinforcement scheme has an extended form of the absolutely expedient learning algorithm (introduced by Lakshmivarahan and Thathachar (1973)) in a single teacher environment.

Remark 4.2   Suppose that the assumptions of Theorem 4.1 hold true. Then, the GAE reinforcement scheme has the following learning performance:

$$E\{p_\beta(t+1)/P(t)\} - p_\beta(t) \geq 0 \qquad \text{for all } t \text{ and } P(t) \qquad (20)$$

Remark 4.3   As examples of the GAE reinforcement scheme, the following two algorithms have been proposed. (Baba (1983a), Baba (1983b))

GL_{R-I} scheme :   When the output from the stochastic automaton B at time t is y_i, and the responses from the n-teacher environment are m rewards and (n - m) penalties,

$$p_i(t+1) = (1 - m\theta)p_i(t) + m\theta$$

$$p_j(t+1) = (1 - m\theta)p_j(t)$$

$$m = 0,\ldots,n; \quad 1 \leq j \leq r, \quad j \neq i; \quad 0 < n\theta < 1.$$

If we let $\phi_k \triangleq 0$ (k=1,...,r) and $\psi_k \triangleq - n\theta p_k$ (k=1,...,r), then we can get the above algorithm. Since this algorithm is an extension of the reward-inaction scheme L_{R-I}, we call it GL_{R-I} scheme.

GNA scheme :   When the output from the stochastic automaton B at time t is y_i, and the responses from the n-teacher environment are m rewards and (n - m) penalties,

$$p_i(t+1) = p_i(t) - k\theta(1 - \frac{m}{n})(1 - p_i(t))\{H/(1-H)\} + \theta(\frac{m}{n})(1 - p_i(t))$$

$$p_j(t+1) = p_j(t) + k\theta(1 - \frac{m}{n})(p_j(t))\{H/(1-H)\} - \theta(\frac{m}{n})(p_j(t)) \qquad (j\neq i)$$

$$0 < \theta < 1, \quad H = \min[\ p_1(t),\ldots,p_r(t)\ ], \quad 0 < k\theta < 1.$$

If we let $\psi_j(P(t)) = - \theta p_j(t)$ and $\phi_j(P(t)) = - k\theta(p_j(t))\{H/(1-H)\}$, (j=1,...,r), we can easily get the above algorithm.

Computer Simulation Results :   In the following example, we consider the three-teacher environment in which two teachers (Teacher 1 and Teacher 3) agree on the best action ($\beta = 2$), but one teacher (Teacher 2) makes mistakes. A learning behavior of the GL_{R-I} scheme under the three-teacher environment (TA3) with the characteristics described in Table I is simulated by computer and compared with those under the single-teacher environment (TA1) and the two-teacher environment (TA2). The changes in the probability $p_\beta(t)$ ($\beta = 2$) and the average weighted reward $W(t)$ are shown in Figure 3 and Figure 4, respectively.

The speed of learning of the stochastic automaton under the two-teacher environment (TA2) is not faster than that under the single-teacher environment (TA1). It appears that this result comes from the fact that Teacher 2 makes mistakes but Teacher 1 agrees on the best action y_2. However, the speed of learning of the stochastic automaton under the three-teacher environment (TA3) is faster than those under (TA1) and (TA2). This means that the speed of learning increases as more teachers who agree on the best action are included. (See Figure 3 and Figure 4.)

Table I

Three-Teacher Environment (TA3)

	c_i^1	c_i^2	c_i^3	c_i^4	c_i^5	($i = 1,2,3$)
Teacher 1	0.65	0.35	0.50	0.45	0.83	
Teacher 2	0.35	0.38	0.40	0.85	0.95	
Teacher 3	0.85	0.23	0.75	0.85	0.57	
Sum of the penalty probabilities	1.85	0.96	1.65	2.15	2.35	

(TA1)	Single-teacher environment with Teacher 1
(TA2)	Two-teacher environment with Teacher 1 and Teacher 2
(TA3)	Three-teacher environment with Teacher 1 - Teacher 3

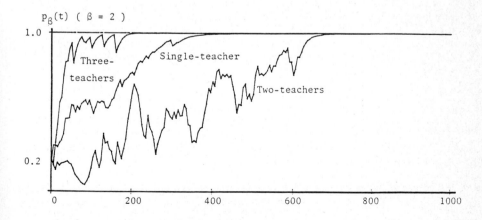

Figure 3
Changes in probability $p_\beta(t)$

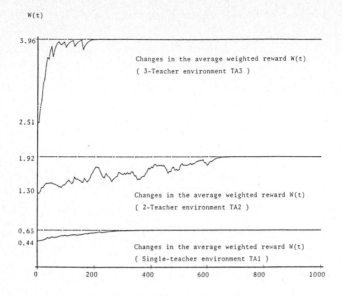

Figure 4
Changes in the Average Weighted Reward W(t)

From the above computer simulation results, we can derive the following induction.
The GL_{R-I} scheme has a nice convergence property which is very close to optimality.
We have derived the theorems that the GAE reinforcement scheme is absolutely expedient
and ε-optimal in the general n-teacher environment. The above computer simulation
results confirm our theoretical study.

As to learning performances of another reinforcement schemes such as GNA, we have
obtained several interesting computer simulation results. If you are interested in
them, please read the book written by the author. (Baba (1985))

5. LEARNING BEHAVIORS OF STOCHASTIC AUTOMATA UNDER NONSTATIONARY MULTI-TEACHER ENVIRONMENT

In this section, we generalize further the model given in the previous section and
discuss the learning behaviors of the stochastic automaton D in the nonstationary
multi-teacher environment (NMT) as illustrated in Figure 5. Here, we deal with
the S-model nonstationary multi-teacher environment from which the stochastic automaton D receives s_j^i having an arbitrary number between 0 and 1. (s_j^i is a
function of time t and point of Basic ω-space. (j = 1,...,n))

Assume that the stochastic automaton D performs action y_i on NMT at time t. Then,
in response to y_i, the jth teacher R_j emits output s_j^i. Here, s_j^i is a function
of t and ω. ($\omega \in \Omega$; Ω is the basic ω-space of the probability measure space
(Ω,B,μ), and B is the smallest Borel field including $\bigcup\limits_{t=0}^{\infty} F_t$, where $F_t = \sigma(P(0),.$
...,P(t),S(0),...,S(t))   (S(t) means the outputs from NMT at time t.))   Therefore,

from now on, we shall often use the notation $s_j^i(t,\omega)$ in order to represent the input into D.

We consider the nonstationary multi-teacher environment (NMT) in which the relation

$$\int_0^1 s \, dF_{\gamma,t}(s) + \frac{\delta}{n} < \int_0^1 s \, dF_{j,t}(s) \tag{21}$$

, where $F_{i,t}(s)$ $(i=1,\ldots,r)$ is the distribution function of $\sum_{j=1}^n s_j^i(t,\omega)/n$, holds for some state w_γ, some $\delta > 0$, all time t, all j $(\neq \gamma)$, and all ω $(\in \Omega)$.

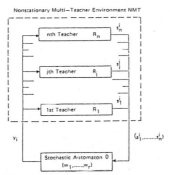

Figure 5
Stochastic Automaton D Operating in the Nonstationary Multi-Teacher Environment NMT

The objective of the stochastic automaton D is to reduce $E\{\sum_{j=1}^n s_j^i(t,\omega)\}$, the expectation of the sum of the penalty strengths. Therefore, by analogy from the definitions introduced in the previous section, we arrive at the following definitions:

Definition 5.1   The stochastic automaton D is said to be "optimal in NMT", if

$$\lim_{t\to\infty} E\{p_\gamma(t)\} = 1 \tag{22}$$

Definition 5.2   The stochastic automaton D is said to be "ε-optimal in NMT", if the parameters of the reinforcement scheme can be chosen so that

$$\lim_{t\to\infty} E\{p_\gamma(t)\} \geq 1 - \varepsilon \qquad \text{for any} \quad \varepsilon > 0 \tag{23}$$

Let us introduce the MGAE reinforcement scheme which can be used for the S-model environment.

MGAE Scheme

Suppose that $y(t) = y_i$ and the responses from NMT are $(s_1^i, \ldots, s_n^i)$. Then,

$$p_i(t+1) = p_i(t) + [\frac{s_1^i + \ldots + s_n^i}{n}]\{\sum_{j \neq i}^r \phi_j(P(t))\} - [1 - \frac{s_1^i + \ldots + s_n^i}{n}]\{\sum_{j \neq i}^r \psi_j(P(t))\}$$

$$p_j(t+1) = p_j(t) - [\frac{s_1^i + \ldots + s_n^i}{n}]\{\phi_j(P(t))\} + [1 - \frac{s_1^i + \ldots + s_n^i}{n}]\{\psi_j(P(t))\} \quad (j \neq i)$$

, where $\phi_i, \psi_i \ (i=1,\ldots,r)$ satisfy the conditions given from (12) to (14).

As to the learning performance of the MGAE reinforcement scheme, the following theorem has been obtained.   (Baba (1984))

Theorem 5.1   Suppose that $\lambda(P(t))$ and $\mu(P(t))$ satisfy the assumptions of the
Theorem 4.2. Then, the stochastic automaton D with the MGAE reinforcement scheme
is ε-optimal under the nonstationary multi-teacher environment NMT satisfying the
condition (21).

Although we have obtained several computer simulation results, we shall omit them
due to limitations of space.

6. LEARNING BEHAVIORS OF THE HIERARCHICAL STRUCTURE STOCHASTIC AUTOMATA SYSTEM OPERATING IN THE GENERAL UNKNOWN MULTI-TEACHER ENVIRONMENT

Recently, the concept of the hierarchical structure automata was introduced by
Thathachar and Ramakrishnan (1981). This work was followed by Ramakrishnan (1982).
Since many living beings follow hierarchical plans and our daily decision makings
are often done in a hierarchical fashion, the concept of the hierarchical structure
automata system would become one of the most important promising tools in various
application areas.

In this section, we generalize the hierarchical structure automata model proposed
by Thathachar and Ramakrishnan (1981) (Ramakrishnan (1982)) and consider the learning behaviors of the generalized hierarchical automata system operating in the multi-
teacher environment.

Figure 6 shows the learning mechanism of the hierarchical structure stochastic automata system operating in the general multi-teacher environment. Since almost all of
the symbols used in Figure 6 are identical to those used in Thathachar et al (1981),
we will only introduce brief outline of the learning mechanism described in Figure 6.

$\bar{A}$ denotes the first level automaton. Initially, all the action probabilities are
set equal. $\bar{A}$ chooses an action at time t from the action probability distribution
$(p_1(t),\ldots,p_r(t))$. Suppose that α_{j_1} is the output from $\bar{A}$ and $\beta_1^{i_1} \ (i_1=1,\ldots,r_1)$
is the response from the i_1th teacher (environment). Depending upon the output
α_{j_1} and the responses ($\beta_1^{i_1} \ (i_1=1,\ldots,r_1)$) from r_1 teachers, the first level
automaton $\bar{A}$ changes its action probability vector $P(t) = (p_1(t),\ldots,p_r(t))'$ govern-

ing the choice of the actions α_i $(i=1,\ldots,r)$.

In the second level, the automaton $\bar{A}_{j_1}$ is actuated. This automaton chooses an action from the current action probability distribution. Depending upon the action $\alpha_{j_1 j_2}$ and the environmental responses $\beta_2^{i_2}$ $(i_2=1,\ldots,r_2)$, the automata in the second level change their probability vectors. This cycle of operation repeats from the top to the bottom.

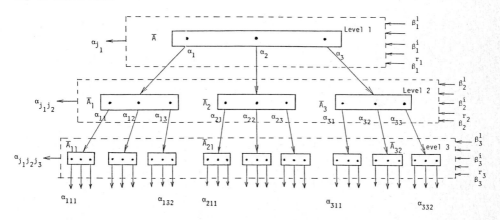

Figure 6

Hierarchical Structure Stochastic Automata System Operating in the General Multi-Teacher Environment

By the simple extension of the algorithm proposed by Thathachar and Ramakrishnan (1981), we are able to derive the following reinforcement scheme.

Ist Level   Assume that the j_1th action α_{j_1} is selected by the first level automaton $\bar{A}$ at time t and the environmental responses are β_1^i ($i = 1,\ldots,r_1$).

Then,

$$p_{j_1}(t+1) = p_{j_1}(t) + L_1(t)(1 - p_{j_1}(t))$$

$$p_{i_1}(t+1) = p_{i_1}(t)(1 - L_1(t)) \qquad (i_1 \neq j_1 ; i_1 = 1,\ldots,r)$$

Nth level   Assume that the actions α_{j_1}, $\alpha_{j_1 j_2}$,\ldots, and $\alpha_{j_1 j_2 \ldots j_{N-1} j_N}$ are selected by the automata $\bar{A},\ldots,\bar{A}_{j_1 j_2 \ldots j_{N-1}}$ at time t and the environmental responses at the Nth level are β_N^i ($i = 1,\ldots,r_N$). ($N = 2,\ldots,N$)

Then,

$$P_{j_1 j_2 \ldots j_N}(t+1) = P_{j_1 j_2 \ldots j_N}(t) + L_N(t)(1 - P_{j_1 j_2 \ldots j_N}(t))$$

$$P_{j_1 j_2 \ldots j_{N-1} i_N}(t+1) = P_{j_1 j_2 \ldots j_{N-1} i_N}(t)(1 - L_N(t))$$

$$(i_N \neq j_N ; i_N = 1, \ldots, r)$$

All other state probabilities at the Nth level of other automata remain unchanged.

Here, $L_i(t)$ ($i = 1, \ldots, N$) are defined as follows.

Let

$$\bar{\eta}_s(t) = 1 - \frac{\beta_s^1 + \ldots + \beta_s^{r_s}}{r_s} \qquad (s = 1, \ldots, N)$$

Then,

$$L_1(t) = \sum_{s=1}^{N} \bar{\eta}_s(t) \lambda_s, \ldots, L_N(t) = \frac{\sum_{s=n}^{N} \bar{\eta}_s(t) \lambda_s}{P_{j_1}(t+1) \ldots P_{j_{n-1}}(t+1)}$$

The following theorem can be easily obtained. (Baba (1985))

Theorem 6.1   Assume that there exists a unique path called the optimal path in the hierarchical tree such that at each level, the average sum of the penalty probabilities in the optimal path corresponds to the minimum of those at that level. This means:

Let $\phi_{j_1^* \ldots j_N^*}$ be the optimal path.

Then,

$$E\{\frac{\beta_s^{1, j_s^*} + \ldots + \beta_s^{r_s, j_s^*}}{r_s}\} < E\{\frac{\beta_s^{1, j} + \ldots + \beta_s^{r_s, j}}{r_s}\}$$

for all s ($s = 1, \ldots, N$) and all j ($j = 1, \ldots, r$).

($\beta_s^{i,j}$ ($i=1, \ldots, r_s$; $j=1, \ldots, r$) is the response from the ith teacher at the s level when jth action has been actuated.)

Further, assume that

$$0 < \sum_{s=1}^{N} \lambda_s < 1$$

Then,

$$\Delta \P_{j_1^* \ldots j_N^*}(t) = E[\P_{j_1^* \ldots j_N^*}(t+1) - \P_{j_1^* \ldots j_N^*}(t) \mid P(t)] > 0$$

in the open simplex of the action probabilities.

$$(\P_{j_1, \ldots, j_N} = P_{j_1}(t) P_{j_1 j_2}(t) \ldots P_{j_1 j_2 \ldots j_N}(t))$$

7. FUTURE PERSPECTIVES CONCERNING THE APPLICATIONS OF THE LEARNING AUTOMATA THEORY

The applications of learning automata have been considered by many researchers. McMurtry and Fu (1966), Shapiro and Narendra (1969), and Baba (1978) used stochastic automata for parameter self-optimization problem with unknown performance criteria. The applications of stochastic automata to games have also been reported. (Chandrasekaran and Shen (1968), Lakshmivarahan (1981), Baba (1985)) Walz and Fu (1965) and Riordon (1969) used stochastic automata as a learning controller of an unknown system. Recently, the application of the learning automata theory to routing problems in communication networks was proposed by Mason (1972) and since then developed in great detail by Narendra et al.

In this section, we discuss briefly how the learning automata theory could contribute in the coming artificial intelligence era. We would like to suggest that research efforts in the following two directions would produce fruitful results and give revolutionary impacts to the knowledge engineering.

1) A stochastic automaton operating in an unknown environment could be considered as a stochastic inferential engine utilized as an expert system / problem solver. We should carefully investigate this idea and extend it in order to advance the study of knowledge engineering.

2) As an application of the learning automata theory, we have considered a robot manipulator working in a room having obstacles with unknown characteristics. We have obtained several computer simulation results which prove the effectiveness of learning performance of the stochastic automaton. This idea could be extended to the multi-robot (distributed learning machine) environments where local learning elements can be agglomerated through appropriate broadcasting / transmission in order to achieve a higher level of (global) knowledge.

ACKNOWLEDGMENT

The author would like to thank Prof. T.I. Ören who gave him several valuable advices. He would also like to thank Prof. Y. Sawaragi (Kyoto Sangyo Univ.), Prof. T. Soeda (Tokushima Univ.), and Prof. T. Shoman (Tokushima Univ.) for their kind encouragement. He is also indebted to his students Mr. H. Takeda and Mr. T. Miyake for their assistance.

8. REFERENCES

Baba, N. and Sawaragi, Y (1975). On the learning behavior of stochastic automata under a nonstationary random environment, IEEE Trans. SMC, Vol. 5, nr. 2, pp. 273-275.

Baba, N. (1978). Theoretical consideration of the parameter self-optimization by stochastic automata, International Journal of Control, Vol. 27, nr. 2, pp. 271-276.

Baba, N. (1983a). The absolutely expedient nonlinear reinforcement schemes under the unknown multi-teacher environment, IEEE Trans. SMC, Vol. 13, nr. 1, pp. 100-108.

Baba, N. (1983b). On the learning behaviors of variable-structure stochastic automaton in the general n-teacher environment, IEEE Trans. SMC, Vol. 13, nr. 2, pp. 224-231.

Baba, N. (1984). ε-optimal nonlinear reinforcement scheme under a nonstationary multi-teacher environment, IEEE Trans. SMC, Vol. 14, nr. 3, pp. 538-541.

Baba, N. (1985). Learning behaviors of the hierarchical structure automata system operating in the general multi-teacher environment, IEEE Trans. SMC, Vol. 15, pp. 585-587.

Baba,N. An application of the hierarchical structure automata to the cooperative game with incomplete information, International Journal of Systems Science, (to be published)

Baba, N. (1985) New topics in learning automata theory and applications, Springer-Verlag, 131p.

Chandrasekaran, B. and Shen, D.W.C (1968). On expediency and convergence in variable-structure automata, IEEE Trans. SSC, Vol. 4, pp. 52-60.

Doob, J.L. (1953) Stochastic processes, Wiley, New-York, 654p.

Koditschek, D.E. and Narendra, K.S (1977). Fixed structure automata in a multi-teacher environment, IEEE Trans. SMC, Vol. 7, pp. 616-624.

Lakshmivarahan, S. and Thathachar, M.A.L (1973). Absolutely expedient learning algorithms for stochastic automata, IEEE Trans. SMC, Vol. 3, pp. 281-286.

Lakshmivarahan, S. and Narendra, K.S (1981). Learning algorithms for two person zero sum games with incomplete information, Mathematics of Operations Research, Vol. 6.

Lakshmivarahan, S. (1981) Learning algorithms Theory and applications, Springer-Verlag, 279p.

Mason, L.G. (1972) Self-optimizing allocation systems, PH.D. University of Saskatchewan, Canada.

McMurtry G.J. and Fu, K.S (1966). A variable-structure automaton used as a multi-modal search technique, IEEE Tans. AC, Vol. 11, pp. 379-387.

Narendra, K.S. and Thathachar, M.A.L (1974). Learning automata - a survey, IEEE Trans. SMC, Vol. 4, pp. 323-334.

Narendra, K.S. and Thathachar, M.A.L (1980). On the behavior of a learning automaton in a changing environment with application to telephone traffic routing, IEEE Trans. SMC, Vol. 10, pp. 262-269.

Narendra, K.S. (1983) Recent developments in learning automata - theory and applications. In: Proceedings of the Third Yale Workshop on Applications of Adaptive Systems Theory, K.S. Narendra (ed). pp. 90-99.

Norman, M.F. (1968a) On linear models with two absorbing barriers, Jounal of Mathematical Psychology, Vol. 5, pp. 225-241.

Norman, M.F. (1968b) Some convergence theorems for stochastic learning models with distance diminishing operators, Journal of Mathematical Psychology, Vol. 5, pp. 61-101.

Norman, M.F. (1972) Markov processes and learning models, Academic Press, New-York, 274p.

Ramakrishnan, K.R. (1982) Hierarchical systems and cooperative games of learning automata, PH.D. Indian Institute of Science, Bangalore, India.

Riordon, J.S. (1969) Optimal feedback characteristics from stochastic automaton models, IEEE Trans. AC, Vol. 14, pp. 89-92.

Sawaragi, Y. and Baba, N (1973). A note on the learning behavior of variable-structure stochastic automata, IEEE Trans. SMC, Vol. 3, pp. 644-647.

Sawaragi, Y. and Baba, N (1974). Two ε-optimal nonlinear reinforcement schemes for stochastic automata, IEEE Trans. SMC, Vol. 4, pp. 126-131.

Shapiro, I.J. and Narendra, K.S (1969). Use of stochastic automata for parameter self-optimization with multimodal performance criteria, IEEE Trans. SMC, Vol. 5, pp. 352-360.

Srikantakumar, P.R. and Narendra, K.S (1982). A learning model for routing in tele-phone networks, SIAM Journal on Control and Optimization, Vol. 20, pp. 34-57.

Thathachar, M.A.L. and Ramakrishnan, K.R (1981). A hierarchical system of learning automata, IEEE Trans. SMC, Vol. 11, pp. 236-241.

Tsetlin, M.L. (1961) On the behavior of finite automata in random media, Automation and Remote Control, Vol. 22, pp. 1345-1354.

Varshavskii, V.I. and Vorontsova, I.P (1963). On the behavior of stochastic automata with variable structure, Automation and Remote Control, Vol. 24, pp. 353-360.

Walz, M.D. and Fu, K.S (1965). A heuristic approach to reinforcement learning control systems, IEEE Trans. AC, Vol. 10, pp. 390-398.

Modelling and Simulation Methodology
in the Artificial Intelligence Era
M.S. Elzas, T.I. Ören and B.P. Zeigler (Editors)
© Elsevier Science Publishers B.V. (North-Holland), 1986

Chapter IV.3

KNOWLEDGE SEEKING IN VARIABLE STRUCTURE MODELS

P.Hogeweg & B.Hesper
BIOINFORMATICA
Padualaan 8
de Uithof, Utrecht
the Netherlands

Systems with a variable structure are often modelled in
terms of models with a fixed structure. We will argue that
such fixed structure models are conceptually inefficient at
best, and (worse) tend to "beg the question" concerning the
system.
We review modelling methodologies in which the variable
structure of the system is represented as the variable
structure of the model: MIRROR modelling methodology, with
an emphasis on the role of knowledge seeking (by OBSERVERs)
in such models.
We will illustrate our ideas with several, still primitive,
examples of MIRROR models which, we hope, will contribute
to our understanding of the use of knowledge seeking
processes in science.

1. INTRODUCTION

1.1 On the need of knowledge seeking in models, or
Modelling sensu strictu vs studying Paradigm Systems

Most verbalisations and formalisations of the concept modelling presuppose
a "real" system which the model system should mimic. Such a "real" system
is conceived by Zeigler (1976,1984) as a database of potential
observations. In his conceptualisation the real system can be thought of as
being represented by a "base model", i.e. the hypothetical system which
produces exactly the same set of observations as the real system. However,
neither the set of potential observations nor the base model are known.
Therefore at any one time the "working" model represents the base model
only relative to an explicitly defined experimental frame, i.e. a set of
input/output relations which the system should mimic. Likewise, Klir (1984)
recognises an "observation channel", and Wymore (1984) a set of feasible
test items. The "real" system and the model are supposed to produce similar
input/output relations when studied through the appropriately similar
experimental frame. Thus although it is recognised that modelling is a
"multifacetted process" (Zeigler 1984) in which a variety of alternative
experimental frames are employed (which are partly defined in a feedback
process from model studies employing other experimental frames (Elzas
1984)) at any one time a model is studied with a fixed structure (system
specification) in which the potential observables are predefined and
incorporated in the model as observational entities.

However "modelling" in the exploratory phases of science is often done without pinpointing the real system (i.e. a source of potential observations) which the model should (partially) mimic. Instead modelling serves the important purpose of defining sets of coherent observations. In such cases the modelling process starts with defining 'paradigm systems', i.e. interesting relations and/or properties of model entities and proceeds by studying what observables /observations can be generated by these relations/properties. Finally a search in the "real" universe will be undertaken to find out whether such a set of observables is applicable in that universe and if so to recognise these observables as a coherent set. This pathway of scientific modelling can be illustrated with well known examples: (1) The fact that observables are generated by models and are only secondarily sought in the "real" universe is clearly true for Black Holes. (2) A prototype of previously observed observables which unexpectedly were shown to form a coherent set are planet trajectories and apples falling from trees.

In this paper we are concerned with studying paradigm systems. Because no apriori behavior of a target system is chosen, knowledge seeking in the model, and therewith the generation of new observables (not represented in the model as observational entities) is of utmost importance.

1.2 On the need of variable structure models

The need for variable structure models arises simply from the fact that
1. Some systems do have a variable structure; imposing a fixed structure then leads to
    a. redefinition of the system, or
    b. including "quiescent entities" and zero interactions, to simulate
    variable structure (compare cellular automata (which only can be
    specified assuming quiescent states), and partially decoupling in
    random nets (Kaufman 1969) (which make these fixed structures de facto
    variable structure)),
2. We may be interested in how a (relatively) static entity structure arises from the behavior of autonomous entities

Both these cases are often true in bioinformatic studies: If we represent biotic systems in terms of their information processing entities we obtain variable structure systems, and the most outstanding question in bioinformatics is how autonomous entities (like molecules, cell, organisms) form relatively stable structures (like cells organisms ecosystems) without assuming global control.

2. FIXED-STRUCTURE VS VARIABLE STRUCTURE MODELS

2.1 Implicit global control

Fixed structure model formalisms are all those formalisms in which the model consists of a fixed set of entities (modules, subsystems) which interact each with a fixed subset of the other entities all through the existence of the model. All classical model formalisms (e.g. differential equations, difference equations, cellular automata, and also DEVS, etc.) fall into this class. Not withstanding their superficial localness (being built up out of simple interacting subsystems) such systems are inherently global in the sense that:
1. The subsystems represent global properties of the system. This is because of the requirement of a fixed set of subsystems: in many systems only global properties are definable in such an invariant way. For example many biological models are defined for this reason in terms of populations (of organisms, cells or molecules) instead of in terms of individuals: the

latter form a varying collection, whereas the former remain the same entity
(possibly with value zero).
2. The model system is defined as a "whole": the subsystems may not
preserve their identity (model interpretation) except as part of the whole.

In variable structure models the set of entities constituting the system is
variable (in number, types and properties) and the interaction between the
entities change in time (neccesarily so because of the changing set of
entities). Such models can comply much more to local characteristics than
fixed structure models because:
1. the model entities can represent "individuals", i.e. the basic
information processing entities of the system to be modelled;
2. the model entities are defined so as to be self-sufficient: they pursue
their own purposes, they gather their own information and they establish,
maintain and abolish relations with other entities on the basis of their
local experiences. Thus the model entities can exist in different
environments and still maintain their model interpretation. The system as a
whole is not explicitly represented in the model.

Besides the distinction between fixed structure- and variable structure
models there is the distinction between models with a global timing regime
(incorporating the world-view that "everything is changing all the time")
and models with a local timing regime(incorporating ultimately the world
view: "once in a while something interesting is happening somewhere in the
system", (see below)). (Note that this does not imply that an implicit
global time does not exist in models with a local timing regime). We have
shown previously that implicit global control through a global timing
regime can impose unwarranted structure in otherwise locally defined
systems (Hogeweg 1980).

The two distinctions run parallel in the sense that local time is required
in variable structure models, whereas both timing regimes are possible in
fixed structure models.

2.2 Knowledge incorporated

The knowledge incorporated in fixed structure models is the invariant
relation it embodies, and the concepts (i.e. entities and entity structure)
which allow for such an invariant relation. (One should be aware that the
class of invariant relations used in (fixed structure) systems models is
wider than that used in mathematical context, e.g. switches are allowed.)
The knowledge to be gained from such models is about the state-changes
compatible with the invariant relation. This knowledge can be gained
easily: the relevant concepts are apriori defined and the stated values
have only to be recorded.

The knowledge incorporated in variable structure models concerns the
information processing properties of the entities under consideration.
The (ultimate) knowledge to be gained from such models concerns the
patterns of interactions which result from the simultaneous occurrence of
the information processing entities under consideration. One such pattern
can be an invariant relation such as incorporated a priori in fixed
interaction models. However not only invariant relations are of interest,
may be even more important is knowledge concerning 'interesting' events,
i.e. events which redirect the system from one configuration to the next.
The knowledge sought in variable structure models is much harder to obtain
then the (different) knowledge sought in fixed structure systems because
new concepts are to be formed to express the patterns of interaction,
whereas in fixed structure models the concepts are given (i.e. are
identical to those represented in the model) and the patterns of
interaction are fixed.

The role in science of both types of models is also different. Fixed
structure models are implemented to test the invariant relation and to
predict the state of the system: they are indeed employed most often in
"applied" science. Variable structure models can be implemented in the
exploratory phases of scientific enterprise and aid in the process of
pattern discovery and concept formation.

3. MIRROR MODELLING

MIRROR modelling represents our attempt to provide the concepts and tools
(implemented in MIRSYS) to make variable structure modelling feasible
(Hogeweg & Hesper 1979,19811,b,1983,1985a,b; Hogeweg 1985). The name MIRROR
modelling is chosen with "through the looking glass" in mind: our variable
structure models should be "as large as life and twice as natural" and
should "reflect our reflections" (recursively). A summary of the concepts
of MIRROR modelling in the form of the most important requirements and the
resulting structure follows.

3.1 Autonomous entities

The basic units should be autonomous entities ('individuals') which possess
their own information processing capabilities. This directs us in the
direction of the "Process" view modelling formalism or to object oriented
modelling/programming, as used in AI. Because of the variable structure,
and the knowledge aquistiion properites of entities, the entities should
preserve their structure during the simulation, and not be only entities in
an abstract formulation which lose their identity during runtime (as e.g.
in SIMSCRIPT).

Individuals should be selfsufficient, i.e. they should not need the active
cooperation of other individuals to satisfy their informatic needs (Hogeweg
& Hesper 1985b). For example a predator should not need a "here I am"
message from a prey to find it.

Autonomy and selfsuffiency do not imply that the individuals are
independent. On the contrary their behavior is highly determined by the
varying interactions in which they are involved (refer to the TODO
principle in the example section). Indeed MIRROR preeminently implements
Simon's paradigm about the ant (and human): "an ant viewed as a behaving
system is quite simple, the apparent complexity of its behavior in time is
largely a reflection of the environment in which it finds itself; a human
...... etc." (Simon(1969)).

In MIRSYS individuals are INTERLISP functions which posses an indirect
reference to their own local program pointer (the ME pointer). Through this
pointer the entire calling environment of the individual can be accesses,
i.e. individuals can inspect the parameters etc. of other individuals of
which they know the local ME pointer (i.e. of which they have a YOU
pointer). Note that the calling environment (i.e. the 'knowable'
individual) changes dependent on the state (behavior) of that individual.
Note also that an individual can not automatically assess all parameters of
other individuals of which they have a YOU pointer: they need in addition
knowledge of how to decode the information (i.e. they need the appropriate
senses). In this way individuals can have the required autonomy and
selfsufficiency without violating the localness requirements (see also
section 3.5).

3.2 Variable interactions

Interactions between individuals can be established in one of the following ways:
1. knowledge incorporated a priori (= fixed structure)
2. Ancestry based: an individual inherits its interactions from the individual which generates it. Various forms of ancestry based variable structure systems are quite common, e.g. context sensitive grammars, L-systems, but also the "hire/fire" ancestry based variable structure model of Zeigler (chapter IV.1) Our PATCHes (which subdivide SPACEs) employ an ancestry based divide/merge variable structure regime comparable to the above mentioned "hire/fire" regime in the sense that PATCHes are generated at need (see below).
3. Proximity based. For this purpose the individuals should be embedded in (one or more) space(s) and change their location in these spaces. This mode of establishing interactions generates more truely variable structured systems than the previous one: e.g. prediction of the interactions is usually not possible. MIRROR models mostly use proximity based interactions. The spatial structure employed is discussed in the next section.
4. Based on common relations (e.g. A knows B and C and establishes a direct interaction between B and C). Such an interaction is implemented in MIRROR through DEMONs (see below).

3.3 The MIRROR universe

The MIRROR universe consists primarily of SPACEs and DWELLERs. DWELLERs are embedded in SPACEs so that they can establish interactions on the basis of proximity. Note that the definition of proximity is not necesarily the same for every DWELLER although all are subjected to the same SPACE topology: proximity depends on the senses of the DWELLERs, e.g. the proximity definition may include viewing direction, different distances etc. The behavior definition of DWELLERs often includes movements through space which implies that the proximity relations change.
SPACEs are themselves of variable structure. They can be subdivided in PATCHes. PATCHes form a hierarchical structure subdividing SPACEs. New PATCHes are generated if necessary for the DWELLERs (e.g. the SPACE is extended by a new PATCH at the root of the hierarchy when a DWELLER moves into hitherto unoccupied (hence non-existing) regions, and PATCHes at the leaves of the hierarchy subdivide if they contain a very large number of DWELLERs). The interaction of PATCHes is ancestry based.

Moreover SPACEs can be generated and deleted during runtime. Like the PATCH structure the interactions of new SPACEs are ancestry based: SPACEs are associated with DWELLERs (which themselves dwell in some other SPACE) as their SKINSPACE. SKINSPACEs can be used in many different ways. They can harbor for example parasites on the animals which are modelled in SPACESPACE. Alternatively a DWELLER can built up its 'worldview' in its SKINSPACE in the form of a (dynamic) configuration of (interacting) DWELLERs (i.e. the SKINSPACE serves as mental space). In both cases the configuration of DWELLERs in the SKINSPACE of a DWELLER is generated by- and will influence the latter DWELLERs behavior. The MIRROR universe is initiated with at least one SPACE (which often represents physical space and is called SPACESPACE). Fig 1 represents the general structure of a MIRROR universe.

3.4 Interesting events

Every event oriented description should confine itself to some extent to 'interesting events'; otherwise it runs into Achilles and the turtle problems (by introducing 'passing the halfway mark' as event, so many

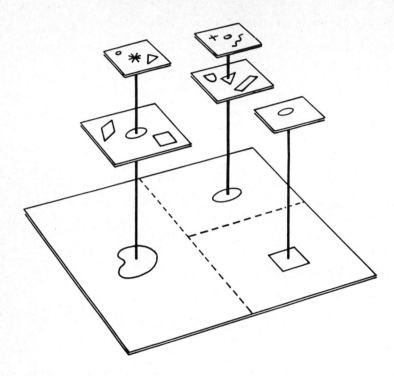

Fig. 1.   Sketch of MIRROR universe which consist of SPACEs (sub divided in PATCHes)
          in which DWELLERs (of different types) dwell. Each DWELLER may possess a
          SKINSPACE in which, again DWELLERs dwell.

events happen that time is effectively stopped; the paradox derives from
talking about never after stopping time). We define 'interesting' events as
those events which redirect the system from its expected behavior, i.e.
interesting events are those events which should happen explicitely in
order to know what happens in future. Which events are interesting depends
on the composition of the universe, not only on single individuals.
Therefore the requirements of autonomous, selfsufficient individuals on one
hand and confining events to interesting events on the other hand are in
conflict. This conflict can (in principle) be resolved in MIRROR by using
its variable structure and knowledge seeking capabilities and the 'shadow
world' (see below). The reasoning is as follows (Hogeweg & Hesper 1981b):
1.Interesting events are those events which redirect the system away from
its expected course of behavior
2. The purpose of modelling is to generate and refine expectancies about
the behavior of the system
3. Such expectancies should not only refer to the system as a 'whole' but
in particular to partial processes (e.g. temporarily decoupled subsystems)
4. Expectancies can be formed by MIRROR entities by monitoring the behavior
of the system (MIRROR entities need such capabilities anyway) and can be
used to confine the events to interesting events by changing the structure
of the system, by replacing (for the time being) the original entities by

entities which only incorporate the interesting transitions.
5. Expectancies are (by definition) generally wrong when interesting events
occur. Thus the system should be able to fall back on its original
definition, i.e. the specification before restructuring on the basis of
expectancies.

This course of restructuring the model is undertaken by DWARFs (which hoard
their "treasure" (knowledge base) of expectancies and make tools out of
them to confine the system to interesting events). DWARFs are part of the
'shadow world'.

3.5 The shadow world

The shadow world is inhabited by DEMONs and DWARFs (and WIZARDs and
SENTINELs) These are locally defined, autonomous, selfsufficient entities
as are the "real world" MIRROR entities. They embody the universal
properties of the MIRROR universe under consideration without violating its
autonomy requirements. They accomplish the ultimate purpose of modelling
itself: embodying expectancies and generating interesting events. This has
always been their role in stories as well.

4. KNOWLEDGE SEEKING IN MIRROR UNIVERSES

In a MIRROR universe three types of entities are definined to communicate
what is happening in the MIRROR universe to the outside, i.e.
RECORDERs
REPORTERs
OBSERVERs

RECORDERs are the simplest. They just record the value of a variable which
is defined in the MIRROR universe, or the events in which a certain entit
is involved. They do not do any information processing to accumulate this
information; they only output it in a reasonable form. They produce for
example a protocol of the behavior of a certain entity or record all
interactions of a special type. RECORDERs are all that is needed in fixed
structure models. They do not suffice in variable structure models. They
tend to produce bulky and irrelevant output.

REPORTERs report on global properties of the system, i.e. properties which
do not occur in the model definition, but can be gathered fairly easily.
Information processing is, however needed to obtain this information. Often
reporters are sent into the system to report on the state of the system
using those concepts which would constitute the primary entities in a fixed
structure model representing a similar system.

OBSERVERs (Hogeweg & Hesper 1981a) are the most versatile: they "observe".
They find interesting phenomena and tell about them in terms appropriate to
the situation, i.e. their information is context dependent. Thus they are
not defined in terms of what to observe, but in terms of how to observe and
possess some criteria of interestingness. Interesting in MIRROR worlds are,
as mentioned, patterns of interaction and the resulting differentiation
between otherwise similar individuals. Such patterns have as interesting
features both the individuals conforming to the pattern as those which do
not conform to the pattern.
OBSERVERs can use the information gathered by RECORDERs, and they profit
from the focus on interesting events caused by the DWARFs. They can also
make use of the concepts formed by other OBSERVERs to evaluate their own
concepts and to focus attention on interesting features.
So far only relatively simple OBSERVERs have been implemented. The most

powerful of them make use of non-supervised pattern analysis procedures, in particular cluster analysis.

Cluster analysis is routinely used in science for concept formation. Some methods (e.g. agglomerative clustering with minimal mean sum of squares as clustering criterion, Ward 1963) are very powerful filters to find consistent patterns, even if the pattern is weak. By its space dilating properties this method finds detailed patterns in those parts of the state space in which much information is available, i.e. it focusses attention on those parts, and, by taking a coarser view of other parts, the method pinpoints exceptional cases (Hogeweg 1976, Hogeweg & Hesper 1981).

The validity of cluster analysis and the generated clusters should not be sought in statistical properties (its power is to provide context dependent information), nor in the ability to recover a priori well defined concepts (compare Michalski & Stepp (1984), who reintroduced cluster analysis in AI context, but modified, to conform to apriori notions about classes). Instead the validity lies in the interpretability (e.g. consistency, local order preservation, (partial) coincidence with other known concepts etc.) of the label information of the extensively defined classes (Hogeweg & Hesper 1981). Thus cluster analysis can (slightly) redefine apriori notions so as to give rise to consistent patterns (see e.g. Van Honk & Hogeweg 1981, Mastenbroek et al 1984), which would not be found otherwise.

In MIRROR worlds OBSERVERs using cluster analysis can for example be used to find groups of individuals which do interact with a similar group of other individuals, using as primary information a record of all interactions (of a certain type). If the groups of individuals selected in this way remain the same during some time, interesting information about the structuring of the interactions is found: later changes in this pattern are very interesting events!
These groups of individuals can be lumped in a next step of pattern seeking processes. The groups become even more interesting if the same groups can be found in other characteristics of the individuals under consideration (e.g. their SKINSPACE configuration). Moreover supervised pattern analysis techniques can be used to characterise the groups, to find typical and exceptional cases etc.
Examples of the use of such OBSERVERs are given in the next section.

More sophisticated OBSERVERs should be able to trace the interesting events which lead to such patterns and tell stories about how it all came about.

Note that OBSERVERs are not alien entities in a MIRROR universe: DWELLERs and DWARFs also gather knowledge. The difference between OBSERVERs and those other entities is that observers do not leave traces in the environment and do not change the structure of the system: they only observe. In addition OBSERVERs establish relations with other OBSERVERs REPORTERs and RECORDERs on the basis not of proximity in SPACESPACE but on proximity in 'knowledge'space.

5. <u>EXAMPLES OF MIRROR MODELS</u>

The examples given aim to demonstrate:
1.the need for variable structure models
2. the complex structures that can be generated by relatively simple variable structure models
3.the need for knowledge seeking in such models
4.how knowledge can be incorporated in biotic systems as 'side effect' of other concerns

5.1 <u>Social structure of bumble bee colonies, or
how do Bumble bees know when the season ends?</u>

Bumble bees are truly social insects somewhat more primitive then honey
bees. Only the queens survive the winter and start a "solitary" life in
spring. They build a nest, lay eggs,forage etc. Later the worker offspring
take over all duties except egglaying. At the end of the season the
workers, however, "rebel", the queen is thrown off the nest and some of the
workers start laying unfertilised (=drone) eggs, and the last eggs laid by
the queen are reared so as to produce not workers but new queens. By timing
the rebellion (and therewith the switch to the production of generative
offspring) at the appropriate time (i.e. as late as possible, but early
enough to get the generative offspring "off the line"), ergonomic
optimality of the nest as a whole can be achieved (Oster 1976, Oster &
Wilson 1978). The question is how the appropriate "collaboration" (i.c.
rebellion) is achieved without introducing some global control mechanism,
or introducing a prepattern like a change in the environment
(experimentally the switch occurs at the appropriate time in a constant
environment) or senility of the queen (experiments show that old queens
still can "manage" young nests).

This is obviously a variable structure system: the number of individual
bees (the relevant information processing entities) increases from 1 to
about 500. Moreover they interact with each other in various ways. This
interaction seems, moreover, to cause a differentiation between initial
identical workers: some lay eggs at the end of the season and others do
not. Van Honk and Hogeweg (1981) have shown that in experimental nests the
dominance interactions between bees and the laying of eggs are related.

Simulating this system as a fixed structure system would require either
lumping bees in apriori defined compartments and defining transitions
between these compartments (which would beg the question of how the
differentiation comes about and which factors influence the nest
composition) or including not yet born individuals as quiescent entities
and accepting a tremendous overhead in (the selection of) interactions (all
bees interacting but many interactions amounting to nothing).

In contrast, the variable structure MIRROR model is very simple (Hogeweg &
Hesper 1983,1985). The universe consists of the nestSPACE, in which the
bees dwell. The interactions between bees are regulated by proximity in
nest space (which is simply subdivided in the PATCHes CENTER, PERIPHERY,
POT (i.e. the honey pot in which food is stored) and OUTSIDE; proximity is
in this case determined by random drawing in the PATCH in which a bee is).
On interaction the BUMBLEs simply do what there is to do (we call this the
TODO principle) with the type of entity they meet: they feed larvae,
dominate (or are dominated by) adults etc. When hungry (this is signaled by
a DEMON which monitors the amount of food not yet digested or given to
larvae) they go to POT; when they find POT empty they go foraging. In this
way, what the BUMBLEs do depends on
                                    the composition of the nest, but no
global control whatever is included.

The dominance interaction causes the differentiation in the MIRROR
universe. When DOM is a numerical value representing the dominace of an
individual, this interaction (called DODOM) is defined as:

1.Display of the current DOM value of each of the bees
2.Determining who wins:
        if rand(0,1)<DOMi/(DOMi + DOMj) then k=1 (i wins)
                                        else k=0 (j wins)
3.Updating of the DOM values:
        DOMi = DOMi + (k-DOMi/(DOMi + DOMj))

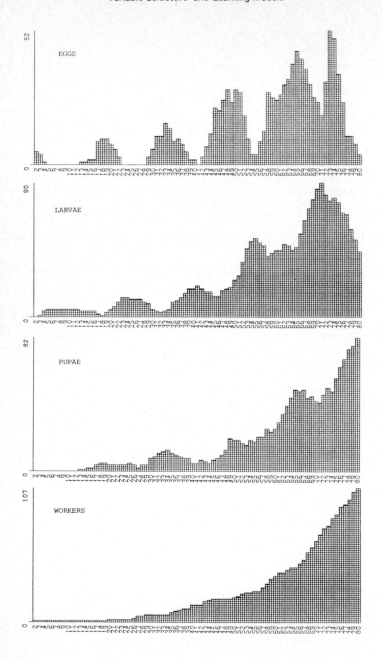

Fig. 2.

Population structure of a (simulated) Bumble Bee nest through time. Horizontal axis: time in days. Vertical axis: number of eggs, larvae, pupae and workers respectively.

DOMj = DOMj - (k-DOMi/(DOMi + DOMj))
This updating causes an "expected win" to generate little change and an
unexpected one a big change: DODOM is a form of ritualised dominance
behavior. We think that such a ritualised dominance behavior underlies much
social organisation.

We have shown (Hogeweg & Hesper 1983,1985) that the so defined MIRROR world
generates all the social complexities of a bumble bee colony known so far.
In fact it generated several behavior patterns which we did not know
existed in bumble bee colonies but which were confirmed by experimental
studies later.
However to find this out we needed all our information gathering entities:
RECORDERs, REPORTERs and OBSERVERs.
RECORDERs provided us with basic protocols similar to those gathered by
experimenters (in our case van Honk (see Van Honk 1981, van Honk & Hogeweg
1981, and Van Doorn (see Van Doorn & Heringa 1985): i.e. a recording of all
pairwise interactions (and who wins) and sometimes protocols of the
behavior of individual bees.
REPORTERs provided us with an overview of the nest composition in terms of
population numbers of the various developmental stages (eggs, larvae pupae,
workers, newqueens and drones, see fig 2). It shows that the population
structure shows the same uneven composition as is the case in experimental
nests.
OBSERVERs were used to observe the differentiation of workers (as a result
of differential interaction patterns). Using cluster analysis on the
interaction data gathered by the RECORDERs they recognized elite workers
and common workers as well as a transition group. The behavior of these
groups was similar to that observed by van HONK & Hogeweg (who used cluster
analysis to find the groups) although in fast growing nests the groups were
less stable then the ones observed by them. Later Van Doorn found that this
is also the case in experimental nests (van Doorn & Heringa 1985).

A very striking property of the MIRROR bumble bee nests was the fact that
the switch from worker to generative offspring production occurred at a
fixed time, was caused by the interaction pattern in the nest, but was
independent of growth rate of the nest (Hogeweg & Hesper 1985). Although
the time of the switch (=killing of the queen) is of course easily
recordable, the timing could only be understood in relation to the dynamics
of the elite vs the common worker group as elucidated by the OBSERVER: In
fast growing nests the elite was much less elite then in slow growing nests
where the elite resembles the queen closely at the end of the nest
development.

We conclude that knowledge about the duration of the season is incorporated
in the DODOM interaction in combination with the TODO of bumble bees. By
coding in this way this knowledge is preserved notwithstanding variations
in climate or individual idiosyncrasies of the bees (Hogeweg & Hesper
1985).

5.2 <u>SKINNIES: their world view and personal aquaintances</u>

In contrast to the previous example (which can be considered as either
modelling s.s. of Bumble bee colonies or as defining a TODO/DODOM paradigm
system in the context of bumble bee population dynamics and maintenance
behavior) the present example is a pure paradigm study: SKINNIES are not
supposed to represent any real world object. Instead SKINNIES were defined
as a minimal informatic system in which the DODOM/TODO principle operates
and in which the individuals know each other personally.

Knowing each other personally only makes sense when relevant information

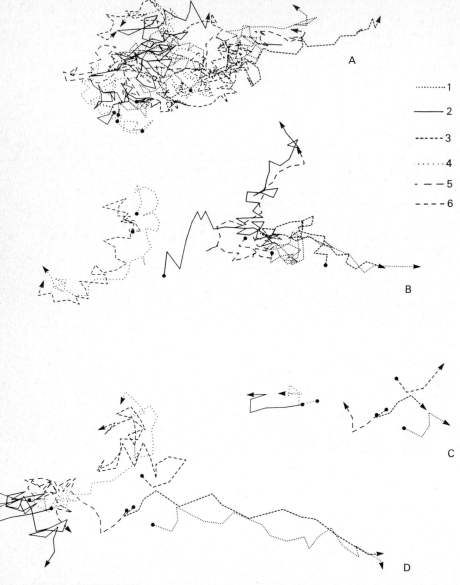

Fig. 3. Paths of SKINNIES.
   3a.Period 0-70: the SKINNIES, who started their life with an undifferentiated
      "world view", initially stay roughly together and move back and forth in
      an unstructured manner.
   3b.Period 70-120: Pairs of SKINNIES split off and move away together.
      When such pairs meet again, or
   3c.When the SKINNIES are reinitiated in a random configuration they quarrel but
   3d.Walk off in the same pairs again.

cannot be sensed directly on encounter. Indeed bumble bees do not seem to know each other personnally but the DOM value seems to be directly sensible as pheromone (= chemicals used for communication between animals) composition and concentration. In SKINNIES the DOM value is supposed not to be sensible, in fact it does not exist as such (see below). On encounter SKINNIES however recognise each other and refer to the internal representation of the other SKINNY in their SKINSPACE to access its (assumed) relative DOM value. In this most simple case the internal representation of the SKINNY only constitutes its DOM value (i.e. its location in a one dimensional SKINSPACE).

DODOM operates both in SKINSPACE and in SPACESPACE. In SKINSPACE it is defined identically to DODOM in the bumble bees, i.e. direct sensing of the mutual DOM values, determining who wins by random drawing and the relative dominances and finally updating of both dominances in accordance with the probability of the outcome of the interaction (see previous section). In SPACESPACE DODOM is defined similarly but:

1. The display of dominance is the relative dominance in each of the SKINSPACEs, i.e.
   $D_i = DOM_i/(DOM_i + DOM_j)$ in SKINSPACE of SKINNYi
   D_j is defined similarly in the SKINSPACE of SKINNYj
(Note that in MIRSYS no absolute indices i and j exist but that each individual refers to "me" and "you")

2. The winning is defied as before but using D_i and D_j

3. The updating happens in SKINSPACE It is based on who wins in SPACESPACE and the expectancies available in the SKINSPACE under consideration (Note that this is the only possible interpretation of "expected" in this context), i.e. is identical to the SKINSPACE updating described above.

Thus a straight forward generalisation of the DODOM interaction is achieved.

TODO is defined very rudimentarily as yet. It only includes some spatial behavior associated with the DODOM interaction. On encounter of another SKINNY (a SKINNY is obliged to react if anybody is nearer then a certain distance (compare the critical distance known of many animals) it first performs a DODOM in its SKINSPACE. If it looses this imagined interaction it moves away. If it wins it displays its relative dominance (which not withstanding its winning may be relatively low) to the other and a DODOM in SPACESPACE takes place. If it wins it moves towards its opponent, if it looses it moves away. The only extra assumption in the SKINNY paradigm is that they are gregarious: if they are too far from other SKINNIES they move towards them.

The so defined SKINNIES show interesting behavior. If they all start with an equal "world view" (i.e. with the same configuration in SKINSPACE, i.e. with an equal estimate of all dominances which are in addition assumed initially equal) they first stay roughly together moving back and forth without covering much distance (see fig 3a). After some time, however, pairs of SKINNIES split off from the rest and start making "mileage" (fig 3b). When such pairs meet each other later on (the SPACESPACE is toroidal) there is some quarrelling but sooner or later they move apart again, forming the original ("harmonious") pairs (fig 3c,d). (this is not always the case but there is a clear preference for the old pairs). This differential coupling between SKINNIES is, of course easily observable when their movemements are displayed. However, why on earth (in SPACE) do SKINNIES form such "friendships"?

OBSERVERs found an answer:

On clustering SKINSPACE configurations the same pairs are formed as those walking off in SPACESPACE (fig 4). Apparently such pairs build up a similar

"worldview" (because they see the same). Having the same worldview they
behave similarly towards "foreigners" and so stay together (they bounce of
in the same direction in SPACESPACE). Note that the SKINNIES forming pairs
are by no means the same: they only agree about their mutual dominance.
OBSERVERs also observed that if individuals are characterised by how they
are represented in the SKINSPACE of other individuals a (stable) dominance
hierarchy was recognised (fig 5)

These results are intriguing. Clearly SKINNIES have severe shortcomings as
representations of organisms: their TODO is only social and does not
contain any maintenance constraints. This fact is probably responsible for
the counterintuitive phenomenon (not often observed in animals) that
dominant SKINNIES follow submissive ones.
Nevertheless we think that the worldview, spatial configuration, alliance
relationships displayed by the SKINNIES under influence of DODOM
interactions are observables interesting enough to try to use them in
studying groups of animals, e.g. monkeys.

ON WORLD VIEW

MEAN CHARACTER DIFFERENCES IN Q-MODE WARD'S AVERAGING

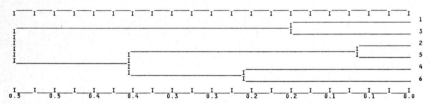

Fig. 4.

Clustering the SKINNIES on the basis of the configuration of DWELLERs (representing the SKINNIES) in their SKINSPACE (i.e. on their world view) at
time=200. The pairs of SKINNIES emerge which walked off together (see fig. 3).

ON OTHERS ESTIMATE

MEAN CHARACTER DIFFERENCES IN R-MODE WARD'S AVERAGING

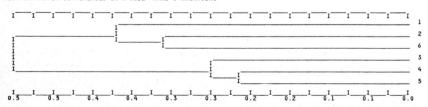

Fig. 5.

Clustering the SKINNIES on the basis of the location of their representations
in the SKINSPACES of other SKINNIES (i.e. on the others estimate) at time=200:
a dominance pattern emerges: SKINNIES 1, 2, 6 are dominant ones and 3, 4, 5
are submissive ones. The latter tend to be in front when the SKINNIES walk
in pairs (see fig. 3).

6. EPILOGUE

Most modelling and simulation studies and most AI work is strongly "supervised": desired behavior of the systems is predefined (as input/output relations. as solution to problems, as correct diagnosis, as conforming to behavior of experts etc.). In contrast our work on knowledge seeking in (variable structured) paradigm systems is strongly non-supervised and aims at discovering new observebles, entities, concepts and relations. Likewise, the work of e.g. Lenat (Lenat 1975,1984; Davis & Lenat 1981, in the the program called AM) aims at discovering new concepts (at least new for the program; no concepts new to mankind were discovered so far), in his case the concepts of number theory given elementary set theoretic concepts (the program discovered for example the concept prime number). There are several similarities between his approach and ours although these similar structures may appear at different levels in the two cases.
1. Both emphasize the use of paradigm systems. Studying paradigm systems is an a priori goal in our approach whereas AM invents (in its simple universe of numbers) paradigm systems in order to have material to find patterns.
2. Both are variable structured individual oriented systems. The individuals communicate via a common environment (the MIRROR universe, the knowledge base).
3. Both are scheduling events (time axis in MIRROR, agenda in AM).
4. Both relate concepts via their extensive definitions (individuals to which they apply in MIRROR, numbers to which they apply or which they generate in AM)
5. Both use similar general heuristics, e.g. find extreme cases, find typical cases etc.)
6. Both use criteria for "interestingness" (e.g. an definition of "interesting" as concepts which share a similar extensive definitions is used in both systems).

Important differences stem from the fact that:
1. in MIRROR knowledge is sought in an autonomously changing universe, whereas in AM numbers are numbers and only what we know about them changes. Therefore AM seeks only invariant relations whereas we seek semi-invariant relations and the interesting events changing the structure of the system
2. comparison of numbers is easy (they are the same or different) whereas the comparison of individuals or relations are more difficult (we need the concept 'similar' and non-supervised pattern detection methods)
3. communication in AM is unlimited (the entire universe (=knowledge base) is accessible to all modules) whereas in MIRROR the MIRROR universe consists potentially of many (possibly imcompatible) worlds (SPACEs). The latter is certainly the case in socio- or ecosystems and we think it is true also in epistemic systems (which we simplistically circumscribe as 'insight seeking' systems).

Finally we note that the most exciting possibilities for merging modelling methods and AI methods is in employing variable structured modelling in modelling epistemic processes (the ultimate goal of AI). After all not all our thought is of the form of an inference machine. A rather large amount has the form of interesting event simulation: stories reflect such epistemic processes. Likewise we think that a knowledge representation in the form of sequences of interesting events instead of in the form of invariant relations would enhance science.

ACKNOWLEDGEMENTS

We thank D. Smit for designing figure 1 and C.J. Stryland for converting the color graphics plots of the paths of the SKINNIES to quite acceptable black and white drawings.

REFERENCES

Davis R & Lenat DB (1981) Knowledge based systems in artificial intelligence. McGraw-Hill Book Comp, New York.

van Doorn & Heringa (1985) Ontogeny of dominance hierarchy in some colonies of the bumble bee Bombus terrestris (hymenoptera. Apidae) and the reproductive success of its members Insect Sociaux (in press)

Elzas MS (1984) Systems Paradigms as Reality Mappings in Simulation and Model-Based Methodologies: an Intergative View (eds. TI Oren et al) NATO ASI Series, Vol.F10

Hogeweg P (1976) Topics in biological pattern analysis, Thesis RU Utrecht

Hogeweg P (1980) Locally synchronised developmental system, conceptual advantages of discrete event formalism INT.J. General Systems 6:57-73

Hogeweg P and Hesper B (1979) Heterarchical, selfstructuring simulation systems: concepts and applications in biology, in: Zeigler BP et al. (eds.) Methodologies in systems modelling and simulation, North-Holland Publ Co Amsterdam pp221-231

Hogeweg P & Hesper B (1981) Oligothetic characterisation of clusters Pattern recognition 14 131-139

Hogeweg P & Hesper B (1981a) On the role of OBSERVERS in large scale systems. in: UKSC Conference on Computer Simulation, Westbury House, Harrogate pp420-425.

Hogeweg P & Hesper B (1981b) Two predators and one prey in a patchy environment an application of MICMAC modelling, J.Theor Biol. 93:411-432.

Hogeweg P & Hesper B (1983) The ontogeny of the social structure of bumble bee colonies, a MIRROR model Behav Ecol & Sociobiol 12, 271-283

Hogeweg & P Hesper B (1985) Socioinformatic processes: MIRROR modelling methodology J. Theor Biol 113, 311-330

Hogeweg P. & Hesper B.(1985) Interesting events and distributed systems, Scs Multiconference 1985, 81-87, San Diego

Hogeweg, P (1985) Heterarchical systems as simulation modelling formalism, Encyclopeadia of systems and control (Singh ed.) Pergamon (in press).

Honk CJG van (1981) The social structure of bumble-bee colonies, Thesis RU. Utrecht

Honk CJG Van & Hogeweg P. (1981) The ontogeny of the social structure in a captive Bombus terrestris Colony Behav. Ecol Sociobiol 9:111-119

Kauffman, S (1969) Metabolic stability and epigenesis; randomly structured genetic networks J. Theor Biol 22 437-467

Klir GJ (1984) Chapter 3 of Simulation and Model-Based methodologies: an intergrative View (eds. Ti Oren et al) NATO ASI Series Vol.F10

Lenat DB (1975) BEINGS: Knowledge as interacting experts IJCAI4, Tbilisi USSR

Lenat DB (1984) The role of heuristics in learning by discovery: three case studies, in Machine Learning, an artificial intelligence approach (Michalski, Carbonell & Mitchell eds.) Springer pp 243-306

Michalski RS & Stepp RE (1984) Learning from observation: conceptual clustering in: Machine learning, an artificial intelligence approach (Michalski, carbonell & Mitchel eds) Springer, Berlin pp331-363

Oster GF (1976) Modelling social Insect Populations I Ergonomics of foraging and population growth in bumble bees, Am. Nat. 110:215-245

Oster GF & Wilson EO (1978) Caste and ecology in the social insects Princeton University Press, Princeton New Yersey.

Simon H (1969) The Science of the artificial, MIT press, Cambridge

Wymore AW (1984) Chapter 5 of Simulation and Model-Based Methodologies: an intergrative View (eds. TI Oren et al) NATO ASI Series Vol.F10.

Zeigler BP (1976) Methodology of systems modelling and Simulation, Wiley

Zeigler BP (1984) Multifacetted modelling and Discrete Event Simulation. AP London.

Modelling and Simulation Methodology
in the Artificial Intelligence Era
M.S. Elzas, T.I. Ören and B.P. Zeigler (Editors)
© Elsevier Science Publishers B.V. (North-Holland), 1986

Chapter IV.4

USE OF EXPLICIT CONSTRAINTS TO EVALUATE A POTENTIALLY UNIQUE, NEURAL MODEL FOR SINGLE-INTERVAL CONCEPT MANIPULATION

Rolf Martin

Department of Chemistry
Brooklyn College of the
City University of New York
Brooklyn, NY 11210

Slightly more than 10,000 constraints on permissible connection values within an otherwise ordinary nerve network are discussed and shown to enable certain aspects of concept use to be simulated. The model is of interest because a number of "high-level" operations that appear fundamental to intelligent behavior can be completed after one round or interval of communication between adjacent layers in a multilayered network. The approach taken may be the only approach that enables concepts to be manipulated as described during one time interval.

1. INTRODUCTION

The approach to be described is one of a class of methods that rely on <u>learning</u> <u>rules</u> which govern the growth of branches or connections between nerve cells ("neurons") or neuron-like processing elements. Simulations of this type have in the past been used to illustrate how nerve networks can support key aspects of associative and sequential recall (Hebb 1949, Gardner-Medwin 1976, Fukushima 1973), feature detection and pattern recognition (Anderson et al. 1977, Nagano, Kurata 1981, Reilly et al. 1982, Fukushima 1983, Martin 1985a) representation of topologically correct feature maps (Takeuchi, Amari 1979, Kohonen 1982) and certain types of concepts (Nakano 1972, Cooper 1974, Amari 1977, Anderson 1983, Hampton, Kibler 1983, Martin et al. 1984) game-playing (Nakano 1972, Martin et al. 1984), similarity assessment, risk benefit evaluation, representation of concept hierarchies and cognitive maps, and learning by simile (Martin et al. 1984), sorting into categories (Martin 1985b), and production of simple but logical sentences (Martin 1986b, 1986c). (See Hinton, Anderson 1981, Anderson 1983, Fukushima et al. 1983, Hampton, Kibler 1983, and Martin et al. 1984, for relatively recent reviews.)

Of these capabilities, associative recall, pattern recognition, short-term risk benefit evaluation, sorting into categories, retrieval of information from concept hierarchies and learning by simile, have been simulated within one time interval or round of communication between cell layers (cf. Nakano 1972, Fukushima et al. 1983, Martin et al. 1984, Martin 1985a,b and others) where one time interval corresponds to the amount of time required for one set of cells to trigger another.

"Single-interval" simulations such as these can be contrasted with
others that require more than one interval for each cell layer
involved. For example, Winston's (1979) description of learning by
simile requires at least three and as many as eleven separate steps,
and Anderson's (1983) simulations of pattern recognition involve up
to 45,000 intervals.

The major aims of this paper are to:

> 1) evaluate the adequacy of a particular variant of the
> single-interval approach with respect to approximately
> 10,000 constraints that severely limit permissible model
> structure and behavior, and

> 2) raise the following questions: Are these constraints
> applicable, in either a strict or a general sense, to other
> qualitatively different models of concept representation?
> And are there any alternative methods for concept represen-
> tation that can generate, within one time interval, respon-
> ses that satisfy these constraints?

2. A GENERAL DESCRIPTION OF METHODS

Several relatively detailed descriptions of our simulation methods
have been published recently (Martin et al. 1984, Martin 1985a,
1986a), so only a brief, complementary discussion is included here
and in Section 4.

The approach taken has been for the most part a rather ordinary one,
and many aspects will be familiar to readers who have followed recent
investigations of neural nets. The overall network architecture is
that of the multilayered hierarchy illustrated in Figure 1. From the
top layer downward, layers in this figure are devoted, respectively,
to propositions, concepts, concept attributes and relatively unpro-
cessed input from the "outside environment". Each square in this
figure signifies a cluster of neurons that respond selectively to,
and hence recognize, a particular proposition, concept, attribute or
input feature.

Input from the environment affects only cells within the lowest
layer. Neural discharge activity spreads to deeper or higher layers
and then is "reflected" back down to the lower levels (cf. McClelland, Rumelhart 1982). Of the layers shown, only the second and
third are discussed in detail in the sections that follow. In all
simulations, discharge at either of these levels leads to a response
at the other level within one time interval.

Connections within this hierarchy extend between cells of the same
layer and between adjacent layers. All connections are initially of
equal strength but vary during each simulation according to the following learning rules:

> 1) Hebb's (1949) rule: the connection or link between two
> neurons is strengthened when both cells fire concurrently;

> 2) the link from cell a to cell b is strengthened when
> cell a discharges a short time before cell b, however the
> link from b to a is not strengthened;

> 3) the link from cell a to cell b is weakened when a dis-
> charges while b is silent;

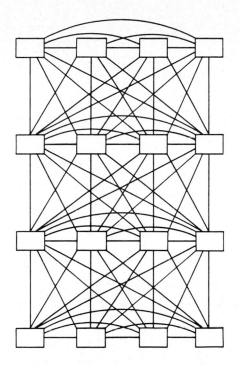

Figure 1
General architecture of the neuron layers simulated.

4) the link from <u>a</u> to <u>b</u> is also weakened when <u>b</u> fires while <u>a</u> is silent;

5) links leading to each neuron or cluster of equivalent neurons tend to reach relatively similar maximum values; and

6) rules 1 to 4 are operative only in the presence, and in proportion to the amount, of neurotransmitters or other hormones or nutrients that signify important metabolic or hormonal states.

Neurons within a "cluster" are defined as those within a broad region of the brain that respond optimally to equivalent stimulus patterns, and that in turn stimulate a similar range of postsynaptic or target cells. As a result, each cluster can be treated as a single, very large neuron with potential connections to and from other clusters in the same and adjacent layers. Readers who are primarily interested in parallel computers may wish to regard each cluster as a computational center or processing unit that repeatedly evaluates and sums input values and then releases a response to its neighbors.

As a consequence of the six learning rules, a trail of strengthened connections is formed whenever two or more neurons or neuron clusters discharge concurrently or within a short time interval. These connection trails form pyramid- and tree-like connection structures which have qualitatively distinct functional properties that enable the network to behave "reasonably" in a number of respects.

Sequential pyramids form whenever neuron clusters within one layer discharge in sequence while at least one cluster in the adjacent, higher layer is firing. As a consequence of the second learning rule, connections along the base of this pyramid are unidirectional or "one-way", so that recall of the firing sequence proceeds stepwise in the forward direction. Sequential discharge of this kind can provide a basis for sequential recall, game-playing, concept inference, sentence production and very likely many other aspects of intelligent behavior.

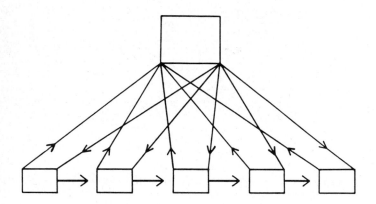

Figure 2
Strengthened connections that form a "sequential pyramid".

Notice in Figure 2 that discharge of the apical cluster (at the top of the pyramid) can reactivate clusters forming the base of the pyramid, and may also be triggered by cells at the base. Since basal clusters may each comprise the apex of a lower pyramid, cells within higher-level pyramids have the power, under appropriate circumstances, to activate chains of firing sequences within the neural layers beneath them. Apical clusters within the uppermost layers thus have some of the properties of Minsky's agents in his "Society of the Mind" theory of intelligence (Minsky, 1979).

Associative pyramids are similar to sequential pyramids except that connections between clusters within the base are strengthened in both directions. As a result, these basal cells stimulate one another to discharge concurrently (rather than in sequence) and the entire base can be reactivated simultaneously by the apical cluster. This type of connection structure forms when several clusters at one level discharge concurrently, while one or more clusters at the adjacent, higher level is firing. Associative pyramids can provide a basis for representing certain kinds of concepts, with neurons at the base representing concept attributes and the apex functioning as a label or recall key.

<u>Figure 3</u>: A "horizontal tree" of strengthened connections that ties together neurons which represent key attributes of semantically related concepts. This type of connection structure enables members of related categories to be listed in the approximate order of their position within a classification tree. Firing activity or "activation" is transmitted primarily along strengthened connections that comprise the main branches of the tree. Note that activation of neurons corresponding to key features of any concept within the mammalian hierarchy results in activation of cells representing key features of neighboring concepts. Discharge of cells corresponding to key features may then lead to firing of cells that represent concept names, so that the names of related concepts can be recalled. Concept names are indicated by quotation marks; key features are capitalized. The simulation that produced this connection pattern is described in Tables I, II and III.

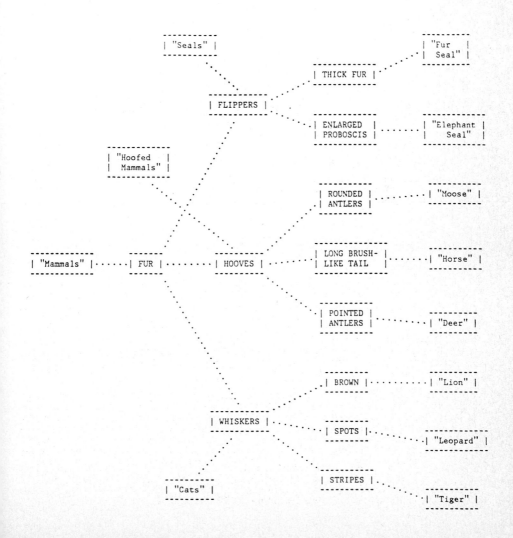

<u>Horizontal trees</u> are formed when information about related concepts
is input into the net. Notice in Figure 3 that neurons representing
the key attributes of various mammals are linked within an inverted
tree of connections that is analogous to the classification tree of
Figure 4. Nodes within this connection tree are neuron clusters
within a single layer of the neural hierarchy of Figure 1. Hence
this tree can be viewed as horizontal, while the neural hierarchy
itself can be viewed as vertical and comprised of layers of horizontal classification trees. Nodal clusters within horizontal trees may
of course also be apical and basal clusters of pyramids that extend
to and from adjacent levels.

The functional properties of these connection structures depend critically on the <u>relative</u> strength of connections within them. It is
apparently not sufficient that specific connections be strengthened:
for networks to make reasonable decisions within the simulation
framework described, each link must be strengthened to a value that
satisfies from several dozen to several hundred constraints, and sets
of links within small or moderately-sized trees must satisfy on the
order of 10,000 constraints.

3. CONSTRAINTS ON PERMISSIBLE MODEL BEHAVIOR AND STRUCTURE

The behavior of any model must resemble, at least in key respects,
the behavior of the system that is modelled. Models can therefore be
viewed as subject to "behavioral constraints" that prohibit behaviors
not exhibited by the modelled system. Such constraints on model
behavior can be translated into constraints on structure if the relationship between model structure and behavior is clearly understood.

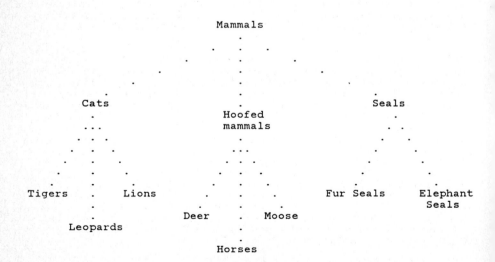

Figure 4
Illustration of the mammalian concept hierarchy discussed in the
text. This hierarchy is an example of what has elsewhere been called
a "specialization hierarchy" (Zeigler 1985, p. 185) or "Linnaean
hierarchy" (Buck, Hull 1966, Salthe 1985, p. 118).

Notice that in this view the same set of behavioral constraints
applies with equal force to all models of a particular aspect of any
system or subsystem, while structural constraints apply to each model
individually, in accordance with specific relationships between the
model's structure and behavior. In this section, behavioral constraints that (apparently) apply to all models of concept naming and
learning by simile are described and then translated into structural
constraints that apply only to neural net models of the kind discussed above. These constraints are described in some detail to
enable interested investigators to consider 1) whether any other models of these aspects of concept manipulation satisfy the behavioral
constraints and produce a response within one interval of processing,
2) whether any qualitatively different network models satisfy the
structural constraints, and 3) whether these two sets of constraints
are in fact generally valid or useful measures of model adequacy.

3.1 Constraints enabling learning by simile

Learning by simile is essentially the transfer of information from
one concept to another, a critically important capability for concept
construction and modification. As an example, consider the sentence
"The fish resembles a tiger." In most cases this statement causes a
tiger's stripes - but not whiskers - to be transferred to the mental
image of a fish. To transfer whiskers rather than stripes, a more-
inclusive ("superordinate") concept is necessary: a cat-like fish or
catfish has whiskers. And to transfer both stripes and whiskers, a
statement similar to "This catfish resembles a tiger" is required.

Both communication and internal mental speech would be confusing
indeed if use of "catfish" transferred not only whiskers but also the
eyes, ears, legs, fur, claws, tails, spots, stripes, colors and all
other attributes of cats, onto the mental image of a single fish.
Appropriate learning by simile thus requires that some attributes of
a concept be transferred and that other attributes not be transferred.

To achieve this specific transfer of attributes, the word "cat" must
be associated with whiskers more strongly than with other attributes
of cats or mammals, else the term "catfish" will not reliably call to
mind bewiskered fish; and "tiger" must be linked more strongly to
stripes than to whiskers or other attributes of cats and mammals.
(Learning by simile is of course much more complicated than described
here since cells representing concepts that "receive" transferred
information apparently help to select the information that is transferred (Winston 1979, Martin et al. 1984). This brief description is
sufficient for present purposes, however.)

For similes involving the twelve concepts within the mammalian hierarchy illustrated in Figure 4, links from cells representing each
concept name to those representing key attributes of the concept must
be stronger than links from cells representing that name to cells
representing any of the eleven other attributes, else non-key attributes will be transferred. Thus:

$$STR(\text{"Tiger"} \rightarrow \text{stripes}) > STR(\text{"Tiger"} \rightarrow \text{fur})$$

$$STR(\text{"Tiger"} \rightarrow \text{stripes}) > STR(\text{"Tiger"} \rightarrow \text{whiskers})$$

$$STR(\text{"Tiger"} \rightarrow \text{stripes}) > STR(\text{"Tiger"} \rightarrow \text{spots})$$

STR("Tiger" → stripes) > STR("Tiger" → antlers)

STR("Leopard" → spots) > STR("Leopard" → fur)

STR("Leopard" → spots) > STR("Leopard" → whiskers)

STR("Leopard" → spots) > STR("Leopard" → stripes) ...

Each of the above constraints can be read: The strength of connections from neurons triggered by Stimulus A to those triggered by
Stimulus B must be greater than the strength of connections from neurons triggered by Stimulus A to those triggered by Stimulus C. For
similes involving the twelve concepts under consideration, connections from neurons representing each concept label to those representing the single appropriate and eleven inappropriate attributes
considered, must conform to 12 x 11 or 132 constraints of this type.
Stimulus patterns corresponding to concept labels are indicated by
quotation marks; key attributes for the twelve concepts are listed in
Section 4.1; and simulation results are provided in Martin et al.
(1984).

3.2 Constraints required for novel examples of familiar categories to be named

Novel examples of familiar categories require use of superordinate
labels. For instance, a person who is only familiar with the animals in the mammalian hierarchy of Figure 4 should identify a black
panther as a "Cat" rather than as a "Tiger", "Leopard", "Lion" or
"Mammal", and should identify a kangaroo as a "Mammal" rather than
with any of the lower level names. The most appropriate response to
a novel creature is the name of the least-inclusive (lowest level)
category that includes the nearest relatives of the creature.

To simulate this type of response, connections that link neurons representing attributes shared by members of each category to those representing the name of the category must be stronger than connections
linking shared attributes to names corresponding to any other category. An additional 44 constraints (eleven for each of the attributes shared by members of four superordinate categories) are
required for this to be ensured.

3.3 Constraints required for groups to be correctly named

The ability to correctly label or name groups composed of examples of
related concepts requires a much larger set of constraints. This
ability can be illustrated as follows: a pride of lions may conveniently and appropriately be referred to as "Lions"; a group containing a lion, lynx, tiger, leopard and jaguar may conveniently and
properly be referred to by the more inclusive, superordinate label
"Cats"; and a group containing a wolf, leopard, beaver, horse, mouse
and fur seal can most easily be identified as "Mammals". Notice the
shift to more inclusive labels as the diversity of lower-level concepts increases.

For correct superordinate labels to be chosen, connections from
attributes of lower-level, subordinate concepts to superordinate
labels must be stronger than connections to each subordinate name
when groups contain approximately three or more different kinds of
animals, and must be weaker than connections to subordinate labels
when only one or two kinds of animals are present.

For example, if "Mammals" is to be selected as the correct name for a group containing tigers, leopards, deer, horses and elephant seals, then:

> STR(fur → "Mammals") + STR(whiskers → "Mammals") +
> STR(fins → "Mammals") + STR(hooves → "Mammals") +
> STR(spots → "Mammals") + STR(stripes → "Mammals") +
> STR(antlers → "Mammals") + STR(brush-like tail → "Mammals") +
> STR(brown → "Mammals") + STR(large proboscis → "Mammals")

> \>

> STR(fur → "Cats") + STR(whiskers → "Cats") +
> STR(fins → "Cats") + STR(hooves → "Cats") +
> STR(spots → "Cats") + STR(stripes → "Cats") +
> STR(antlers → "Cats") + STR(brush-like tail → "Cats") +
> STR(brown → "Cats") + STR(large proboscis → "Cats")

But if a group of tigers, lions and leopards is to be named "Cats" rather than "Mammals", then:

> STR(fur → "Cats") + STR(whiskers → "Cats") +
> STR(spots → "Cats") + STR(stripes → "Cats") +
> STR(brown → "Cats")

> \>

> STR(fur → "Mammals") + STR(whiskers → "Mammals") +
> STR(spots → "Mammals") + STR(stripes → "Mammals") +
> STR(brown → "Mammals")

Choosing appropriate names for groups of animals is complicated by the large number of possible combinations of animals. Even if groups that contain different numbers of animals but the same combination of species are treated as equivalent (i.e., 3 tigers, 2 deer and 5 horses are considered equivalent to 5 tigers, 6 deer and 2 horses because both groups contain tigers, deer and horses), there are still 256 different combinations of species that must be considered. (Since each of the eight species may or may not be represented in a group, 2^8 or 256 qualitatively different combinations of species are possible - and each combination must be evaluated by a different set of neurons and interconnections if an appropriate label for the group is to be selected. Omitting the single combination that includes <u>no</u> members of any species leaves 256 less 1 or 255 combinations to be considered.)

Because it is possible to have 255 different combinations of the eight mammals, and because connections corresponding to each must be subject to eleven constraints if the most appropriate of twelve available labels is to be selected, connections between neurons representing the eight mammals and twelve names under consideration must conform to 11 x 255 or 2,805 additional constraints.

Certain groups may appropriately be identified by combinations of low and high-level names. For example, a group consisting of 10 lions, 10 tigers, a horse, a deer, a wolf and a mouse may appropriately be labelled "lions, tigers and other mammals", and 3 lions, 3 tigers, 3 leopards, 3 jaguars and a horse, deer, wolf and mouse can be named "cats and other mammals." The additional constraints required for selection of appropriate combinations of subordinate and superordinate labels are noted but will not be considered further here.

3.4 Constraints that limit the severity of errors

The tendency to commit errors involving semantically related words suggests a strategy of limiting errors to "near misses". Mechanisms to limit the severity of errors will be useful if nearly-correct responses are, on average, more advantageous than responses that are completely off target.

The degree of error can be minimized relatively simply if connections linking the attributes of each concept to names of closely-related concepts are stronger than connections to names of more distantly-related concepts. For example, connections linking the attributes of a tiger with the name "Lion" must be stronger than connections linking the tiger's attributes with the name "Horse", and even stronger than connections to the label "Fish". And of course connections to the correct name ("Tiger") must be strongest of all.

In addition, there must be stronger links from tigers' attributes to the name "Tiger" than to "Cat" and stronger links to "Cat" than to "Mammal". And there must also be progressively weaker sets of links to increasingly inappropriate labels for groups of animals. For example, a group containing many different kinds of cats is most appropriately referred to as "Cats", somewhat less appropriately referred to as "Mammals", even less appropriately as "Tigers", and much less appropriately as "Seals" or "Fur Seals". For a collection of neurons to "prefer" the more appropriate names for this group, connections linking the features of each cat to names that are less appropriate must in the aggregate be weaker than corresponding connections to more appropriate names.

Because there are 255 possible combinations of the eight species; because each combination can be named either correctly, almost correctly, somewhat incorrectly or completely incorrectly; and because connections to each of the correct, somewhat less correct, slightly incorrect and completely incorrect names for each of the 255 groups are constrained to be either stronger or weaker than connections to the eleven other names; 255 x 3 x 11 or 8,415 additional constraints are needed, in this example, to ensure that semantic errors most frequently involve closely-related labels when groups are identified.

This view of constraints is almost too complex. Even for the very limited hierarchy considered, several hundred constraints limit the permissible value of each connection, and individual constraints apply to as many as twenty four connections. (For instance, if "Mammals" is a more appropriate label than "Cats" for a diverse group of animals, then connections from the twelve groups of neurons representing the key and shared features of mammals within this group to apical neurons initiating production of the word "Mammals" are constrained to be stronger, in the aggregate, than the twelve alternative connection paths leading to apical cells that initiate production of "Cats".)

It does not appear possible to readily comprehend or visualize the large number of constraints that must simultaneously be satisfied for learning by simile to occur correctly, for novel and familiar examples of familiar categories to be appropriately named, for groups containing members of several categories to be named, and for the severity of errors to be minimized when inappropriate names or labels are selected. How then can connection patterns that conform to every constraint be constructed and verified? The approach taken was to simulate neural interactions during learning and use the simulation program to generate possible sets of connection values.

4. SIMULATION METHODS AND RESULTS

Numerical values are first assigned to each of the essential components of a network, including the number of neurons, their initial firing rates, the number of neural connections, the number of bound and unbound neurotransmitters and receptors in each synapse, and the discharge frequency of each cell. When neurons fire, values corresponding to neurotransmitters are placed in an array representing all synapses. A value derived from the number of transmitter-receptor complexes in each synapse is then used to determine whether and at what rate other neurons subsequently discharge. When firing frequencies are recalculated, the new values are printed, a new set of transmitter values is added to those already in each synapse, and all calculations are repeated. This cycle of computation continues for the duration of the simulation. It is considered equivalent to one step or interval of communication because only a single value is transmitted from each cell to its neighbors.

At the end of each step or interval, bound and free transmitter values are decreased to simulate transmitter-receptor dissociation and reabsorbtion and degradation of unbound transmitter molecules. Stimulus input into the network is effected by addition of an arbitrary number of units to the firing rate of neurons triggered directly by external stimuli. And the strength of connections between neurons that fire, concurrently or not, is adjusted in accordance with the learning rules described above. Further details of the simulation procedures are provided in Martin et al. (1984) and Martin (1985a, 1986a).

4.1 Concept representation

To represent concepts within the mammalian hierarchy under consideration, a neural net was arbitrarily divided into 25 clusters or sets of neurons, with each set responding to the shared or key attributes or label of one of the concepts in the hierarchy. For example, cells triggered by stripes and the colors black and yellow (i.e. cells that recognize this combination of input) were placed within the set of cells representing the key features of tigers; while cells triggered by brown spots on a light background were placed within the set representing key features of leopards. These groups may conveniently be referred to by the most salient attribute represented by each, or by numbers:

Group no.	Key attribute	Group no.	Name
1	fur	13	Tiger
2	whiskers	14	Lion
3	stripes	15	Leopard
4	solid brown color	16	Horse
5	spots	17	Deer
6	hooves	18	Moose
7	long, brush-like tail	19	Fur Seals
8	sharply pointed antlers	20	Elephant Seals
9	rounded antlers	21	Kangaroos
10	flippers	22	Mammals
11	Thick fur	23	Cats
12	Enlarged proboscis	24	Hoofed mammals
		25	Seals

During simulations, cells that respond to the same stimulus were represented by a single neuron, as if sets of equivalent cells behave more or less like large, single neurons. By treating sets of equivalent neurons as single cells, a significant reduction - from many thousands to 625 - in the number of connections within the net was achieved. Constraints on permissible connection values were tallied after this reduction and thus reflect a much less complex analysis than would have been necessary if the network had not been simplified and reduced in size.

This network was then "informed" of the relationships between concepts by concurrent input of associated attributes and labels. For example, input to cells 1, 2, 3 and 13 enabled association of fur, whiskers, stripes and the label "Tiger" since connections between cells corresponding to these attributes and label were strengthened. Input to neurons 1, 2, 3 and 23; and then to 1, 2, 3 and 22 enabled a similar association of tigers' attributes with the labels "Cat" and "Mammal" as well. Labels from each level of the hierarchy were each paired with appropriate attributes approximately three times during this "training" so that one level of response to subsequent input would not overshadow others.

4.2 Testing the neural net

After training, a series of inputs was used to determine whether this neural net would correctly respond to a variety of inputs. Correct responses were selected in each case, demonstrating that the connection pattern within the network conforms in large part to the constraints described above. A formal proof that every constraint is actually satisfied has not been attempted however. Table I summarizes results that were obtained during a typical simulation.

4.3 Simulation of semantic errors

Production of semantic errors was simulated by altering the simulation program so that certain apical or basal clusters (representing either concept names or attributes) were unable to discharge. The probability of each semantically-related response was then calculated as the combined strength of connections from discharging, basal neurons to associated apical cells. Selection of the most intensely stimulated response was assumed.

Two types of results were obtained. 1) When discharge of apical cells capable of initiating the correct response was blocked, the next-most appropriate response was most likely to be chosen, and if the second-best response was also blocked, the third-best was most probable. For example, input of the attributes of a tiger (fur, whiskers, stripes) triggered most effectively the response "Cat" when "Tiger" was blocked, and the response "Mammal" when "Cat" was also blocked. Similarly, input to neurons corresponding to attributes of cats (fur and whiskers) resulted in the response "Mammal" when "Cat" was blocked, and to subordinate cat names when both "Cat" and "Mammal" were blocked. Thus damage to apical cells generally led to inappropriate use of semantically-related, superordinate names. Subordinate names were selected only as a last resort. 2) When discharge of cells triggered by the defining attributes of one or more animals was blocked, fourth-best and fifth-best responses involving subordinate names were more often selected. For example, input of the attributes of tigers resulted in the responses "Lions", "Leopards" and "Mammals" with equal frequency so that the two subordinate responses outnumbered this superordinate response by almost two to one. The model therefore suggests that the site of damage may influence the relative number of superordinate and subordinate responses made. In all cases, semantically related concepts were favored. Representative results are shown in Table II; Table III contains the connection values within the network that were formed during this simulation.

5. DISCUSSION

5.1 Alternative measures of processing time

When a multilayered network such as the brain processes continuous streams of input, it is possible to view all cognitive processes as requiring at least one processing interval for each cell layer traversed as input passes from sensory to motor regions of nervous system. These same cognitive processes can also be considered to require essentially no time if they are completed without delaying, even by one interval, the spread of activation from sensory to motor cells. The phrase "single-interval manipulation" reflects the intermediate view that the time needed can appropriately be considered to be the average number of intervals required for activation to pass from each layer to the next. But regardless of the measure one prefers, it is clear that learning networks of the type described can process information quite rapidly, with no additional time necessary when complex hierarchies are accessed, when information is transferred from one concept to another, or when alternative, semantically-related names are selected.

5.2 Key questions

While the neural model just described provides a general explanation for certain aspects of concept naming and production of semantic errors, a large number of questions remain unanswered. Among the most important are: 1) Have all 10,000 of the constraints actually been satisfied by connections formed within the net? How can this be proven generally? 2) Can these constraints be met by connection patterns that are qualitatively unlike those described here -- or is this basically the only approach that can succeed in networks similar to those formed by neurons? And how can this be determined? 3) Are there any other sets of learning rules that can satisfactorily guide construction of acceptable connection patterns? 4) What additional constraints must also be satisfied for concepts to be represented usefully? And 5) what other learning rules will be required to satisfy these additional constraints?

Acknowledgement

The author is very grateful to Stanley N. Salthe and Aaron Lukton for the years of patient advice and criticism they have given, to Roy, Evelyn and Lee Martin, John A. Evans, James Nishiura, Jay Hindle, Robert Dong, Kostas Piperis, Anthony Stergianopoulos and Anacletos T. Padua for their assistance while this paper was being prepared, and to the Chemistry Department and Computer Center at Brooklyn College for their support and computer facilities.

Table I: Firing rates during the mammalian concept hierarchy simulation. Comments indicated at the right refer to the explanatory footnotes on the following page.

```
                                     Stimulus for discharge

         Key visual attributes                           Auditory input

                          s
                          h    d
                     b    a    u
                     r    r    l                                             H
           w         u    p    l              p                         E    O
      h    s         u    p    l         t    r                         L    K      O
      i    t         h    s    a    a    h    r                    F    E    A    M O
      s    r    b    s    o    h    n    i    o         L           U    P    N    A F
      k    i    r    p    o    t    n    n    c         E    O    H M    R    H.   G M    D    S
      f    e    p    o    o    t    t    t    f    k  s T    O    H M    R    H.   G M    D    S
 f    u    r    w    t    e    v    a    l    l    i  f c G    I    P O    D    O    S S    C    M    E
 u    r    e    w    t    e    i    r    r    n    u  i E    O    A D    O    E    E A    A    M    A
 r    s    s    n    s    l    s    s    s    r    s  s R    N    R E    R    E    L L    S    S.   S    Comment

 87  87  87   0   0   0   0   0   0   0   0   0    0 87   0   0   0   0   0   0   0   0   0   0   0   0    a
 87  87   0  87   0   0   0   0   0   0   0   0    0  0  87   0   0   0   0   0   0   0   0   0   0   0    b
 87  87   0   0  87   0   0   0   0   0   0   0    0  0   0  87   0   0   0   0   0   0   0   0   0   0
 87   0   0   0   0  87  87   0   0   0   0   0    0  0   0   0  87   0   0   0   0   0   0   0   0   0
 87   0   0   0   0  87   0  87   0   0   0   0    0  0   0   0   0  87   0   0   0   0   0   0   0   0
 87   0   0   0   0  87   0   0  87   0   0   0    0  0   0   0   0   0  87   0   0   0   0   0   0   0
 87   0   0   0   0   0   0   0   0  87  87   0    0  0   0   0   0   0   0  87   0   0   0   0   0   0
 87   0   0   0   0   0   0   0   0  87   0  87    0  0   0   0   0   0   0   0  87   0   0   0   0   0    c
 87   0   0   0   0   0   0   0   0  87  87   0    0  0   0   0   0   0   0   0   0   0   0   0   0  87
 87   0   0   0   0   0   0   0   0  87   0  87    0  0   0   0   0   0   0   0   0   0   0   0   0  87
 87   0   0   0   0  87  87   0   0   0   0   0    0  0   0   0   0   0   0   0   0   0   0  87   0
 87   0   0   0   0  87   0  87   0   0   0   0    0  0   0   0   0   0   0   0   0   0   0  87   0
 87   0   0   0   0  87   0   0  87   0   0   0    0  0   0   0   0   0   0   0   0   0   0  87   0
 87  87  87   0   0   0   0   0   0   0   0   0    0  0   0   0   0   0   0   0   0  87   0   0   0    d
 87  87   0  87   0   0   0   0   0   0   0   0    0  0   0   0   0   0   0   0   0  87   0   0   0
 87  87   0   0  87   0   0   0   0   0   0   0    0  0   0   0   0   0   0   0   0  87   0   0   0
 87   0   0   0   0  87  87   0   0   0   0   0    0  0   0   0   0   0   0   0   0  87   0   0   0
 87   0   0   0   0   0   0   0   0  87  87   0    0  0   0   0   0   0   0   0   0  87   0   0   0


  0   0   0   0   0   0   0   0   0   0   0   0    0 87   0   0   0   0   0   0   0   0   0   0   0   0    e
  6  12  24   0   0   0   0   0   0   0   0   0    0  0   0   0   0   0   0   0   0   0   0   0   0   0
  0   0   0   0   0   0   0   0   0   0   0   0    0  0   0  87   0   0   0   0   0   0   0   0   0   0
  6   0   0   0   0  12  24   0   0   0   0   0    0  0   0   0   0   0   0   0   0   0   0   0   0   0
  0   0   0   0   0   0   0   0   0   0   0   0    0  0   0   0   0   0   0   0   0  87   0   0   0   0
 12   0   0   0   0   0   2   0   0   6   6   0    0  0   0   0   0   0   0   0   0   0   0   0   0   0
  0   0   0   0   0   0   0   0   0   0   0   0    0  0   0   0   0   0   0   0   0   0  87   0   0   0
 12  24   0   2   6   0   0   0   0   0   0   0    0  0   0   0   0   0   0   0   0   0   0   0   0   0
 87  87  87   0   0   0   0   0   0   0   0   0    0  0   0   0   0   0   0   0   0   0   0   0   0   0    f
  0   0   0   0  48   2   0   0   2  12  12   0   48  0   2   0   0   0   0   0   0   0  12  24   2   0
 87  87  87  87   0   0   0   0   0   0   0   0    0  0   0   0   0   0   0   0   0   0   0   0   0   0
  0   0   0   0  48   2   0   0   2  12  12   0   48 48   2   0   0   0   0   0   0   0  12  24   2   0
 87  87  87  87  87   0   0   0   0   0   0   0    0  0   0   0   0   0   0   0   0   0   0   0   0   0
  0   0   0   0   0   0   0   0   4   4   0  16   16  8   0   0   0   0   0   0   0   4  64   0   0   0    g
 87   0   0   0   0  87  87  87  87   0   0   0    0  0   0   0   0   0   0   0   0   0   0   0   0   0
  0   0   0   0   0   0   0   0   2   2   0   0    0  8   8   4   0   0   0   0   2   0  64   0
 87  87  87  87   0  87  87  87   0  87  87   0    0  0   0   0   0   0   0   0   0   0   0   0   0   0
  0   0   0   0   2   0   0   0   4   0   0   0    2  2   0   2   2   0   0   0   0  68   0   2   0    h
 87   0   0   0   0   0   0   0   0   0   0   0    0  0   0   0   0   0   0   0   0   0   0   0   0   0
  0   0   0   0   0   2   0   0   2  12  12   0    0  0   0   0   0   0   0   0   0   6   0   2   0    i
 87  87   0   0   0   0   0   0   0   0   0   0    0  0   0   0   0   0   0   0   0   0   0   0   0   0
  0   0   0   0  48   2   0   0   2  12  12   0    0  2   0   0   0   0   0   0   0   6  12   2   0    j
 87   0   0   0   0  87   0   0   0   0   0   0    0  0   0   0   0   0   0   0   0   0   0   0   0   0
  0   0   0   0   0   0   0   0  48   6   6   0    0  0   0   0   0   0   0   0   0   2   0  12   0
```
(Left margin labels: Training — rows of the upper block; Testing — rows of the lower block.)

Comments to Table I:

a) Each horizontal row of numbers indicates firing activity during a
particular computation cycle or time interval. Each number represents the average firing rate of a cluster of attribute-level neurons
during one time interval, or the probability that any single cell
within that cluster is firing. External input during the first time
interval (indicated by firing rates of '87') triggered neuron sets 1,
2, 3 and 13, which correspond to fur, whiskers, stripes and the label
"Tiger". This firing pattern signifies that the network was "presented" with a tiger and (concurrently) informed that an appropriate
label for this animal is "Tiger".

b) Input in this row corresponds to similar information about lions.
Transmitter levels were reset to zero between each training interval,
as if a period of time had elapsed.

c) Information entered during this and all previous computation
cycles was entered twice more - once in reverse order and again in
forward order - so that each label was used from three to five times.

d) Information about five mammals was entered, along with the label
"Mammal".

e) The label "Tiger" was entered here to elicit a response from the
net. The response, which is indicated on the following line, was
primarily by the neuron group corresponding to stripes, the salient
feature of tigers. Note that this and all other responses were produced one time interval after stimulus input.

f) Information about a tiger was input, so that neuron groups representing the attributes of tigers fired. Cells corresponding to the
name "Tiger" were subsequently triggered more strongly than neurons
corresponding to any other name.

g) After input of information about three different cats, the
response is clearly dominated by neurons representing "Cats", a
superordinate label, rather than those corresponding to any other
name.

h) After input of information about two cats, two hoofed mammals and
a seal, the response is appropriately dominated by neurons corresponding to the label "Mammals". Notice that this response was
selected after one interval even though "Mammals" is at the "top" of
a multilevel hierarchy, as if the hierarchy is horizontal.

i) In response to fur, and no other attribute, the label most
strongly activated is, once again, "Mammals".

j) And in response to fur, whiskers and the color black (corresponding to a black panther) the dominant response among labels is, appropriately, "Cat". None of the neuron groups included in this simulation is triggered by black, so only groups triggered by fur and
whiskers discharge in response to information about this panther.

TABLE II: Simulation results indicating the probability of semantic errors involving each concept.   Note   that correct reponses are the most probable and that the likelihood or "priority" of each incorrect response reflects its semantic distance from the correct response. For example, the attributes of a tiger are most likely to elicit, in order of probability, "Tiger", "Cat", "Mammal", "Leopard", "Lion" and finally the names of even less-closely related mammals. Values following each selection indicate the actual summed strengths of connections triggering neurons corresponding to each label, reduced by a factor of three for convenience.   Comments indicated within the table clarify certain aspects of the response pattern.

INPUT TO NEURONS CORRESPONDING TO:

	Fur, whiskers and stripes	Fur, flippers and heavy fur	Attributes of three cats	Attributes of a tiger, horse and fur seal	Attributes of all eight mammals
First choice:	Tiger (a)(51)	Fur Seal (56)	Cats (f)(77)	Mammals (78)	Mammals (107)
Second choice:	Cat (b)(43)	Mammal(d)(51)	Lion (g,h)(56)	Fur Seal (60)	Hoofed Mammals (87)
Third choice:	Mammal (30)	Elephant Seal (35)	Leopard (55)	Horse (57)	Cats (85)
Fourth choice:	Leopard (28)	Seal (24)	Tiger (55)	Tiger (55)	Elephant Seal (76)
Fifth choice:	Lion (26)	Hoofed Mammal (16)	Mammal (47)	Hoofed Mammals (48)	Fur Seal (70)
Sixth choice:	Hoofed Mammal (16)	Cat (14)	Hoofed Mammals (19)	Cats (46)	Deer (69)
Seventh choice:	Elephant Seal (13)	Moose (e)(11)	Elephant Seal (17)	Elephant Seal (39)	Moose (68)
Eigth choice:	Fur Seal (12)	Deer (10)	Fur Seal (15)	Moose (35)	Horse (67)
Ninth choice:	Moose (11)	Horse (9)	Moose (14)	Deer (32)	Lion (67)
Tenth choice:	Deer (9)	Leopard (9)	Deer (13)	Leopard (32)	Leopard (65)
Eleventh choice:	Horse (9)	Lion (8)	Horse (12)	Lion (30)	Tiger (65)
Twelfth choice:	Seal (c)(2)	Tiger (8)	Seals (6)	Seals (28)	Seals (54)

(left margin, vertical: RESPONSE PRIORITY)

Comments to Table II:

a) Notice that the correct response is assigned the highest priority in each case and is therefore more likely to be selected than any single, incorrect response. Initial evidence suggesting that correct responses are generally the most probable, for three types of aphasia patients, has been reported by Ostergaard (1984) and Howard et al. (1984).

b) Responses of the second through twelfth priority are of course not usually taken and most often will not even be accompanied by awareness. Thus the majority of entries in this table suggest a possible view of unconscious neural activity, rather than of conscious reasoning or decision-making.

c) The response "Seal" receives the lowest rating in all but one of these examples because neurons capable of initiating this response were not discharged during the second half of training, when training with subordinate labels was twice repeated (cf. comment (c) of Table I). Many of the connections triggering "Seal" were thus weakened (according to the third and fourth "learning" rules) so that the likelihood of sufficient stimulation reaching neurons representing "Seal" was reduced. Aphasic patients are also less likely to select or recognize words they have not used frequently (Wepman et al. 1956, Newcombe et al. 1964, Howard et al. 1984).

d) The seal category contains only two members and thus has not been fully "recognized" by the net. As a result, the second most likely response to the attributes of a fur seal may be either "Seal" or "Mammal", according to whether a fur seal was identified most recently as a "Mammal" or "Seal" during training. If a fur seal had more recently been identified as a "Seal", then "Seal" would have been the second most likely response instead of "Mammal". The tendency to select recently used labels is a potentially useful side-effect of the learning rules used that inevitably influences the selection of alternative responses when categories contain relatively few members.

e) Notice in this column that responses assigned the six lowest priority ratings (from "Moose" on down to "Tiger") are listed here in the reverse order of their occurrence during training. Connections leading to cells that represent recently used labels are somewhat stronger so these labels receive slightly higher priority ratings.

f) There is no mechanism at the present time to distinguish singular and plural labels.

g) Note that subordinate names are chosen here, rather than the label "Mammal", as if the net has decided instead to list the names of each cat. "Mammal" is consequently rated as the fifth-best response rather than second-best.

h) In this set of responses there appears to be a tendency to list individual members of the group when information about three animals is input. In contrast, superordinate labels are the second and third choices in the column at the right, when information about eight animals is input. This seems "natural" since superordinate labels that correctly describe the group require less effort to produce than the eight subordinate labels.

Table III: Conductivity values formed within the network. Concurrent firing of these neuron clusters, as outlined above, resulted in the following conductivity values for connections between each cluster and the others. Each row of values indicates the degree to which firing within one cluster stimulates the others to discharge. At least two types of connection structures are embedded within this set of conductivity values: "associative pyramids" of the kind discussed in Section 2, and a "tree" of strengthened connections corresponding to Figure 3.

Stimulus for discharge and postsynaptic group no.

```
        Key visual attributes                              Auditory input

                              s
                              h  d
                           b  a  u
                           r  r  l              p
              w            u  p  l           t  r
              h  s         p  l  h  o               L                  E                 H
              i  t      h  s  a  a  i  b            E           F  E  A  M  L  K           O
              s  r  b  s  o  h  n  n  c  o  T    L  O  H        U  P  N  A  H. G           O  F
              k  i  r  p  o  t  t  t  f  k  s  I  L  P  O  D  O  S  S  A  M  R. S  A  M  C  M  E
           f  e  p  o  o  v  a  l  l  i  f  c  G  I  A  R  E  O  E  E  R  A  A  M        D  S
           u  r  e  w  t  e  i  r  r  n  u  i  E  O  R  S  E  S  A  A  O  L  T  L  L
           r  s  s  n  s  s  l  s  s  s  r  s  R  N  D  E  R  E  L  L  O  S  S  S. S

           1  2  3  4  5  6  7  8  9 10 11 12 13 14 15 16 17 18 19 20 21 22 23 24 25
```

Presynaptic group no.

#	1	2	3	4	5	6	7	8	9	10	11	12	13	14	15	16	17	18	19	20	21	22	23	24	25
1	99	56	17	20	49	70	22	25	59	79	67	35	17	18	20	21	23	27	30	35	0	51	39	44	1
2	56	99	55	62	86	0	0	0	0	0	0	0	51	55	58	0	0	0	0	0	0	20	66	0	0
3	17	55	97	4	3	0	4	5	3	0	4	4	86	6	6	6	6	6	6	6	11	21	25	5	6
4	20	62	4	97	3	0	4	3	3	0	4	4	6	86	6	6	6	6	6	6	11	27	36	5	6
5	49	86	3	3	98	0	3	4	2	0	3	3	5	5	75	5	5	5	5	5	9	23	66	4	5
6	70	0	0	0	0	99	56	60	87	0	0	0	0	0	0	52	55	59	0	0	0	18	0	67	0
7	22	0	4	4	3	56	97	5	3	0	4	4	6	6	86	6	6	6	6	6	11	23	5	25	6
8	25	0	5	5	4	60	5	95	4	0	5	5	7	7	7	88	7	7	7	7	13	4	6	36	7
9	59	0	3	3	2	87	3	4	98	0	3	3	5	5	5	5	75	5	5	5	9	30	4	66	5
10	79	0	0	0	0	0	0	0	0	99	88	74	1	1	1	1	1	1	62	66	4	50	0	0	43
11	67	0	4	4	3	0	4	5	3	88	97	4	6	6	6	6	6	6	77	6	11	52	5	5	29
12	35	0	4	4	3	0	4	5	3	74	4	97	6	6	6	6	6	6	6	86	11	3	5	5	60
13	17	51	86	6	5	0	6	7	5	1	6	6	90	9	9	9	9	9	9	9	15	5	7	7	9
14	18	55	6	86	5	0	6	7	5	1	6	6	9	90	9	9	9	9	9	9	15	5	7	7	9
15	20	58	6	6	75	0	6	7	5	1	6	6	9	9	90	9	9	9	9	9	15	5	7	7	9
16	21	0	6	6	5	52	86	7	5	1	6	6	9	9	9	90	9	9	9	9	15	5	7	7	9
17	23	0	6	6	5	69	0	88	5	1	6	6	9	9	9	9	90	9	9	9	15	5	7	7	9
18	27	0	6	6	5	59	0	7	75	1	6	6	9	9	9	9	9	90	9	9	15	5	7	7	9
19	30	0	6	6	5	0	6	7	5	62	77	6	9	9	9	9	9	9	90	9	15	5	7	7	9
20	35	0	6	6	5	0	6	7	5	66	6	86	9	9	9	9	9	9	9	90	15	5	7	7	9
21	0	0	11	11	9	0	11	13	9	4	11	11	15	15	15	15	15	15	15	15	25	0	0	0	0
22	51	20	21	27	23	18	23	4	30	50	52	3	5	5	5	5	5	5	5	5	9	98	4	4	5
23	39	66	25	36	66	0	5	6	4	0	5	5	7	7	7	7	7	7	7	7	13	4	95	6	7
24	44	0	5	5	4	67	25	36	66	0	5	5	7	7	7	7	7	7	7	7	13	4	6	95	7
25	1	0	6	6	5	0	6	7	5	43	29	60	9	9	9	9	9	9	9	9	15	5	7	7	90

REFERENCES

Amari, S.I. (1977). Neural theory of association and concept-forma-
    tion. Biol. Cybernetics, Vol. 26, pp. 175-285.

Anderson, J.A. (1983). Cognitive and psychological computation
    with neural models, IEEE Trans. SMC, Vol. 13(5), pp. 799-815.

Anderson, J.A., Silverstein, J.W., Ritz, S.A. and R.S. Jones (1977).
    Distinctive features, categorical perception, and probability
    learning: some applications of a neural model, Psych. Rev.,
    Vol. 84(5), pp. 413-451.

Buck, R.C. and D.L. Hull (1966). The logical structure of the
    Linnaean Hierarchy, Syst. Zool., Vol. 15, pp. 97-111.

Cooper, L.N. (1974). A possible organization of animal memory and
    learning. In: Proc. Nobel Symp. on Collective Properties of
    Physical Systems, Lundquist, B. and S. Lundquist (eds.),
    Academic Press, New York, pp. 252-264.

Fukushima, K. (1973). A model of associative memory in the brain,
    Kybernetik, Vol. 12, pp. 58-63.

Fukushima, K. Miyake S. and T. Ito (1983). Neocognitron: a neural
    network model for a mechanism of visual pattern recognition,
    IEEE Trans. SMC, Vol. 13(5), pp. 826-834.

Gardner-Medwin, A.R. (1976). The recall of events through the
    learning of associations between their parts, Proc. R. Soc.
    Lond. B, Vol. 194, pp. 375-402.

Hampton, S. and D. Kibler (1983). A boolean complete neural model
    of adaptive behavior, Biol. Cybernetics, Vol. 49, pp. 9-19.

Hebb, D.O. (1949). The Organization of Behavior, Wiley & Sons,
    New York, 335 p.

Hinton, G.E. and J.A. Anderson (1981). Parallel Models of
    Associative Memory, Erlbaum, Hillsdale, New Jersey, 295 p.

Howard, D., Patterson, K., Franklin, S., Morton, J. and V. Orchard-
    Lisle (1984). Variability and consistency in picture naming
    by aphasic patients, Adv. Neurol. 42, pp. 263-276.

Kohonen, T. (1982). Self organized formation of topologically
    correct feature maps, Biol. Cybernetics, Vol. 43, pp. 59-69.

Martin, R. (1985a). Assessment of proportions: an efficient method
    for single neuron recognition of letters, numbers, faces and
    certain types of concepts. In: Artificial Intelligence and
    Simulation, W.M. Holmes (ed.). Society for Computer Simulation,
    San Diego, pp. 52-57.

Martin, R. (1985b). Evaluation and sorting of multicomponent
    descriptions, in one interval or in constant time, by simple
    neural nets. In: 1985 Summer Computer Simulation Conference
    Proceedings., Society for Computer Simulation, San Diego,
    pp. 696-701.

Martin, R. (1986a). A neural approach to concept representation suggests explanations for certain aspects of aphasia, alexia and agraphia. In: The International Journal of Mathematical Modelling, special issue on disease, M. Witten (ed.), in press.

Martin, R. (1986b). An initial framework for simulations of discontinuous recall and concept inference in multilayered nerve networks. The 1986 SCS Multiconference Proceedings, forthcoming.

Martin, R. (1986c). A preliminary network model of neural mechanisms for sentence production. Proceedings of the 1986 Eastern Simulation Conference, forthcoming.

Martin, R., Lukton, A. and S.N. Salthe (1984). Simulation of simple cognitive maps, concept hierarchies, learning by simile, and similarity assessment in homogeneous neural nets. 1984 Summer Computer Simulation Conference Proceedings. Society for Computer Simulation, San Diego, vol. 2, pp. 808-821.

McClelland, J.L. and D.E. Rumelhart (1982). An interactive model of context effects in letter perception: part 2. The context ual enhancement effect and some tests and extensions of the model. Psychol. Rev., Vol. 89, pp. 60-94.

Minsky, M. (1979). The Society Theory of Thinking. In: Artificial Intelligence: an MIT Perspective, P.H. Winston and R.H. Brown (eds.), MIT Press, Cambridge, MA), vol. I, pp. 421-450.

Nagano, T. and K. Kurata (1981). A self organizing neural network model for the development of complex cells, Biol. Cybernetics, Vol. 40, pp. 195-200.

Nakano, K. (1972). Associatron: a model of associative memory, IEEE Trans. SMC, Vol. 2(3), pp. 380-388.

Newcombe, F. and J.C. Marshall (1984). Task- and modality-specific aphasias, Adv. Neurol. 42, pp. 139-144.

Ostergaard, A.L. (1984). The effect of sentence boundaries upon aphasic patients' immediate memmory for connected speech, Cortex 20, pp. 591-597.

Salthe, S.N. (1985). Evolving Hierarchical Systems, Columbia Univ. Press, New York, 343 p.

Takeuchi, A. and S. Amari (1979). Formation of topographic maps and and columnar microstructures in nerve fields, Biol. Cybernetics, Vol. 35, pp. 63-72.

Wepman, J.M., Bock, R.D., Jones, L. and D. Van Pelt (1956). Psycholinguistic study of aphasia: a revision of the concept of anomia, Speech Hear. Dis. 21, pp. 468-477.

Winston, P.H. (1979). Learning by creating and justifying transfer frames. In: Artificial Intelligence: an MIT Perspective. Winston, P.H. and R.H. Brown (eds.), MIT Press, Cambridge, Massachusetts, vol. I, pp. 347-374.

Zeigler, B.P. (1984). Multifacetted Modelling and Discrete Event Simulation. Academic Press, New York, 372 p.

SECTION V
ARTIFICIAL INTELLIGENCE
IN
SIMULATION QUALITY ASSURANCE

Modelling and Simulation Methodology
in the Artificial Intelligence Era
M.S. Elzas, T.I. Ören and B.P. Zeigler (Editors)
© Elsevier Science Publishers B.V. (North-Holland), 1986

Chapter V.1

ARTIFICIAL INTELLIGENCE IN QUALITY ASSURANCE OF SIMULATION STUDIES

Tuncer I. Ören
Computer Science Department
University of Ottawa
Ottawa, Ontario, Canada

The highlights of three types of quality assurance problems in simulation are given. They are: 1) Quality assurance in cognizant simulation, i.e., where simulation environment and/or simulation system have cognitive abilities. 2) Cognizant quality assurance which consists of either enhancement of quality assurance operations via cognizant techniques or assurance of quality via cognizant techniques.

1. COGNIZANT SYSTEMS

Artificial intelligence systems can better be called cognizant systems. A cognizant system is a computer or computer embedded system which has cognitive abilities such as: 1) knowledge-processing abilities including acquisition, learning, reasoning, and dissemination of knowledge, 2) asking and answering questions, 3) explanation including explanation of the trace of its own knowledge processing, 4) goal-setting, 5) adapting to new situations, 6) improving performance, 7) monitoring itself, its environment and its user for 7a) knowledge acquisition and learning, 7b) adaptation, and 7c) improving performance (its own performance or the performance of the system being monitored).

The concept of "computer embedded system" is suggested in Ören (1986b, c) as a generalization of knowledge processing system. A taxonomy of machine learning and its implications in simulation are given in Ören 1986c. Artificial intelligence in simulation is covered in Ören 1984, Birtwistle 1985, Holmes 1985, Zeigler 1985, Elzas et al. 1986, Kerckhoffs and Vansteenkiste 1986, and Luker and Adelsberger 1986.

Basically one has artificial intelligence applications in modelling, model referencing, model processing, specifications of experimental conditions and parameter values as well as behavior generation and behavior processing. Cognizant simulation models may allow goal directed modification of model structure during a simulation study. Logic modelling is yet another application of artificial intelligence techniques to generate state or output trajectories of a model. Cognizant simulation environments can be used to specify models, parameters, experimental and run control conditions, as well as to monitor simulation process and enhance and/or assure quality. Furthermore, several knowledge bases which may exist in an advanced simulation environment (Ören 1986a) may be updated as a result of machine learning (Ören 1986c) to provide knowledge-rich environments for specification and execution of simulations.

2. QUALITY ASSURANCE PROBLEMS IN SIMULATION

Quality assurance of an element of a simulation study is assessment of its characteristics to certify its acceptability or to recommend ways and means for its improvement or to recommend its rejection. An element of a simulation study is either an object in a simulation study (such as a model or a parameter set) or an activity (such as modelling or spe cification of experimental conditions) leading to a simulation object.

An extensive bibliography prepared by Balci and Sargent (1980) provides a good source of knowledge in the field. Two systematizations of the quality assurance issues are given in Ören 1981 and 1984. A systematization of the assessments needed in complex social sys- tems, including ethical assessments, are given in Ören 1983. A list of definitions of the most common concepts of simulation quality assurance is provided in Ören et al. 1985 In this article important research directions are highlighted.

Quality assurance problem in simulation has a multitude of aspects (Ören 1981). There-fore, simulation of complex systems require consideration and scrutiny of elementary quality assurance activities.

As given in Ören 1984 (p. 482) quality assessment studies fall under two major categories as follows:

- descriptive assessment
    - syntactic assessment
    - morphological assessment
    - semantic assessment
- normative assessment
    - pragmatic assessment
    - ethical assessment.

Descriptive assessment of an element of a simulation study is its evaluation with respect to the value free rules used to represent it. It consists of syntactic, morphological, and seman- tic assessments.

Syntactic assessment of an element of a simulation study is its evaluation with respect to the rules of representing the symbols or the expressions constructed from these symbols.

Morphological assessment of an element of a simulation study is its evaluation with respect to norms to represent relevant forms and structures. Both problem-dependent and methdology-based elements can be subject to scrutiny of morphological assessment.

Semantic assessment of an element of a simulation study is its evaluation of the meaning attached to it.

Normative assessment of an element of a simulation study is its evaluation with respect to some norms of a value system which can be pragmatic or ethical.

Pragmatic assessment of an element of a simulation study is its evaluation with respect to practical results such as implementability, useability, usefulness, clarity, comprehension, sensitivity, or cost effectiveness.

Ethical assessment of an element of a simulation study is its evaluation with respect to a set of moral codes.

A systematization of quality assurance problem in simulation can be developed by considering two sets: 1) the set of criteria with respect to which assessments have to be done and 2) the set of elements of simulation.

One can then consider a matrix where the elements of simulation may have a corresponding line and each of the criteria a corresponding column. Some of the elements will correspond to assessment of an element with respect to a criteria (Ören 1981). The number of assessment possibilities is rather high. As an example, Figure 1 provides a list of assessments available for models only (Ören 1984). The set of criteria to be used in assessment is given in Figure 2.

3. THE ELEMENTS OF A SIMULATION STUDY

The basic activities of simulation and related quality assurance issues are summarized in Figure 3. The objects of simulation can be conceived as problem independent and problem dependent. The elements of both of the categories have to be quality assured. Figures 4 and 5 provide problem independent and problem dependent objects of the simulation study.

4. QUALITY ASSURANCE IN COGNIZANT SIMULATION

Cognizant simulation is a simulation where the modelling simulation environment and/or the simulation system have cognitive abilities such as perception, interpretation, reasoning, explanation goal-setting, or learning (Ören 1986c). Cognizant simulation creates additional needs for quality assurance. Some of the fundamental issues are related to knowledge bases of the modelling and simulation studies (Ören 1986a).

In a learning simulation system or learning simulation environment, one or more knowledge bases are updated to reflect the learning process of the system. Everytime there is learning in a knowledge base, integrity and consistency of the knowledge base need to be assured via relevant syntactic and semantic checks. Since we are at the very beginning of

model acceptability
model accuracy
model accuracy, range of
model adequacy
model aggregation, assessment of
model analysis
model analysis, descriptive
model analysis, evaluative
model analysis, spectral
model applicability, scope of
model appropriateness
model assessment
model calibration
model certification
model characterization
model coarseness analysis
model comparison
model comparison, behavioral
model comparison, structural
model comprehensibility
model consistency
model controllability
model credibility
model documentation
model equivalencing
model fitting
model homomorphism
model identification
model integrity
model isomorphism
model modifiability
model morphism
model plausibility
model qualification
model realism
model referability
model relevance
model robustness
model sensitivity analysis
model simplification assessment
model stability

Figure 1.   Assessment possibilities of simulation models (continued)

model testing
model testing with respect to technical specifications
model tracing
model Turing test
model understandability
model useability
model usefulness
model utility
model validation
model validity
model validity, behavioral
model validity, historical
model validity, internal
model validity, replicative
model validity, statistical
model validity, structural
model ventilation
model veracity
model verification
model verisimilitude

Figure 1. Assessment possibilities of simulation models (continuation)

- Goal of the study
- Conceptual aspects of the study
    - Conceptual experiments
    - Conceptual models
    - Conceptual parameters
- Real system
- Behavior
    - Real system behavior
    - Model behavior
- Simulation program
    - Components
        - Simulation experiment
        - Simulation model
        - Simulation parameters
    - Overall code
- Norms of
    - Experimental design and data analysis
    - Simulation methodology
        - Modelling formalism
        - Behavior generation (simulation technique)
    - Software engineering

Figure 2. Criteria to be used for quality assurance of simulation

Activities:	Quality Assurance:
- Instrumentation	- Instrumentation adequacy
- Specification of experimental conditions	- Qualification of experimental conditions
- Modelling	- Model realism

- Parameter
  - identification
  - fitting
  - calibration
	- Adequacy of parametrization

- Computerization of
  - experimental conditions
 	
  - models
 	
  - parameters
	
	- Verification of experimental conditions
	- Model verification
	- Structural model validity
	- Parameter verification

- Program synthesis	- Program testing - Program benchmarking

- Simulation
  (i.e., behavior generation)
  - same model
  (different conditions)
  - different models
  (same conditions)
	
	- Sensitivity
	  of model behavior
	- Behavioral comparison
	  of models
	- Benchmarking

Figure 3. Simulation activities and related quality assurance issues

- Simulation environment
    (for computer-aided - specifications of a study,
                            - synthesis/compilation of programs
                            - running a simulation,
                            - knowledge-base management)

    - Experimentation environment
        - Experimentation specification advisor and certifier
        - Experimentation base and its manager

    - Modelling environment
        - Modelling advisor and certifier
        - Model base and its manager

    - Parameter environment
        - Parameter specification advisor and certifier
        - Parameter base and its manager

    - Programming environment
        - Program synthesizer/translator/compiler
        - Program base and its manager

    - Interactive environment
        - Dialog facilities
        - Utilities

- Methodology/technique selected/used
    - Experimental design technique

    - Simulation methodology
        - Modelling formalism
        - Behavior generation technique

    - Behavior processing technique
        (statistical/analytical compression of behavior)

    - Software engineering technique

- Norms of
    - Design of experiments
    - Simulation methodology
        - Modelling formalism
        - Behavior generation technique
    - Behavior processing
    - Software engineering

Figure 4.   Problem-independent objects of a simulation study

- Goal of the study

- System under consideration
    - Real system   (for analysis problems)
    - Object system   (for control systems)
    - Target system   (for design problems)

- System behavior
        (collected under or specified for specific conditions)

- Model behavior

- Conceptual aspects of the study
        (one or more aspects)
    - Conceptual experiments
    - Conceptual models
    - Conceptual parameters

- Simulation program(s)
        (representation(s) and execution(s))
    - Simulation experiments
    - Simulation models
    - Simulation parameters

Figure 5.   Problem-dependent objects of a simulation study

learning simulations, the problem will be better realized when we face practical situations (which might be catastrophies so far as knowledge processing is concerned). Until the im plications of the problem are well understood and solutions are embedded in such systems knowledge bases should not be used unmonitored.

In a rule-based simulation system, the rule base requires special attention. Due to the na ture of logical programming, the inference engine can function and generate answers even in the absence of a rule or if another rule is added to the original rule base. Rule-based systems are therefore open to a very easy way of degradation. One needs to have automated consistency checks of the rule base after every change of the rules. One pos sibility is to develop logical programming languages with declarative abilities, i.e., strongly typed logical programming languages. In such a case, one can declare all logical variables with their range of acceptable values. Then, the rules can be checked to assure whether or not each logical value has been used consistently.

To assure quality in an autonomous simulating system, a cognizant module can be provi ded to monitor either 1) run-time activites such as checking values of some variables with respect to threshold values or 2) intra-run activities where run-time monitoring activity the knowledge acquired from previous runs or studies can also be used.

5. COGNIZANT QUALITY ASSURANCE

Cognizant quality assurance (cqa) is a short form to refer to application of cognizant tech niques to quality assurance problems. There are two approaches to the problem: 1) en hancement of quality assurance operations via cognizant techniques, 2) assurance of qual ity via cognizant techniques.

5.1 Enhancement of Quality Assurance Operations via Cognizant Techniques

A category of activities which can be applied to a large number of quality assurance opera tions is using logical programming or rule-based programming for their realization.

A fundamental similarity of rule-based programming and procedural programming in a well structured language is that there are rules in both of them. In a procedural program ming environment the sequence of rules is fixed in advance by the programmer. In a rule-based programming, the inference engine has to find first the order in which the rules have to be applied and then has to apply them. A rule-based programming of qual ity assurance operations helps build an explicit knowledge base, i.e., a rule base for such operations. Such a rule base has definite superiority of being easily updateable.

Another important category of applications is embedding learning abilities in quality assu rance operators and use dynamically enhanceable knowlege bases which will hold knowl edge or knowledge-processing knowledge relevant to quality assurance operations.

5.2 Assurance of Quality via Built-in Cognizant Techniques

Built-in cognizant quality assurance is an important shift of paradigm in assurance of quality. The gist of the matter is that cognizant techniques can be used to guide the user in specification or realization phase of activities or elements of simulation to eliminate some types of errors, rather than having additional techniques (including cognizant ones) to check the existence of cases which need to be improved or certified as quality assured.

For example, specification of input/output interface of model modules, i.e., their coupling specification, can benefit from this type of assurance of quality. A knowledge based system can assure completeness and compatibility of all connections and eliminate the need for any further checks to assure the quality of the specifications. This approach has been taken in Magest (Ören 1986d).

User-friendly explanation ability provided by cognizant techniques makes it easy to handle the detected errors in the user specifications. The system can either explain the errors and or can suggest alternatives to correct them.

REFERENCES

Balcı, O. and R.G. Sargent (1984). Bibliography on Validation of simulation models, ACM Simuletter, Vol. 15, Nr. 3, July 1984, pp. 15-27.

Birtwistle, G. (Ed) (1985). Artificial intelligence, graphics, and simulation. SCS, La Jolla, CA, 119 p.

Elzas, M.S., T.I. Ören, B.P. Zeigler (Eds) (1986). Modelling and simulation in the artificial intelligence era, North-Holland, Amsterdam.

Holmes, W.M. (Ed) (1985). Artificial intelligence and simulation, SCS, San Diego, CA, 75 p.

Kerckhoffs, E.J.H. and G.C. Vansteenkiste (Eds) (1986). Artificial intelligence in simulation, SCS, San Diego, CA.

Luker, P.A. and H.H. Adelsberger (Eds) (1986). Intelligent simulation environments, SCS, San Diego, CA, 167 p.

Ören, T.I. (1981). Concepts and criteria to assess acceptability of simulation studies: A frame of reference, CACM, Vol. 24, nr. 4, pp. 180-189.

Ören, T.I. (1983). Quality assurance of system design and model management for complex problems. In: Adequate modelling of systems, H.Wedde (Ed), Springer-Verlag, Heidelberg, Germany, pp. 205-219.

Ören, T.I. (1984). Model-based activities: A paradigm shift. In: Simulation and model based methodologies: An integrative view, T.I. Ören, B.P. Zeigler, and M.S. Elzas (Eds), Springer-Verlag, Heidelberg, Germany, pp. 3-40.

Ören, T.I. (1986a). Knowledge bases for an advanced simulation environment. In: Intelligent simulation environment, P.A. Luker and H.H. Adelsberger (Eds), Proceedings of SCS conference on intelligent simulation environments, San Diego, CA, 1986 Jan. 23-25, pp. 16-22.

Ören, T.I. (1986b). Artificial intelligence and simulation. In: Proceedings of Artificial intelligence in simulation, Ghent, Belgium, 1985 Feb. 25-27, SCS, San Diego, CA.

Ören, T.I. (1986c). Implications of machine learning in simulation. In: Modelling and simulation in the artificial intelligence era, M.S. Elzas, T.I. Ören, B.P. Zeigler (Eds), North-Holland, Amsterdam.

Ören, T.I. and Z.K. Aytaç (1986d). Magest: A model-based advisor and certifier for Gest programs. In: Modelling and simulation in the artificial intelligence era, M.S. Elzas, T.I. Ören, B.P. Zeigler (Eds), North-Holland, Amsterdam.

Ören, T.I., M.S. Elzas, and G. Sheng (1985). Model reliability and software quality assurance in simulation of nuclear fuel waste management systems. In: Waste management '85, Vol. 1, R.G. Post (Ed), pp. 381-396.

Zeigler, B.P. (Ed) (1985). Expert systems and simulation models, lecture notes of the seminar in expert systems and simulation models, the University of Arizona, Tucson, AZ, 1985 Nov. 18-19.

Modelling and Simulation Methodology
in the Artificial Intelligence Era
M.S. Elzas, T.I. Ören and B.P. Zeigler (Editors)
© Elsevier Science Publishers B.V. (North-Holland), 1986

Chapter V.2

AN EXPLORATION OF POSSIBILITIES FOR EXPERT AIDS IN MODEL VALIDATION

Robert G. Sargent

Department of Industrial Engineering
and Operation Research
Syracuse University
Syracuse, New York
U.S.A.

This chapter describes an exploration by the author on expert aids for model validation. It identifies potential expert aids for model validation, develops a hypothetical expert system for the identified aids, and identifies the major issues of implementing these expert aids in three different ways: (i) the aids implemented separately for independent use, (ii) the aids integrated into an expert system for model validation, and (iii) the aids integrated into an expert system for modelling and simulation.

1. INTRODUCTION

The purpose of this chapter is to discuss an exploration of possibilities for expert aids in model validation. This exploration consisted of (i) identifying those aspects of model validation which the author believes expert aids would be of help to model developers and (ii) developing a hypothetical expert system containing these expert aids for the purpose of helping to identify what the major issues would be in developing real expert aids to assist in model validation. The expert aids identified can be used separately, be integrated into an expert system for model validation, or be part of an expert system for modelling and simulation. The hypothetical system is used for identifying the major issues in each of these three implementations of expert aids for model validation.

Model validation is a process within the model development process. It usually consists of performing a series of tests and evaluations on a model (or series of models) until one or more individuals obtain "confidence" that the model is valid for its intended purpose or until it is determined that the model is invalid. (For an introduction to model validation, see, for example, Sargent 1984a, 1984b, or 1985 and for a recent bibliography on validation, see Balci and Sargent 1984.)

An expert aid, as used here, is an user friendly interactive computer program, software module, or software system which contains and uses knowledge from an expert and possibly other relevant information in a specific domain and it differs from an expert system in two major ways. The first difference is that an expert aid is concerned with only a subtask (a portion of the problem or sub-problem) instead of the total task (the total problem) as an expert system is. (The task or problem under consideration in this chapter is whether a model is valid or not.) The second difference is that an expert aid does not provide justification or explanations in the conclusions reached as an expert system does. Expert aids cover a spectrum of capabilities as expert sytems do; i.e., they can present alternatives, specify a course(s) of action, or make a decision. However, in validation, most of the expert aids will only be able to provide "guidance" or "list a set of possible actions", i.e., be advisory, for at least the near future. The major reason is that considerable research is still needed in model validation to bring it to a level that will allow expert aids or an expert system to be developed beyond being advisory.

The assumption used in this exploration of expert aids for model validation are the following:

(1) The user has had at least one course in modelling and simulation,

(2) The user desires to have the assistance of a validation expert to assist in the validation of a model being developed for a specific purpose,

(3) The expert aids will provide expertise to a user similar to what this author would supply,

(4) The expert aids would be in an interactive computer system which has graphics, and

(5) Validation is performed with respect to a simplified version of the modelling process.

2.   VALIDATION AND A SIMPLIFIED VERSION OF THE MODELLING PROCESS

Recent research (e.g., Gass and Thompson 1980, Sargent 1981, 1982, 1984a) has related model validation to specific steps of the model development process. We will follow the development of Sargent (1982, 1984a) and use the simplified version of the modelling process in Figure 1. The problem entity is the system (real or proposed), idea, situation, policy, or phenomena to be modelled; the conceptual model is the mathematical/logical/verbal representation (mimic) of the problem entity developed for a particular study; and the computerized model is the conceptual model implemented on a computer. The conceptual model is developed through an analysis and modelling phase, the computerized model is developed through a computer programming and implementation phase, and inferences about the problem entity are obtained by conducting computer experiments on the computerized model in the experimentation phase.

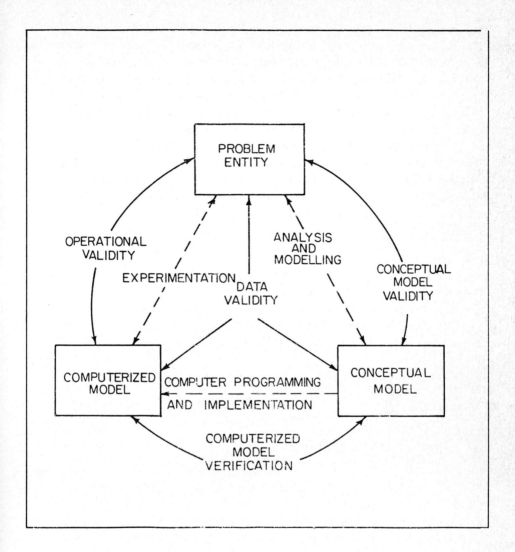

Figure 1: Simplified Version of the Modelling Process

We relate validation and verification to this simplified version of the modelling process as shown in Figure 1. Conceptual model validity is defined as determining that the theories and assumptions underlying the conceptual model are correct and that the model representation of the problem entity is "reasonable" for the intended use of the model. Computerized model verification is defined as ensuring that the computer programming and implementation of the conceptual model is correct. Operational validity is defined as determining that the model's output behavior has sufficient accuracy for its intended purpose or use over the domain of the model's intended application. Data validity is defined as ensuring that the data necessary for model building, model evaluation and testing, and conducting the model experiments to solve the problem are adequate and correct.

Several models (or modifications of a model) are usually developed in the modelling process prior to obtaining a satisfactory valid model. During each model interaction, model validation and verification are performed (Sargent 1984a). The specific validation techniques used and the amount of in-depth evaluation performed usually varies from one model interaction to the next.

3. IDENTIFICATION OF EXPERT AIDS

In this section, sets of expert aids which the author believes would be useful in model validation are identified. For each type of expert aid, the problem it is to address is stated, and its goal is specified, i.e., the results desired form the expert aid. This will be done separately for conceptual model validation and operational validity.

3.1. Conceptual Model Validation

With respect to conceptual model validation, there are three levels of assistance that expert aids could provide as shown in Figure 2. The goal of the first level of assistance is to determine the appropriate set of validation techniques which can or should be used for conceptual model validation of the specific model being validated. This is usually done in two parts. The goal of the first part is to determine the set of validation techniques which can or should be used to validate the underlying assumptions and theories of this specific model. The goal of the second part is to determine the set of validation techniques which can or should be used to validate that this specific model's representation of the problem entity being modelled (e.g., a system) and its structure, logic, and mathematical and causal relationships are "reasonable" for the intended use of the model. An expert aid could be developed for each of these two parts.

For the next level of assistance, an expert aid could be developed for each validation technique. The goal of each expert aid would be to determine the set of

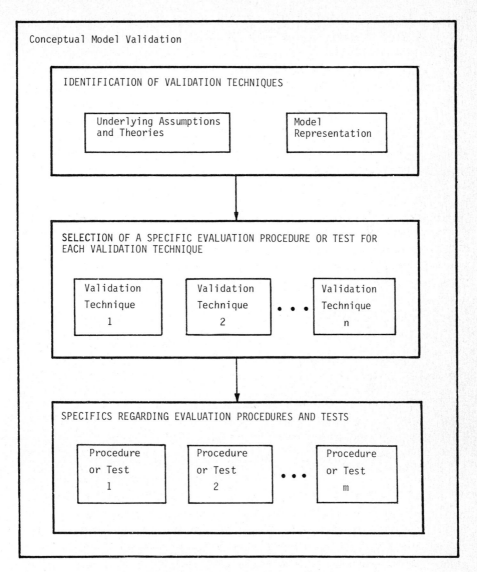

Figure 2: Levels and Relationships of Expert Aids for
Conceptual Model Validation

evaluation procedures and tests that can or should be used for the specific model
being validated if that validation technique was used. Two examples of what is
meant here are (1) if a Poisson assumption is to be validated for a model of an
observable system by using actual data from the system, then an appropriate
statistical test would be selected by the user from a set of tests provided and
(2) if a model's logic is to be validated by using the face validity technique
(which involves using people knowledgable about the system being modelled to help
determine its validity, see Sargent 1984a, 1984b, 1985 for further discussion)
then an appropriate evaluation procedure would be selected by the user from the
procedures provided by the expert aid.

At the third level of assistance, an expert aid could be developed for each
evaluation procedure and test with the goal of determining or giving the specifics
on the use of that evaluation procedure or test. In some cases, this may not be a
true "expert aid" but a "standard" or "intelligent" computer program or package
(see Hahn 1985). Two examples of what is meant here are (1) if a specific statistical test is to be used, a discussion on this test, how to select the sample size,
and how to perform the data analysis could be in this expert aid or intelligent
statistics package and (2) if it is a procedure, the expert aid or computer program could contain the steps to be used (course of action to take) and how to
draw the appropriate conclusions (make a decision).

3.2 Operational Validity

With respect to operational validity, there are three levels of assistance that
expert aids can provide as shown in Figure 3. The goal of the first level of
assistance is to identify the appropriate set of validation techniques which can
or should be used for operational validity of the specific model being validated.
An expert aid could be developed for this.

For the next level of assistance, an expert aid could be developed for each validation technique. The goal of each expert aid would be to determine the specific
set of evaluation procedures or tests which can or should be used for the specific
model being validated if that validation technique was selected for use. An example of what is meant here is if the operational validity of the steady state mean
and variance of a response variable is to be determined by using the historical
data validation technique, then the expert aid for this validation technique would
present to the user the set of statistical procedures and tests which could be
used and should include, e.g., the two sample standardized time series statistical
tests for the means (Chen and Sargent 1984a) and the variances (Chen and Sargent
1984b).

For the third level of assistance, an expert aid could be developed for each
evaluation procedure or test. The goal of each expert aid (or perhaps a "standard"

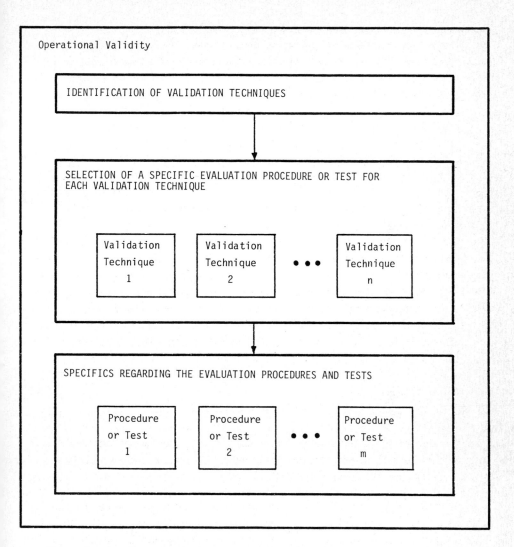

Figure 3: Levels and Relationships of Expert Aids for Operational Validity

or "intelligent" computer program or package) would be to provide specifics on
the use of that specific evaluation procedure or test. An example of what is meant
by this is that the specifics of the steps of an evaluation procedure would be
given if a subjective approach for the face validation technique is to be used on
the model's output (behavior) data for various sets of model inputs.

4. A HYPOTHETICAL EXPERT SYSTEM FOR MODEL VALIDATION

In this section, a simple hypothetical expert system for model validation containing the expert aids discussed in the previous section is presented. The major
purpose of this hypothetical system is for it to help determine the issues that
need to be addressed in order to develop expert aids and eventually an expert
system for model validation. Two assumptions were made in developing this hypothetical system. The first assumption is that it would be imbedded in a larger
software system which supports modelling and simulation. The second assumption is
that the expert aid could be implemented into a multilevel expert system in two
different ways: (i) the expert aids are integrated in the expert system and are
used to solve subproblems and (ii) the expert aids are used independently of each
other. These two assumptions were made because the author believed that they
would allow the major issues involved with implementing the expert aids separately,
integrated into an expert system for model validation, and integrated into an
expert system for modelling and simulation to be identified while minimizing the
exploration effort.

4.1. Software System

Figure 4 shows the simple software system used in this study to support modelling
and simulation. (For information on integrated software systems to support
modelling and simulation, see, for example, Ören, Zeigler, Elzas 1984). The major
components of this simple software system are a user interface which has interactive
and graphics capabilities, a model database which contains the various models and
information on each of them, a system database which contains the information on
the various systems, a software support system which contains the other elements
of a modelling and simulation software support system, the hypothetical expert
system for model validation, and a temporary storage for use by the expert system.

4.2. Hypothetical Expert System Conceptualization

The hypothetical expert system consists of three parts as shown in Figure 4: the
knowledge base, a problem solver, and the interface. The knowledge base contains
the knowledge for the expert aids discussed in section 3. The problem solver
operates on the knowledge contained in the knowledge base and the information about
the specific model being evaluated to obtain the goal of the expert aid being used.

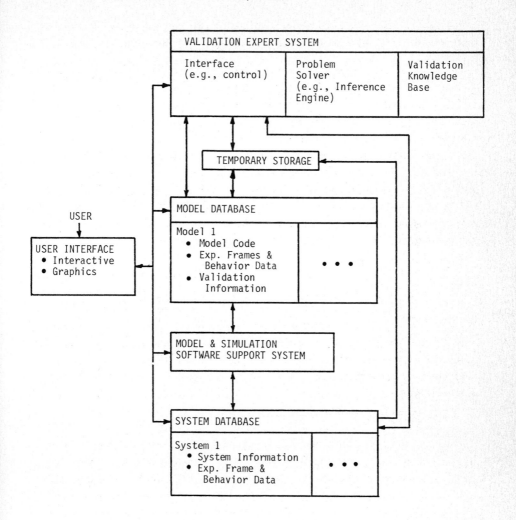

Figure 4: Simple Software System

The interface controls the use of the problem solver, interfaces with other components of the software system, interprets and justifies the results, etc.

The hypothetical expert system has the expert aids organized into three levels and thus we have a multilevel expert system as shown in Figure 5. The purpose of level 1 is to identify the validation techniques to be used. This level contains the three expert aids identified for this purpose in Section 3. These three expert aids serve different purposes and thus will be assumed to operate independent of each other. The purpose of level 2 is to select the appropriate evaluation procedures or tests to be used for the validation technique(s) identified in level 1. This level contains an expert aid for each of the validation techniques which can be identified by level 1. The purpose of the third level is to give the specifics on each procedure or test that can be identified in level 2. These may be "true" expert aids or "intelligent" computer packages (see Hahn 1985).

The use of the expert aids contained in this hypothetical system can be integrated for use in two different ways. The first way is that the expert aids are used to solve subproblems in an integrated expert system. The second way is that the expert aids are to be used independently of each other. These two ways of implementing the hypothetical system allows the issues for each of the three different ways of implementing the expert aids stated previously to be identified.

To use this hypothetical system to assist in the validation of a specific model, information about the model and the system it represents must be made available to the expert system. A portion of this information must come from the user. We will assume the validation interface will be able to ask questions of the user (querying the user) regarding the model under evaluation. Both general and specific information will be needed. The general information will usually be required for the higher levels of the multilevel expert system and will be used for more than one expert aid. Specific information will usually be only for specific expert aids.

A partial list of the general information desired from the user is listed in Table 1. This information could be stored in slots of frames (data structures). The information on the model and on validation would be stored in the model data base and that on the system would be stored in the system database. Copies of this information would be put into the temporary storage for use by the expert system when needed.

The goal of level 1 is to obtain the set of validation techniques that can or should be used in validating a specific model. A (partial) list of the validation techniques is given in Table 2. (For additional information on validation techniques, see, e.g., Sargent 1984a, 1984b, or 1985). The knowledge base and

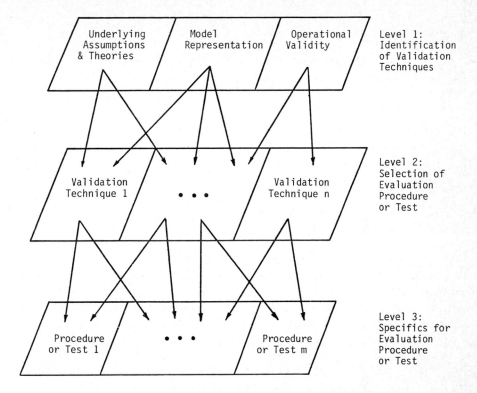

Figure 5:   Multilevel Organization of Expert Aids

Table 1.

Partial List of General Inputs

- System Information
    - Deterministic or stochastic
    - Continuous, discrete or both
    - Stationary or nonstationary
    - Observable or nonobservable
    - Can experiments be performed on it
        - If yes, would it be extremely costly
    - Does historical data on system exist

- Model Information
    - Deterministic or stochastic
    - Continuous, discrete or both
    - Stationary or nonstationary
    - Does it have submodels
    - Linear or nonlinear

- Validation Information
    - Domain of interest
    - Response variable of interest
    - Amount of accuracy required
    - Steady state or terminating
    - Do other models of this system exist

Table 2.

Validation Techniques

- Comparison to other models
- Degenerate tests
- Event validity
- Extreme-condition tests
- Face validity
- Fixed input values
- Historical data values
- Historical methods
    - Rationalism
    - Empiricism
    - Positive economics
- Internal validity
- Multistage validity
- Operational graphics (animation)
- Parameter variability - sensitivity analysis
- Predictive validation
- Traces
- Turing tests

problem solver for level 1 can be implemented in different ways. A production system (Weiss and Kulikowski 1984) could be used where the knowledge base contains If--, Then-- rules and the problem solver is an interface engine. The If portion of the rule would "and" various types of inputs and the Then portion of the rule would consist of one or more validation techniques. Another implemented method is to use decision trees (Weiss and Kulikowski 1984) for the knowledge base and a problem solver which can search them. If the general information did not contain all of the inputs desired, the information desired would be requested from the user.

The goal of level 2 is to select the evaluation procedures and tests to be used for the validation techniques selected for validating a specific model. A partial list of evaluation procedures and tests are given in Table 3 as an example of the different outputs possible. The expert aid for each validation technique could be implemented using either a production system or a decision tree approach. Specific information beyond the general information would usually be required for each validation technique.

The goal of level 3 is to give specifics on the evaluation procedures and tests to be used for the selected validation technique. Specific information would usually be requested from the user for these procedures and tests. This author believes that most of the expert aids at this level would be advisory only. An example of· why this author believes this is, if a comparison is to be made between two sets of data, e.g., data such as that in Figure 6, it is difficult to have this done by the computer instead of by a user subjectively.

4.3. Issues

This hypothetical expert system exploration for model validation raises major issues of concern for the development of a "real" expert system. Two major issues occur independent of the method of implementation. The first one is that an expert system for model validation would be extremely complex. There are two reasons for this. One is that there are a large number of attributes (see, e.g., Sargent 1984a or Ören 1984) which effect how a model is validated. This results in many ways to validate a model. The second reason for the completity is that there is a large number of evaluation procedures and tests which can be used.

The second general major issue is that it will be extremely difficult to develop most of the expert aids. As one example of this difficulty, it would be difficult to develop an expert aid for the standardized time series method of data analysis because little is known about some aspects of this method, e.g., determining the number of observations required. In fact, developing intelligent statistical software and statistical expert systems are a research field itself (Hahn 1985).

Table 3.

Partial List of Evaluation Procedures and Tests

- Graphical Comparison of Model and System Outputs
    - Subjective Evaluation Procedure
    - Schruben's Statistical Test
- Confidence Intervals for Means
    - t-test
    - Standardized Time Series
- Hypothesis Test
    - t-test
    - Hotellings T^2 Test
- Sensitivity Analysis
    - Subjective Evaluation Procedure for Mean Behavior
    - Subjective Evaluation Procedure for Variance Behavior
- Testing for Poisson Behavior
    - Probability Plots
    - Kolmogorov-Smirnov Test
- Face Validation Procedure for Model Structure

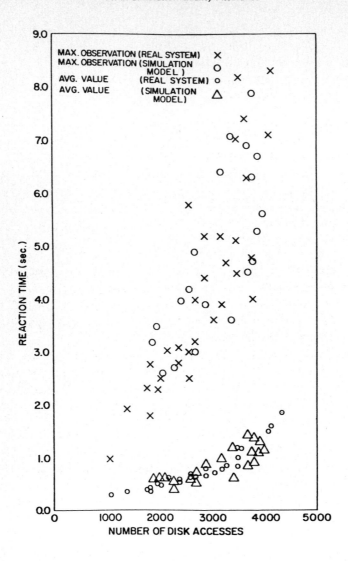

Figure 6: Model and System Data for Comparison

As a second example, consider the difficulty in developing an expert aid for face validity of a model's logic. This difficulty is true of many of the topics for which expert aids for model validation are desired. Basically, what is required is a large number of "expert systems", one for each expert aid, and many of these topics are currently being researched.

If the expert aids were developed to operate separately (i.e., not be part of an integrated system), there is an additional major issue of concern. This additional issue is the large amount and variety of input data which usually would have to be inputted into each expert aid used about the specific model being validated and the system it represents in order for it to function. This would require a significant amount of work on the part of a user in validating a specific model because several expert aids would usually be used in the validation process.

If an expert system for model validation is to be developed, two additional major issues occur beyond the two general major issues of concern. The third major issue is that the subproblems interact (Hayes-Roth, Waterman, Lenat 1983). For example, two different expert aids used independently might require two different statistical experiments be performed whereas only one statistical experiment might be required if the two aids or systems were to interact. The fourth major issue is how to integrate the results from several evaluation procedures and tests to determine if a specific model is valid. This would require a fourth level in our conceptualization of an expert system for model validation. Its goal (purpose) is to determine whether the model is valid or not.

If model validation is to be part of an expert system for modelling and simulation, the four major issues identified for an expert system for model validation apply. One advantage of a total expert system over an expert system for model validation only is that some of the expert aids identified for level 3 of the hypothetical expert system would be useful for other areas of modelling and simulation, e.g., output analysis.

5. CONCLUSIONS

The basic conclusion which must be drawn from this exploration is that it is going to be extremely difficult to develop an expert system for model validation. The reason is because of the major issues identified in Section 4.3. Two other issues come forth. One, is there a simpler conceptualization for an expert system for model validation than the one used in the hypothetical expert system. Two, is there a simpler and better way to do model validation than what is currently being done. This author does not believe a better way to do model validation will be forthcoming at least in any reasonable time frame. Therefore, even if a simpler conceptual model for an expert system is found, it will still be extremely complex and difficult to develop an expert system for model validation.

This author believes that the only way to begin to develop any knowledge-based assistance for model validation is to begin to develop some expert aids. Some expert aids will be much more difficult than others to develop and some will be much more useful than others. Preliminary thinking on what knowledge-based assistance to develop as an initial prototype suggest that either (i) one valida- tion technique be chosen along with some evaluation procedures and tests for it or (ii) one of the expert aids at level 1 be developed. Expert aids would be developed initially ignoring the interactions of subproblems.

REFERENCES

Balci, O. and R.G. Sargent (1984). A bibliography on the credibility, assessment, and validation of simulation and mathematical models, Simuletter, Vol. 15, nr. 3, pp. 15-27.

Chen, B. and R.G. Sargent (1984a). Confidence interval estimation for the difference between stochastic processes using standardized time series, Working Paper #84-004, Department of Industrial Engineering and Operations Research, Syracuse University, Syracuse, New York.

Chen, B. and R.G. Sargent (1984b). Asymptotic variance estimation for stationary phi-mixing processes, Working Paper #84-006, Department of Industrial Engineering and Operations Research, Syracuse University, Syracuse, New York.

Gass, S.I. and B.W. Thompson (1980). Guidelines for model evaluation: An abridged version of the U.S. General Office Exposure Draft, Operations Research, Vol. 28, nr. 2, pp. 431-479.

Hahn, G.J. (1985). More intelligent software and statistical expert systems: Future directions, The American Statistician, Vol. 38, nr. 1, pp. 1-8.

Hayes-Roth, F., D.A. Waterman, and D.B. Lenat (Eds) (1983). Building expert systems, Addison-Wesley Publishing Co., Reading, Mass.

Ören, T.I. (1984). Quality assurance in modelling and simulation: A taxonomy, In: Simulation and Model-Based Methodologies: An Integrative View, T.I. Ören, B.P. Zeigler, M.S. Elzas (Eds), Springer-Verlag, New York, pp. 477-517.

Ören, T.I., B.P. Ziegler, and M.S. Elzas (Eds) (1984). Simulation and model-based methodologies: An integrative view, Springer-Verlag, New York.

Sargent, R.G. (1981). An assessment procedure and a set of criteria for use in the evaluation of computerized models and computer-based modelling tools, Final Technical Report RADC-TR-80-409, Rome Air Development Center, Griffiss AFB, NY.

Sargent, R.G. (1982). Verification and validation of simulation models, Chapter IX in Progress in Modelling and Simulation, F.E. Cellier (Ed), Academic Press, London, pp. 159-169.

Sargent, R.G. (1984a). Simulation model validation, Chapter 19 in: Simulation and Model-Based Methodologies: An Integrative View, Ören, T.I., B.P. Ziegler, and M.S. Elzas (Eds), Springer-Verlag, New York, pp. 537-555.

Sargent, R.G. (1984b). A tutorial on verification and validation of simulation models, In: Proceedings of 1984 Winter Simulation Conference, S. Sheppard, U. Pooch, and D. Pegden (Eds), Dallas, Texas, pp. 115-121.

Sargent, R.G. (1985). An expository on verification and validation of simulation models, In: Proceedings of 1985 Winter Simulation Conference, D. Gontz, G. Blais, and S. Solmon (Eds), San Francisco.

Schruben, L.W. (1980). Establishing the credibility of simulation, Simulation, Vol. 34, nr. 3, pp. 101-105.

Weiss, S.M. and C.A. Kulikowski (1984). A practical guide to designing expert systems, Rowman and Allanheld, Totowa, New Jersey.

Modelling and Simulation Methodology
in the Artificial Intelligence Era
M.S. Elzas, T.I. Ören and B.P. Zeigler (Editors)
© Elsevier Science Publishers B.V. (North-Holland), 1986

Chapter V.3

MAGEST: A MODEL-BASED ADVISOR AND CERTIFIER FOR GEST PROGRAMS

Zühtü K. Aytaç
Dept. of Computer Science
University of Hacettepe
Beytepe, Ankara, Turkey

Tuncer I. Ören
Computer Science Dept.
University of Ottawa
Ottawa, Ontario, Canada

Gest is a high-level model and simulation experimentation specification language. Magest (Modelling Advisor and Certifier
for Gest programs) provides a knowledge-based specification
and certification environment for Gest. Magest system uses
knowledge on Gest modelling formalism and incremental
knowledge obtained from user to assist the user to specify models, parameter sets, and experimentations. Model reliability is
assured through checks of completeness, correctness, and compatibility. Acceptable Gest programs are certified by the
Magest system.

1. INTRODUCTION

Magest (Modelling Advisor and certifier for GEST programs) is a knowledge-based
modelling and simulation system and provides a user-oriented specification and certification environment for Gest which is a high-level model and simulation experimentation
specification language. Gest provides modular model and simulation specification
facilities (Ören 1971, 1982). A detailed discussion of the language is given in Ören 1984
The architecture of Magest system is given in a recent article (Ören and Aytaç 1985).

Magest system consists of an executive and three programs: 1) a template generator for
models, 2) Magest certification and advisor program, 3) Gest translator. A Gest source
program can be generated by using a general purpose text editor or a model template
generator which generates, for every component model, a template of static and dynamic structures to be filled in. An interactive dialogue system was also developed for a
macrocomputer (Aytaç and Ören 1984).

A Gest source program generated by using the possibilities given above must be certified
by Magest certification and advisor program before it is translated into Simscript language. Several activities are performed by the program to assist the user to specify mod
els, parameter sets, and experimentations to have a complete and correct Gest program
and to assure compatibility of several modules of a Gest program. In the article model
reliability in Magest system is highlighted.

2. MAGEST CERTIFICATION AND ADVISOR PROGRAM

A Gest source program has to be certified by Magest before it is translated into Simscript representation. The user request for translation automatically invokes the Magest certification. Figure 1 shows the major elements of the Magest system.

Magest certifier and advisoris invoked by the Magest executive. For the safe of integrity of Gest programs in an appropriate model base, any Gest source program has to undergo the certification to ensure that the text is state without inconsistent alterations. Gest source program can be updated several times during the certification. All updates are performed on copied files and Gest source program remains in its original form until it has been completely checked and certified.

The Magest certifier has four outputs: a complete and certified Gest program and three other lists. Cross reference list is one of the output files of Magest which might be useful for users to overview models and their variables in alphabetical order. Another output file DIALOGUE consists of all dialogues made between the user and Magest during the certification process. If any error is detected in Gest source program, an error file is generated.

3. MODEL RELIABILITY IN MAGEST

Magest modelling advisor and certifier uses available knowledge to generate reliable models using modular structure of Gest. Knowledge available to Magest consists of 1) knowledge about Gest morphology and 2) incremental knowledge obtained from user program and gathered from the user feed back via dialogue during the certification. Figure 2 shows how available knowledge is obtained. Domain- specific knowledge on different application areas such as population models, ecological models, economic models or engineering design models, are not yet included in Magest knowledge base. Magest uses the available knowledge to assist the user to specify models, parameter sets, and experimentations, and to perform checks for completeness, correctness, and compatibility.

The following checks are performed by Magest before accepting the declaration of a variable or an identifier:

- Models with the same identifier are not allowed.
- Variables with the same identifier and in similar type are not allowed (such as STATES A, B, C, A; is not accepted since second "A" is ambiguous).
- Identifiers in input, parameter or tabular function type must be uniquely declared.
- State variables can be declared if necessary as output, auxiliary, or interpolated variables.
- Output variables can be declared as state, auxiliary, or interpolated variables.
- Auxiliary variables can be declared as state, output, interpolated variables.
- Interpolated variables can be declared as output or auxiliary variables.

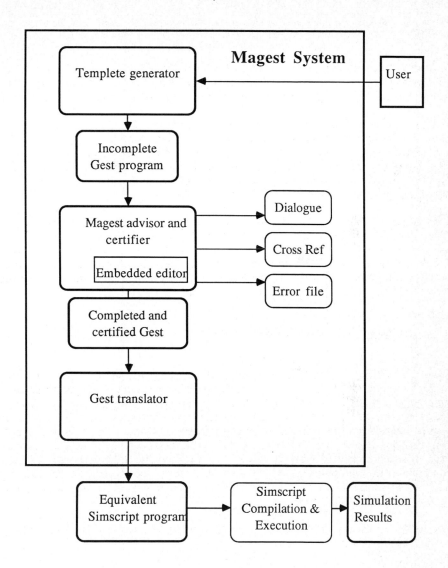

Figure 1. Elements of Magest system

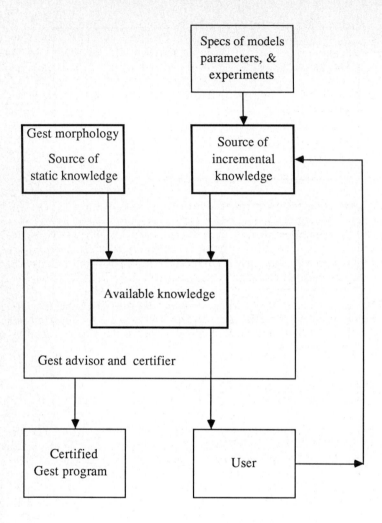

Figure 2. Sources of available knowledge in Magest

- State and output variables cannot be declared as random variables.
- State variables should appear at the left hand side of assignment statements in state transition functions.
- Output variables should appear at the left hand side of assignment statements in output functions.
- Input variables should not appear at the left hand side of assignment statements in dynamic structure.

The following checks are performed if all statements up to the current line are syntactically correct:

- Each component variable of a coupled model must be completely declared and specified.
- State variables must appear in their derivative form (') at least once at the left hand side in one of the equations of derivative blocks for a continuous type of model.
- Each variable or parameter appeared in derivative block are checked to see if they have been declared as input, state, auxiliary variable or parameter. If an auxiliary variable is used at the right hand side of an equation, it must have a value assigned in the same block.
- Output variables must be assigned at least once in the output function block of the dynamic structure of a continuous type model.
- Each of the external inputs or outputs must appear in equivalencing block.
- Coupling of component models of a coupled model must be completely specified without ambivuity. Each variable and model name specified in the coupling block has to exist in a model specification.

4. ERROR HANDLING IN MAGEST SYSTEM

Since Magest provides a partly interactive environment for Gest user, error handling is performed in different ways according to the position of the statement or specification in which an error occurs. Categories of error handling are the following: 1) error handling without guiding the user and 2) error handling by providing guidance to the user. Errors can be corrected by using either Magest editor or CMS editor or both. Magest editor is handy in making corrections on the current line on which an error is detected by Magest. Figure 3 shows the editors of Magest Executive.

4.1 Error Handling Without Guiding the User

This type of error handling is applied to the declarations or statements which exist in external blocks of a coupled model, or static and dynamic blocks of component models. Since the blocks above are used to declare main structures of models, any update on them may necessitate modifications in the remaining part of the program. Therefore the whole specification needs to be certified from the beginning after performing any modification in one of these blocks. For this reason, if an error occurs in these blocks, Magest points out the type of the error and then the user is allowed to update the current line using either the Magest editor or CMS editor. In this case, Magest starts to certify the program from the beginning.

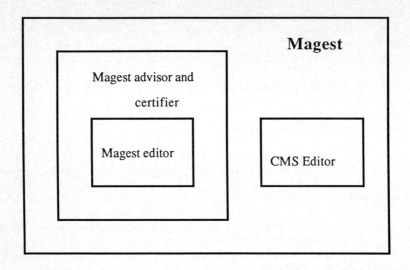

Figure 3. Editors in Magest

4.2 Error Handling by Providing Guidance to the User

Magest guides the user to update or complete the specifications of models and certain other blocks. These blocks are the following:

- equivalencing and coupling for a coupled model,
- parameter sets,
-experimental frames,
-run, control and output modules.

Error Handling for Equivalencing and Coupling Blocks.   Complete information of coupling specification of component models and equivalencing external and internal inputs as well as external and internal outputs are given in Ören 1984 (pp. 298-311) and are not repeated here.

Guidance is provided for two different situations: 1) equivalencing and/or coupling blocks of a coupled model have not yet been specified, 2) equivalencing and/or coupling blocks of a coupled model exist but some specifications are not correct or external variables need to be specified or some component models have not yet been coupled.

In the first case, if these blocks have not been specified, Magest simply points out this error condition and asks the user if he wants to insert these blocks. Then Magest sets up the left hand side of an equivalencing input/output specification and the user is requested to complete the right hand side of the current line on the screen. The following types of checks are performed:

- The name of the component model should be part of the list of coupled models and it should be available.
- The input variable should be part of the input variables of the component model.
- The ranges of input and corresponding output variables should be compatible.

The completeness of the coupling specification is assured by Magest which generates the left had sides of the input/output relationships of the variables. Magest uses the following knowledge about coupling specification:

Every input variable of every component model has to receive information from a unique information channel which can be an output variable of the same component model (in case of feedback coupling) or of another component model. Input variables which receive information from external input channels to the coupled model are specified in the equivalencing section. This knowledge is used by Magest which does not request and does not accept coupling specification from an output variable of one of the coupled models.

In the second case, incorrect specifications are updated by a system-driven dialogue. At the end of these blocks if external variables still need to be assigned or some component models need to be coupled, blocks are completed by appropriate system-driven dialogues.

Specifications in these blocks are certified line by line. The user can use the CMS editor for corrections and the program is certified from the beginning.

Error Handling for Parameter Sets. In the blocks of parameter sets, values are assigned to parameters declared in component models of a coupled model or in an uncoupled model. If this block has not been specified in the text, the user can assign values to parameters of each model by a user friendly dialogue of Magest. The name of the parameters of each model are known by Magest. The names are displayed on the screen by Magest and the user is requested to enter the corresponding values. If the range of acceptable values of parameters have already been declared in a model's static structure, this knowledge is used by Magest to accept the value entered by the user or advise the user why the value is not acceptable.

Error Handling for Experimental Frames, Run Control and Output Modules. Declarations of experimental frames are checked. If these blocks do not exist, Magest guides the user to complete these blocks in a user firendly dialogue.

Statements in the simulation run and the output modules are syntactically and semantically checked using the available knowledge of the whole model. Incorrect statements can be corrected interactively by the user.

ACKNOWLEDGEMENT

This study was supported by a fellowship to the senior author from the United Nations and by a grant to the second author from the Natural Sciences and Engineering Research Council of Canada (NSERC).

REFERENCES

Aytaç, Z.K. and T.I. Ören (1984). Interactive modelling with GEST on a microcomputer, Technical Report TR-84-11, Computer Science Department, University of Ottawa, Ottawa, Ont., Canada.

Ören, T.I. (1971). GEST: A combined digital simulation language for large scale systems. In: Proceedings of the 1971 AICA (Association Internationale pour le Calcul Analogique) symposium on simulation of complex systems,Tokyo,Japan, Sept 3-7, 1971, pp. B-11-14.

Ören, T.I. (1982). Model reliability in interactive modelling in GEST 81. In: Proceedings of the 10th IMACS Word congress on system simulation and scientific computation, Aug. 8-13, 1982, Montreal, PQ, Canada, Vol. 4, pp. 201-203.

Ören, T.I. (1984). GEST - A modelling and simulation language based on system theoretic concepts. In: Simulation and model-based methodologies: An integrative view, T.I. Ören et al. (Eds), Springer-Verlag, Heidelberg, Germany, pp. 281-335.

Ören, T.I. and Z.K. Aytaç (1985). Architecture of MAGEST: A knowledge-based modelling and simulation system. In: Simulation in Research and Development, A. Javor (Ed), North-Holland, Amsterdam, pp. 99-109.

SECTION VI
ARTIFICIAL INTELLIGENCE TECHNIQUES
IN
MODELLING OF ORGANIZATIONAL PROBLEMS

Modelling and Simulation Methodology
in the Artificial Intelligence Era
M.S. Elzas, T.I. Ören and B.P. Zeigler (Editors)
© Elsevier Science Publishers B.V. (North-Holland), 1986

Chapter VI.1

ARTIFICIAL INTELLIGENCE AND MODELLING OF SOCIETAL SYSTEMS:
A SYNOPSIS.

M.S. ELZAS

Agricultural University
Department of Computer Science
Wageningen/The Netherlands

The presence of emotions, unimpedable interactions
and a high degree of variability of the (human)
components in social entities, make them extremely
difficult to model adequately.
Notwithstanding the large number of publications on
the subject, advances have been disappointing until
now.
The use of generative approaches, based on techniques
developed for Artificial Intelligence, may offer more
hope for the future.

1. TYPICAL GOALS FOR SOCIETAL MODELS

In 1982 an international working conference was held in which
attention was mainly focussed on the adequacy of models for
man-machine and organisational models (Wedde 1983).
As adequacy can only be assessed with respect to the goal of the
exercise, this conference led to a renewed interest in their
definition.
An overview of such goals was contained in a previous publication by
the author (Elzas 1984), which was based on several years of
observation of- and experience with some major projects in this
field.
Limiting the list of goals for such exercises to the (most)
practical ones, yields the following enumeration:

- strategy design (see Elzas 1982)
- policy construction (see Elzas 1982)
- policy evaluation (see Beer 1981)
- planning of activities (see Schiffers 1983)
- conflict resolution (see Bowen 1981)
- consensus generation (see Young et al. 1980)
- management of change (see Elzas 1980)
- organizational design (see Elzas 1985)
- decision support (see Heeren and Hopmans 1983)
- business information system design (see Gessford 1980)

Note that the order in this enumeration does not imply any judgment
on the relative importance of these goals.

2. TYPICAL FUNCTIONS OF SUCH MODELS

It is generally known that - even when using the best possible
modelling methods and the best data available - the reliability of
models of societal systems is mostly very poor, and validation often
not realistically possible (see also Elzas 1986a and 1986b).
Therefore these type of models can clearly not be used for
prediction, optimalization or similar tasks.
At best they help the user to fathom certain general behavioral
characteristics, reason about trends or roughly compare
alternatives.
Therefore models used for these purposes are, in most cases, less
computational vehicles than:

- rough behavioral analogies, or
- *mirrors* that reflect possible consequence of actions, or
- trend extrapolators.

In order to perform these functions within reasonable margins of
trustworthiness, the models will have to be able to display similar
variable characteristics as the systems they represent.
That is where Artificial Intelligence-like knowledge representations
and retrieval techniques can be used to advantage in order to allow
the sufficiently powerful adaption stratagems which are needed for
this purpose.

3. ROLE OF ARTIFICIAL INTELLIGENCE TECHNIQUES

Based on the expectation that experts in the social sciences, though
they might not be as well versed in mathematical modelling as the
traditional (physics-oriented) simulationists, will certainly be
able to reason about the circumstances that lead to changes of
behavior in social groups, this expertise could be used to provide
inference mechanisms which, when associated to a good model base,
can lead to situation dependent model compositions.
This means that models will come into existence that do not have
their variability expressed by varying the couplings between
submodels that have all been included at model specification time,
but will be able to completely change their composition by inference
from circumstantial evidence.
Hogeweg and Hespers' "Knowledge Seeking Models" (Chapter IV.3 of
this book), can be considered to be a first experiment to achieve
something of this kind.
This would not be the only use of Artificial Intelligence in this
context.
The Artificial Intelligence experience in *pattern analysis* can be
extremely helpful for extracting typical modes of behavior from the,
often massive, amount of data collected about some social
phenomenon. These modes of behavior can then be used for reference
when building new model components for the model base mentioned
before.
Because more often than not, more than one submodel will be suitable
for "explaining" certain behavior patterns, it is also important
that the degree and frequency of recorded satisfactory resemblance
should be monitored and stored, in order to be able to associate
certainty factors with these (sub)models and use them as indicated
in Chapter I.3 of this book.

This then requires such a model manager to be able to retrieve
(sub)models on basis of "most probable candidates".
It is clear that in this way completely different modelling
paradigms will get to be used than those applicable to more
deterministic fields.
Moreover, the added possibility to reason about the inherent
fuzziness of these type of models, is expected to allow a major
step forward in the development and utilization of better models
of societal systems.

4. EPILOGUE

The inherent capability of Artificial Intelligence systems to
produce varying organizational patterns for the elements present
in their knowledge bases, create the possibility to build model
generators that deliver models that are specialized on basis of
inferences from circumstantial evidence.
An extremely high degree of adaptability is achievable in this way.
It is to be expected that the inference mechanisms that will be used
for this purpose will closely resemble present-day Expert Systems.
The following Chapters in this Section can also serve to illustrate
the emergence of this approach.

5. REFERENCES

Beer, S. (1981). Brain of the Firm. John Wiley & Sons, Chichester,
    2nd. Edition.

Bowen, K. (1981). A Conflict Approach to the Modelling of Problems
    of and in Organizations. In: Operations Research '81, Brans, J.
    (Ed.), North-Holland, Amsterdam.

Elzas, M.S. (1980). Simulation and the Processes of Change. In:
    Simulation with Discrete Models: A State-of-the-Art View, Oren,
    T.I. et al. (Eds.), IEEE, New York.

Elzas, M.S. (1982). A Simplified Macro-Economic Model of Israel.
    (Elements for an Income Strategy). In: A Framework for the
    formulation of Income Policies in Israel, Wiener, A. et al.
    (Eds.), Report PNØ2/ØØ1/82, The Neamann Institute for Advanced
    Studies in Science and Technology, Haifa/Israel.

Elzas, M.S. (1983). The use of Structured Design Methodology to
    Improve Realism in National Economic Planning. In: Adequate
    Models of Systems, Wedde, H. (Ed.), Springer-Verlag,
    Heidelberg.

Elzas, M.S. (1984). Concepts for Model-Based Policy Construction.
    In: Simulation and Model-Based Methodologies: An Integrative
    View, Oren, T.I. et al. (Eds.), Springer-Verlag, Heidelberg.

Elzas, M.S. (1985). Organizational Structures for Facilitating
    Process Innovation. In Real-time Control of Large Scale
    Systems, Tzafestas, S. et al. (Eds.), Springer-Verlag, Berlin.

Elzas, M.S. (1986a). <u>The relation of simulation methodology tosystems control/management</u>.

..... (1986b). <u>Assessing the credibility of a simulation study</u>. In: Encyclopedia of Systems and Control, Madan Singh (Ed.), Pergamon Press, Oxford.

Gessford, J.E. (1980). <u>Modern Information Systems, designed for decision support</u>. Addison-Wesley, Philippines.

Heeren, Th.F.J. and A.C.M. Hopmans (1983). <u>Decision Support System for bankhall Organization</u>. In: Proc. ESC'83, First European Simulation Conference, Ameling, W. (Ed.), Springer-Verlag, Heidelberg.

Schiffers, M. (1982). <u>An Exercise in Achieving Goals in Distributed Systems</u>. In: Loc.cit. sub Elzas (1983).

Wedde, H. (1982). <u>Adequate Modelling of Systems</u>. Proc. of the International Working Conference on Modeal Realism Held in Bad Honnef, Federal Republic of Germany, Springer-Verlag, Heidelberg, 1983.

Young, H.P., N. Okada and T. Hashimoto (1980). <u>Cost allocation in water resources development - a case study of Sweden</u>. Report RR-80-32, IIASA, Laxenburg, Austria.

Modelling and Simulation Methodology
in the Artificial Intelligence Era
M.S. Elzas, T.I. Ören and B.P. Zeigler (Editors)
© Elsevier Science Publishers B.V. (North-Holland), 1986

Chapter VI.2

APPLYING ARTIFICIAL INTELLIGENCE TECHNIQUES TO
STRATEGIC-LEVEL GAMING AND SIMULATION

Paul K. Davis

The Rand Corporation and the Rand Graduate Institute
1700 Main Street
Santa Monica, California 90406-2138
The United States

This paper describes a large-scale program melding rule-based modelling and traditional simulation in the problem domain of game-structured military strategic analysis. It then draws on the program's experience to discuss paradigms from artificial intelligence, concepts and techniques for representing knowledge in a policy domain having no body of acknowledged experts or experimental data, and lessons from managing the related research and software development. Finally, it discusses implications for the ability to reflect in policy analysis concepts of bounded rationality and organizational behavior.

1. INTRODUCTION

This book explores ways in which knowledge-based modelling can be integrated with traditional simulation modelling to produce something transcending the separate activities. This paper describes an operational prototype system accomplishing precisely this kind of synthesis, and a related research effort that may well be unique in scope, complexity, and relevance to interdisciplinary policy analysis. The paper proceeds chronologically to provide a realistic image of how a successful development evolved and of the extent to which concepts and techniques from AI have proved useful in each phase of the work.

2. PHASE ONE: THE CONCEPT OF AUTOMATED WAR GAMING

2.1 The Problem Domain and Initial Concepts for an Approach

The work described here had its origins in a U.S. government request in 1979 for a new approach to strategic analysis that would combine features of human political-military war gaming and analytic modelling. The request reflected rejection of sole reliance on traditional system analysis and strategic simulation models with their focus on stereotyped scenarios, simple measures of effectiveness, and purely quantitative analysis. From war gaming was to come an enriched global view with strategic nuclear forces present in a context of military campaigns, political constraints, alliances, escalation and de-escalation, and imperfect command and control (Marshall, 1982; Davis and Winnefeld, 1983). However, it was recognized that war gaming itself was no solution: War games are slow, expensive, manpower intensive, and narrow in scope. Working through a single war game, however interesting, does not justify drawing conclusions because results depend sensitively on the players and because cause-effect relationships can be quite unclear. The government hoped, then, for a change of approach that would somehow retain the game character but permit greater analytic rigor.

Upon reviewing the government's request, Rand concluded that to gain control over the enormous number of variables in a war game it would be necessary to automate the war game as suggested in Figure 1. In this concept, which was deemed radical in 1980, Rand proposed a game-structured interactive simulation in which any of the human teams could be replaced by automated models called "agents." Thus, one could have a closed simulation with agent pitted against agent, a mixed simulation with one or more human teams, or a computer-assisted human war game (Graubard and Builder, 1980).

Even at this stage of thinking the concept involved a synthesis of knowledge-based modelling (the Red, Blue, and Scenario Agents of Figure 1) and more traditional simulation modelling (the Force Agent, which would keep the game clock, move and keep track of military forces, assess the results of battle, and generally cope with the consequences of decisions). The concept also assumed that the decisionmaking agents (Red, Blue, and Scenario Agents) would depend primarily upon qualitative heuristic rules rather than on optimizing algorithms.

Red Agent: Makes decisions for Soviet Union and Warsaw Pact
Blue Agent: Makes decisions for United States and NATO
Scenario Agent: Makes decisions for nonsuperpower countries
Force Agent: Simulates results of combat and other military operations; also, controls simulation time

Figure 1
Schematic Representation of the Automated War Game

2.2 The Mark I System

Serious work began in 1980 when Rand was asked to build quickly a rudimentary demonstration system to illustrate its notion of automated war gaming. A conservative approach using existing capabilities at Rand was taken, but integration was complex. Some characteristics of the Mark I system were as follows:

o The Red Agent made decisions by (a) comparing a 15-dimensional characterization of the current world state with a set of world states previously considered and identified in data, (b) choosing the world state in data that was "closest" to the current one (as defined with a Euclidean metric), and (c) following If ... Then ... instructions associated with that of the state in data.

o The Scenario Agent was an experiment with rule-based modelling in an English-like Rand AI language called ROSIE (Fain, Hayes-Roth, Sowizral, and Waterman, 1982) that allowed users to review and change rules interactively.

o The Force Agent consisted of simple combat simulation models developed in previous Rand work.

o There was a Blue team rather than a Blue Agent, all interfaces were manual, and the system lashed together three computers and three programming languages.

The Mark I system successfully conveyed to government reviewers a sense for the project's vision and demonstrated not only that decisionmaking agents could be built, but also that automated war gaming could allow users to examine a wide range of scenarios. Indeed, it strongly encouraged focusing on the very scenario variables that are so often taken for granted in policy studies (Builder, 1983). The reviewers were also impressed with the experimental Scenario Agent (Dewar, Schwabe, and McNaugher, 1982), because they placed great value on being able to review and change the underlying rules of a model. This endorsement of transparency by senior and mid-level officials had a major impact on subsequent work.

In spite of their interest, the reviewers were by no means sanguine. They were skeptical about moving from a simple demonstration system to something with a high degree of military content. They feared that the Mark I system might be "another example of computer scientists making great promises on the basis of a 'toy problem'." Nonetheless, the Phase One effort was successful in gaining support for further work and laying an empirical base of experience for the research team that would prove important for the next five years.

3. PHASE TWO: CONCEPTS FOR IMPROVING THE SUBSTANTIVE CONTENT

3.1 Prelude

After a year's funding hiatus, work began again in earnest in early 1982 with the government stipulating that there was to be no additional computer activity until the concepts had been developed for greatly improving the military content of the approach.

Key decisions were made rather quickly. The Mark I pattern-matching approach to the Red and Blue Agents was inappropriate for advanced work because it was neither transparent nor readily scalable to more complex work. After a review of alternatives based on a survey of the AI literature (Steeb and Gillogly, 1983), it was decided early in 1982 that decision modelling would revolve around "analytic war plans," which would be new constructs (Davis, 1982) based loosely on the scripts of AI (see, for example, Schank and Abelson, 1977, and Carbonell, 1978). The rationale for this was that by using script techniques one could make early use of the substantial knowledge that exists about real-world military operations and plans. The alternative of developing a goal-directed model to create such complex plans within the simulation appeared (at least to the author) to be a prescription for delays and potential failure.

The script approach was itself no panacea and would have to be extended significantly to permit the Red and Blue Agents to change their analytic war plans at appropriate times and to orchestrate the change of plans intelligently. Although there is an insidious temptation to turn strategy problems into decision trees, which would make scripts easy to use, the reality is that one does not know even which events will occur, much less in what order or precisely when.

This implied the need for a building-block approach in which primitive plans in the form of scripts would be combined and used to fit the circumstances (Davis, 1982).

The model for Red and Blue Agents emerging from this thinking was to have three "levels." The National Command Level (NCL) would pick analytic war plans, which would be the scripts containing general instructions for Area Command Levels (ACLs), with different ACLs for different regions worldwide. The ACLs would refine the action instructions based on the current state of the simulation (e.g., they might choose one or another branch of an analytic war plan). The Tactical Command Level (TCL) submodels, which have subsequently been reinterpreted, would refine instructions to the level of tactics and would determine more precisely what the Force Agent would be asked to do with military forces. Thus, one could say that the NCL submodel would pick a script and the ACL and TCL would "fill in slots of that script." Precisely how this would be accomplished was unclear, although some of the workers envisioned something akin to AI chess-playing programs with large numbers of look-ahead projections searching for good stratagems within the general structure imposed by the analytic war plan (Steeb and Gillogly, 1983).

There were two other important concepts affecting the Red and Blue Agents: (1) because of fundamental uncertainties about superpower behavior, there would be alternative Red and Blue Agents referred to informally as "Sams" and "Ivans," and (2) as suggested above, the Red and Blue Agents would conduct look-aheads to test potential analytic war plans before making final decisions, look-aheads consisting of a game within the game using Red's image of Blue and vice versa (more on this below).

Another part of the early thinking in 1982 dealt with the characteristics desired for a future Force Agent. Several conclusions were especially important (Davis, 1982; see also Bennett, Bullock, Jones, and Davis, 1985):

o The emphasis would be on breadth rather than depth, and well-intended suggestions to add ever-increasing detail would be resisted. The goal was to be the capability to answer many "What if?" questions quickly, with a strategic rather than tactical perspective. This implied aggregation and parameterization.

o The simulation would be self-contained with no special effort to insert other large-scale models as modules (something likely to increase technical problems and confusion).

o To the extent permitted by finite imaginations, the attempt would be made to reflect all phenomena having an important bearing on the strategic-level outcome--even if the phenomena were difficult to quantify or simulate. As a matter of principle, "scripted models" would be used, which would draw upon separate studies, judgments, or prudent speculation, rather than omit important phenomena altogether (Davis, 1982).

A scripted model might be as simple as a provision allowing one of the superpowers to create a crisis in region x as the result of events in region y, with the precise nature of the crisis left unspecified. In this case, the model would merely post a symbol in the world state: "Crisis exists in region x." In other cases, a scripted model might be quantitative but simple. For example, it might decree that the military forces of Side A would advance through a particular region on a rigid timescale based on a separate study.

There was nothing novel about the individual examples of scripted models, but establishing their widespread use as a matter of principle was unique. It also met resistance until the scripted models began proving their value by allowing the research team to address issues policymakers know are important but that modellers commonly ignore because of uncertainties or "softness." The scripted models are especially valuable in dealing with issues of escalation, where nations react to symbols (e.g., the fact of an invasion or the crossing of some other tacit boundary) more than to details, and in examining parametrically the potential significance of military events that are difficult to simulate in detail (e.g., events affecting command and control). In passing, it might be observed that resistance to treating qualitative ill-defined events in simulations with scripted models was analogous to the resistance received in the 1960s and 1970s by those who first questioned rational-analytic models (Simon, 1980) and those who insisted on including important but subjective cause-effect relations in policy simulations (Forrester, 1969).

3.2 The Mark II System

Although most computer work had been deferred, it was deemed essential to gain additional empirical experience. Thus, by the summer of 1982 manual walkthrough experiments were conducted to gain experience with analytic war plans, an improved Scenario Agent (Schwabe and Jamison, 1982), and the use of multiscenario experiments to derive policy conclusions. These experiments improved intraproject communications and morale and provided the basis for a coherent status report. Their value was analogous to that of the rapid prototyping frequently discussed in the literature.

Some of the principal lessons from this period of theorizing and experimenting were the following:

o Even simple analytic war plans could effectively communicate a sense for objectives, strategy, and interrelationships. Although the plans existed only in notebooks, it would clearly be possible to encode them.

o The notion of Red's Blues and Blue's Reds (i.e., each side's perceptions of the other) could reflect analytically something discussed by international relations specialists for years: that misunderstandings about the opponent can be the origin of unintended escalation and other forms of disaster (see Glaser and Davis, 1983, and classic references therein; see also the more general discussion of policy-relevant games by Elzas, 1984).

o As noted earlier, the script concept would have to be extended substantially to cope with plan changing and resynchronization (one of the general problems facing variable-structure simulation, as discussed by Zeigler elsewhere in this volume).

o Interdisciplinary work was greatly hindered by the jargon of AI and computer science more generally; domain-specific language was greatly to be preferred if misunderstandings were to be minimized and the vision sharpened. There were serious culture gaps among AI specialists, other computer scientists, and modellers/programmers concerned with military issues.

o The transparency of individual rules in English-like computer code was misleading: it was very difficult to review and

comprehend entire rule modules, in part because it was difficult
to judge completeness and to see the logic in a compact physical
space.

o There was an insidious side to the practice of heuristic
  modelling--in taking the pendulum swing away from rigorous
  quantitative modelling, there was a tendency to write ad hoc
  rules without appropriate structure or theory. It was sometimes
  difficult to judge the quality of rule sets.

The Phase Two work led to a government decision authorizing construction of a prototype system over a two-year period (1983 and 1984),
an effort that would require approximately twice the previous phases'
efforts (approximately 70 man-years were expended between 1980 and
the end of 1984).

4.   PHASE THREE: DEVELOPMENT OF A PROTOTYPE SYSTEM

Phase Three began early in 1983 and continued intensively for two
years (and, in a sense, for 2-1/2 years, since consolidation of
progress required at least six months in 1985). The result was a
prototype system for automated and interactive war gaming. This
section describes the design and implementation of that prototype,
again with a view toward indicating realistically how progress was
made. At present (late 1985), work is under way to develop and
transfer to the government a first-generation operational version of
the Rand Strategy Assessment System (RSAS). That work will continue
through 1986.

4.1 Choosing a Programming Language

One of the earliest decisions in 1983 was to choose a programming
language. The requirements were: (1) speed (less than a half day for
an automated war game processing thousands of rules and large numbers
of numerical algorithms with programs having tens of thousands of
lines of code); (2) transparency of decision rules and decision
processes (explanation facilities); and (3) transportability of the
eventual system for automated war gaming. The decision was to work
with two programming languages, one for the Force Agent simulation,
the other for the rule-based decision models. The former would be the
existing C language; the latter would be new and would require
considerable development. What follows summarizes the principal
considerations (Shapiro, Hall, Anderson, and LaCasse, 1985a):

SIGNIFICANT FEATURES OF LANGUAGES USED

C Language and UNIX Operating System (major characteristics)

        o portable among modern computer systems
        o available and familiar at Rand
        o efficient
        o powerful and flexible (e.g., C/UNIX allows
              hierarchical files, complex data structures
              accessed by strongly-typed pointers,
              long variable names improving readability of
              self-documenting code, and structured programming)
        o suitable for building a fast readable preprocessor
              language for the decision models (using UNIX
              utilities such as LEX and YACC)

RAND-ABEL^{TM} Programming Language (initial requirements)

- o fast (execution speeds of seconds for decision models)
- o readable and modifiable by nonprogrammers
- o easily extended
- o identify errors early (via strong typing)

Adopting C/UNIX raised difficulties for the Force Agent programmers familiar with languages such as Fortran and PL/1, but they came rather quickly to like C/UNIX, which is not usually mentioned in connection with simulation modelling. The basic reason for their enthusiasm was that the simulation has many features akin to those of operating systems (e.g, extensive use of pointers to a centralized database necessitated by interactions among parts of the simulation, interactions of special interest for strategic-level global war gaming). C/UNIX is a strong language for such applications.

The history and rationale for the RAND-ABEL language are described in Shapiro et al (1985a). Two factors were especially important. The first was the speed requirement, which ruled out Rand's ROSIE language, even though ROSIE has been successfully used on many other AI applications successfully. The second factor was more subtle: it was observed that early decision models such as the Scenario Agent did not rely upon generalized inference with AI-style "search," although the ROSIE language in which it was written had such capabilities; this, and the impression that the same would be true for more advanced models, suggested that the new programming language could be highly procedural and would not have to possess a general inference engine. Thus, RAND-ABEL was originally conceived as a fairly simple pre-processor for the C language. In reality, it has developed into a sophisticated language with some unique and attractive features (especially tables) that will be discussed later in the paper. It has indeed proven very fast (only three times slower than C itself), resulting in execution times less than 1 millisecond per rule on a VAX 11-780.

4.2 Model Architecture and System Design: Managing Complexity

The next issue was to tighten the conceptual model and develop some-thing approximating system specifications. Because concepts were still evolving rapidly and because those concepts were often abstract because of their novelty, it was infeasible to develop rigorous system specifications and a conscious decision was made to forego attempting to do so except in specific problem areas. Indeed, the reality is that many system specifications were not developed until 1985--after the prototype system had been successfully constructed and demon-strated.

What did exist in 1983 was a conceptual model designed with a strategic-level perspective and a rather high-level system overview (Hall, Shapiro, and Shukiar, 1985). Figure 2 describes the conceptual model as conceived early in 1983 (Davis and Stan, 1984).

The first column of Figure 2 describes the top level of the game: Red, Blue, Scenario, and Force Agents "take turns," although the order and time spacing of moves vary with events in the simulation and moves by one agent are based on only imperfect knowledge of other agents' prior moves because of time delays and command and control limitations. Recall that the Force Agent is conducting the simulation and keeping the simulation's clock; the role of the other agents is to make decisions about the actions to be simulated by Force Agent.

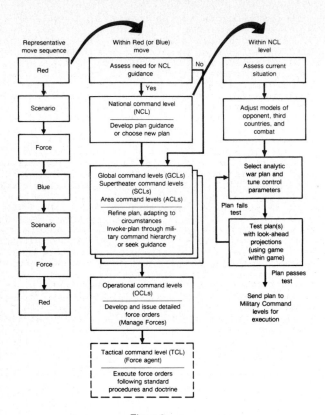

Figure 2
Conceptual Model of the RSAC Simulation

Using Red for the sake of example, the second column shows that within a given Red move the first issue is whether Red is satisfied with results using its current analytic war plan. If so, Red merely continues with that plan--although it may be necessary to refine the plan or to decide which of several plan branches to take. The refinement and execution of a plan is accomplished by modules identified with military command levels.

If the Red Agent is not satisfied with its current analytic war plan-- as determined by tests contained within that plan (e.g., tests of whether Blue is escalating or successfully defending)--then Red's NCL must have the opportunity to change that plan. The process for doing that is suggested in the third column (and discussed at more length later in the paper). The character of the NCL decision process is not that of a script, but rather something more nearly like rational-analytic thinking--but with mostly heuristic decision rules.

The third column of Figure 2 indicates that after the NCL has tentatively chosen a new plan it can test that plan by conducting a look-ahead--a game within a game. However, in doing so it must make

assumptions about its opponent, third countries, and the laws of war--
all of which may be wrong. Just as there are alternative Red and Blue
Agents (the Sams and Ivans), so also can there be alternative Red's
Blues and Blue's Reds. In principle, this perception-related
recursion could extend to infinite depth, but actual practice avoids
look-aheads within look-aheads: Agents within a look-ahead can
project their opponent's behavior using current information and
heuristics or simple algorithms, but they do not call upon the full
game machinery for a game within a game within a game. Realistically,
this seems to sacrifice very little credible information.

Figure 3 elaborates on the internal structure of the Red and Blue
Agents, emphasizing a more complex hierarchical character than
originally conceived. The Global Command Level (GCL) is an abstraction combining, for example, the Blue functions of the Joint Chiefs
of Staff, State Department, and White House Staff. The Supertheater
Command Level corresponds to something like NATO's Supreme Allied
Commander in Europe (SACEUR) and, simultaneously, the U.S. Commander
in Chief in Europe. The Area Command Levels, then, correspond to
individual theater-level commands (e.g., the NATO commander for
Europe's Central Region). The number of subordinate commands (i.e.,
SCLs and ACLs) can be changed easily, as can the physical regions over
which they have authority. The Operational Command Level (OCL) models
are really service models for managing forces. One function of an OCL
model might be to decide on a daily basis what fraction of a given
theater's air forces should be used for interdiction bombing rather
than air defense. These models rely upon a mixture of quantitative
algorithms and qualitative heuristics and are responsible for
reasonably fine-grained decisions about operations.

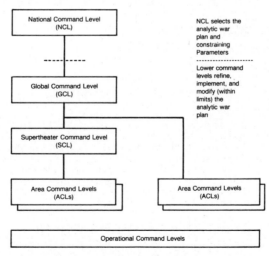

Figure 3
Hierarchical Structure of Red and Blue Agents

The outputs of the GCL, SCL, ACL, and OCL models are the force orders
to which the Force Agent responds when it next conducts the
simulation. In executing force orders, the Force Agent can apply
different tactical logic for Red and Blue to reflect asymmetries

between Red and Blue military forces, doctrine, and capability. Thus, part of the logic defining the abstractions known as the Red and Blue Agents is actually located within the Force Agent rather than the decision models, but the decision models can guide the Force Agent's logic by setting appropriate parameters. For example, an ACL may specify a forward defense rather than a fallback to some defense line in the rear and an OCL may specify certain constraints on the use of different national forces within an alliance; the Force Agent will then perform regular reallocations of ground forces among combat axes consistent with the guidance received.

Figure 4 is an influence diagram showing that the various command levels communicate through a rigid line of authority. By writing appropriate rules, however, the real-world phenomenon of a national leader communicating directly with a tactical commander can be simulated: the mechanism for doing so amounts to having the intermediate command models pass on the NCL's instructions without delay or adjustment. The design also specifies that (a) diplomatic exchanges occur between GCLs and (b) the NCL uses information resulting from Force Agent and Scenario Agent activities, but does not send instructions back, communicating instead with its lower command levels.

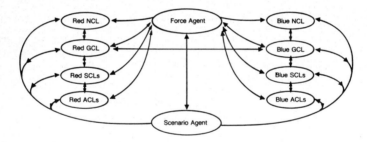

Figure 4
Influence Diagram for RSAS

Figure 5 shows an aggregated data-flow diagram of the system as it existed in late 1985 (Davis, Bankes, and Kahan, 1985). The system is highly centralized because of the many interrelationships that exist among types of decision and types of military actions worldwide. Thus, there are many global data variables for both the decisionmaking agents and Force Agent. Access to information is controlled through a data dictionary. Humans can interact through a data editor or a currently separate Force Agent interface.

It is impractical to show a control-flow diagram for the system because the control flow varies drastically from run to run. Figure 6 shows the system's subprograms (or, loosely, "objects"), with System Monitor represented as the Main Program determining control flow. It is System Monitor, for example, that contains the "wake-up rules" determining when a particular agent should have a move, and the order of moves among agents when several wish to move at the same time. The mechanism for wake-up rules is fairly complex. For example, if a Red Area Command Level model decides on a course of action and issues a series of orders, it will also specify the conditions under which it will want to move again (e.g., every day, or if any of certain events occur). These conditions will be reflected by data items in the World

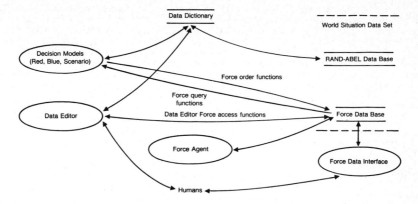

Figure 5
Data Flow Diagram for RSAS

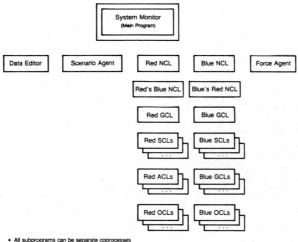

- All subprograms can be separate coprocesses
- "Red Agent" and "Blue Agent" are abstractions

Figure 6
Top-level Subprograms (Objects) of the RSAS

Situation Data Set (WSDS). As the Force Agent conducts the
simulation, it tests the conditions on a regular basis; if one of them
is met, it sets another data value indicating that one or more
particular agents want to awaken and move. It is then System Monitor
that takes control and decides which Agent is to be awakened next.

It was recognized early in 1983 that implementation of analytic war
plans with a script-like character would be greatly simplified by
using co-routines, so a co-routine capability was provided in
RAND-ABEL by Edward Hall for the UNIX environment (Shapiro et al.,

1985a,b). By late 1983, it was decided to use hierarchical
co-routines structured to correspond reasonably well to command and
control relationships in the real world (i.e., relations of the sort
suggested in Figure 3).

One reason for including the design diagrams is to emphasize the
difference between the system discussed here and more typical expert
systems. Those differences include: (1) complexity (the system
discussed here can be considered to include many separate expert
systems as well as programs of a rather different character); (2) the
requirement for hierarchical structuring; and (3) the requirement for
difficult system programming rather than application of generic expert-
system software.

It may also be worth noting that the system is definitely "object
oriented" intellectually. The various agents represent a nearly
decomposable hierarchy (Simon, 1980) of natural entities that operate
independently to a first approximation but interact significantly in
controlled ways (e.g., by engaging in crisis or conflict). They also
communicate in the normal sense of that term (e.g, through diplomatic
messages). On the other hand, RAND-ABEL does not have some of the
features of object-oriented languages such as SMALLTALK (Goldberg and
Kay, 1976) or Rand's ROSS (McArthur and Klahr, 1982). In particular,
the mechanisms for message passing and other interactions are quite
different.

4.3 Representation of Knowledge: General Comments

The design of the Rand Strategy Assessment System (RSAS) had to
address many basic issues, including: (1) what entities should be
focused upon in the game-structured simulation, (2) when should each
entity move, (3) how should the various entities communicate, and (4)
how should the various entities decide what to do in a move (decision
style). The answers required domain-specific knowledge if the
resulting simulation was to be comprehensible and achieve a level of
phenomenological verisimilitude (or, at least, a naturalness and
plausibility).

A sometimes implicit consideration in system design, but one about
which the author was especially concerned, related to the absence of
experts and empirical data. There are national security specialists
(including the author), but there are no "experts" in the sense that
term is used in AI. And, fortunately, there have been few superpower
crises in the last forty years, and none of them have brought the world
into general war. One consequence of this is that a system attempting
to simulate a variety of potential crises and conflicts had to achieve
higher standards of transparent logic than would, for example, an
expert system that could demonstrate its validity empirically. Also,
if the system were to be useful in understanding issues of deterrence,
crisis stability, and military strategy more generally, the various
rule-based agents would have to exhibit human-like behavior and
thought processes. At the same time, model development would have to
be highly analytic: For this application no expert was available to
provide all the rules from his intuition, and yet it was essential
that care be taken to assure some level of completeness--holes in the
knowledge base could be much more serious here than in a typical
expert system.

These factors had many consequences, among them the use of substantial
domain-specific knowledge in every facet of system design. By
contrast with expert-system models in which it has proved useful to

separate discrete entities such as a scheduler, inference engine, and knowledge base (see, for example, Hayes-Roth, Waterman, and Lenat, 1983), in the present work such an approach was neither feasible nor desirable. To the contrary, knowledge has been reflected in many different places and in a variety of different representations. Furthermore, the logic of RSAS models makes only minimal use of "general search" or generic inference techniques. Instead, the control logic tends to be highly structured (procedural)--something consistent with many classic AI efforts (e.g., those involving decisionmaking theory, organizational theory, or script), but quite different in character from much of the current expert-system work on goal-directed search with programming languages possessing inference capabilities using generalized search.

4.4 Knowledge Representation in System Architecture

The RSAS system design, then, employs substantial "meta knowledge" in the sense of Hayes-Roth et al (1983). This meta knowledge about the domain (military strategic analysis) affected both system architecture (e.g., the objects of attention) and the system's top-level control structure.

SYSTEM CHARACTERISTICS REFLECTING DOMAIN-SPECIFIC META KNOWLEDGE

    Number of high-level players in game (Red and Blue)
    Command-control hierarchy for players (see Figures 3,4)
    Order of moves
    Top-level process model for Red and Blue Agent moves (see
      Figure 2)
    Process model for Scenario Agent moves (Perception-Response)

Meta knowledge also determined the characters of the various Red and Blue submodels (which will be discussed further below):

MODELS AND MODEL CHARACTER

National Command Level	Rational, analytic, global in perspective, and not bound by history: Strategic Behavior
Military Command Levels (GCL, SCL, ACL)	Follows a prescribed plan, albeit with key decision points and adaptations, using many building-block procedures that are individually complex but practiced: Organizational (Cybernetic) Behavior
OCL	Manages forces on a routine basis using a combination of algorithms and heuristics (Service Behavior)

Given the variety of models and the complexity of the simulation, there is no single "knowledge base" in the RSAS, nor a single way to change knowledge. Conceptually, however, one can still talk about the knowledge base and how to change it. The options available are summarized below, with the number of pluses indicating how easily the change can be made.

WAYS TO CHANGE KNOWLEDGE IN THE RSAS SIMULATION

	NCL	GCL,SCL, ACL	OCL	Scenario Agent	Force Agent
Substitute entire rule sets (e.g., switch Sams, Ivans, or the scripts available to Red and Blue Agents)	+++	+++			
Change individual rules or algorithms	++	++	++	++	+
Change parameters within rules or algorithms	+++	+++	+++	+++	+++
Change parameters characterizing forces, capabilities, laws of war, etc.					+++

This listing also indicates the RSAS' hierarchical approach to model modification. All of the models are constructed so that usually one can implement changes (e.g, for sensitivity tests) by merely changing a parameter--either in data beforehand, or interactively during a simulation. In addition, however, the rules written in RAND-ABEL can be read and changed so easily that they can also be considered, in a sense, part of "data." By the end of 1985 RAND-ABEL will also have interpretive features making recompilation unnecessary after most changes of decision-model rules. Currently, a reasonably typical recompilation can take 15 minutes.

4.5 Knowledge Representation Within Analytic War Plans

As mentioned earlier, the GCL, SCL, and ACL models are supposed to demonstrate organizational behavior. Scripts are especially suitable here because they can capture detailed procedural knowledge (i.e., knowledge about how to do things, which may require dozens or hundreds of individual instructions). The scripts of theatrical plays are a good metaphor for military war plans because both proceed from start to finish without backtracking, and both have natural phases (e.g., one must alert forces before they deploy, and one must deploy them before they can enter combat). Just as an actor knows what to say or do next because he already understands where he is, so also is it easy to write military-command-level decisions within a coherent analytic war plan: the script format reflects implicitly a great deal of context that otherwise would have to be explicit. In effect, if the plan is applicable, then various actions go together and certain decision points and adaptations are predictable and to some extent schedulable. The participant in the plan need not worry about the larger context.

The analytic war plan describing the decision logic for a particular ACL commander is organized hierarchically by phases, within phases by moves, and within moves by technical complexity. For example, the first phase of a given plan might involve placing forces on alert; this might occur over a series of moves because of political factors and the need to call forces up from reserve status. Within a move that, for example, alerted military airlift, there would be a number of specific orders understandable by the Force Agent, or by an OCL model that would in turn issue detailed orders understandable by the Force Agent.

Although simple scripts might consist of nothing but a sequence of instructions, analytic war plans must also possess decision rules determining (as a function of the world state): when to proceed from one move or phase to another; whether to take one or another branch of the plan; what type of guidance should be given to OCL models managing forces; whether to request something from higher authority (e.g., more forces or authorization for some action); and whether to notify higher authority that the plan is no longer working as intended and that higher authority may wish to modify the plan or change it altogether.

Since the analytic war plans are to be building blocks for reasons discussed earlier in the paper, they must also contain logic allowing them to adapt to circumstances. That is, when a given plan (script) is first invoked, it must establish its own context. As a minimum, it must determine what the previous plan has already accomplished (Are the forces already alerted? Have they been deployed?). In principle, the plan might have to undo some of what the previous plan had ordered (e.g., disengage forces prior to starting a separate offensive).

In the general case, such resynchronization would be an extremely difficult problem in variable-structure simulations such as this. However, in practice it has proven possible to proceed with relatively simple domain-specific expedients. The principal technique is to build analytic war plans in families, with all plans of a family having a common understanding of plan phases so that if one plan replaces another it can test to see where it should begin. Using only a few indicators of context, it has been possible to develop a fairly large number of building-block scripts for the Red and Blue Agent prototypes.

4.6 Knowledge Representation In National Command Level Models

Clearly, knowledge representation for the National Command Levels must be altogether different from that of the script-based models if the NCLs are to exhibit "strategic" behavior. The most important issues in representing knowledge are probably (Davis and Stan, 1984; Davis, Bankes, and Kahan, 1985): (1) decision style, (2) strategic framework for organizing information, and (3) characterization of alternative NCL models (the various Sams and Ivans alluded to earlier).

The issue of decision style is especially interesting because the choices range from decision-analytic styles, with decision trees and utility calculations, to various styles associated with cybernetics or bureaucratic politics (Simon, 1980, 1982; and Steinbruner, 1974). Consistent with the desire for phenomenological fidelity and transparency, the approach adopted is akin to the idealization of what many real-world decisionmakers attempt (see, for example, Janis and Mann, 1977). Figure 7 illustrates this idealized decisionmaker as a process in which the decisionmaker first decides whether to decide, then examines a broad range of options (taking pains to assure that he receives a good set of choices to consider), contemplates the options with a variety of objectives and values in mind, searches for tie-breaking information, assimilates that information, reviews, and decides. Also, the decision model includes plans for implementation, contingencies, feedbacks, and control.

The NCL model is described in Figure 8. Note that the NCL model makes a situation assessment that includes "learning" as well as "projecting." It then specifies escalation guidance, operational objectives, operational strategy, and detailed controls within more generic war plans. Each such decision limits further the number of

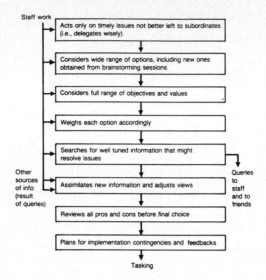

Staff work

Acts only on timely issues not better left to subordinates
(i.e., delegates wisely)

Considers wide range of options, including new ones
obtained from brainstorming sessions

Considers full range of objectives and values

Weighs each option accordingly

Searches for well tuned information that might
resolve issues

Other
sources
of info
(result
of queries)

Assimilates new information and adjusts views

Queries
to
staff
and to
friends

Reviews all pros and cons before final choice

Plans for implementation contingencies and feedbacks

Tasking

Figure 7
Actions of a Mythical Ideal Decisionmaker

• Assumes specific Ivan/Sam with associated grand strategy and values

Establish Context

• Assess current situation
• Adjust assumptions about opponent, third
  countries, and laws of combat
• Project future situation

• Establish escalation guidance (consistent
  with grand strategy)

• Establish operational objectives

• Establish operational strategy (and war plans)

• Establish special controls (set parameters in
  plan)

Test plan with look-ahead, implement or
reconsider choice of plans

reconsider

Implement plan

Figure 8
Decision Process Within NCL

available plans to be considered until a single plan is selected. The
NCL then performs a look-ahead projection to see whether the tentative
plan is likely to succeed; if so, it proceeds (or compares results for
two or three plans); if it is unsuccessful, it reconsiders (with
feedback logic determined by rule-based preference orders for plan
testing and the requirement that alternative controls be tested first,
then strategies, then objectives, then escalation guidances).

The relationship between the NCL model and the idealized decisionmaker
of Figure 7 is that both describe decisionmaking as a process, both
rely primarily upon heuristic rules rather than optimization or
general search algorithms, both recognize the potential for obtaining
and using special information, and both involve trading off
conflicting objectives and values. The NCL model makes explicit the
process of situation assessment and has the options (plans) as inputs
rather than producing the options itself. In summary, then, the
overall decision styles are similar, but there are significant
technical differences. Finally, it should be noted that the design
permits treatment not only of very good decisionmaking but also
decisionmaking degraded by limitations of information, perception,
mindset, and style. This is essential if the models are to be a
useful analytic mechanism for studying issues such as deterrence and
crisis stability.

As mentioned earlier, the fundamental uncertainties about national
behavior necessitate use of alternative Red and Blue NCL models.
Before building a given model, one must form a strong image of the
particular NCL--its personality, grand strategy, and "temperament."
There is a variety of techniques for crystallizing concepts on these
matters before beginning to write the decision rules that constitute
an NCL model. For example, essays such as the following prove useful:

> Model X is somewhat aggressive, risk-taking, and
> contemptuous of the opponent, but is ambivalent--
> believing that the opponent can sometimes be
> aggressive and irrational. He believes his military
> doctrine is essentially correct, although not always
> applicable. He is strongly averse to nuclear war....

Such essays communicate a sense for a given model, but they are
imprecise. More useful are some tree-like diagrams that one can work
out on blackboards to suggest the decision points and predispositions
a given type of national leadership might have (Davis, Bankes, and
Kahan, 1985). Also useful is a methodology involving formal
attributes within which one fills out a check list for the decision
model, a check list characterizing the model's attitude toward use of
nuclear weapons, its willingness to engage in risky tactics, and other
factors. The purpose of the essays, grand-strategy trees, and some
formal attribute lists is to clarify an image of the particular Red or
Blue NCL before the rule-writer attempts to write rules. This type of
procedure is essential for achieving coherence and logic.

Next to be considered is the question of how to organize information
within a strategic framework. Three concepts have proved especially
useful: conflict levels, conflict states, and a hierarchy of variables
for situation assessment.

The concept of conflict level has become familiar in strategic
analysis since the seminal work of Kahn and Schelling in the 1960s.
One constructs an escalation ladder in which, for example, nuclear war
is "higher" than conventional war. There can be a large number of
rungs on the ladder if one wants to distinguish carefully between

levels and types of nuclear use, types of crisis, and so forth. The ladder concept can be quite useful, although there are serious ambiguities when one applies it to complex problems (e.g., is war in one theater higher or lower than war in another theater?). A more sophisticated concept is that of conflict state (Davis and Stan, 1984), where the state is described in several dimensions such as conflict level by theater and side, and the presence or nonpresence of certain symbolic actions, again by theater and side. Figure 9 shows a simplified version of such a conflict state in which dots indicate the types and locations of certain military activities within a large but constrained set of scenarios focused on Southwest Asia, Europe, the high seas, and the intercontinental arena. Although rather simple, Figure 9 summarizes much of what senior players tend to focus upon in pondering high-level abstractions in political-military war games.

Conflict Level	Theater of Warfare				
	SWA	Naval	Europe	Space	Interconti-nental
General Strategic Nuclear					
Counterforce Strategic Nuclear					
Demonstrative Strategic Nuclear					
General Tactical Nuclear	•	•	•		
Demonstrative Tactical Nuclear					
Biological					
Chemical	•				
General Conventional	•	•	•	•	
Demonstrative Conventional					
Regional (one superpower)					
Crisis					

Figure 9
A Simplified Conflict State Space

The last concept to be mentioned here is that of hierarchical situation assessment. The objective in this concept is to have models capable of summing up a situation as follows, much as would a human decisionmaker:

> Well, gentlemen, if I understand what you've been telling me... then...our current situation is pretty good: we've achieved our principal objectives (though not everything we sought). We could push on, but prospects are marginal and risks high. Therefore,...

Note the emphasis, in this summary, on high-level abstractions such as situation, prospects, and risk. There is no mention here, for example, of the detailed force ratio on the third axis of advance in the second of three active theaters. However, the abstractions depend on layers of staff work that do reflect numbers and other details.

It follows, then, that situation assessment in an NCL model should depend primarily on a few high-level variables, each of which depends on a number of intermediate variables, which each depend on still more lower-level variables, and so on. An example here is that the assessment of Risks should depend on strategic warning, tactical warning, sensitivity of projections to assumptions, ultimatums

received from the opponent, and assessment of the opponent's
intentions and will. These, in turn, would all depend on more
detailed events in the simulation (the current state and history).

The current NCL prototype models contain about 4000 lines of RAND-ABEL
code each, which is the equivalent of 10,000-20,000 lines of C code.
The rules are expressed primarily in terms of RAND-ABEL decision
tables more or less as follows, although the example is contrived.

```
      If Current-situation is Eur-gen-conv
      Then
        Decision Table
        Basic-status Other-status  Prospects Risks   / Decision
        ============ ============  ========= ======    ========.
        goals-met    good          good      low       terminate
        goals met    good          good      medium    terminate
        [... many other lines...]
        losses       bad           bad       high      surrender.

      Else If Current-situation is Eur-demo-tac-nuc
      Then ...
```

Thus, the rules are modularized first by Current-situation using a
fairly complex escalation ladder to identify current-situation's
values. Within those modules, the rules are hierarchically structured
to depend primarily on high-level variables such as Risks, which are
then assessed elsewhere in the program in terms of strategic warning,
tactical warning, and other variables.

The RAND-ABEL decision table is to be read as follows. The first line
of the table's body is a rule saying that "If Basic-status is goals-
met, other-status is good, prospects are good, and Risks are low, then
the NCL decision is to terminate." This table is executable RAND-ABEL
code (not data) equivalent to a decision tree. The table format
allows the reader quickly to "see the whole" and to assess
completeness and flow. There exists an interactive table generator to
assist analysts writing rules to specify format, cover all the cases,
use the correct variable values, and so on.

There are many versions of RAND-ABEL tables, and many special
features. For example (Shapiro et al., 1985a,b): (1) the number of
and logical relationships among variables in a decision table can be
varied; (2) automatic explanations can be produced reproducing the
lines of decision tables that fire, and attaching the appropriate
comments that appear in the code as footnotes to the table; (3) one
can use relational operators like < and > in tables to reduce the
number of lines; and (4) there exist different types of tables that
provide lengthy sets of instructions in a natural format.

By contrast with software engineering techniques for using tables for
pseudocode system specifications or techniques for entering rules as
formatted data (see discussion in DeMarco, 1979), RAND-ABEL tables
appear directly in source code--replacing long chains of If... Then...
Else clauses. Properly designed rule-based programs can use tables
for a large fraction of the rules, producing highly transparent,
flexible, and self-documenting code.

In practice, these features of RAND-ABEL have proven extremely
valuable to analysts, programmers, and reviewers, and should be
seriously considered for other languages as well. In effect, the
table features exploit human capability to work two-dimensionally when

studying information. In this respect, they (as well as the
increasingly familiar spread-sheet programs and full-screen editors)
represent a new paradigm of computer science.

4.7   The Prototype System

The prototype system for automated war gaming was demonstrated to the
government late in 1984 and greatly improved over the course of the
next six to nine months, with research continuing. The RSAS program
currently contains the equivalent of about 120,000 lines of C-code
(much of it in RAND-ABEL). An automated war game requires about 6
megabytes of storage, with current mass storage being 50 megabytes or
more, and takes less than a half day (the time required depends in
part on how many look-ahead projections the agents make). By and
large, reactions to the prototype were highly favorable, particularly
with respect to: (1) the natural representations (i.e., objects
corresponding to important commands); (2) the hierarchical treatment
of agents; (3) the NCL's situation assessment structure; (4) the
overall emphasis on user interfaces, interactivity, and graphics; (5)
the architecture allowing enrichment without change of structure; (6)
the highly flexible nature of the models; (7) speed; (8) the inclusion
of realistic command and control heuristic rules in preference to
highly simplified optimizing algorithms; and (9) compactness (the
potential exists for a single analyst to comprehend and operate the
entire system).

As of late 1985, the development of decision models and Force Agent
was reasonably balanced with a number of synergisms. Force Agent
modellers had absorbed the expert-system paradigm and developed
heuristic command and control models (in C) on the basis of experience
with human play; those developing analytic war plans were efficiently
calling on the Force Agent's capabilities to avoid having to reproduce
clumsily, in rule-based code, the types of operational- and tactical-
level decisions and orders for which algorithmically structured models
are especially suited.

Although it is dangerous to make such statements, it seems that with
respect to the principles of interest in this book--and in particular
the feasibility of constructing large-scale complex systems combining
features of both knowledge-based and simulation modelling, the most
difficult conceptual and technical problems have been surmounted.
What exist, however, are prototypes. The effort to enrich those
models and apply them will be an exciting and challenging effort for
years into the future, as will expanding the newer techniques to reach
their full potential.

5.   CONCLUSIONS

This final section of the paper attempts to draw lessons from the
experience of a large and complex effort, lessons related to the
paradigms from AI, the management challenges of developing software
mixing knowledge-based and simulation techniques, and the
opportunities for contributing to policy analysis.

The first conclusion should probably be that the paradigms of AI have
proven enormously powerful in Rand's work. Especially significant are
such concepts as nearly decomposable hierarchies, process models of
behavior, and heuristic decisionmaking under conditions of complexity
and uncertainty (see especially Simon, 1980, 1982; and Cyert and

March, 1963). All of these are an excellent basis for system
architecture and are still insufficiently appreciated after two
decades of exposition.

Another set of paradigms with origins in AI relates to transparency
and comprehensibility. In the author's experience, modern computer
science techniques have proven invaluable in comprehending, managing,
and explaining complexity--in both software development and
applications of the game-structured simulation. The effort to develop
a programming language that could be read and modified by good
analysts with only modest programming skills has been extremely
worthwhile and has served to narrow the man-machine gap significantly,
as have such techniques as postprocessor color graphics to describe
simulation results (Bennett et al., 1985).

The paradigms from current expert-system work are more arguable as the
basis for work of the type described here. In particular, the author
is skeptical about finding generic knowledge engineers (as distinct
from domain specialists collaborating with computer scientists to
learn the necessary paradigms and techniques of AI) and about generic
software environments as a panacea for problem solving: the limiting
factor will continue to be finding individuals capable of exploring
the particular problems in depth. Also, while it is important to have
general concepts to guide work in knowledge-based modelling and
simulation (e.g., concepts well described in Hayes-Roth, Waterman, and
Lenat, 1983), it can be highly counterproductive to allow the language
of abstractions and AI jargon to permeate the work place--especially
if success depends upon interdisciplinary work, or even on a
combination of AI conceptualizing, analytic modelling, and complex
system programming. In part because of communication problems, the
value of early prototypes, walkthroughs, and other mechanisms for
producing something tangible early cannot be easily exaggerated. So
also should modellers adopt software engineering techniques for design
(e.g., DeMarco, 1979).

Another conclusion supported by work at Rand and elsewhere is that
success in combining knowledge-based modelling and simulation for
complex problems will require an astute combination of AI thinking and
more traditional "hard" analysis: adopting heuristic approaches can
be an excuse for fuzzy thinking and the failure to develop sound
theories or straightforward algorithms. One suggestion is that AI
specialists be used as conceptual architects, analysts (including
decision analysts) used as the knowledge engineers, and system
programmers be used for rigorous system design and implementation.

One conclusion from the development effort described here should be
evident to readers: large and complex problems require time, money,
and effort. Rand's work to develop the RSAS began in 1980, with the
first prototype system not emerging until the end of 1984. This time
could have been shortened somewhat, but not dramatically.

Lastly, it seems appropriate to observe that the advent of techniques
combining knowledge-based modelling and traditional simulation will
make it possible to exploit for the first time some of the richest
ideas of the last thirty years--ideas arising from the social sciences
on such issues as organizational behavior, bounded rationality, and
the role of cognitive style in decisionmaking. In the past, it has
been difficult to apply these ideas to practical problems in part
because they did not lend themselves well to predictive modelling of
the sort easily accomplished with more classical concepts such as
profit maximization, game-theoretic solutions of simplified problems

ignoring uncertainty, and simulation. As a result, there continues to
be a widespread tendency to approach policy-relevant modelling with
the classic tools even when they are inappropriate. Now, it would
seem (at least to the author) that it should be possible to do much
better--primarily because it is now far easier to build rule-based
models that can be large, complex, and realistic--and yet efficient
and transparent. If this notion proves valid--in applications going
beyond what this paper has discussed--simulation modellng will become
an essential tool at the fingertips of managers and other
decisionmakers (or at least their trusted staff).

REFERENCES

Bennett, Bruce W., Arthur M. Bullock, Carl M. Jones, and Paul K. Davis (1985). The RSAC Theater Warfare Model, The Rand Corporation, Santa Monica, California.

Builder, Carl (1983). Toward a Calculus of Scenarios, N-1855-DNA, The Rand Corporation, Santa Monica, California.

Carbonell, J. (1978). POLITICS: Automated Ideological Reasoning, In: Cognitive Science, 2.

Cyert, Richard M., and James G. March (1963). A Behavioral Theory of the Firm, Prentice-Hall, Inc., Englewood Cliffs.

Davis, Paul K. (1982). Concepts for Improving the Military Content of Automated War Games, P-6830, The Rand Corporation, Santa Monica, California.

Davis, Paul K., Steven C. Bankes, and James P. Kahan (1985). A Prototype Model of National Command Level Decisionmaking, R-3290-NA, The Rand Corporation, Santa Monica, California.

Davis, Paul K., and Peter J. E. Stan (1984). Concepts and Models of Escalation, R-3235, The Rand Corporation, Santa Monica, California

Davis, Paul K., Peter J. E. Stan, and Bruce W. Bennett (1983). Automated War Gaming As a Technique for Exploring Strategic Command and Control Issues, N-2044-NA, The Rand Corporation, Santa Monica, California.

Davis, Paul K., and James A. Winnefeld (1983). The Rand Strategy Assessment Center: An Overview and Interim Conclusions About Potential Utility and Development Options, R-2945-DNA, The Rand Corporation, Santa Monica, California.

DeMarco, Tom (1979). Structured Analysis and System Specification, Prentice Hall, Inc., Englewood Cliffs.

Dewar, James A., William Schwabe, and Thomas L. McNaugher (1982). Scenario Agent: A Rule-Based Model of Political Behavior for Use in Strategic Analysis, N-1781-DNA, The Rand Corporation, Santa Monica, California.

Elzas, M. S. (1984). Concepts for Model-Based Policy Construction. In: Simulation and Model-Based Methodologies: An Integrative View, T. I. Oren et al (eds). Springer-Verlag, Heidelberg.

Fain, J., F. Hayes-Roth, H. Sowizral, and D. Waterman (1982). Programming in ROSIE: An Introduction By Means of Examples, N-1646-ARPA, The Rand Corporation, Santa Monica, California.

Forrester, Jay W. (1969). Urban Dynamics, M.I.T. Press, Cambridge.

Glaser, Charles, and Paul K. Davis (1983). Treatment of Escalation in the Rand Strategy Assessment Center, N-1969-DNA. The Rand Corporation, Santa Monica, California.

Goldberg, A. and Alan Kay (1976). Smalltalk-72 Instruction Manual, Xerox PARC, SSL 76-6.

Graubard, Morlie H., and Carl H. Builder (1980). Rand's Strategic
    Assessment Center: An Overview of the Concept, N-1583-DNA. The
    Rand Corporation, Santa Monica, California. Also in: Rand's
    Strategic Assessment Center: An Overview of the Concept (1982),
    Policy Sciences.

Hall, H. Edward, Norman Z. Shapiro, and Herbert J. Shukiar (1985).
    Overview of RSAC System Software: A Briefing, N-2099-NA, The
    Rand Corporation.

Hayes-Roth, Frederick, Donald A. Waterman, and Douglas B. Lenat (Eds)
    (1983). Building Expert Systems, Addison-Wesley Publishing
    Company, Inc., Reading, MA.

Janis, Irving L., and Leon Mann (1977). Decision Making, The Free
    Press, New York.

Kahan, James P., William L. Schwabe, and Paul K. Davis (1985).
    Characterizing the Temperament of Red and Blue Agents--Models of
    U.S. and Soviet Decisionmakers, N-2350-NA, The Rand Corporation,
    Santa Monica, California.

Marshall, A. W. (1982). A Program to Improve Analytic Methods Related
    to Strategic Forces, In: Policy Sciences 15, Elsevier Publishing
    Company, Amsterdam.

McArthur, D. and Phillip Klahr (1982). The ROSS Language Manual,
    N-1854-AF, The Rand Corporation, Santa Monica, California.

Schank, R., and R. Abelson (1977). Scripts, Plans, Goals and
    Understanding, Lawrence Erlbaum Associates, Hillsdale, New
    Jersey.

Schwabe, William, and Lewis M. Jamison (1982). A Rule-Based
    Policy-Level Model of Nonsuperpower Behavior in Strategic
    Conflicts, R-2962-DNA, The Rand Corporation, Santa Monica,
    California.

Shapiro, Norman Z., H. Edward Hall, Robert H. Anderson, and Mark
    LaCasse (1985a). The RAND-ABEL Programming Language: History,
    Rationale, and Design, R-3274-NA, The Rand Corporation, Santa
    Monica, California.

Shapiro, Norman Z., H. Edward Hall, Robert H. Anderson, and Mark
    LaCasse (1985b). The RAND-ABEL Programming Language: Reference
    Manual, N-2367-NA, The Rand Corporation, Santa Monica, California

Simon, Herbert A. (1980). Sciences of the Artificial, M.I.T. Press,
    Cambridge.

Simon, Herbert A. (1982). Models of Bounded Rationality: Behavioral
    Economics and Business Organization, M.I.T. Press, Cambridge,
    1982.

Steeb, Randall, and James Gillogly (1983). Design for an Advanced Red
    Agent for the Rand Strategy Assessment Center, R-2977-DNA, The
    Rand Corporation, Santa Monica, California.

Steinbruner, John D. (1974). The Cybernetic Theory of Decision: New
    Dimensions of Political Analysis, Princeton Press, Princeton.

Modelling and Simulation Methodology
in the Artificial Intelligence Era
M.S. Elzas, T.I. Ören and B.P. Zeigler (Editors)
© Elsevier Science Publishers B.V. (North-Holland), 1986

Chapter VI.3

A MODEL-BASED EXPERT SYSTEM FOR DECISION SUPPORT IN NEGOTIATING

Syed V. Ahamed

Computer Science Department
College of Staten Island
City University of New York
Staten Island, New York 10301
U.S.A.

Evelyn G. Roman

Computer Science Department
Polytechnic Institute of New York
333 Jay Street
Brooklyn, New York 11201
U.S.A.

In this paper, we show how an expert system superstructure may be used as a decision support tool in a negotiating process model. This superstructure is built around a model blending a systems approach with a mathematical framework for inter-organizational interaction. After chaining the highlights of the negotiation process as sequential and logical events in a systems framework, the dollar value of the assets exchanged and their utilities for the beneficiaries are compared to investigate the conditions for acceptability, rejection, further negotiations, or eventual stalemate. Expert system rules help to evaluate the actual cost of agreement and cost of disagreement. Segments of the solution space leading to little or no probability of success in the negotiating process are pruned. Expert system software techniques for automatic propagation of probabilities through the inference network are used. Behavioral and perceptual factors are also introduced in the expert system to explain the (non-linear) irrational attitudes/patterns of behavior. The strength of the systems approach in the representation of the essential chain of events and of the feedback processes to emulate the learning process is fully exploited. Likewise, the strength of mathematical tools to transform the actual composite assets donated from one organization to the utility array of the other by an evaluation matrix is also utilized. The effects of the feedback in the systems approach becomes an iterative computation of marginal utility in the mathematical framework. The convergence of this iterative process leads to essentially acceptable values in the utility array, and, likewise, instability in the iterative process leads to a divergence in the negotiating process.

1. INTRODUCTION

In a unified approach to the mapping of reality by system models, the contributions of Elzas and Zeigler (Elzas, '84.1, Zeigler, '76) have established the methodology leading to the construction of models for complex human and economic situations. The discussion presented by Elzas (Elzas '84.1, Elzas '84.2) is especially relevant to the particular model presented here. A diversity of corporate, economic, legal and behavioral forces interact to produce an intercorporate decision such as a merger or an acquisition. Such decisions have a critical and long range influence on the survival of the corporation. The corporate survival is generally influenced by the economic stability, product leadership and both the tangible and intangible corporate assets.

Further, the advances in three unrelated sciences have also paved the way for the development of a mathematical and computable basis for human and organizational negotiations. The first one deals with the principles of game theory in economics. The second and third relate to the concepts of systems analysis and expert systems, both in the field of computing sciences. The first two can be merged to produce a highly legitimate discipline relating to the development of corporate strategy and planning. Each parent science having been endowed with the wealth of ideas, supports each other where one may fail independently. Systems science yields a methodic approach to the pursuit of objectives by a systematic accumulation of the constituents of success in achieving the objectives. Certain game theory aspects are applicable to decisions that the corporate bodies may undertake along the pathway to success in achieving the objectives. Typical examples of games applicable to the intercorporate and social interactions are the zero sum game and the prisoners dilemma (Overstreet, '71). Finally, the development of expert systems (Hayes-Roth, et.al. 1983) facilitates the application of a knowledge base extracted from the experience and wisdom of organizational negotiators. The languages that have emerged from the rule-based programming assure that the basic rules and the fine points which finally shape the outcome of a negotiation are not overlooked and overwritten by the game theory rules or by an unsophisticated application of the systems considerations. Heuristic rules may be conveniently incorporated in such languages to deal with exceptional circumstances.

The chief strength of systems science is its capability to separate and seek the conditions leading to a goal on a step by step and day by day basis. Generally in computing science, where Systems Analysis is extensively used, information is manipulated, sought, used and processed. In the interaction process, assets, tangibles, and intangibles or organizations or individuals are sought and processed. System Science can also accommodate most feed-back processes effectively. Feed-back loops are more or less essential to represent situations where the game participants learn from the interaction to modify their behavioral pattern (Ahamed, '84). To this extent System Science can be very effective in adjusting its procedures according to the predictions of game theory. Major feed-back loops can be represented in systems notations; the quantity of the feed-back signal (stimulus) carried in System loops is determined by the outcome of game theory. In computer systems the quantity and consequence of this feed-back signal is programmed. In organizational and human interaction both the quantity and consequence of these feed-back signals are fuzzy and ill-defined. As rationality is assumed to dominate the transactions, the behavior pattern becomes more predictable.

The chief strength of game theory lies in its capability to seek and direct behavior and understand the consequence of one player's behavior on the reaction of the other, thus filling the very gap created when one tries to use System Science in its crude form while dealing with human organizational systems.

For the remainder of this paper, we use intercorporate negotiations to illustrate the use of expert system decision making for negotiations. Typical of such interactions may be merger and acquisitions, large order buy/sell negotiations, Labor-Management negotiations, (Ahamed, et.al. 1985, Roman, et.al. 1984) international development ventures, Industry-Government interactions, Industry-University research, project negotiations, etc.

It is clear that the negotiating process between two organizations or that between two individuals are not radically different. The primary motivation for both may be derived, the basic laws of economic behavior may be anticipated, and the outcomes may be those of achieving a "feasible" compromise which "satisfies" with a basic "security level" for both parties involved. However, the path and goal defining activity for interpersonal negotiation can be highly individualistic, whereas the corresponding activity for intercorporate negotiation arising from the collective intelligence of the group is likely to more or less be consistent and predictable.

2. EXPERT SYSTEM CONCEPTS

When negotiations take place, a team of experts is often brought in to gather the facts and optimize the decision-making process. Particularly when time is of the essence, as in the recent hostage crisis, it would be useful to have much of the expertise incorporated beforehand in a computer expert system. The large amounts of knowledge necessary to reach a successful settlement and the heuristic nature of many of the rules underlying organizational behavior, make negotiations an ideal domain for an expert system.

Recently computer expert system software tools have been developed to encode and deductively combine the heuristic rules an expert in a particular field is assumed to use to solve problems in his area of expertise. These computer systems differ from conventional computer programs in that there is a clear separation between the knowledge base of rules and a control module which decides which rules should be looked at first, and which rules' consequents should be performed if the antecedents of several rules hold simultaneously. This separation facilitates the addition, deletion, and modification of rules. Typical control mechanisms are forward chaining, in which given pieces of evidence lead to a hypothesis being formulated by the rules, and backward chaining, in which a hypothesis is tested by recursively testing the antecedents of rules whose consequents are the given hypothesis. The user may be queried as to the certainty of some evidence, and, in some tools, may respond with a probability value rather than just a true or false value. These probabilities may be propagated through the rule base to then deduce the probabilities of various hypotheses. Some of these tools include explanation facilities for justifying the system's conclusions, and some include sophisticated knowledge acquisition facilities to aid in building the rules. Some include interacting knowledge sources of production rules, each of which gets scheduled depending upon which data gets posted on a common blackboard structure, allowing for the incremental construction of competing hypotheses. (We envision a separate primary knowledge source for each side to the negotiations, with a common supervisor. Each of these three would be further refined into specialized knowledge sources for the different types of knowledge). Some allow for inferences involving fuzzy terms such as "High profits" programmed by defining probability distributions for these terms. These features are all relevant to the negotiations scenario.

Guidelines for the Construction of the Expert System Rules

(a) Organizations have needs.

(b) Society has resources to satisfy organizational needs.

(c) Organizational assets are consumed, conserved, or wasted.

(d) Organizational motivation and ensuing behavior stems from unsatiated needs, external stimulation (which gives rise to a reaction) and/or internal conditions (which give rise to a motivation).

(e) Under complex conditions, the simple maximizing behavior becomes that of "Satisficing", the search for an optimal solution becomes that for a "feasible" solution, and the search for certainty in goal achievement becomes that of finding a "Security Level" for the outcome of the solution.

(f) Organizations learn from interactions with society and other organizations and modify their behavior.

The axioms (a) through (d) are self explanatory, but the effects of (e) and (f) are far reaching. It is due to such effects and their dynamic combinations, that the corporate interactions can neither be completely programmed nor completely predicted. Consider the concept of satisficing. This function is human and personality dependent. It stems from the past experiences of the interacting individuals who represent the corporation and the managerial objectives. Such objectives are generally not even documented and lie buried in the collective ambitions of the upper management. When two corporations interact, the "satisficing" effort is sought by two different bargaining parties. Further, the same set of agreements drawn out in successful negotiations by the parties should be "satisficing" enough for both, and likewise should be "feasible" enough for both and finally should provide acceptable "security levels" for both.

Next consider the concept of one side learning from the behavior of the other side. Numerous factors enter into the learning process. First, the perception of behavior is again a personality dependent effect. Communications skills of the participants, cultural backgrounds, personal norms of communication, and of body language, all play a role in transmitting and perceiving the behavioral patterns of the other side. Second, a feed-back process immediately becomes necessary to monitor the present behavior from the past learnings. Third, the feed-back effort has profound effects on the stability of the interacting process itself.

3. MATHEMATICAL ASPECTS OF THE INTERACTION PROCESS INCORPORATED IN THE EXPERT SYSTEM

3.1 The Need Vector (N)

Corporate needs like human needs can be classified. To a certain extent, such needs arise from the long range objectives of the top management. The very existence of a stable corporation implies planning and achieving goals of financial solvency, participating in a viable economic activity, and ascertaining the continued existence of the corporation. The basic security needs thus exist and are continuously satisfied. The balanced cash flow requirements, good social and labor relations etc., form a secondary tier of needs necessary for participation in viable economic activity. Finally, the higher needs arise from the long term goals to grow and expand, earn a reputation, provide a sound emotional and intellectual atmosphere for the employees, and satisfy their own higher needs, etc. It is thus feasible to envision a need structure for corporations like that for individuals. The relative importance of needs becomes important in assigning the numbers in the need vector.

3.2 The Asset Vectors (A)

Assets have been classified by the accounting profession. Tangible assets generally satisfy the more basic needs of corporations, even though intangible assets may play a dominant part in the very existence of the corporation. Assets, by definition tend to be scarce and the price of assets depends strongly on the scarcity of such assets in relation to their needs. Corporate assets include productive resources (raw materials, plant, equipment, patents, goodwill, services, etc.), contractual rights to future services and products, and human resources.

3.3 The Consumption Vector (C)

Needs are satisfied by the consumption of assets. These assets may be regenerated over a period of time. The surplus (such as retained earnings of corporations) may be reinvested or accumulated. During a corporate interaction it thus becomes essential to be aware of the present consumption of the existing assets within one's own corporation producing its basic need satisfaction.

3.4 The Motivational Vector (M)

The lack of total satisfaction of all the corporate needs produces a sense of motivation to achieve a further satisfaction and derive further utility by the consumption of more assets. Such assets may be self generated or obtained by corporate interactions. The dynamic nature of the need vector also provides a sense of motivation. Ensuing interactions could be highly streamlined, routine, and stylized, or they could be distinct, unique, and highly customized.

An interaction may develop between two motivated corporations, or between one motivated and one reacting corporation. The former situation leads to a case where one may expect a cooperative game structure during a majority of the interaction process, the latter situation leads to a case where at least one party may hole a cooperative game structure during a majority of the process. This condition itself does not imply that the cooperative or uncooperative attitude of one or the other party will not reverse during the interaction. Frequently, attitudinal and behavioral factors lead to very pertinent changes in the game structure.

Legal and social constraints may not only force an interaction from corporations, but under different conditions also specifically prohibit interaction between them.

3.5 The Resource Balance Vector (B)

When assets are retained, they accumulate and grow. Under-utilized assets provide a strong incentive for corporate executives to seek some satisfaction of their outstanding needs. If they can be reinvested to generate additional utilization within the corporation or through the standardized and stylized mechanisms of interactions, no major corporate interaction results. However, if greater than normal enhancement or corporate utility is desired, it becomes essential to seek and interact with other corporations (e.g., mergers, acquisitions, etc.).

3.6 The Donation Vector (D)

During interactions, assets are exchanged and one corporation agrees to commit a certain array of assets from the resource balance vector B. These donations depend on the cost of the assets and the balance after the consumption.

3.7 The Valuation Matrix (V)

The utilization of assets generates utility for the corporation. Assets can be used many ways and different types of utilities may be derived from the same assets. Hence, by making the valuation (or utilization) function be in a matrix format, one can generate a utility array from the asset vector.

3.8 The Utility Array (U)

This is obtained by multiplication of the valuation matrix by the asset vector and represents the state of need satisfaction. If all the needs are completely satisfied a unit utility array is generated. By default, organizations tend to maximize their utility arrays or generate some particularized weighted sum of all the terms.

3.9 The Marginal Utility Array (ΔU)

This is the change in utility derived by assimilating the donated assets of the other corporation by the recipient organization, and ΔU equals the new utility if the donations were made and utilized minus the old utility with no donations.

3.10 The Weighted Marginal Worth (ΔW)

This is a single number derived from the marginal utility array. It indicates the dollar value of the benefits (or losses) derived from the change in utility due to the corporate interaction.

Since all the various elements of the marginal utility array (ΔU) do not carry the same importance, it becomes necessary to weigh the relative importance of each elements by assigning a weighing factor b_i, so that the net dollar worth of the marginal utility may be derived.

3.11 The Weighted Price of Donations (P)

This is a single number used to determine the cost of the donations vector (D). Here, the cost for the donator for making such a donation is important. The donation vector (D) has numerous elements and all the elements are not equally expensive for the donor. Hence it becomes necessary for the donor to attach a weighing dollar value to each element for the donation vector, so that the net dollar value of the entire Donation may be aggregated.

3.12 The Perceptual and Behavioral Variables

Behavioral variables inherent in the individual negotiators, and perceptual variables estimating how particular facts are perceived determine state transition probabilities for the negotiation process which give rise to a cusp catastrophe model which may be incorporated in the expert system for predicting nonlinear behavioral shifts (Roman, E.G., et.al. 1985).

4. THE COST OF AGREEMENT (COA), COST OF DISAGREEMENT, AND DEMAND INTENSITY

These exist on a symmetrical, bilateral and reciprocal basis. When the demands of one corporation are listed, the dollar value of the benefit demanded should be divided by the dollar value of the compensations offered to get the Demand Intensity. (To computer the value of benefits, the expectation of such benefits should be calculated from an estimate of probability if there are uncertainties beyond the immediate negotiation. The dollar value of the compensation offered is well defined, at least during the time of negotiation.)

Where there is a perfect trade, the Demand Intensities (DIM1 for Corporation 1, DIM2 for Corporation 2) both computed simultaneously by both corporations are both 1, and the negotiation a completely open and one step success. When DIM1 as calculated by Corporation 1, and DIM2 as calculated by Corporation 2 are both greater than one (non-zero sum game situation), then the negotiation becomes mutually beneficial and completely acceptable to both. The negotiation itself starts to assume its proper dimensions when the first corporation maximizes DIM1 and likewise corporation two maximizes DIM2 when there is a zero sum game situation.

The cost of agreement and disagreement arises from a specific set of demands being made at a certain instant of time during the negotiating process. The dollar value of meeting all demands of the other party are calculated as the cost of agreement. The cost of disagreement would be the total loss incurred in terminating the interaction or agreement to a less desirable contract or interaction.

Step 1:   The negotiating function consists of examining the following events for the two corporations.

CORPORATION 1   CORPORATION 2

Basic Conditions: Basic Conditions:

$$M^1 = N^1 - C^1 \qquad\qquad M^2 = N^2 - C^2$$

$$B^1 = A^1 - C^1 \qquad\qquad B^2 = A^2 - C^2$$

<u>Expected Marginal Utility & Worth:</u>   <u>Expected Marginal Utility & Worth:</u>

$$\Delta U^1 = D^2 \cdot V^1 \qquad\qquad \Delta U^2 = D^1 \cdot V^2$$

$$\Delta W^1 = \sum_{i=1}^{i=m} b_i^1 \cdot \Delta U^1 \qquad\qquad \Delta W^2 = \sum_{i=1}^{i=m} b_i^2 \cdot \Delta U^2$$

<u>Expected Donations & Price:</u>   <u>Expected Donations & Price:</u>

$$D^1 = D^1 (P^1, B^1) \qquad\qquad D^2 = D^2 (P^2, B^2)$$

$$P^1 = \sum_{i=1}^{i=n} a_i^1 \cdot D_i^1 \cdot P_i \qquad\qquad P^2 = \sum_{i=1}^{i=n} a_i^2 \cdot D_i^2 \cdot P_i$$

<u>Step 2</u>: The result of the negotiating process ends in one of the five following situations:

a) <u>SUCCESSFUL NEGOTIATION:</u>

$$\Delta W^1 \gg P^1 \quad \text{(as viewed by Corp. 1)}$$

$$\Delta W^2 \gg P^2 \quad \text{(as viewed by Corp. 2)}$$

b) <u>AGREEMENT, PERCEIVED FAIRNESS:</u>

$$\Delta W^1 \approx P^1 \quad \text{(as viewed by Corp. 1)}$$

$$\Delta W^2 \approx P^2 \quad \text{(as viewed by Corp. 2)}$$

c) <u>AGREEMENT, GENUINE FAIRNESS:</u>

$$\Delta W^1 \approx P^1 \approx \Delta W^2 \approx P^2$$

d) <u>EXPLOITATION BY CORPORATION 1:</u>

$$\Delta W^1 \gg P^1 \quad \text{(in actuality)}$$

$$\Delta W^2 \approx P^2 \quad \text{(in actuality)}$$

Corporation 2 comprehends (from its own stand point) that $\Delta W^1 \approx P^1$, or it has no mechanism to reduce or redistribute the terms in D^2 appropriately.

e) <u>EXPLOITATION BY CORPORATION 2:</u>

$$\Delta W^1 \approx P^1 \quad \text{(in actuality)}$$

$$\Delta W^2 \gg P^2 \quad \text{(in actuality)}$$

Corporation 1 comprehends (from its own stand point) that $W^2 \approx P^2$ or it has no mechanism to reduce D^2 or redistribute the terms in D^1 appropriately.

f)   UNSUCCESSFUL NEGOTIATION:

$$\Delta W^1 \ll P^1 \quad \text{as viewed by Corp. 1}$$

$$\Delta W^2 \ll P^2 \quad \text{as viewed by Corp. 2}$$

It can be seen that over a long period of time (implying repeated interactions) situations (c) and (d) are the only stable conditions. Situations (a) and (b) are not stable over a long period since the true perception of ΔW^1 and ΔW^2 in relation to P^1 and P^2 gets established thus leading to situation (c). Constant violation of the situation (c) by situations (d) and (e) by one corporation leads to exploitation by that corporation thus leading to mistrust and withdrawal by the other. This leads to the other stable situation (f) over a long period of time. The other conditions (a), (b), (d) and (e) even though unstable over a long period of time may find stability over the life span of the contract. The most important factor for the agreement hinges on the approximate equality of the net worth of the increased utility to the price of the donation.

5.   THE SYSTEMS MODEL OF THE INTERACTION PROCESS INCORPORATED IN IN THE EXPERT SYSTEM

Our basic purpose of using system science is not to develop an entirely quantitative basis for the strategy selection as is done in computer simulation but to evolve a methodology similar to PERT (Program Evaluation and Review Techniques) or CPM (Critical Path Method) for interorganizational interaction. Figures 1 and 2 represent a structural configuration depicting the sequence of events, their interactions, and the various decision making processes involved during intercorporate negotiations.

The bilateral symmetry is established by the center line through the boxes A, B, C and D. The contents of boxes 2, 4, 6,...... 42 are identical or converse of boxes 1, 3, 7,...... 41 respectively.

5.1 Sequence of Events

When the managements of the two eligible corporations become aware of their needs, they have to initially discover each other. The circumstances or events leading to this mutual discovery are not discussed here since it is outside the realm of the actual negotiation. When it does become apparent that there can be mutual benefit or that a reaction is essential, then the actual interaction starts. The preliminary effort for both managements lies in evaluating their residual needs and residual assets (boxes 5 and 7; 6 and 8). It is here that the actual motivation for interaction is rooted.

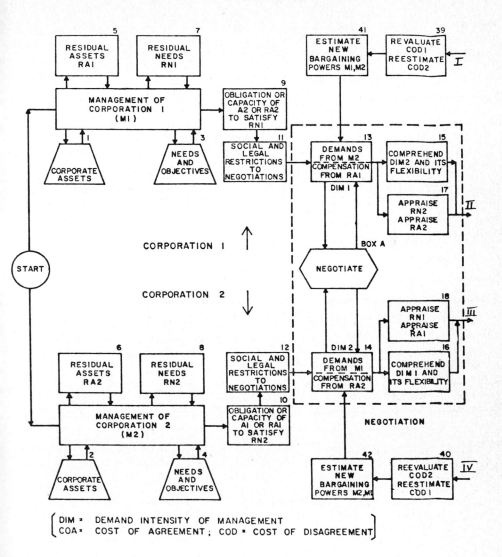

Figure 1. The Start and the Continuation (Loop II to I for Corporation 1 and Loops III to IV for Corporation 2) of the Intercorporate Negotiation Process

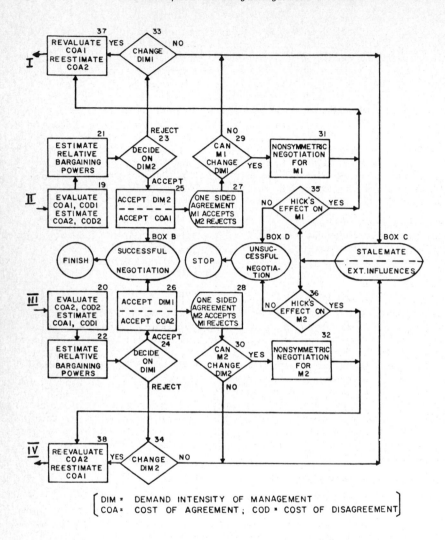

Figure 2. The Continuation (II to I and III to IV) and the Finish (Box B, C, or D) of the Intercorporate Negotiation Process

Boxes 9 and 11 or 10 and 12 corresponds to the investigation prior to the negotiation. Here, there is an evaluation of potential reward by interaction and a determination of the legality and/or social acceptance of the potential negotiation. Boxes 13 through 17 or 14 through 18 depict the actual negotiation where there is an exchange of information regarding the reciprocity of assets for mutual need satisfaction. Also exchanged is a framework of reasoning and fairness in the trade of assets conforming to the social mores and the economic valuation of such assets at that particular time and at that particular place. Boxes 19 and 21 or 20 and 22 establish the costs of agreement if the Demand Intensities appear reasonable or the costs of disagreements if the Demand Intensities appear to be hopelessly out of line (i.e., far from their ideal value of unity). Considerable subjectivity and the valuation (based on scarcity and the potential use) of the assets become critically important for reaching the decision in boxes 23 or 24. Here, all the behavioral traits of the executive decision making process becomes active in accepting or rejecting the Demand Intensity presented from the other side.

If corporation 2 accepts DIM1 and corporation 1 rejects DIM2, we have a situation where a one-sided agreement results and boxes 28, 30, C etc. are encountered. Conversely, a one-sided agreement for corporation 1 is equally possible. It is during such a situation that the effects of feed-back and learning from the negotiating process becomes critically important.

5.2 Feed—back Loops

There are two major types of feed-back loops in the negotiation process. As the duration of the disagreement between the two corporations start to increase, the frustration in not achieving the desired goals of both corporations exerts an influence in relaxing their respective demands. This tendency was first detected by Hicks in Labor Management Negotiations (Roman, et.al. 1984). These feedback loops depend on the duration for the parties to traverse them. The effects of the first type of loop are generally felt during the interaction. It provides a minute to minute, hour to hour or day to day correction for demands and expectations. The continuity of the negotiation is rarely lost. The second type of loop provides for correction of a long drawn stalemate situation where a major overhaul of demands and expectations becomes essential. In the former type of correction procedure, small and minor concessions are made. In the latter type of correction procedure, the effect of long term needs still unsatisfied provides a major restructuring of the demands made on the other side.

5.3 The Stalemate and its Consequences

When a stalemate condition forces a Hicks effect on the demands from the corporation, then there is a correction for the DIM1 and/or the DIM2 thus edging towards a gradual convergence to Box B, a successful end to the negotiations. On the other hand, the absence of a Hicks effect leads each corporation holding dogmatically to its own demands and gradually diverging to Box D, thus terminating the negotiation.

The effect of time without a conclusion of the interaction also motivates corporations to look for many solutions, one of which is the search for an alternate, more flexible corporation to interact with. The termination of the interaction with one may be only the start of an interaction with another. The reaction to a stalemate situation depends on the personality and style of the upper management. The outcome in such cases further depends on evaluating the bargaining powers of the individual corporations. Federal agencies and Social organizations (with the aid of courts or legal mechanisms) can hold an enormous amount of bargaining power. In such cases the cost of disagreement becomes not only high but increases with time.*

6. PRUNING AND PREDICTING THE OUTCOME OF NEGOTIATIONS

6.1 The Smooth Convergence

A smooth convergence of negotiation essentially entails no feedback loops in the block diagram (Figs. 1 and 2), where there is an explicit change of DIM1 or DIM2. This essentially eliminates the loops 13, (15, 17), 19, 21, 23, 33, 37, 39, 41, 13 and its image loop 14, (16, 18), 20, 22, 24, 34, 38, 40, 42, 14 or the loops passing through boxes 29 or 30. Hicks effects discussed in Section 5.2 and depicted in boxes 35, or 36 are also eliminated. The expert system rules will guide the users towards this type of a convergence process in expediting the negotiation. Pruning becomes imperative in the search towards an optimal and expedient solution.

6.2 The Smooth Divergence

The prerequisites for smoothly diverging negotiations are weak motivations and/or lack of compensating assets that are offered. From the systems consideration, this condition exists if the demand intensities of both corporations are so high that the negotiation ends in box D via the paths 13, (15, 17), 19, 21, 23, 33, box C, 35, box D and its image loop 14, (16, 18), 20, 22, 24, 34, box C, 36, box D. The demand intensities DIM1 or DIM2 are never changed in boxes 29 and 30 or at boxes 33 and 34.

From a mathematical consideration, the smooth divergence occurs if $\Delta W^1 >> P^1$ as seen by 2 and also $\Delta W^2 >> P^2$ as seen by 1, thus there is no incentive to alter P^1 by 2 or conversely P^2 by 1. The expert system will evaluate these quantities and guide both sides accordingly.

6.3 The Oscillatory Convergence

This type of outcome of negotiation is by far the most commonly encountered agreement between parties. Here the demands are explicitly spelled out in proposals. Initially they are quite high and are tapered down. Lowering of demands from their artificially high initial values is a common feature of such an oscillatory process. Oscillations could be weak or strong; over-damped or persistent. Weak oscillations occur when one party fails to put up a long and meaningful resistance to the demands of the other party, and the second party easily convinces the first about its position.

Fram a systems viewpoint the demand intensity of the first corporation DIM1 is high but the second corporation convinces the first that the cost of agreement on its part would be much too high; the first corporation thus reduces its own DIM. From a mathematical consideration, this situation calls for a relatively high value of ΔW^1 as seen by the corporation at a disportionately low value of P^1, thus making Π^1 excessive; the first party thus either reduces ΔW^1 by reducing D^1 or increases P^1 to increase Π^2 (profit of corp. 2).

On the other hand, strong oscillation occurs when there is a severe lasting conflict over demands of major importance to either corporation. Very severe and strong oscillations can lead to divergence, thus exposing each corporation to the risk of wasted efforts and unsatisfied needs. Persistent weak oscillations are sometimes tolerated because the parties cannot agree on every microscopic detail of every issue. At this level, the compromise achieved by equalizing the weighted averages of the costs involved may be logical. Issues dealing with valuable assets (assets being too close to non-negotiable assets) lead to persistent oscillations. Issues of major importance involving highly valuable (bordering on being non-negotiable)

---

*   When corporations or unions are fined on a daily basis for noncompliance to a code, court order, etc.

assets are a major source of oscillatory divergence leading to unsuccessful negotiations. Here both the dimensions of negotiations (behavioral and economic) become entirely important to alter the course of agreement.

In an oscillatory convergence of negotiations both parties arrive at box B (Figs. 1 and 2). Feed-back loops in Figures 1 and 2 through boxes 13, (15, 17), 19, 21, 23, 33, 37, 39, 41, 13 or 13 (15, 17), 19, 21, 23, 25, 27, 29, 31, 37, 39, 41, 13 and its corresponding image loops 14, (16, 18), 20, 22, 24, 34, 38, 40, 42, 14, or 14 (16, 18), 20, 22, 24, 26, 28, 30, 32, 38, 40, 42, 14 should be traveled at least once for an oscillation to be present. Further, the more number of times these loops are traversed, the more persistent these oscillations are going to be. Feed-back loops via box C may also be traversed during the feedback process. The expert system keeps track of long drawn oscillatory negotiation and suggests cooling-off periods further used to reevaluate their positions. The expert system would eliminate those sources of oscillation due to the behavioral dimension of negotiation if they are present.

From an economic consideration, let Π^1 and Π^2 be the total profit levels for both corporations. Their sum is viewed as being essentially constant, however their relative values take an oscillatory path before becoming acceptable. In a zero sum game, such oscillations arise due to an incomplete knowledge of probabilities and costs. These probabilities and cost levels are altered due to the negotiation process and due to mutual learning effects. Further causes of these oscillations are due to an incomplete analysis of the organization about the details of expected and donated asset levels. Costs and prices having been derived by non-linear relations to the scarcity of assets can be another major, reasonable, and persistent source of oscillations, not only in evaluating the cost of agreement and cost of disagreement for the party itself, but also for the other party.

6.4 The Oscillatory Divergence

From a systems consideration, oscillatory divergence almost always implies one party reaching Box B and then the other party increasing its demand intensity (DIM), due to a reversal of position on the part of the first party. During divergent oscillations the expert system would indicate to the users a modified demand intensity, and suggest concessions to make the cost of agreement attractive to control the divergence in the negotiating process.

7. CONCLUSION

Intercorporate negotiations are based on the behavioral foundations of organizations. The corner stones in such behavioral foundations are the Economic, Accounting, Social and Transactional laws. First, the economic basis of donations and expectations, proposals and counter proposals, demands and concessions, stems from the marginal price theory of assets. When conditions of bilateral monopoly are encountered between informed parties, and the zero sum constraint on profits exists in its entirety, the fair distribution of profits forms an equilibrium condition. When these conditions are not ideal, the maximization of profit (defined as the difference between the expected net worth of donations received and the price paid for the compensating donations) is a popular form of economic activity in negotiations. Cooperative or non-cooperative game structures are chosen by individual parties depending on the relative knowledge levels.

Second, the accounting principles become dominant in evaluating the allocations and/or availability of corporate assets. Such assets being actively traded and bartered during negotiations form the cards in the hands of corporate players.

Third, the social laws sets the outer limits on the negotiation per se. The legal framework defines which assets may or may not be negotiated, the types of prices, the use of assets by either corporation, etc. This aspect of negotiation becomes particularly important in international negotiation.

Finally, the transactional aspect of the negotiation is perhaps where the greatest amounts of effort is spent. While making demands and offering compensation, an economic justification is necessary. The basis of the transaction rarely stops here. Each party maximizes the expected profit after partially establishing a knowledge base for itself and for the other side. Full exploitation of the positions is expected and each transaction (proposal and counter proposal) is thus a manifestation of the corporation to the other three positions: economic, accounting, and social.

All of these aspects can be incorporated in an expert system for negotiations. Such a system may include a selection from the following components:

(a)   The systems and mathematical components we have modelled.

(b)   One or several interacting knowledge sources implementing the aspects from (a), together with a Control module for logical inference.

(c)   Other expert system features available in current software tools including automatic propagation of probabilities, fuzzy reasoning, explanation facilities, and knowledge acquisition facilities. Least commitment control strategies (Rich, '83), adaptive learning, constraint satisfaction, dependency directed backtracking, criticality levels, etc., are also applicable.

(d)   Behavioral and perceptual factors incorporated in, perhaps a cusp catastrophe model built into the system. The resulting system can calculate costs, probabilities, and bargaining powers, monitor oscillations, suggest cooling-off periods and concessions, and learn and predict.

With many major breakthroughs evolving in the technologies, man is still at the frontier of the complex process he commands during his association with others. The paths and mazes through the labyrinth of association and interaction have been explored by philosophers with a candlelight. We believe the techniques mentioned here will provide a more practical scientific light.

REFERENCES

Ahamed, S., "A Systems Model for Labor-Management Negotiations", in <u>Proceedings of 1984 Summer Computer Simulation Conference</u>, North Holland Publishing Co.

Ahamed, S., Roman, E., "Extensions in the Application of Expert System Concepts to Labor Management Negotiations", in <u>Proceedings of 1985 Summer Computer Simulation Conference</u>, North Holland Publishing Co.

Elzas, M. S. (1984.1), "System Paradigms as Reality Mapping", <u>Simulation and Model Based Methodologies: An Integrative View</u>, Springer-Verlag Berlin Heidelberg, 1984.

Elzas, M. S. (1984.2), "Concepts For Model-Based Policy Construction", <u>Simulation and Model Based Methodologies: An Integrative View</u>, Springer-Verlag Berlin Heidelberg, 1984.

Hayes-Roth, F., Waterman, D., Lenat, D., <u>Building Expert Systems</u>, Addison Wesley, 1983.

Rich, Elaine, <u>Artificial Intelligence</u>, McGraw-Hill Publishers, 1983.

Roman, E. G., Ahamed, S., "An Expert System for Labor-Management Negotiations", in <u>Proceedings of 1984 Summer Computer Simulation Conference</u>, North Holland Publishing Co.

Zeigler, B. P. (1976), <u>Theory of Modelling and Simulation</u>, John Wiley & Sons, N.Y.

Modelling and Simulation Methodology
in the Artificial Intelligence Era
M.S. Elzas, T.I. Ören and B.P. Zeigler (Editors)
© Elsevier Science Publishers B.V. (North-Holland), 1986

Chapter VI.4

EXPERT SYSTEMS FOR MODELLING OF DECISION SUPPORT AND INFORMATION SYSTEMS

Dr. Henk G. Sol
Professor of Information Systems
Department of Informatics
Delft University of Technology
Julianalaan 132
2628 BL Delft, The Netherlands

For problem—solving in general, and thus e.g. for simulation modelling, for decision support and for information systems design, the development of conceptual models is of great importance. We observe that the relevance of application domain models is greatly overlooked, mainly because in many decision—making situations emphasis has been on the exploration of alternative solutions, not on the activities of problem identification and problem specification.

Effective and efficient modelling requires a lot of expertise. The consultation of a base of conceptual models from various application areas may speed up the specification of an appropriate model of the specific application domain. This brings us to some requirements on how expert systems could be used and what their contents should be to support effective modelling during the design of decision support and information systems.

1. INTRODUCTION

Although the interest for artificial intelligence (AI) in general and for expert systems (ES) in particular should be welcomed, one has to bear in mind that these topics are not an aim in itself. On the other hand, contributions from AI and ES may be fruitful to improve the process of problem—solving in organizations.

For problem—solving in general, and thus e.g. for simulation modelling, for decision support and for information systems design, the development of application domain models is of great importance. This is illustrated in Section 2, where we refer to the proces of problem—solving and the methodology of simulation. Emphasis on the activities of problem identification and problem specification does require the specification of various application areas. These application domain models, as described in Section 3, guide the construction of conceptual and empirical models, of which various types can be identified.

Section 4 describes the large amount of expertise that is needed for effective and efficient modelling. This support can only partly be generalized in expert systems as is discussed in Section 5, even if one focusses the discussion on decision support systems and on the design of information systems.

2. PROBLEM SOLVING AND SIMULATION

The question how an effective use can be made of computers for the solution of problems in organizations is not getting the attention it deserves. Simulation plays an important role, when a contribution is sought in the computer supported activity of expressing the premises behind individual decision—making and in instruments for decision support, especially for problem specification, for generation of alternatives and for solution finding.

Following Shannon (1975) we define SIMULATION rather broadly as the process of designing a model system of a real system and conducting experiments with this model system in order to understand the behaviour of the system and/or to evaluate various strategies for its operation.
We look upon simulation as a problem—solving methodology. We identify the following stages in a problem solving process: problem as perceived in reality, conceptual model, empirical model and solution, see Figure 1. The stages are connected by the activities of conceptualization, model—construction, solution finding, implementation, consistency check, and correspondence check, see Sol (1982).

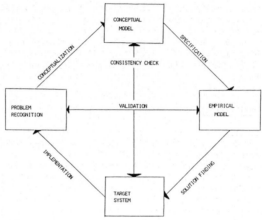

Figure 1

The activity of CONCEPTUALIZATION comprises firstly the choice of a vehicle for communication and of a metatheory comprises a worldview and a construction para—digm. Thereafter a conceptual model of the problem at hand is formulated with the help of these. The conceptual model defines the variables that will be used, to specify the nature of the problem in broad terms. It presents a vision of the problem situation described in a specific application domain.

Once the conceptual model of the problem at hand has been arrived at, an empiri—cal model has to be specified. By analysing the empirical model of the existing situation the PROBLEM SPECIFICATION has to become clear. The connection between the empirical model and the problem as perceived in reality reflects the degree of correspondence between these two. This can guide the problem owner in the selection and acceptation of courses of action.

Given the problem specification, the activity of SOLUTION FINDING is initiated. Solution finding is an iterative process of questioning and answering, or of ANALYSIS and SYNTHESIS, where computers might be of great help. After a des—cription of the problem situation in a descriptive conceptual and empirical model the creation of prescriptive or normative conceptual and empirical models is started. Theories in the conceptual models and empirical model are rejected or modified during this process. Answers, generated by an empirical model that shows a good correspondence, have to be consistent. When a solution is found, a course of action is IMPLEMENTED in reality, which influences the problem situa—tion.

Simulation has a number of advantages for performing practical research in the field of decision—making in organizations, decision support systems and information systems, see Sol (1982), namely
— the possibility to emphasize the activity of conceptualization;
— the possibility to experiment in view of the data available;
— the possibility to generate alternatives and analyse these in comparison with the initial specification.

In methodological discussions around simulation, see e.g. Zeigler (1976) and Zeigler et al. (1979), not much attention is paid to the process of problem solving itself. The emphasis is put on the phases of solution finding and implementation. Recently, there is argumentation to focus on the phases of problem identification and problem specification, see e.g. Elzas (1984), Landry et al. (1985), Sol (1982).

Before one can start looking for a problem solution, or designing an information system, one has to understand the problem situation or the actual object system. Of course, design of an application or choice of a solution has to be done within constraints of time and resources. But, ´thinking before doing´ does apply to any modelling situation. Therefore, more emphasis should be placed on the activities of problem identification and specification, especially in a simulation approach.

3. **APPLICATION DOMAIN MODELLING**

We remark that in many methodologies for problem—solving, and also for the construction of decision support systems (DSS), the ill—structured character of a problem situation is not taken as point of departure. However, most problems in organizations can be characterized as being ill—structured.
We define a problem as well—structured if the following conditions are met:
1. The set of alternative courses of action or solutions is finite and limited.
2. The solutions are consistently derived from an empirical model that shows a good correspondence with the real system.
3. The effectiveness and efficiency of the courses of action can be numerically evaluated and are reproducible.
Problems that do not fulfil these requirements are defined as being ill—structured. In Sol (1982) we conclude that ill—structured problems especially demand specific emphasis on the activities of conceptualization and problem specification, leading to a good correspondence between the problem situation and the empirically supported model of it. The latter model as systems description of the existing situation is the frame of reference for creating and evaluating alternative courses of action.

The distinction between a conceptual model and an empirical model reflects the special character of conceptualization on the one hand, and problem specification and solution finding through experimentation on the other. Data are needed to construct an empirical model and to accept its degree of correspondence with the actual problem situation. However, in analyzing individual decision—making processes, it is often very difficult to catch up detailed data. As we have to give an empirical content to the conceptual model, we demand a methodology which may generate these data. Therefore, in the process of problem—solving, we do have to specify explicitly conceptual models and empirical models. We have to describe the way the models are placed in an empirical environment in the search for a solution. This clearly has consequences for knowledge representation and expert systems.

For the construction of conceptual models and empirical models one needs a

language system which does not restrict the capabilities of inquirers and decision—makers in using knowledge to make models and to create insight. We make a
distinction between on the one hand a description form using equations and on
the other hand process or rule—based models.
The EQUATION MODELS are frequently encountered in DSS for strategic and organizational problems, especially in corporate or financial models. In these models
one has to define functional relationships in terms of definition equations or
behavioral equations. Although these may be specified in a non—procedural way as
in several DSS—generators, they still apply to the outside of a phenomenon, seen
as a black—box.

In the PROCESS OR RULE—BASED MODELS one does not try to summarize a process in
equation form. Instead, one tries to describe the sequence of events in a
system. We introduce the notion of an ENTITY as an identifiable set of associated ATTRIBUTES. An entity may portray behaviour by applying one or more
transformation rules to change the values of some of its attributes and by
interactions with other entities. We define in a SCENARIO related to an entity
the possible transformation rules and the possible interaction paths of an
entity, as well as the conditions under which these can be actualized. This can
be done in various modes. One mode is the ´declarative´ mode, as e.g. encountered in interpreted predicate logic, see Bubenko (1982), Sernadas (1982).
Another mode is the ´procedural´ mode, as we know this style from a great many
procedural programming languages. It is sometimes suggested that these modes are
antagonistic. We prefer to see them as complementary. Depending on the application domain and the users involved, one might prefer one of the modes.

In combining within an entity a data part and an action part, we come close to
the concept of object—representation in object oriented—languages, see e.g. Cox
(1984).
The notions of an entity and a scenario enable us to ´open the black—box´ of an
individual decision—maker and specify the concepts and rules applied. We are
able to specify their own language system, knowledge system and problem processing system. As to the construction of a conceptual model of an individual
decision—maker, we have to describe how scenarios of entities with their attributes are actualized. We may specify various psychological types of a decisionmaker in a multidisciplinary way by introducing entities with corresponding
attributes and scenarios for processing data and making decisions. In a scenario
for an individual we may even describe the changes in the data input mode and
decision—making during the process of problem—solving. We observe that scenarios
for portraying behaviour may bring about transformation rules not previously
thougt of, as well as attributes and interaction paths involved. We may have to
describe that a decision—maker has a local specialisation: As an entity he only
deals with a specific set of attributes and specific access—paths to other
entities. He only observes a ´representative state´ of an entity, i.e. those
attributes and that part of the scenario which have meaning to him. However,
this representation may change dynamically during the problem—solving process.

With the distinction between conceptual and empirical models and between equation and process models in mind, we like to have a closer look at the activities
of conceptualization and specification.
Let us first start modelling from the ´equation perspective´: When a problem is
perceived, a number of relationships are hypothesized from a specific worldview.
In the activity of conceptualization the variables are defined that will be used
to specify the nature of the problem in broad terms. The parameters in the
relationships between the variables are to be specified by measurement or by
estimation during the activity of problem specification. In an iterative process, hypotheses may be rejected until a valid model of reality is achieved.
Alternative solutions can now be calculated by playing with the parameters as
well as the values of the variables. This approach is e.g. followed in financial
and marketing models when sensitivity analysis or goal—seeking is used.

It is known from e.g. marketing that families of candidate equations exist for specific application areas, cf. Naert and Leeflang (1978). A base of formal candidate equations can be used as 'application domain model' during the activity of conceptualization. Then the normal hypothetic—inductive process is followed to generate a valid empirical model. The resulting numerically specified models may be compared with other numerical models from the application domain.

In a 'process perspective' one may proceed as follows:
The activity of conceptualization consists of three distinct steps: The first step is the choice of a vehicle for communication and of a context for conceptualization or application domain model. Using this description form, the application domain model should present instruments in view of a problem area under consideration. As our vehicle we choose the entity—attribute—action construction as the corner stone for possible contexts. The second step comprises the identification of entity—categories in a given problem situation using the application domain model. This step may be performed using a metaphor. An example is: 'look for co—ordinating agents'. A metaphor could even be brought into the application domain model as an entitity—category, to be used as an example. In the third step, the specification, instances of the identified entity—categories are created to form a conceptual model of the object system.
The activity of model construction comprises the transition of the conceptual model to an empirical model which has to be executed on a machine with a number of physical constraints. The conceptual model defines the scope for the specification of an empirical model without referring to available data. The problem is, what attribute parts and action parts of what entities are to be described in which amount of detail.

A general application domain model often used in the design of information systems is based on the specification of the object system in terms of flows of labour, money, assets, articles and intermediate products, controlled by the processes of inflow, treatment, transport and outflow.
For the development of decision support systems often reference is made to an application domain model on a high level of abstraction which sees organizational entities as loosely coupled systems.

Similar remarks as to the construction of process models also apply to the construction of dynamic empirical process models, or shortly simulation model systems.
The activity of conceptualization proceeds in the same way. The transformation to an empirical model is a data bound activity where refinement and extension are given to the conceptual model.
Reduction can be achieved by:
— as to the attribute part:
  — replacing one or more deterministically valuated attributes by stochastic attributes, taking the availability of data into account;
  — coarsening the range set of one or more attributes;
— as to the action part:
  — simplification of entity—entity interaction by entity—categories, which define specializations, and by functions and procedures;
— as to the system entity:
  — aggregating entities together in instances of new entity—categories. This may involve the introduction of new data—items as attributes, new reference attributes or new action parts. Also new aggregates can be formed through nesting.
To place a simulation model as a system description in an experimental frame, a simulation model system is constructed under control of a modeller. The simulation model is extended to an executable simulation model system entity by a specification of a treatment. An experimental frame is a set of possible treatments.
We make a distinction between a simulation model and a simulation model system,

because we can now clearly pay attention to the considerations to achieve model reduction and for exposing treatments to the model in an experimental frame. The steps in the construction of simulation models and framework for simulation based inquiry is depicted in Figure 2.

4. EXPERTISE FOR MODELLING SUPPORT

The experimentation or generation of evidence from the simulation model system in an experimental frame is done in four phases controlled by the experimenter, see e.g. Kleijnen (1974, 1975).
1. verification;
2. validation;
3. pruning;
4. investigation.

In the verification phase, the distributions of the exogenous attributes are tested against actual data, available in the administration or collected specifically for this purpose. The model system is checked for consistency. The initialization conditions, i.e. the conditions that control the creation of entities, are looked into and the runlength as well as the number of replications are determined.

The validation of a model system of an existing situation entails the comparison of the values of the endogenous attributes with the ones found in the object system, as far as these are measurable. We denote this form of validation by replicative validation. We refer to structural validation, if hypotheses on the behaviour of the simulation model system as specified by the endogenous attributes are checked. This can be done, for instance, by giving impulses to the system and looking for correspondence between the measured values of attributes inside the model system and in the object system.

In the pruning, the model system of the existing situation is explored for possible relationships between endogenous and exogenous attributes. The hypotheses that result from this analysis are to be tested in the investigation.

The investigation requires an experimental design which may maximize the discriminating power for testing the hypotheses.

The various treatments in the experimental design are, of course, to be verified and validated. Now the validation is a predictive validation for which plausibility or expert tests may be applied.

We use the notion experimentation in a broad meaning, not in the restricted one of performing a set of experiments in an experimental design. We want to stress that a simulation model is placed as model system in an experimental frame in order to create insight by exposing treatments to it. The contents of the experimental frame, i.e. the set of possible treatments, evolve during the phases of verification, validation, pruning and investigation. For the investigation phase, one mostly chooses in a rational way a set of treatments in the form of an experimental design with specific requirements to create evidence.

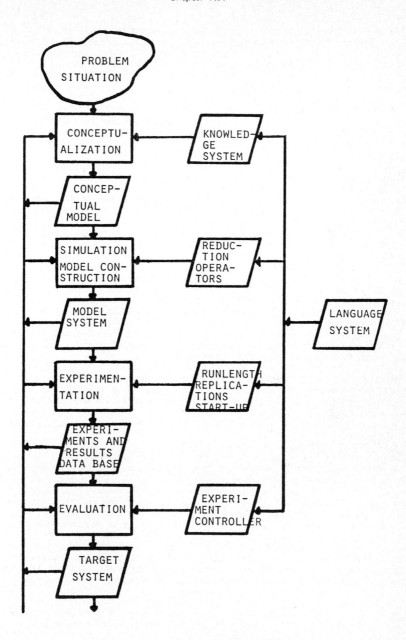

Figure 2: A framework for simulation

The framework expresses that a language, the tools and the activities are close—
ly related. This is realized by the introduction of the notion INQUIRY SYSTEM.
An inquiry system serves as a ´context for conceptualization´, a conceptual
model for problem specification, a model system for solution finding and as a
target system for implementation. An inquiry system integrates what in the area
of decision support systems is called a language system (LS), a knowledge system
(KS) and a problem processing system (PPS), see Bonczek (1981).
The inquiry system reflects an extensible LS with various contexts and data
models. We are able to define various conceptual models as conceptual schemata
reflecting the KS. Our inquiry system, as a PPS, explicitly addresses the phases
of verification, validation, pruning and investigation.

A family of simulation based inquiry systems can be implemented in various
programming languages like e.g. Simula. We identify instruments for a concep-
tualizer, a modellor, an experimentor and an evaluator. Various entity—categories present the building blocks of a simulation methodology in specific application areas. Great flexibility exists as to the conceptualization of the problem situation at hand. The specification of a conceptual model and the transi—
tion to a simulation model system in an experimental frame is done in explicit
transformation steps, subject to requirements of consistency and correspondence.
The inter—relations between the various activities find form in successive
models, building on each other in layers. This is easily implemented in Simula
by making the context, the conceptual model, the simulation model and the simulation model system ´prefixed´ CLASSES, see Sol (1982). In the latter an experimentation data base is invoked. This is shown to be capable of avoiding the
confusion of evolutionary model building and experimentation.

This approach has been applied to several cases in the field of decision support
systems and prototype development of information systems, from which the follo—
wing lessons can be learned (Sol, 1983).
The concepts to specify a conceptual model determine, to a large extent, the
effectiveness of simulation, e.g. concepts like a resource or a bin may define
away alternative specifications. A complete specification of interactions between entities gives more insight in co—ordination problems than a specification
in terms of transactions, events or monitors.

5. **EXPERT SYSTEM SUPPORT**

A useful framework for research on DSS is introduced in Sprague (1980). He
discusses the perspective of the end—user, the builder and the toolsmith from
which a DSS can be viewed. In accordance with this distinction the concept of a
DSS—generator is put forward to bridge the gap between general tools and specific DSS. Sprague distinguishes as the main components of a DSS a data base, a
model base, and an intermediate software system which interfaces the DSS with
the user.

Within the data base for decision support one can distinguish between external
data from public data sources, administrative data produced by the transaction
processing system, and internal data created by personal computing. The models
in the model base as envisaged by Sprague are mostly of the ´equation´ type: a
great number of so called corporate models or financial models consists of
definition equations and behavioral equations. Econometric models also consist
of equation models. Another category is formed by optimalization models based on
linear, dynamic or stochastic programming.

A first generation of so—called DSS—generators focusses on equation models with
data base and interactive facilities like data—, model— and text manipulation,
cf. Klein and Manteau (1983) and Bergquist and McLean (1983). By now, the
integrated facilities are not only offered on mainframes, but also on micro—

computers together with facilities for ´down—loading from and up—loading to central computer systems through data—communication´.

A less technological framework is put forward by Bonczek et al. (1981). They replace the components mentioned by the concepts of a language system, a knowledge system and a problem processing system. The language system is the sum of all linguistic facilities made available to the decision—maker by a DSS. A knowledge system is a DSS´s body of knowledge about a problem domain. The problem processing system is the mediating mechanism between expressions of knowledge in the knowledge system and expressions of problems in the language system.

The framework put forward by Bonczek et al. makes it easy to relate the work in the field of artificial intelligence to DSS. We define an expert system as ´a computer system containing organized knowledge, both factual and heuristic, that contains some specific area of human expertise, and that is able to produce inferences for the user´, see Chang, Melamud and Seabrook (1983).
When one looks upon an inference engine as a special kind of problem processing system and upon the knowledge base as a special kind of knowledge system, then these expert systems fit neatly into the framework.

We distinguish between ´strategic knowledge of the application domain´ and ´actual knowledge´ or expertise in an empirical situation. The first type of knowledge is encountered in the construction of conceptual models, the second one in empirical models. Both notions of knowledge play a key role in expert systems.

The inquiry system mentioned supports the process of problem—solving, firstly by creating an epistemological specification of processes in an empirical situation. This specification is based on a conceptual model formulated against the background of knowledge of an application domain.
Subsequently, the inquiry system facilitates the generation of alternatives and the choice of a solution. By keeping track of the subsequent steps in the process of a problem—solving we may acquire knowledge, not only about the actual problem situations, but also perhaps for future situations.

The inquiry system can be seen as a problem—solving environment. When it is supported on a computer, we are dealing with a DSS—environment. How can we apply these environments to create supporting inquiry systems for individual decision—makers?
The construction of the descriptive understanding model and the prescriptive target solutions can be facilitated by a design environment in which various expert systems and knowledge bases have their place. The process of producing the epistemological representation can be facilitated by an expert system with a knowledge base characteristic for the application domain.
Further expert systems with a different knowledge base, to support the process of problem—solving are dedicated at
— verification and validation of the descriptive model;
— pruning and evaluating this model and setting up an experimental design;
— creating suggestions for alternative target specifications.

The approach in applying these knowledge bases is then:
— choose appropriate building blocks for a system description of the existing situation;
— identify decision entities and describe rules in the existing situation;
— develop a simulation model and analyse the problem;
— transform the target prototype to a concrete DSS/IS.
Pilot applications of this approach are reported in Sol (1984a, 1984b).

The efficiency of a simulation—approach is mainly determined by appropriate mechanisms, namely for controlling simulated time, for generating input data from a data base, for interactive run control, for output data collection on direct access files, for experimentation control through special data bases and for evaluation of results. The experimentation phases in the simulation methodology can be supported only partially by software. The experimentation efficiency still largely depends on the insights of the inquirer in dealing with the screening and the experimental design.

REFERENCES

Bergquist, J.W., McLean, E.R. (1983), Integrated Data Analysis and Management Systems: An APL—Based Decision Support System, in: Sol, H.G. (ed.), Processes and Tools for Decision Support, North—Holland, Amsterdam.

Bonczek, R.H., Holsapple, C.W., Whinston, A.B. (1981), Foundations of Decision Support Systems, Academic Press.

Bubenko, J.A. et al., CIAM (1982), in: Olle, T.W., Sol, H.G., Verrijn Stuart, A.A. (eds.), Information Systems Design Methodologies: A Comparative Review, North—Holland, Amsterdam.

Chang, C., Melamud, Y. and Seabrook, D. (1983), Expert Systems, The Butler Cox Foundation, Report Series no. 37.

Cox, B.J. (1984), Message/Object Programming: An Evolutionary Change in Programming Technology, IEEE Software, January.

Elzas, M.S. (1984), Systems Paradigms as Reality Mappings, in: Oren, T.I. et al., Simulation and Model—Based Methodologies: An Integrative View, Springer, Berlin.

Klein, M., Manteau, A. (1983), Optrans: A Tool for Implementation of Decision Support Centers: Sol, H.G. (ed.), Processes and Tools for Decision Support, North—Holland, Amsterdam.

Kleijnen, J.P.C. (1974), Statistical Techniques in Simulation, part I, Marcel Dekker, New York.

Kleijnen, J.P.C. (1975), Statistical Techniques in Simulation, part II, Marcel Dekker, New York.

Landry, M., Pascot, D., Briolat, D. (1985), Can DSS Evolve Without Changing Our View of the Concept of ´Problem´?, Decision Support Systems, Vol. 1, nr. 1.

Naert, P.A., Leeflang, P.S.H. (1978), Building Implementable Marketing Models, Martinus Nijhoff, Leiden.

Sernadas, A. (1982), Software Behaviour Specification with Triggering Logic, Infolog Research Report RR02, Lisbon.

Sol, H.G. (1982), Simulation in Information Systems Development, Ph.D. Thesis, University of Groningen.

Sol, H.G. (1983), Developing Decision Support Systems by Simulation, Proceedings 11th Simula Users´ Conference, NCC, Oslo.

Sol, H.G. (1984a), The Emerging Role of Simulation Based Inquiry Systems, in: Bemelmans, Th.M.A. (ed.), Beyond productivity, Information Systems Development for Organizational Effectiveness, North—Holland, Amsterdam.

Sol, H.G. (1984b), <u>Prototyping: A Methodological Assessment</u>, in: Buddle , R. et al. (eds), Approaches to Prototyping, Springer, Berlin.

Sprague, R.H. (1980), <u>A Framework for Research on Decision Support Systems</u>, in: Fick, G. Sprague, R.H. (eds.), Decision Support Systems: Issues and Challenges, Pergamon Press, Oxford.

Zeigler, B.P. (1976), <u>Theory of Modelling and Simulation</u>, John Wiley.

Zeigler, B.P. et al. (1979), <u>Methodology in Systems Modelling and Simulation</u>, John Wiley.

Modelling and Simulation Methodology
in the Artificial Intelligence Era
M.S. Elzas, T.I. Ören and B.P. Zeigler (Editors)
© Elsevier Science Publishers B.V. (North-Holland), 1986

Chapter VI.5

A KNOWLEDGE-BASED MODELLING APPROACH
TO OFFICE FORM-FLOW SYSTEMS

Kappel G. [1], Tjoa A M. [1], Wagner R.R. [2]

1) Institute of Statistics and Computer Science, University of Vienna, Austria, A-1010 Vienna, Liebiggasse 4/3-4
2) Institute of Computer Science, University of Linz, Austria A-4040 Linz/Auhof

A form modelling approach based on NF^2-relations (non-first-normal-form relations) is introduced. The aim of the paper is to present a concept of embedding knowledge into an office information system which is modelled as a form-flow system. Since the major task of this paper is the knowledge engineering aspect of form-flow systems emphasis is given to the problem of the conceptual design of form-flow systems. Therefore the knowledge base aspect of form flow systems which concerns the notion of integrity constraints in dynamic models and the notion of triggering resp. flow-control is described in some detail.

1. INTRODUCTION

In the last few years the relevance of the form interface as an instrument of communication in office information systems is explored by many researchers LOU 81 , EMBLEY 82 , GIBBS 82 .

Recently semantic data models have been used by some authors for the logical conception of form views (e.g. EMBLEY 82). A more system-theoretical view of different modelling concepts is given in ELZAS 84, ZEIGLER 84 and ÖREN 79.

In this paper a form modelling concept based on NF^2-relations (non-first-normal-form relations) with the characteristics of a knowledge based system is introduced.

In section 2 a brief description into the architecture of a knowledge based form-flow system is given.

In section 3 the advantages of the semantic concept of NF^2-relations for the internal representation of form flows are described.

In section 4 the problems concerning the time dimension and integrity check are discussed.

The form flow system described in this paper has been implemented as a prototype at the University of Vienna. The system is called CBIS (Computerunterstütztes BüroInformationsSystem).

2. THE ARCHITECTURE OF A KNOWLEDGE BASED FORM FLOW SYSTEM

2.1 BASIC CONCEPTS

2.1.1 FORM SCHEMA AND FORM EXTENSION

A form may be thought of as an unnormalized relation (CODD 70) or a file containing nested repeated groups. In analogy to the relational model of data which distinguishes between the relational scheme and the extension of a relation, one can distinguish between the form scheme (i.e. description of the form by means of its attributes, domains and constraints) and the form extension ("filled-in form").

Example:

Form scheme INSTITUTE given by the following unnormalized relational scheme

INSTITUTE(INSTITUTENO,PROFESSOR(PROFESSORNO,PROFESSOR-NAME),
          STUDENT(STUDENTNO,STUDENT-NAME,COURSE(COURSENO,SEMESTER)))

- form scheme

INSTITUTE FORM			
INSTITUTENO:			
PROFESSORS OF THE INSTITUTE:			
PROFESSORNR	PROFESSOR-NAME		
STUDENTS OF THE INSTITUTE:			
STUDENTNO	STUDENT-NAME	COURSENO	SEMESTER
		⋮	⋮
		⋮	⋮

- 'filled-in' form

```
INSTITUTE FORM
INSTITUTENO: 00442
PROFESSORS OF THE INSTITUTE:
PROFESSORNO | PROFESSOR-NAME
   1111          Tjoa
   1112          Wagner
    ⋮             ⋮
```

STUDENTS OF THE INSTITUTE:

STUDENTNO	STUDENT-NAME	COURSENO	SEMESTER
7825845	Miller	111000	
		112345	
		235645	
		⋮	
7935450	Babbage	123123	
		111000	
		⋮	⋮

In the following we will consider the usage of a form in the context of a form flow system. In this environment forms are used on the one hand as a non-procedural user interface of a database and on the other hand as a medium of communication between (office-) work stations.

The user can manipulate office forms in the following ways:

a) Filling-in a form scheme

In this mode the system requires from the user the specification of data to be filled in.
If the form scheme is initially filled-in the identification-attributes of the objects handled in the form-scheme must be specified. The remaining attribute values can be deduced from the database by the user.

b) Send facility

After manipulating an office form the user can send a form to another working station.

c) Filing facility

If a form has reached its 'final-state' the user can file the form for future applications.

2.1.2 TIME DIMENSION

To represent documents it is necessary to conserve informations which were valid at a certain moment, even if these informations have been updated afterwards.

A representative example concerning this problem is the generation of birth-certificates at any time with the original information, e.g. maiden name.

In the concept described in this paper for each object an attribute for the 'absolute time' (i.e. 'time-stamp') and if necessary an additional attribute for the 'entity-state' can be defined. The valid transition from one entity-state to another can be described by a so-called transition-graph relation.

2.2 SEMANTIC CONCEPTS

In this section we will introduce the basic semantic concepts of a form-flow system as it is used in the CBIS-prototype which is implemented at the University of Vienna.

2.2.1 CONCEPTUAL DESCRIPTION OF THE FORM FLOW WITH 3NF-NF²-RELATIONS

The form-flow definition in CBIS is described by NF^2-relations itself. For semantic reasons a new form of relations (3NF-NF^2-relations) is used. This concept has been introduced by the authors in KAPPEL 85 . The main characteristic of 3NF-NF^2-relations is the absence of strict-transitive dependencies as in NF^2-relations. It has been shown by the authors that a semantic interpretation of these relations leads to an unique distinction of every 3NF-NF^2-relation as either a kernel entity type or a characteristic entity type or an association.

2.2.2 THE IS-A GENERALIZATION OF ARTIFICIAL INTELLIGENCE

Using the concept of the entity-state for every object-type the entity-state can be used as a generic-attribut in the sense of semantic nets. Therefore, for every entity-state a subrelation can be created which interacts in an is-a relationship to a superset in the database.

Example:

Let us consider the entity type 'student' with the following entity-states:

- matriculation (S_0)
- 1st degree   (S_1)
- Master degree (S_2)
- ph.D   (S_3)
- ex-matriculation (S_4)

(Note: This example is perhaps only typical for Austrian Universities)

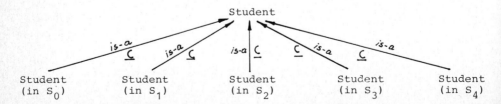

For the entity-type "Student" the generalization hierarchy shown above can be constructed (is-a hierarchy).

The following valid state-transitions exist between the entity-states resp. subrelations of the is-a hierarchy:

PRE	POST	
0	S_0	
S_0	S_1	
S_1	S_2	
S_2	S_3	0 means the initial state before an entity
S_0	S_4	is stored.
S_1	S_4	
S_2	S_4	
S_3	S_4	

2.2.3 THE PETRI-NET CONCEPT USED IN FORM-FLOW SYSTEMS

On the conceptual level in CBIS the form-flow component is modelled as a Petri net. The more interested reader in modelling concepts with Petri nets is refered to FUSS 82 . In section 3 the mapping of the Petri net into NF^2-relations (the internal level) is discussed.

In our approach all office procedures are described by form-flows, which again are modelled as Petri nets. A form-flow is a set of transactions whose succession is defined in a deterministic manner and which are dependent from each other.

Each transaction needs some input-data and produces some output-data.

The states of the Petri net are used for the representation of the subrelations of the is-a hierarchies built by several entity state generic attributes. These subrelations are input-data resp. output-data for the transactions. The transitions of the Petri net are used for the representation of the transactions at the work stations resp. for the triggering components.

Until now we have only dealt with the meta-information about form-flows, i.e. about the description of object-types involved in the form-flow system. In analogy to the concept of form scheme and form extension it is possible to define the notion of a <u>Petri net scheme</u> and its <u>Petri net extensions</u>.

Example: (Student Miller)

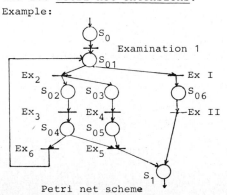

Petri net scheme

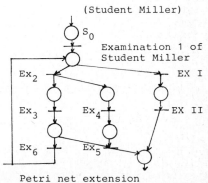

Petri net extension of Student Miller

2.2.4 THE USE OF THE SURROGATE CONCEPT

The surrogate concept can be used in the form-flow environment described in this paper to identify:

a) objects in the database
b) objects which represent a Petri net extension (e.g. the form-flow
   of the student Miller)

The concept of surrogates allows also that different forms can refer
to the same object by different key attribute sets in an easy manner.

3. DESIGN OF THE FORM-FLOW MODEL WITH NF²-RELATIONS

3.1 THE MODELLING OF THE PETRI NET BY MEANS OF NF²-RELATIONS

Using NF²-relations a Petri net can be modelled with every transition
defined by a surrogate.

Example:

NF²-relation for the description of the Petri net of the previous
example

Transitionsurrogate	Preconditions	Postconditions
Ex_1	$\{S_0\}$	$\{S_{01}\}$
Ex_2	$\{S_{01}\}$	$\{S_{02}, S_{03}\}$
Ex_3	$\{S_{02}\}$	$\{S_{04}\}$
Ex_4	$\{S_{03}\}$	$\{S_{05}\}$
Ex_5	$\{S_{04}, S_{05}\}$	$\{S_1\}$
Ex_6	$\{S_{04}\}$	$\{S_{01}\}$
Ex I	$\{S_{01}\}$	$\{S_{06}\}$
Ex II	$\{S_{06}\}$	$\{S_1\}$

3.2 THE MODELLING OF THE IDENTIFIER OF THE PETRI NET EXTENSION

Every Petri net extension can be viewed as an association between
the objects which define the form-flow and the form-flow itself. Or
with other words for every Petri net which represents a form-flow
the objects (resp. input objects) which are handled must be defined.
In our approach we model this fact by creating an association between the objects and the Petri net.

Each association represents one form-flow.

3.3 A REFINEMENT OF THE NF²-REPRESENTATION OF THE PETRI NET

In this section we will introduce a refinement of the NF²-represen-
tation of the form-flow-Petri-net introduced in section 3.1. This
refinement is necessary to provide a better integrity-check of the
form-flow. Therefore, we distinguish between two kinds of transactions on the states (i.e. subrelations of an is-a hierarchy) by each
transition:

a) d-type: The subrelation is used to deduce data from the database
           (input-mode).
b) f-type: Data are filled-in (resp. updated) in a subrelation (out-
           put-mode).

This distinction is not necessary. Nevertheless, with its use the
role of every relation can be modelled in a clearer manner with

respect to the form scheme (section 3.4).

Example:

For our Petri-net example the NF^2-relation (see section 3.1) can be extended in the following way:

Transitionsurrogate	Preconditions	Postconditions
Ex_1	$\{(S_0,d)\}$	$\{S_{01},f\}$
Ex_2	$\{(S_{01},d)\}$	$\{(S_{02},f),(S_{03},f)\}$
Ex_3	$\{(S_{02},d)\}$	$\{(S_{04},f)\}$
Ex_4	$\{(S_{03},d)\}$	$\{(S_{05},f)\}$
Ex_5	$\{(S_{05},d),(S_{04},d)\}$	$\{(S_1,f)\}$
Ex_6	$\{(S_{04},d)\}$	$\{(S_{01},f)\}$
$Ex\ I$	$\{(S_{01},d\}$	$\{(S_{06},f)\}$
$Ex\ II$	$\{(S_{06},d)\}$	$\{(S_1,f)\}$

As shown in the example above the roles of every subrelation with respect to a transition is defined more precisely, even if it seems to be redundant until now.

3.4 THE MODELLING OF THE FORM SCHEME WITHIN THE PETRI NET

With the help of the different roles of the subrelations within the Petri net we can define the logical linkage between the roles of sub-relations and form schemes. (It should be emphasized here that in the form-flow system proposed in this paper the concept of a form is the only interface between every user class (i.e. office administrator, but also end-users) and the form-flow system, since 'meta-informations' are also modelled in NF^2-relations.) The binding of a form scheme to relations is shown in the following example:

Example:

Transitionsurrogate	Form-scheme-surrogate	Subrelations
⋮	⋮	
$\underline{Ex_5}$	F_1	$\{(S_{04},d),(S_{05},d),(S_1,f)\}$
	F_2	$\{(S_{04},d),(S_1,f)\}$
	F_3	$\{(S_{04},d)\}$
Ex_4	F_4	$\{(S_{03},d),(S_{05},f)\}$
⋮	⋮	⋮

In this example the transition Ex_5 is performed by transactions of the form schemes F_1, F_2 and F_3. The different role of the subrelation S_{05} within the forms F_1 and F_4 can be seen clearly.

4. KNOWLEDGE ENGINEERING ASPECTS

4.1 PETRI NET EDITOR

Although as described in section 3 relatively complex office situations can be modelled in CBIS, it turns out that there are processes which can not be modelled solely by form declarations. Therefore at the University of Vienna an additional tool called PNE-CBIS (Petri Net Editor) is being developed in PROLOG which allows to define more complex situations. The PNE can be used interactively by the user.

As set of facts the PNE can use the NF²-relations (resp. subrelations) which are defined in the corresponding database of the form-
flow system.

The aim of the office administrator in PNE is the exact definition
of pre- and post conditions which can not be modelled by forms.

The most frequent application of this kind of definition is given if
decisions have to be made at a working station. In this case transitions of the Petri-net can be interpreted as logical predicates. The
support of graphic tools for PNE is planned but not yet realized.

4.2 COMPLEX TEMPORAL TOOL

Another important tool which is on development at the University of
Vienna is the embedding of a tool for the handling of time intervalls.
The aim of this tool is inferrencing facts concerning time inter-
valls by means of logical rules.

Since two time intervalls can interact in several ways (e.g. X over-
laps Y, X begins Y, X before Y, X during Y, etc.) one can modell
integrity rules for time intervalls in an office environment. For
instance it is possible to derive transitivity rules of time intervalls. The easiest case is:

(X before Y and Y before Z) implies (X before Z).

For the other cases this task is not a trivial one, and still a topic
for furture research work.

5. CONCLUSION AND FURTHER INVESTIGATIONS

In this paper a form-flow system is introduced which allows the conceptual modelling of form-flows for complex office applications. The
tools used in the model are inspirated by AI-concepts concerning
semantic-network modelling and semantic data models. The extensions
of the system for more sophisticated applications are written in
PROLOG.

REFERENCES

Elzas, M.S. (1984). Concepts for model-based policy construction. In:
       Simulation and Model-Based Methodologies: An Integrative View,
       T.I. Ören (ed), Springer Verlag.

Embley, D.W. (1982). A natural form query language - an introduction
       to basic retrieval of office objects. In: Improving Database
       Usability and Responsiveness, P. Scheuermann (ed), Academic
       Press, pp 121-133.

Fuss, H. (1982). Reversal simulation with Place-Transactor-Nets. In:
       Model Adequacy: Proceedings of the International Working Con-
       ference on Model Realism, H. Wedde (ed), Springer Verlag.

Gibbs, S.J. (1982). Office information models and the representation
       of office objects, ACM-SIGOA Conference 1982.

Kappel, G., A M. Tjoa and R.R. Wagner (1985). Form Flow Systems based on NF²-Relations. In: GI-Fachtagung: Datenbanksysteme für Büro, Technik und Wissenschaft, Springer Verlag.

Luo, P. and S.B. Yao (1981). Form operation by example: A language for office information processing, Proc. ACM SIGMOD, pp.212-223.

Makinouchi, A. (1977). A consideration on normal form of not-necessarily-normalized relations in the relational data model. In: Int. Conference on Very Large Data Base, Tokyo.

Ören, T.I. (1979). Concepts for advanced computer assisted modelling. In: Methodology in Systems Modelling and Simulation, B.P. Zeigler, M.S. Elzas, G.J. Klir and T.I. Ören (eds), North-Holland.

Schek, H.J., and M. Scholl (1983) The NF²-relational algebra for the uniform manipulation of external, conceptual and internal data structures. In: Languages for databases (in german), Springer Verlag, pp. 113-133.

Vinek, G., P.F. Rennert, and A M. Tjoa (1982). Datenmodellierung: Theorie und Praxis des Datenbankentwurfs, Physica Verlag.

Zeigler, B.P. (1984). System theoretic foundations of modelling and simulation. In: Simulation and Model-Based Methodologies: An integrative View, T.I. Ören (ed), Springer.

Zisman, M.D. (1977). Representation, specification and automation of office procedures, Ph.D. Thesis, Dep. of Decision Science, The Wharton School, University of Pennsylvania, Scrancton.

SECTION VII
RELATED TOOLS AND TECHNIQUES

Modelling and Simulation Methodology
in the Artificial Intelligence Era
M.S. Elzas, T.I. Ören and B.P. Zeigler (Editors)
© Elsevier Science Publishers B.V. (North-Holland), 1986

Chapter VII.1

AN EXPLORATION OF THE APPLICABILITY OF
PRODUCTION RULE BASED TECHNIQUES TO PROCESS MODELLING

V.R. Voller and B. Knight

Centre for Numerical Modelling and Process Analysis
School of Mathematics, Statistics and Computing
Thames Polytechnic
London.

Process modelling is a highly skilled task requiring the
application of knowledge from a wide variety of domains.
Although it is possible to list the steps that have to be
taken in the modelling process it is difficult to identify
the areas where the modeller uses 'intuitive' or experiential
skills. With artificial intelligence and in particular
rule based systems, however, it does become possible to
represent this intuition. In this contribution we identify
areas where the modeller's intuitive knowledge interacts
with the model system. A potential methodology is then
proposed for representing this knowledge in the form of a
production rule base. Finally, possible applications of such
a rule base in the modelling process are noted and discussed.

1. INTRODUCTION

Process modelling is typically an example of the classical generate and test
paradigm that has been the hallmark of AI programs for two decades (Feigenbaum
1979). In this framework heuristic generation methods are used in a constructive
phase which is succeeded by critical analysis and appraisal of results. This is
just the same framework as is used in process analysis, where model construction
and validation are the key elements.

Efficient process modelling requires a highly skilled modeller who can configure
and run the models and interpret the results in the appropriate numerical and
engineering environments. Hence, the success, or otherwise, of a modelling
exercise will rely heavily on the modeller's knowledge, both of the process being
modelled and the modelling tools used. The important word here in the context of
rule based systems is "knowledge".

- What are the essential elements of this knowledge?

- Can the knowledge be represented as a set of production rules?

- If so, how can such rules be used to enhance the techniques of process
  modelling.

The intention of this chapter is to determine, and represent, the steps in a
modelling exercise which are outside the formal definition of modelling, yet
still essential if a valid model is to be produced. Essentially we are examining
the heuristics for model generation and testing.

The Mathematical Model   AI Model

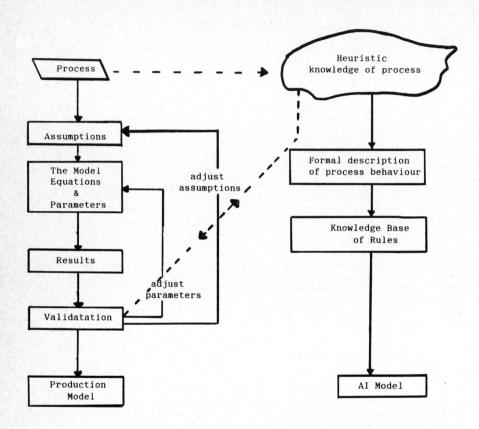

Figure 1:   The steps in Mathematical Modelling compared with AI

            Modelling.

2. THE CONCEPTUAL MODEL OF A PROCESS

The first question to be looked at is how and where does a modeller use his knowledge in process modelling. A way of gaining some insight is to look at the basic steps involved in the construction of the model. Many modelling/problem solving methodologies have been proposed [see Elzas (1984), Gass (1983), Noble (1982), Aris (1978) and Polya (1957)]. These are all essentially similar in nature with the main steps along the lines of those shown on the left of Figure 1. Initially simplifying assumptions are made about the process to be modelled. The exact nature of these assumptions will depend on the requirement of the final model and to some extent on the current understanding of the process itself. From the assumptions the preliminary model is derived. This consists of a set of equations (linear, non-linear, pde's, ... etc) and a set of independent parameters. The next stage involves using the model to produce a set of predictions. This is followed by a validation stage where the predictions are examined against what is required of the model and what is expected of the process. The outcome of the validation is that the model parameters are perturbed and sometimes the assumptions adjusted or modified. This validation procedure continues until the model predictions are at the required standard. The modelling cycle is then complete.

From the above it is clear that at every stage of the modelling cycle the modeller must have access to a sound knowledge about the process. For this the modeller can be imagined to have his own internal conceptual model of the process distinct from the mathematical computer model of the process. The conceptual model does not exist in any formal sense it is simply an heuristic understanding of the process (see RHS of Figure 1). Clearly, however, a formal description of such an understanding, via a rule base for example, would have wide ranging and useful benefits.

3. PRODUCTION RULES: AN EXAMPLE

One formal description could be obtained by using AI techniques to build a rule base as is done in expert systems. Such a rule base would represent an alternative AI model of the process, (see RHS of Figure 1) which in some cases may address and solve the same process problems as the mathematical model would.

As a simple illustrative example of how an AI model can be generated the following process is introduced. Fluid is contained in a long unit square duct, shown in cross-section in Figure 2a. Three faces of the duct (South, East and West) are kept fixed at a temperature of 0°C. The fourth face (North) is kept at a temperature of 100°C. The process problem is to find the steady state temperature distribution in the fluid within the duct. Under the following assumptions:

    i)   the duct is long enough to neglect end effects;
    ii)   heat transfer is by conduction, and
    iii) thermal properties are constant (ie. have no dependence on space or temperature)

the mathematical model of the above process problem is

$$\frac{\partial^2 T}{\partial x^2} + \frac{\partial^2 T}{\partial y^2} = 0 \tag{1}$$

This model can be solved analytically to give the required temperature

2a. Setup

2b. Mathematical Model. Eq. 2.

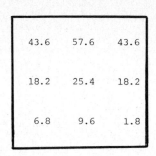

	North	
(1).	(4).	(7).
(2).	(5).	(8).
(3).	(6).	(9).
	South	

west ← O → east

100

O

43.6	57.6	43.6
18.2	25.4	18.2
6.8	9.6	1.8

Figure 2: Mathematical Model of Temperature Duct Process

3a. No knowledge

3b. Max. and Min. (Rules 1-2)

4	391	O
198	25	55
-77	2	-468

7	22	95
33	69	56
48	12	3

3c. Symmetry (Rules 3-5)

3d. Order (Rules 6-10)

7	22	7
33	69	33
48	12	48

48	69	48
22	33	22
7	12	7

Figure 3: Development and Application of Expert Rules in Table 1.

distribution as

$$T(x,y) = \frac{400}{\pi} \sum_{n=1,3,5}^{\infty} \frac{Sin(n\pi x)Sinh(n\pi y)}{n\,Sinh(n\pi)} \qquad (2)$$

(see Bajpai et al (1977)). The given temperatures are given at nine internal points in Figure 2b.

A process "expert" looking at the results in Figure 2b would accept them as reasonable. This is not surprising since the model given by equation (1) is based on sound engineering mathematical principals. Clearly then some knowledge has been used in generating the model in the first place. To some extent it can be said that this knowledge is implicitly represented by the model. The process expert, however, might only have a limited appreciation of engineering mathematics and his knowledge of the process may be more explicit in nature. Knowledge in this form is more accessible to a rule based representation.

A method by which rules associated to a process and related to a model can be generated is to consider the model of the process as a 'black box' number generator. The accuracy and validity of the model will then depend on the quality of the rules used to 'sieve out' 'good' numbers from 'bad'. The development of such a rule base is illustrated in Figures 3a-3d and outlined below on considering increasing levels in sophistication of process knowledge.

No knowledge:- with no understanding of the process there will be no way of knowing what is a good or bad value for the nine internal temperatures. Any temperature field generated at random will be acceptable, such as the values given in Figure 3a.

Maximum and Minimum temperatures:- it does not require much knowledge of heat transfer to realise that the temperature field in Figure 3a is not reasonable. Clearly all internal temperatures must be bounded by the face temperatures. This bit of knowledge leads to the first two rules in the expert model rule base given in Table 1. The values given in Figure 3b, obtained by generating a group of random numbers between 0-100 on a BBC micro computer, represents a possible state of the model at this stage.

Symmetry:- another piece of data in the knowledge base results in noting the symmetry on points equi-distant from the North South meridian. This leads to Rules 3-5 in the knowledge base of Table 1. The state of the expert model can be adjusted on giving preference to points on the West side of the meridian, see figure 3c.

Order:- some elementary ordering can also be done on the point temperatures. Clearly points near the top and centre are hotter than points near the bottom corners. Appropriate rules are given in Table 1. Readjustment of the random numbers (1-100) of Figure 3c leads to the temperature field of Figure 3d.

At this point rules 1-10 in Table 1 represent a fair amount of process knowledge and may be considered as a formal conceptual model of the temperature duct process. Although the quantitative agreement between this conceptual model and the 'qualitative' model (ie. equations (1) and (2) and Figure 2b) is not good, the qualitative agreement is complete.

4. APPLICATIONS

The above represents a somewhat simple example of a rule based process model, in that the associated physics and mathematics is at a relatively low level. The methodology of the black box random number generator for obtaining process rules, however, should carry over to more complex systems.

<u>Table 1</u>

<u>Expert Rule Base for Temperature Duct Process</u>

Rule 1:- No internal temperature can be greater than the largest face temperature.

Rule 2:- No internal temperature can be less than the smallest face temperature.

Rule 3:- Temp. at 1 = Temp. at 7.

Rule 4:- Temp. at 2 = Temp. at 8.

Rule 5:- Temp. at 3 = Temp. at 9.

Rule 6:- Temp. at 1 > Temp. at 2 > Temp. at 3.

Rule 7:- Temp. at 4 > Temp. at 5 > Temp. at 6.

Rule 8:- Temp. at 4 > Temp. at 1.

Rule 9:- Temp. at 5 > Temp. at 2.

Rule 10:-Temp. at 6 > Temp. at 3.

If such a rule base can be obtained then what applications could it be put to? There are a number of possibilities:-

<u>Stand Alone Model</u>: In applications where the process patterns are more important than the process values, for example in process control on selection, qualitative validity of the rule base may be a sufficient requirement for the model to work.

<u>First Stage Validation</u>: The rules given in Table 1 represent redundant data. Redundant in the sense that the correct mathematical model will contain all of this knowledge. Therefore results from the mathematical model should fit the rule base model. If this is not the case then something is wrong in the system and a correction is required. Note that redundancy is a typical feature of rule based systems and is present in all cognitive models.

<u>Validation</u>: Identifying that something is wrong with the system is, unfortunately, only first stage validation. For a correction to be made the exact error needs to be located. A disagreement between the mathematical model and rule based model could come about for three classes of errors:

    1) the model formulation is wrong
    2) the numerical solution has broken down, or
    3) the available process knowledge is incomplete.

The first two classes of these errors would need additional rules which could identify such things as inconsistent assumptions, or stiff and unstable systems. The third class of errors would be investigated after the first two classes have been exhausted of possibilities. Once again this would require additional rules.

5. CONCLUSIONS

By its nature building a model of a process is an expert task. No matter how carefully modelling taxonomies are put together it is difficult to represent and define the areas of modelling where knowledge is applied. Here, by examination of the main steps of the modelling exercise, areas where knowledge is applied have been identified. It has been shown via a simple example how this knowledge can be formally represented in a rule base. Such rule base can be:

  - Used as a stand alone model.

  - Used as a first line means of model validation.

  - Extended and used as a complete model validation.

In the movement towards user friendly software tools for modelling and simulation the development of rule based models of the type suggested here could and should have a significant impact.

REFERENCES

Aris, R. (1978). <u>Mathematical modelling techniques</u>, Pitman, London.

Bajpai, A.C., Mustoe, L.R. and Walker, D. (1977). <u>Advanced engineering mathematics</u>, John Wiley, Chichester.

Elzas, M.S. (1984). <u>System paradigms as reality mappings</u>. In: Simulation and model-based methodologies: An integrated view, T.I. Oren et al (eds). Springer-Verlag, Berlin Heidelberg, pp.41-67.

Feigenbaum, E.A. (1979). <u>Themes and case studies of knowledge engineering</u>. In: Expert systems and the micro electronic age, Edinburgh University Press, Edinburgh.

Gass, S.I. (1983). <u>What is a computer-based mathematical model</u>?, Mathematical Modelling, Vol.<u>4</u>, pp.467-472.

Noble, R.D. (1982). <u>Mathematical modelling in the context of problem solving</u>, Mathematical Modelling, Vol.<u>3</u>, pp.215-219.

Polya, G. (1973). <u>How to solve it</u>, 2nd Ed., Princeton University Press, Princeton, N.J.

Zeigler, B.P., (1976). <u>Theory of modelling and simulation</u>, John Wiley and Son, New York.

Modelling and Simulation Methodology
in the Artificial Intelligence Era
M.S. Elzas, T.I. Ören and B.P. Zeigler (Editors)
© Elsevier Science Publishers B.V. (North-Holland), 1986

Chapter VII.2

PROBLEMS AND ADVANTAGES OF SIMULATION
IN PROLOG

I.Futó   T.Gergely

Institute for Coordinations   Applied Logic Laboratory
Computer Techniques   SZÁMALK
Budapest 1251. P.O.Box 19.   Budapest,15o2,P.O.Box 146
        Hungary   Hungary

A very perspective way to renew simulation is
connected with involation of logic programming.
This approach at the same time presupposes the
combination of two programming paradigms, logic
programming based on constructive logic and
object oriented programming based on simulation.
It is shown in the case of PROLOG that this
combination cannot be done by using a logic
programming language for simulation directly, but
it should be extended with appropriate devices
nesessary for model building, execution and model
modification.

1.INTRODUCTION

Logic programming as a new paradigm of programming implements
constructive logic to provide a universal language as to solve
problems represented in an apprppriate formalism.
An other important programming paradigm is the object oriented
one motivated by the simulation languages particularly by
SIMULA 67. The conceptual background of this paradigm is
provided mainly by system theory. Namely simulation languages
realize a consistent family of notions from system theory to
model real objects.
One of the main objections against simulation in general is
connected with the system theoretic origin, namely simulation
is not a direct optimum or solution-seeking method, because
it only imitates the normal working of the modeled object,
and if the original object fails in a given situation simulation
itself cannot say anything about how to solve the problem. The
human intervention thus needed is not even an element of a
partnership, e.g. which may involve automated backtracking:
Existing popular simulation systems (see e.g. Birtwistle et
al (1973), Kiviat (1968)) only allow a different alternative
to be tried after the intervention has terminated a previous
run. There seems to be no way around this difficulty in current
simulation languages, because they have no built-in mechanisms
to preserve the intermediate states of a computation. Therefore
simulation languages allow to illustrate problem situations and
check out some suggestions but they have no tools to solve the
problems.
The constructive branch of mathematical logic provides an
alternative to system theory namely, one that allows not only
to describe an object but also to plan its behaviour. Therefore
joint constructive logic and simulation may renew the latter

one by eliminating e.g. the above mentioned objection.

At the same time logic approach allows the usage of any appropriate signature even the system theoretic notions can be built into the language. Hence object oriented approach is supported by mathematical logic. Therefore constructive logic allows to join the above mentioned two programming paradigm into a new one, namely into logic simulation. How to realize this is the topic investigated in this paper. Namely we analyze if it is possible to use a logic programming language for simulation directly. The analysis is done in the case of the wellknown PROLOG language and we show that this is not possible and that the real issue to be searched is an appropriate modification of logic programming language and therefore PROLOG by augmenting with devices necessary for modelling. At the same time these devices allow their object oriented usage.

2. BASIC NOTIONS OF PROLOG

The main point in logic programming is that the solution of a problem is obtained by the proof of the problem specification as a theorem. Of course as to achieve this the specification is to be presented in an appropriate formalism. In the case of PROLOG this formalism is based on the Horn formulas. A Horn formula is of the form $Q_1 x_1 \ldots Q_n x_n$ $(f_1 \wedge \ldots \wedge f_m)$. Here Q_i is either $\forall$ or $\exists$ and each f_i is either of the form $\neg p_i \vee \ldots \vee \neg p_i$ or of the form $p_{i_1} \wedge \ldots \wedge p_{i_k} \rightarrow p_{i_o}$ where each p_{i_j} is an atomic formula and $\neg$ stands for negation.

An atomic formula or its negation is said to be a literal and the disjunction of one or more literals is called a clause. A formula is said to be in clause form if it is in prenex normal form with the prefix consisting only of universal quantifiers. I.e. if $x_1, \ldots, x_n$ are all the variables occuring in a formula f then its clause form is

$$\forall x_1 \ldots \forall x_n \quad K_1 \wedge \ldots \wedge K_m$$

where each K_i $(i=1, \ldots, m)$ is a clause. The prefix is usually omitted.

Those clauses, $\{B_1, \ldots, B_m, \quad \neg A_1, \ldots, \neg A_n\}$ where $(m \leqslant 1)$ are called Horn clauses.

The various Horn clauses are named as follows:

(i)   m=o, n=o, □ , the empty clause;

(ii)   m=1, n=o, $\{B\}$, the assertion or unit clause;

(iii) m=o, n=o, $\{\neg A_1, \ldots, \neg A_n\}$, the goal or goalsequence;

(iv)   m=1, n=o, $\{B$, $\quad \neg A_1, \ldots, \neg A_n\}$ the rule of inference.

The empty clause means a contradiction. The meaning of a Horn clause $\{B, \neg A_1, \ldots, \neg A_n\}$ which contains variables $x_1, \ldots, x_k$ is the following: forall $x_1, \ldots, x_k$, B if A_1 and $\ldots$ and A_n. Further on we equivalenty use the Horn clause form and the corresponding Horn formulas in the form of $B \leftarrow, A_1 \wedge \ldots \wedge A_n$ and $B \leftarrow A_1 \wedge \ldots \wedge A_n$ corresponding to the Horn clauses (ii), (iii) and (iv) respectively.
A formula is said to be constructive if there is an algorithm

(procedure) which computes (realizes)it. Horn clauses provide a constructive sublanguage of the first order language which is the syntax of PROLOG. Realizability in PROLOG is provided by the SL-resolution calculus with the top-down depth-first search strategy.

Therefore a Horn clause $\{B, \neg A_1, \ldots, \neg A_n\}$ may be viewed as a <u>procedure declaration</u>, where B is the <u>head</u> of the procedure and the <u>procedure calls</u> A_i form the body of the procedure. Assertion of the form $\{B\}$ may be looked upon as procedures with empty bodies, while the empty clause □ is the STOP instruction. The arguments of the literals correspond to the parameters of procedures (procedure calls).

Using the procedural view of Horn clauses, it is possible to step outside of the frame of the first order predicate calculus to introduce other procedures.
There are two types of procedures in PROLOG.

(i)   Procedures defined by the user in the PROLOG language;

(ii)   Procedures provided by the interpreter; that is built-in procedures.

A user defined procedure means that it is the responsibility of the user to provide for each procedure call (a literal of the form of A_i) a procedure definition with an applicable head A. If this is not the case, backtracking takes place and it provides results according to the top-down, dept-first strategy of PROLOG.

Pure logic cannot be used in practice. This is so, because in logic numerical operations must be also defined in an axiomatic way, e.g. by giving the Peano's axioms.To overcome this difficulty we can use so called "built-in" predicates in theorem prover.

An important difference between the use of a built-in predicate and the correct axiomatic definition of the predicate is that when a proper axiomatic definition is given there are no differences between the input and output arguments of the predicate. That is in this case e.g. $5=t+3$ when resolved, gives for t the value 2. If we use built-in predicate, then a distinction is made between the input and the output variables of the predicate. Execution of $5=t+3$ as a built-in predicate will cause an error message. However in practice the use of built-in predicates is a possible and useful solution to make logic adequate for simulation. Such built-in predicates are used to perform arithmetic functions, logical comparisons, I/O,file handling operations. Now let us use PROLOG for simulation. First we look at how it can be used for activity oriented simulation.

3. PROLOG IN ACTIVITY ORIENTED SIMULATION

The activity oriented simulation is not very popular in computer based modelling and only Control and Simulation Language (CSL) (Buxton (1962)) supports this approach.
However this approach is close enough to that of planning and plan generation dealt in AI and (implemented even in PROLOG,see e.g.Warren (1974). Plan generation consists of finding a sequence of actions which transforms the system considered from its initial state into a given final state, the goal state.

In plan generation no time parameters are treated, so for simulation we have to modify this technique so as to handle also the notion of time. At any given moment, say t_i, the object under consideration may be said to be in a state, say s_i. Let $S_i:T_i$ denote that at time T_i the system is in state S_i. Here s_i and t_i are variables ranging over the set of possible states and that of time moments respectively and the corresponding capital letters refer to state and time constants.

A state may be described by means of a Horn formula. For example, state S_1 with attribute values $t_1, \ldots t_n$ at time T_1 can be described by a Horn formula: (1) $Q(t_1, \ldots, t_n, S_1:T_1) \leftarrow$ where Q is the predicate describing the state, t_i (i=1,...,n) are terms.

Changes in states are the result of performing actions and sequence of actions. An action can be represented by a function that maps states into new states (achieved by executing the action).

A Horn formula describing the effect of an action is typically of the form
(2) $P(t_1, \ldots, t_n, f\ (s_i:t_i):t_j) \leftarrow Q(t_1, \ldots, t_n,\ s_i:t_i) \wedge plus\ (t_i, T, t_j)$
where all variables are universally quantified and

    P is a predicate describing the new state,

    s_i is a state variable

    t_i, t_j are time variables,

    f^i is an action function (corresponding to some action) that maps a state into a new state (achieved by executing the action),

    Q is a predicate describing the old state,

    T is the ellapsed time during the execution of the action function f.(If T=$\emptyset$ then plus (t_i, T, t_j) is quantified,

    t_i (i=1,...,n) are terms.

The goal state is given by a formula of the form
(3) $\leftarrow P(t_1, \ldots, t_n, s_k:t_k)$

To use resolution first we have to transform the above Horn formulas into their clause form

$C_1 = \{Q(t_1, \ldots, t_n, S_1:T_1)\}$

$C2 = \{P\ (t_1, \ldots, t_n, f(s_i:t_i):t_j\ ,\ \neg Q(t_1, \ldots, t_n, s_i:t_i), \neg plus\ (t_i, T, t_j)\}$

$C3 = \{\neg P\ (t_1, \ldots, t_n, s_k:t_k)\}$

To prove that a state $P(t_1, \ldots, t_n, s_k:t_k)$ can be reached from state (1) using action function f defined by (2), we need to prove that the set of clauses $S = \{C_1, C_2, C_3\}$ is unsatisfiable. To keep track of the unifications, a special predicate, the "Answer" predicate will be used in the goalsequence. It can be considered as a special built-in predicate printing out its argument value. We will concentrate our attention on the variables "s_k" and "t_k". Let us see two steps in the proof tree:

$\{\neg P\ (t_1, \ldots, t_h, s_k:t_k),\ Answer\ (s_k:t_k)\}$

    $\{\ P(t_1, \ldots, t_k, f(s_i:t_i):t_j),\ \neg Q(t_1, \ldots, t_n, s_i:t_i), \neg plus(t_i, T, t$

    $sk/f(s_i:t_i)$

    t_k/t_i

$\{Q\ (t_1, \ldots, t_n, s_i:t_i), \neg plus(t_i, T, t_j),\ Answer\ (f(s_i:t_i):t_j)\}$

    $Q(t_1, \ldots, t_n, S_1:T_1)$

    s_i/S_1

    t_i/T_1

$\neg plus\ (t_1, T, t_j),\ Answer\ (f(S_1:T_1):t_j)$

    Fig.1: Proof tree of a goal

Here x/t denotes the substitution of all occurences of the variable
x by the term t. Suppose that Plus (T_1,T,t_j) is a built-in procedure
giving in its third argument the sum of its first two arguments and
suppose that $T_1+T=T_2$. Then Answer $(f(S_1:T_1):T_2)$ says that state P
$(t_1,\ldots,t_n,s_k:t_k)$ can be reached at state S_1 at time moment T_1. By
Backtracking and taking new alternatives - i.e. modifying the model
automatically - plan generation performs a very high level simulation.
Another activity oriented approach provides the description of an
activity or state by an appropriate formula which also specifies its
time duration. Note that according to Nance (1981) a state of a system
unchanged over a time internal is said to be activity. To use PROLOG
for this approach we use two extra arguments to describe the time
interval attached to the activities. Namely a formula $p(t_1,\ldots,t_k,T_s,T_e)$
can be considered as the definition of an activity (state) p of
the modeled system between the instances T_s and T_e. This activity is
described by the predicate p and attributes $t_1,\ldots,t_k$. Morever we are
also interested in the notion of process consisting of activities.
For this a formula

$$p(t_1,\ldots,t_k,T_s,T_e) \leftarrow q_1(t_1,\ldots,t_k,T_{s_1},T_{e_1})\wedge\ldots\wedge q_n(t_1,\ldots,t_k,T_{s_n},T_{e_n}).$$

is to be used which is the definiton of the process p with attributes
$t_1,\ldots,t_k$ consisting of activities $q_1,\ldots,q_n$. Duration of p is
$[T_s,T_e]$. If activities $q_1,\ldots,q_n$ of a process p do not depend on the
activities of other processes then $T_s=T_{s_1}, T_{e_1}=T_{s_2},\ldots,T_{e_{n-1}}=T_{s_n}, T_{e_n}=T_e$

where T_s is the starting instance of process p, T_e is the final
instance of process p, T_{s_i} is the starting instance of activity q_i
while T_{e_i} is its termination time moment. Therefore the typical
Horn formula for the activity description is of the form

$$p(t_1,\ldots,t_k,T_s,T_e) \leftarrow$$
$$p(t_1,\ldots,t_k,T_s,T_e) \leftarrow q_1(t_1,\ldots,t_k,T_s,T_{e_1})\wedge\ldots\wedge q_n(t_1,\ldots,t_k,T_{e_{n-1}},T_e)$$

$\leftarrow p(t_1,\ldots,t_k,T_s,T_e)$, where the latter formula can be considered as a
goal state (process) p with attributes $t_1,\ldots,t_k$ starting at T_s and
terminating at T_e.
Now let us see how PROLOG can be used to simulate processes by the use
of the execution of logic programs which is but the proof of the
corresponding formulas.

4. PROCESS ORIENTED APPROACH IN PROLOG

Let us suppose that we have the following set S of Horn formulas:

(1) $A \leftarrow B \wedge C$
(2) $B \leftarrow D$
(3) $B \leftarrow E$
(4) $D \leftarrow F$
(5) $D \leftarrow G$
(6) $E \leftarrow H \wedge I$
(7) $H \leftarrow \qquad t_H$
(8) $I \leftarrow \qquad t_I$
(9) $C \leftarrow \qquad t_C$

where $H \leftarrow B_1 \wedge \ldots \wedge B_n$ and $H \leftarrow$, are considered as processes in the
following manner:

(i) $H \leftarrow B_1 \wedge \ldots \wedge B_n$ denotes a process H composed
from activities $B_1,\ldots,B_n$;

(ii) $H \leftarrow$ denotes an activity
(iii) t_H is the time needed to perform activity H.

We can say, that the set S of Horn formulas (1)-(9) describes the
<u>possible behaviour</u> of a system R; where <u>behaviour</u> is an ordered
sequence of activities. We can obtain from the set S a possible behaviour of the system R by defining a <u>path</u> in the execution tree
of S ∪ {← G} starting from ← G, where G is an intended system's
activity, i.e. the goal.

In our case the execution tree is shown on Fig 2. where the numbers
in paranthesis denote the second parent clause of the resolvent.

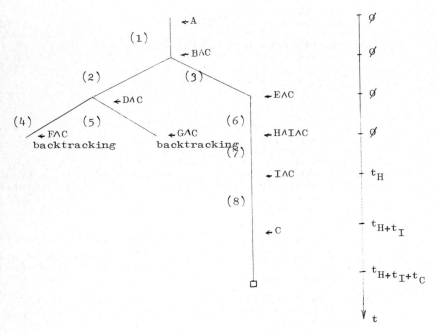

Fig.2: Execution Tree of a Set of Horn Formulas

Note, that the proof is done by using SL-resolution with top-down
and dept first strategy, only instead of using the clause notation
{ A, ⌐B, ⌐C } we used the equivalent A ← B ∧ C notation.

A <u>path</u> in the execution tree of S is a sequence $C_o, C_1, \ldots, C_n$ of
nodes leading from the root node to an empty node $\Box$, where all
C_{i+1} is a <u>child</u> of C_i.

For example
```
        ← A
      ← B ∧ C
      ← E ∧ C
      ← H ∧ I ∧ C
      ← I ∧ C
      ← C
```

is a path in the execution tree of Fig. 2.

Using the process-activity concept of Nance (1981) to the above
example of path, we can give the following schema:

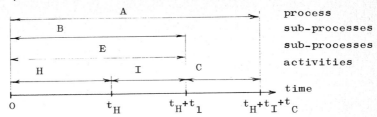

Fig.3. Activities and process corresponding to a path

About Fig.3 we can say that H, I and C are activities (elementary
actions) of system R.A is a process consisting of sub-processes B
and C, where B is a version of sub-process E, and sub-process E
consists of activities H and I. Finally, process A consists of
activities H, I, and C.

The execution of activity A takes $T_A=t_H+t_E+t_C$ time. A is considered
as a system's level activity, which is decomposed into activities
E and C on a lower level. At this point A is a process consisting
of activities E and C. On its turn, E as a sub-process is also
decomposed into activities H and I.

Note some important properties of the use of Horn formulas for
<u>process</u> definition:

(i)   The simulation starts from the goal state A of the system R.

(ii) By backward reasoning the state A is decomposed into a
      sequence of states which are preconditions for reaching A.
      At the same time A is transformed into a <u>process</u> .

(iii) Finding the first elementary activity H with duration t_H
      the <u>time</u> is moved from 0 to t_H simulating the execution
      of activity H.

(iv) The same backward reasoning method is used to find all the
      remaining activities of process A.

(i)-(iv) mean however the simulation starts from the <u>final state</u>
      (the goal state) and by <u>backward reasoning</u> determines the
      antecedent states, it goes <u>forward</u> in the time (!) when
      executing activities as it <u>is common</u> in simulation.

5.PROBLEMS WITH SIMULATION IN PROLOG

There are several problems when PROLOG is used for simulation. The
most important ones are as follows:

(i)   The solvability of the problem depends on the order of
      goals in the goalsequence;
(ii) In PROLOG it is not possible prescribe what type of
      messages are waited for and to check out the type of
      comming messages.
(iii) To model communication among components we need an argument
      for a message and a second argument to design the time
      when it was sent to control the massages through its time
      parameter.

(iv) The model does not reflect explicitly the structure of the system.

(v) There is no global (system) time.

Problem (i) is the most important one, because it cannot be solved in a standard PROLOG system. In a complicate simulation model, where a great number of components can be present in the system it is practically impossible to foresee a good order of goal-execution for the components. This is why PROLOG cannot be used for simultation directly.

To illustrate (i) let us see the following example:

(1) problem_1 (T1, T2,T3,T4) ← wait (M,TM,T1,T2) ∧ send (M,TM,T3,T4).

(2) problem_2 (T1,T2,T3,T4) ← send (M,TM,T3,T4) ∧ wait (M,TM,T1,T2).

(3) wait (M,TM,T1,T2) ← hold (1,TM,T2) ∧ output (T2).

(4) send (M,TM,T3,T4) ← hold (1,T3,TM) ∧ M=2 ∧ T4=TM.

(5) hold (DT,TØ,TE) ← plus (DT,TØ,TE).

(1) means that the processes wait and send start in instant T1 and T3 respectively to run up to the instants T2 and T4.

(3) means that a message M is waited for which arrives at moment TM. Then the process is to be suspended for 1 time unit and then T2 is outprinted.

(4) means that a message M is sent at moment TM if before the process has been suspended for 1 time unit and M=2, T4=TM.

Let us see how the execution runs for problem_1 (Ø,T2,Ø,T4).

(1)
(3)
(5)

← problem_1 (Ø,T2,Ø,T4).

← wait (M,TM,Ø,T2) ∧ send (M,TM,Ø,T4)

← hold (1,TM,T2) ∧ output (M) ∧ send (M,TM,ØT4).

← plus (1,TM,T2) ∧ output (m) ∧ send (M,TM,Ø,T4).

?

Here plus (1,TM,T2) is not defined logically but it is a built in procedure so it cannot be executed since TM is a variable. Now let us see the execution for problem_2 (Ø,T2,Ø,T4)

(2)
(4)
(5)

(1)
(5)

← problem_2 (Ø,T2,Ø,T4)

← send (M,TM,Ø,T4) ∧ wait (M,TM,Ø,T2)
  T3:=Ø

← hold (1,Ø,TM) ∧ M=2 ∧ T4=TM ∧ wait (M,TM,Ø,T2)

← plus (1,Ø,TM) ∧ M=2 ∧ T4=TM ∧ wait (M,TM,Ø,T2)
  TM=1
← M=2 ∧ T4=1 ∧ wait (M,1,Ø,T2)
← T4=1 ∧ wait (2,1,Ø, T2)
← wait (2,1,Ø,T2)
  M:=2,TM:=1
← hold (1,1,T2) ∧ output (T2).

← plus (1,1,T2) ∧ output (2),
  T2:=2
← output (2).

As it can be seen in this case when send and wait are exchanged for one another the execution is succesfully terminated. Here, as we can see, the problem is connected with time handling which is caused by the way how the plus function is introduced. Problem (ii) is not crucial but very inconvenient. As in PROLOG to a variable one can assigne a value only once, if we want to simulate message passing among competents, represented by their respective goals in the goalsequence of the problem, we need as many additional arguments in the goals as many communication will occur during the execution of these goals. Moreover they have to be passed over several level until their value assignement is performed.
Using only one common logical variable as a global communication channel with open ended list solves the problem of the too much arguments, but leads to a similar problem mentioned in (i), and also gives problem (iii).
Suppose we have the following program.

```
(1)  a(X) ←  send(a,X).
(2)  b(Y) ←  wait_for (Z,Y).
(3)  wait_for (M,M̄,L) ←  not (variable (M).
(4)  wait_for (M,K,L) ←  not (variable (K), wait_for (M,L).

(5)  send (M,M,L) ←
```

There are two components "a" and "b" communicating by a common logical variable "X" (see (7)). "a" sends a message "a" through a channel X, "b" waits a "Z" through a channel Y. send is defined as puting the message as the last not variable element of a list. The last element of the list will be a variable (open ended list). "wait_for" tries to take a non-variable element of the open ended list. This element may be the head of the list (3) or an element of the tail of the list (4).

Executing the above program with goalsequence ← a(X) ∧ b(X) it works correctly, see Fig.4. (The communication channel is X.)

```
    ┌←a(X)                          ⎫
(1) │                               ⎬  process "a"
    │←send (a,X)                    ⎭
    │  X := [a | X1]
(6) │
    │←b([a | X1])                   ⎫
(2) │                               ⎪
    │←wait_for (2, [a | X1]).       ⎬  process "b"
(3) │  Z:=a                         ⎪
    │←not (variable( a ) ).         ⎭
    □
```

Fig.4. Succesful Communication Through Variable

But if we change the order of goals ← b(X) ∧ a(X) the program fails, see Fig.5.

```
    ┌←b(X)
(2) │
    │←wait_for b (Z,X).
(3) │  Z:= X̄1 , X:= [X1 | X2]
    │←not (variable (X1)
    failed
```

Fig.5. Unsuccesful Communication Through Variable

The first idea may be to redefine "wait_for" as

$$(3') \text{ wait\_for } (M,M.L)$$
$$(4') \text{ wait\_for } (M,K,L) \leftarrow \text{ wait\_for } (M,L)$$
to be symmetric to "send".

But this definition leads to inproper solutions. If we modify (2)
to
$\qquad (2') \text{ b}(Y) \leftarrow \text{ wait\_for } (c,Y)$ the goalsequence $\leftarrow a \ (X) \wedge b(X)$ is
unsolvable, hence a will send message "a" where b is waiting a
message "c".
However PROLOG will solve the problem if (3') and (4') are used as
definitions for "wait_for", see Fig.6.

(1) $\leftarrow a \ (X)$
$\qquad \leftarrow \text{send } (a,X)$
(5) $\quad X:= [\ a \ | \ X1]$
$\qquad \leftarrow b \ (\ [\ a \ | \ X1])$
(2)
$\qquad \leftarrow \text{wait\_for } (c. \ a \ \ X1 \ ),$
(4) $\quad M:=c \ \ K:=a \ L:= \ X1$
$\qquad \leftarrow \text{wait\_for } (c,X1),$
(3) $\quad M:=c, \ X1:=[c \ | \ X2] \ , \ X:= [a,c \ | \ x_2 \ ]$

Fig.6. Inproper communication through variables

Problem (iv) simply meany, that no explicit definiton of the
structure, that is enumeration of components and description of
their hierarchy with explicit definition of communication channels
is possible in PROLOG. Practically to each component a process is
assigned and communication channels are represented in the program
by common shared logical variables.

Problem (v) means the lack of a central (global) system time in
the model. Processes are executed sequentially and some of them
may be already terminated, one is currently executed (the active
process) and others are waiting for execution. However some time
parameters including the termination time of the already terminated
processes may be uninstantiated.

It is so, because these time parameters depend on the moments of
communication with other processes, not yet executed. PROLOG will
assign the correct values to these time parameters when it will
execute the process in communication with the already "terminated"
ones. At the end of the simulation all time parameters will be
correctly calculated.

For the user the above means that if he has to debug his program,
snapshoots of the intermediate states contains no global information
about the system due to the uninstantiated time parameters or the
already terminated processes.

6. A POSSIBLE MODIFICATION OF PROLOG FOR SIMULATION

As it was shown in the previous section, pure PROLOG cannot be used
for simulation without difficulty.

To make possible simulation in PROLOG we have to modify and extend
it appropriately. We need

    (i)   to solve the problem of sequential solution of some
              goals leading to no_solution;

(ii)   to introduce an appropriate mechanism to handle the time.

To solve problem (i) we can give the following possibilities for simulationists:

(i)   possibility to define activities to be executed in parallel;

(ii)   possibility to define activities to be executed sequentially,

(iii)   possibility of the suspension of the execution of an activity (process) until some conditions do not fulfil.

To handle appropriatly the time, we need also a special clock which is closely related to the scheduler supporting (i)_(iii).
A first solution was the definition of the T_PROLOG (see e.g. Futó Szeredi (1982) and then TS_PROLOG (see e.g. Fotó and Gergely (1983)).

The main features of T_PROLOG are:

(i)   to process corresponding to a component a virtual PROLOG interpreter is assigned;

(ii)   execution of these processes can be synchronized by communication among the underlaying virtual PROLOG interpreters;

(iii)   communication is possible by
        _ sending/receiving messages
        _ writing/reading a common shared database
        _ suspension until a condition is not fulfiled

(iv)   an internal clock and a next event scheduler mechanism is used to handle suspensions and activations of the virtual PROLOG systems .

In TS_PROLOG in addition to T_PROLOG some very special built_in predicates are defined for simulation, e.g:

(i)   sending (M) to send a message of form "M",

(ii)   waiting_for (M) to suspend the solution of a goal until a message "M" does not arrive,

(iii)   wait (C) to suspend the solution of a goal until condition "C" becomes true.

(iv)   create (N) to create a component of name "N".

(v)   hold (T) to suspend the solution of a goal for "T" simulated time units,

(vi)   systemtime (T) to ask the current simulated time in the system.

(vii)   equations_of (N), initialization_of (N) to define set of differential equations for continuous components.

(viii)   wait_for condition (Expr) to suspend the activity of a
           continuous component until a state variable gets an
           appropriate value.

(ix)   formulas to define structure like system (Name),
           component (Name) and elementary_component (Name).

The solution of problems (i)_(iv) and v) in T_PROLOG and TS_PROLOG
respectively for the communicating processes "a" and "b" is shown
in Fig.7. and Fig.8.

Problem ←   new (send, a) ∧ new (wait_for,b)

send ← send (message (a))

wait_for ← wait_for (message (7)) (or wait_for (message(c))

Fig.7. Communication in T_PROLOG.

System (problem) ←
       elementary_component (send, a)   ∧
       elementary_component (wait_for, b)

Communication (a,b, message (X)) ←

Send ← send (message (a))
wai_for ←   wait_for (message (Z)) (wait_for (message (c))

Fig.8. System and communication definition in TS_PROLOG.

In Fig.7. "new" creates the process a (b) with goal send (wait_for)
and in Fig.8 "elementary_component" defines a process a (b), with
activity send (wait_for). The system "problem" consists of two
elementary components "a" and "b" communicating by a message of
the form "message (X)"

The main advantages of T_PROLOG and TS_PROLOG systems are that they

(i)   allow the explicit description of a hierarchical structure
         of the modeled system,

(ii)   provide a very flexible communication mechanism,

(iii)   permit the behaviour of the components at any level to
         be given by a set of differential equations as well as
         by a sequence of procedures.

(iv)   allow backtracking to try several alternatives in case
         of dead_lock or other unwanted situation.

7. CONCLUSION

The two programming paradigms logic programming and object oriented
programming can be combined into a new paradigm logic simulation,
which provides new possibilities for simulation, e.g. the dynamic
model modification. As we have seen in the case of PROLOG it is not
possible to achieve the required new paradigm by using directly a
logic programming language for simulation but this language should

be   augmented by appropriate devices to support model building, experimantation and model modification. Two possible steps of modification of PROLOG are outlined. T_PROLOG is augmented with devices to handle time and processes. TS_PROLOG beyond the devices of T_PROLOG has also devices to handle both structural and behavioural aspects of models of hierarchical and complex systems.

REFERENCES

Birtwistle, G.M. O.J. Dahl and K.Nygaard (1973). Simula Begin , Studentliteratur, Lund Sweden, 1973.

Futó,I., and J.Szeredi. (1982). A Discrete Simulation System Based on Artifical Intelligence Methods, in Discrete Simulation and Related Fields, A.Javor (ed.),North Holland, pp. 136-15Ø.

Futó,I. and T.Gergely. A Logical Approach to Simulation _ TSPROLOG, in Adequate Modelling of Systems, F.Wedde (ed.).Springer Verlag, 1983. pp.26-5Ø.

Kiviat, P.J. (1968). Simulation Using SIMSCRIPT II., Rand Corporation

Nance, R.E. (1981). The Time and State Relationships in Simulation and Modelling, CACM, Vol.24.No.4., pp. 173-189.

Warren, D.H. (1974).Warplan: a System for Generating Plans, University of Edinburgh, Edinburgh.

Modelling and Simulation Methodology
in the Artificial Intelligence Era
M.S. Elzas, T.I. Ören and B.P. Zeigler (Editors)
© Elsevier Science Publishers B.V. (North-Holland), 1986

Chapter VII.3

GRAPHIC INTERFACES FOR MODELLING SYSTEMS

Yoshikazu Yamamoto

Institute of Information Science
KEIO University
Yokohama, JAPAN

It has been greatly emphasized that importance of simulation in various fields. In spite of this fact, it is still not an easy job to develop a simulation model for a certain problem. Considering current state of the art of software and hardware, it is strongly required to facilitate some convenient tool for modelling and simulation. We had designed and partially implemented a model building system called GMBS in these three years. Here we discuss several aspects on modelling systems based on experience of our GMBS project.

1. INTRODUCTION

There are two classes of graphic modelling systems. One for showing a real system as it is, i.e., for keeping the real shape and real motion, and simulating them on the screen. This type of interfaces is utilized for a specific application as in robotic, aerodynamics etc. The other class is used for much broader application area where the model is represented as combination of abstract objects such as a graph connecting circles. In this case, we are paying attention to the relation between system components rather than their actual shape or motion. A picture which is shown on the screen does not reflect the actual shape but it represents physical or logical relationship between the system components, and may reflect behavior of the system. GMBS (Graphic Model Building System) was designed for the purpose of the latter class.

First of all, we briefly review the concept of GMBS in the next section. Then we will point out characteristics of GMBS in section 3. In section 4, we will discuss several problems on modelling systems comparing GMBS with other systems. Finally, we will mention about important points which we should consider for designing an integrated tool for simulation support.

2. CONCEPT OF GMBS

GMBS consists of several modules and support programs. Detailed explanation of the total system and these modules are found in (Yamamoto 1983). Here, we briefly review the basic concept of GMBS. GMBS was originally designed to support entire discrete event simulation process even for people who have no previous knowledge about neither modelling nor simulation languages. For this purpose, we adopt very simple world view much like that of GPSS. We divide a given system into two categories of components. One is a *Packet* which goes through the system while it is processed or served by other components. The other is a *Process* which serves incoming *Packets*.

We use a graph or a network of *Processes* to represent paths in which *Packets* pass through. This graph only shows the structure of logical relation of the model components. The behavior of each *Process* is specified by logical behavior specification which is separated from the structural representation. The *Packet* is an object which carries as much information as we want so that it sometimes may represent a physical component such as a customer, a part and a worker etc., and it may also represent a collection of information such as a signal and a message. The *Process* is a general conceptual object which gives some service to *Packets*. There are two special *Processes* called *Generator* and *Terminator* which creates and destroys *Packets* respectively.

GMBS allows to define a *Submodel* as a collection of *Processes* and other *Submodels*. Thus, we can get together components to have some specific functionality or have some locality as a *Submodel*. We call a closed network which consists of any number of *Generators*, *Terminators*, *Processes* and *Submodels* a picture. By utilizing *Submodels*, we can build hierarchical network structure of any level of pictures by decomposing the system into subsystems. A *Submodel* is also used as a subroutine so that we can call the predefined *Submodel* from any place of the upper level picture if the input/output specification, i.e., the number of lines for input and output, agrees between caller and called *Submodel*.

3. CHARACTERISTICS OF GMBS

GMBS is not only a modelling system but also to be a simulation support system which includes even parallel execution of a model program. We concentrate here the modelling aspect of GMBS.

Let us consider an example of a gas station. The station has two pumps, a washer and a cashier. There is a worker at each pump who serves filling gas to cars and cleans interior of cars. Cars arrive at this station at intervals of time following a certain distribution and select one of two pumps or the washer. After filling gas and interior cleaning, a certain percentage of cars go to the washing machine and the remaining go towards to the cashier to pay. Then they leave the station.

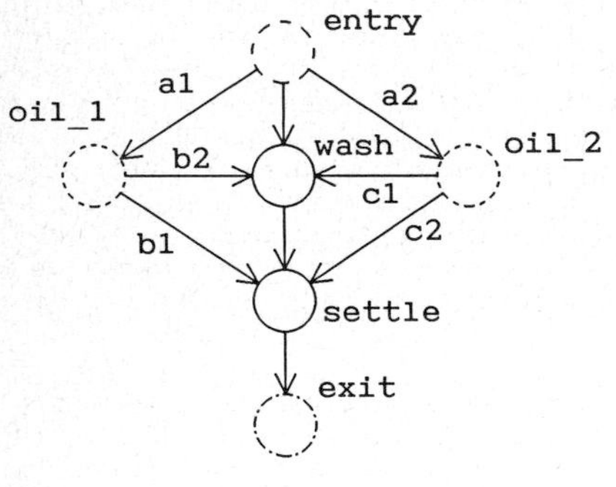

Figure 1 A Gas Station Model 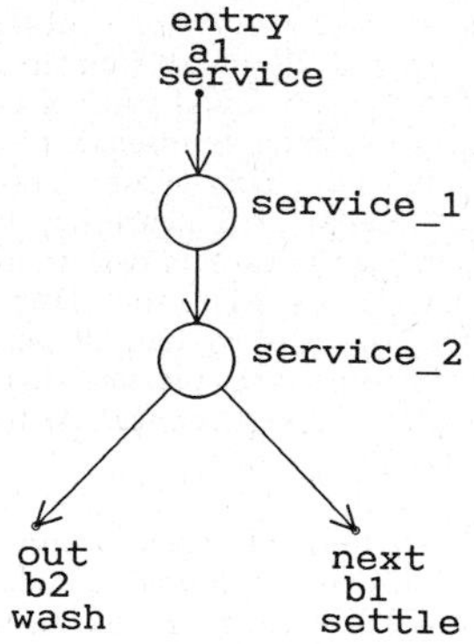   Figure 2 Submodel Picture bound to *oil_1*

We may model the structure of the given system as shown in Figure 1 which is called the top level picture of the model. In this picture, we define a *Generator*, a *Terminator*, two *Processes* which are labeled *wash* and *settle* and two *Submodels* labeled *oil_1* and *oil_2*. Each *Submodel* has an underlying picture. In this case, these two *Submodel* pictures have the same structure. The *Submodel* picture is regarded as a procedure or a subroutine in the sense of usual programming languages and not includes actual parameter binding part. When the *Submodel* picture is bound to the *Submodel* in the upper level picture, then the binding is established at that time. Thus, Figure 2 shows the *Submodel* picture after bound to the *Submodel oil_1*. Notice that the only difference between *Submodel* pictures *oil_1* and *oil_2* is binding of formal and actual parameters for i/o. Namely, referring a *Submodel* from the calling picture specifies only the i/o ports of the picture for the *Submodel* and has no effect to the internal structure of the *Submodel*.

The most important characteristics in modelling of GMBS is the separation between structural specification and logical behavior specification (LBS). LBS has to be done for each *Process* of a model. A *Generator* and a *Terminator* can be treated as a special *Process*. There are two ways for specifying LBS, that is by parametric and dimensional flowcharting. For both of these methods, GMBS will automatically generate a source program module for a *Process*.

Parametric specification of a *Process* is done according to the predefined internal logic structure. That is, packet selection, queuing, server and dispatching specifications. Current version of GMBS achieves this part by utilizing a character display terminal interactively, an example of this parametric LBS was given in (Yamamoto 1983). LBS by dimensional flowcharting is beyond the scope of this paper, but we already implemented a system for it which supports editing of a flowchart, checking of flowchart syntax and source code generation (Yamamoto 1985). It will soon be incorporated into GMBS.

There must be at least one LBS for each *Process* (including *Generator* and *Terminator*) for producing an executable program. Current GMBS allows only one LBS for each *Process*, but we can leave several parameters as variable which will be given values at the start of execution.

4. PROBLEMS ON MODELLING SYSTEMS

In this section, we discuss the following problems of modelling systems comparing GMBS with other systems : Level of abstraction, Reusability of models, Graphic interfaces and Documentation tools.

The level of abstraction of GMBS at modelling is quite high because of the aforementioned submodel-picture decomposition and separation between structural and logical behavior specification. Other systems, such as proposed by Engelke and Willis, utilize more problem oriented graphical symbols. Engelke's system was designed for production systems simulation and Willis's was for wider problem area. Both of these utilize graphical symbols as representative of a fairly small function like blocks of GPSS. Such tight correspondence between a function and a graphical symbol causes to introduce so many symbols. We believe it is better to utilize predefined symbols for which functions are able to define by a user, or to facilitate a tool for defining a new symbol for a specific function. GMBS allows a user to name meaningfully to symbols in a picture for distinguishing their functionality. Thus, GMBS may be used as a special problem oriented modelling system if we utilize *Submodels* which were previously defined as functional units. Due to the loose coupling between symbols and functions, we can design a model by GMBS with relatively small number of components. In addition, the hierarchical submodel-picture structure assists stepwise decomposition of the model. It means that the pictorial representation by GMBS helps us to grasp the bird's eye view or perspective of the target system.

Concern with reusability of a model, current implementation of GMBS is unfortunately poor because there is no model database implemented yet. A *Submodel* is specified by only i/o ports from the calling picture as mentioned before. Thus, GMBS has high potential to reuse formerly defined *Submodel* pictures. In this case, we have to consider about a database for multiple LBS for a *Process*.

The topic about graphic interfaces is very important from usability and user friendliness point of view. There are two types of graphic display terminals, one is a bitmap display and the other is a graphic terminal. Graphic terminals usually accept special control sequences which achieve various functions defined by GKS or CORE standard. The first version of GMBS utilized the VS11 bitmap display for graphic i/o and a character display for command and text i/o. We also partially implemented GMBS on Seillac 3, Yamaha YGT-100 and Xerox SIP1100. The VS11 is the most primitive in its function and we had to implement entire graphic primitives. On the other hand, graphic displays like Seillac 3 or YGT-100 have many graphic primitives such as line or circle drawing, filling, clipping, enlarging, shrinking, rotation, moving and viewport transformation etc. In addition to these functions, they have a large local memory for maintaining picture elements as segment and class data structure. We can sharply reduce response time of interactions from the VS11 version to the YGT-100 version by means of adopting this segment and class data structure.

Table 1 summarizes comparison of hardware specification of display terminals, though the SIP1100 is classified into a workstation.

Table 1 Comparison of Display Terminals (Hardware)

	VS11	Seillac 3	YGT-100	SIP1100
Color	16	256	1024	B/W
Screen size	16"	20"	14"	17"
Resolution	512×512	1400×1024	640×480	1024×808
Pointng device	joy stick mouse	joy stick tablet	light pen mouse	mouse

There still remain several problems for applications such as GMBS even in these highly capable graphic displays. We have to use an additional character display for commands i/o same as the VS11 version or to modify every interaction into pop up menu driven when we utilize the Seillac 3 as a display because it can not allow to coexist both graphic and console modes. It is possible to register predefined menus as segments and to exchange menus instantaneously. But it is still necessary to make up an error message viewport for informing a diagnosis depending on the error, and it take relatively long time due to increased transfer of necessary information. We avoid this problem by introducing a console viewport in the YGT-100 version.

When we want to move a circle while structure modelling, it is possible to move simultaneously the circle itself by dragging and lines which are connected to it by rubber banding on the VS11 version. This function of course had to be implemented by a program. However, GKS or CORE does not allow to use segment dragging and rubber banding at the same time. There is also no preparation to enhance local functions by programming for usual graphic terminals. It is not so difficult to realize this function by programming in the host computer, but it is not suitable for practical use due to inevitable increase of response time.

The last topic about the system as a documentation tool is also very important. As far as a system which has graphic interface concerned, it has advantages over other systems due to its capability of pictorial structure representation. GMBS has a facility for plotting pictures on a color plotter and a laser printer. For the parametric LBS we have no document generator yet, but it certainly will be implemented. The plotting program for a dimensional flowchart is available for the non-parametric LBS (Yamamoto 1985).

5. TOWARDS AN INTEGRATED TOOL FOR SIMULATION

We discuss here the topics which we believe to be key factors for designing an integrated simulation support system, that is model program generation, interactive modification, tracing and monitoring.

The first problem that we want to pick up is automatic model program generation from the given graphic model description. For a graphic modelling system such as GMBS, it is very difficult to represent a model without any textual description. In GMBS, for example, we adopt parametric LBS as textual description for each structural component. There still remains a possibility to represent complete model description graphically by utilizing pictorial representation, such as the dimensional flowchart, for internal logic of components. The pictorial LBS, in this case, constructs a picture which becomes the inner most level of submodel-picture hierarchy. It seems quite possible to generate a model program from these submodel-picture hierarchy by applying the code generation method of the dimensional flowcharting system and the parameter binding mechanism used in parametric LBS.

Such a fully graphical modelling system will have advantages that it will allow us to be free from coding efforts, it will support interactive debugging on the picture and give a chance to observe the model behavior. The latter two are achieved by tracing discussed later.

Concerning about interactive graphic modification of the model, at least changing parameter values in parametric LBS and altering the number of *Processes* are already possible on current GMBS. Further modification, such as changing model structure itself or modifying logical behavior of some *Process* during execution, is impossible as far as we utilize a compiler. We can implement an interpreter for such a system if we can solve the response time problem (speed of interpretation), then we will get complete freedom of modification of the model.

Two tracing modes, that is sequential and parallel, are necessary to consider. The former traces transition of *Packets* step by step and the latter traces concurrent transition of *Packets* as they are. Sequential trace is used for model debugging and parallel trace is used for learning or educating system behavior. We had already implemented both tracing modes. If we interpretively trace a model, parallel tracing causes a problem. That is, if parallel tracing should be exact reflection of model behavior, it is very difficult to reflect duration of active or idle phase of *Processes*, because that the necessary computation time is not always proportional to an active interval of a *Process*. Unless we persist in interpretive execution, we have not found the solution for it. GMBS traces a model in parallel by rearranging sequential trace output.

GMBS allows to interrupt sequential trace mode and then enter to monitoring mode. This facility is implemented by the menu driven manner. Although there is a restriction that we can only monitor a *Process* which is defined by parametric LBS, it is also quite useful for debugging.

6. CONCLUSION

We discussed graphic interfaces for modelling systems by using GMBS as an example. Though there still remain several problems, a pictorial representation certainly has great persuasive power over textual expression. Again we believe that a system for supporting simulation should have not only modelling support but also tracing and monitoring facility.

We are now considering about possibility to utilize GMBS to object oriented programming based on such as Smalltalk-80. It is quite natural to consider a *Packet* of GMBS as a message of Smalltalk-80 and a *Process* as an object, and the concept of message passing will make parallel model program execution possible.

ACKNOWLEDGMENT

The author would like to thank to Professor Yoshio Ohno for his helpful suggestion on implementing graphic primitives for the YGT-100 version of GMBS. And also be grateful to referees for their helpful comments.

REFERENCES

Engelke, H. et. al. (1983). Structured Modeling of Manufacturing Process, Proc. the 16th Annual Simulation Symposium, pp. 69–78.

Willis, R.R. (1983). GMSS - Graphic modelling and Simulation System, Proc. the 16th Annual Simulation Symposium, pp. 137–160.

Yamamoto, Y. and Lenngren, M. (1983). Graphic Model Building System, Proc. the 16th Annual Simulation Symposium, pp. 161–176.

Yamamoto, Y. (1985). A System for Dimensional Flowcharting, Technical Report KIIS-84-02, Institute of Information Science KEIO University, 44 p.

SUBJECT INDEX

A

Ability			47, 276
Absolute	time		368
Abstraction	level		53, 121, 332
Acceptable	value of	parameter	306
Acceptor			47, 84
Action	cluster		166, 169, 171
Action	function		388
Action-cluster	interaction	graph	169
Active	constraints		91, 92
Active	documentation		16
Active	perception		51
Activity	oriented	simulation	165, 170, 172, 387
Adaptive	behavior of	model	206
Adaptive	control		153
Adaptive	experimentation	with models	153
Adaptive	expert-systems	architecture	206
Adaptive	input	generator	158
Adaptive	strategy		203
Adaptive	systems		195, 196, 199
Advisor			41, 299
Agent			15
Aggregation			318
Agreement			345
Algorithm			33, 208, 316, 323
Algorithmic	transformation		170, 208
Analog	computers		4
Analogy			4, 53, 312
Analysis			21, 79, 134, 137, 166, 234, 295, 312, 315, 354, 356
Analytic	modelling		315, 319
Ancestry	based	structure	231
Animation			116
Antecedent			25, 182
Apical	cluster		248
Applicability	knowledge		65
Application	domain	model	353, 355, 357
Applications of	learning	automata	223
Approximately	correct	decomposition	23
Artificial	intelligence	building-block	69
Artificial	intelligence	environments	61, 74, 75

Artificial   intelligence   workbench   69
Artificial   intelligence   workstation   69
Aspect   25,80,87,200
Assertions   182
Assessment   245,268,269,332
Asset   vector   342
Assimilated   knowledge   42,47
Assistant   41,67,81,114
Associative   pyramid   248
Attached   variable   25,78
Automata   theory   84,146,211,220,221,223
Automated   consistency   checks   276
Automated   model   316
Automated   war   317
Automatic   model   formulation   124
Automation   42,124,133,155,316,317
Automaton   211,212
Autonomous   entity   228,230
Autonomous   learning   51
Average   penalty   213
Axiomatic   definition   387

B

Background   knowledge   65
Backward   reasoning   66,70,391
Bargaining   power   349
Base   frame   109
Base   model   26,227
Behave   intelligently   3
Behavior   3,16,27,72,135,156,166,196,198,
                                               206,211,232,241,326,327,390,400
Behavior   generation   267
Behavior   pattern   312
Behavior   planning   385
Behavior   processing   9,41,267
Behavioral   analogy   312
Behavioral   specification   155,158,400
Behavioral   variables   344
Bidding   scheme   208
Binding of   form   scheme   371
Biotic   system   234
Black   box   113,135,381
Blackboard   66
Block   of   knowledge   62,63,303,318
Block   oriented   languages   106
Browsing   33
Building   block   69,318

C

CAD   workstation   133
Calibration   103
Candidate   model   29,109,357
Canonical   rule   scheme   92
Cause   effect   relationship   315
Centralized   data   base   321
Certainty   factor   23,31,38

Chaining			36,37,66,70,149
Changing	mode		197
Class			15,33,62,360,401
Class of	subjects		62
Classification	problem		20
Classification	tree		249,250
Clock	generator		189
Cluster			22,166,169,171,234,247,248
Cognitive	model		8,67
Cognitive	simulation		41
Cognitive	structure		30
Cognitive	system		6
Cognizant	quality	assurance	276
Cognizant	simulation		41,43,267,269
Cognizant	system		267
Communication	channel		393
Comparable	certainty		31
Compatibility			70,71,299
Complex	temporal	tool	372
Complexity	bound		177
Complexity of	models		103,177
Component			16,67,103,113,114,198,303,305, 394
Composite	object		166
Composition	tree		93,103,112
Computer	assistance for	simulation	81,114
Computer	embedded	machine	43,47
Computer	embedded	system	43
Computer	program		4,10,43,133
Computer-aided	decision	system	79
Computerization	of	simulation	42
Computerized	model		280
Computerized	model	validity	281
Concept	formation		230,251
Concept	manipulation		245
Concept	representation		255,370
Conceptual	dependency		108
Conceptual	match		27
Conceptual	model		280,281,321,355,378
Conceptual	model	validity	281
Conceptual	similarity		31
Conceptualization			354
Condition			35,104,154,169,176,177
Condition	specification		165,166,171,176,177
Conflict	resolution		311,331
Conflicting	objective		331
Conjunction of	conditions		169
Connection	pattern		128,254
Consensus	generation		311
Consequent			25,182
Consistency			276,360
Consistency of	knowledge	representation	24,67,121
Consistent	pattern		234
Constraint			16,80,88,91,92,93,199,250
Constraints	on	structure	250
Construction of	models		79,92,109,148
Consultant			6,41
Consultation	task		6,73
Consumption	vector		342
Context			22,26,233,329

Context   dependent   information   233
Contingent   action   cluster   171
Continuous   change   model   102
Continuous   time   simulation   109
Control   85,153,235
Coordination   scheme   202
Cost of   (dis)agreement   344
Coupled   model   303,305
Coupling   16,95,106,115,121,126,200,303,
                                                        305
Coupling   constraint   80,93
Coupling   recipe   95,115
Coupling   relationship   16,80,198
Cross   reference   list   300
Cybernation   42

D

DEVS   specification   181
Data   base   25,286,321
Data   bound   activity   357
Data   dictionary   324
Data   editor   324
Data   input   definition   116
Data   management   systems   10,113,367
Data   validity   281
Database   367
Debugging   51,66,151
Decision   entity   361
Decision   making   21,79,311,331,341,353,354
Decision   model   320,324
Decision   rule   21,322
Decision   support   339,353,355,357
Decision   table   333
Decision   tree   317,329
Declarative   method   107
Decomposition   16,23,30,67,78,80,108,122,126,
                                                        137,198,326,401
Decomposition   transformation   137
Decomposition   tree   87,139
Deducive   modelling   approach   79
Deductive   learning   53
Definitional   model   (in)validation   127
Demand   intensity   344
Demon   35,65
Demon   driven   relation   35
Dependency   108,166,233
Depository of   knowledge   23
Depth   first   strategy   88,390
Derivability   relation   109
Derivatives   105
Description   17,116,121,160,268,361,402
Descriptive   assessment   268
Descriptive   model   361
Design   10,55,83,93,133,135,150,153,
                                                        187,195,311,358
Design   automation   133,155
Design   diagram   326
Design   entity   structure   97

Design	objectives		97
Design for	testability		133
Desired	behavior		241
Determined	action	cluster	171
Deterministic	automaton		160,211
Diagnostic	problem		6,20
Diagram			116,326
Dialogue	facilities		73,299,305
Differential	equation		105,146
Differentiation of		individuals	235
Dimensional	flowcharting		401
Directed	learning		50
Directed	search		327
Direction of	influence		123
Discontinuities			105
Discovery			4,51,230
Discrete	change	modelling	102,107
Discrete	event	simulation	165,181,399
Discrete	event system	specification	84
Discrete	structure	states	196,197
Discrete-Event	System	formalism	181
Distributed	systems		83
Divergence			350,351
Divide &	conquer		200
Divide/merge	regime		231
Documentation			16,105,333,402
Domain	specific	knowledge	6,10,81,300,353,355,357
Domain	specific	language	319
Dominance	interaction		235
Donation	vector		343
Dummy	entity		89
Dynamic	behavior		166
Dynamic	block		303
Dynamic	knowledge	components	67
Dynamic	learning		55
Dynamic	model		62
Dynamic	system		135,153

E

Econometric	model		360
Economic	transaction	layer	209
Editor			66,324
Education			50
Embedded	chain	concept	149
Embedded	learning	abilities	276
Embedded	model		9,43,62
Emotion			311
Empirical	model		353
Eniac	project		3
Entity			25,80,87,89,200,228,230,280, 357,361
Entity	based	structures	22,79
Entity	driven	simulation	147
Entity	lattice		31,38
Entity	structure		22,24,79,80,87,89,97,139,154, 166,228,229,395
Entity	structuring	program	25
Entity	tree		33,79

Entity   type   23,80,357
Enumeration of   components   394
Environment   42,61,74,75,81,219,220,269,
                                                    335,361
Environment   architecture   42,68,74,75
Epistemological   structure   63
Epistomology   63,64,241
Equivalent   stimulus   patterns   247
Error   handling   254,256,303
Ethical   assessment   269
Evaluation   procedure   121,167,282,311
Event   84,165,181,229,231,399
Event   scheduling   165,170,172
Event   subroutine   146,165
Execution   aids   151
Execution   control   85
Existing   AI   environments   74,75
Expected   behavior   232
Expedient   reinforcement   scheme   215
Experiment   applicable to   model   104
Experiment   base   156,157
Experiment   supervisor   10
Experimental   conditions   104,154
Experimental   design   10,150,153,358
Experimental   frame   21,79,84,85,86,104,109,156,157,
                                                    160,357
Experimental   frame   (definition)   83
Experimental   frame   construction   79
Expert   41
Expert   aids   145,149,151,279
Expert   database   systems   25
Expert   simplification aid   149
Expert   simulation   system   155
Expert   system   6,19,20,25,62,69,109,134,161,
                                                    206,286,339,346,353,360
Expert   system   concept   286
Expert   system   shell   69,206
Explanation   41,66,280,320,341
Explanation   facility   66,320,341
Exploitation   345
External   block   303
External   state   transition   185

F

Face   validity   technique   282,295
Fact   15,16,108,182
Familiar   category   252
Fault   prone   systems   195
Feed   back   loop   115,340,349
Feed   back   relationship   115
Filing   367
Filler of a   slot   35
Finite   automata   146
Finite   state   machine   133
Finiteness of   knowledge   representation   25
Fixed   structure   automaton   211
Fixed   structure   formalism   228
Flexible   process   199

Flip   Flop   element   183
Flowchart   401
Form   flow   system   365
Form   modelling   concept   365
Form   scheme   366,371
Formal   knowledge   16,104,109
Formal   model   104
Formalism   109,117,181,228
Forward   reasoning   66
Forward and   backward   chaining   70
Frame   35,70,108,288
Frequency of   learning   50,55
Function   121,140,147,388
Function   evaluation   121,167
Functional   requirements   21
Functional   similarity   31
Future   research   75
Fuzzy   state   machines   140

G

Game   structured   simulation   335
Game   theory   340
Gaming   315,335,340
Gate   elements   187
General   knowledge   21
General   problem   solver   5
Generality of   knowledge   representation   24
Generalized   inference   321
Generate and   test   paradigm   377
Generation of   model   structures   86
Generative   systems   specification   135
Generator   10,73,84,158,189
Generic   attribute   368
Generic   experimental   frame   84,85,86
Generic   software   environment   335
Generic   template   93,123
Generic   variable   type   81
Genetic   algorithm   208
Giving   system   knowledge about 15
Global   control   mechanism   235
Global   information   394
Global   property   233
Global   state   transformations 134
Global   time   392
Goal   7,41,182,311,327
Goal   directed   learning   50
Goal   directed   search   327
Goal   setting   41
Goals for   simulation   studies   7
Goals for   societal   models   311
Graph   138,169,368
Graphic   interface   399
Graphic   model   description   402
Graphic   modelling   system   399
Graphical   model   builder   114,116
Graphical   representation   66,106,160,166,169,280,334,403

H

Hardware   159,187,200,334
Hardware   design   specification   187
Heuristic   decision   rule   322
Heuristic   modelling   320
Heuristics   4,316,323
Hierarchical   coupling   scheme   200
Hierarchical   model   construction   92,200
Hierarchical   situation   assessment   332
Hierarchical   structure   automaton   220,221
Hierarchical   structuring   92,200,220,326
Hierarchical   tree   222
Hierarchy   17,23,92,200,220,222,246,256,
                                                            326,332,369
Hierarchy of   levels   17
Hierarchy of   system   descriptions   17
High-level   knowledge   53
Hire/fire   regime   231
Hiring   and   Firing   201,205,231
Horizontal   tree   249
Horn   clause   65,386
Human   knowledge   acquisition   5
Human   like   behavior   326

I

Icon   66,116
Identification   155,196,355
Ill   structured   problem   355
Implementable   structures   25
Implicit   knowledge   165
Inconsistent   alteration   300
Incremental   knowledge   55,300
Incremental   learning   55
Indicator of   context   329
Individual   oriented   systems   241
Inference   engine   66,133,361
Inference   rule   16,133
Inference   strategy   66
Inferencing   15,66,73,133,182,321,361
Influence   123
Information   channel   305
Information   processing   property   229
Information   purchase   208
Information   retrieval   245
Information   systems   20,21,311,353,355,360
Initial   learning   55
Initiative of   learner   50,51
Input   116,140,149,158,295,305
Input   alphabet   140
Integrative   learning   55
Intelligent   agent   15
Intelligent   machinery   3,42
Intelligent   robot   42
Intelligent   statistical   software   292
Intelligent   system   16
Interaction   165,169,170,173,229,231,235,
                                                            237,311

Interaction	process		346
Interactive	debugger		151
Interactive	dialogue	system	299
Interactive	graphics		280,403
Interesting	event		229,231
Interface			5,10,66,121,288,399
Internal	representation		15
Internal	state	transition	185
Interpretation			41
Intervention	alternative		79
Introspective	learning		51
Invariant	relation		229
Inverted	tree of	connections	250
Is-a	hierarchy		369
Item	name		81
Items of	knowledge		22

J

Justification	280

K

Key	attribute		251
Knowledge			6,10,15,16,20,21,22,33,42,47,
			50,53,55,62,63,65,70,71,80,81,
			101,104,106,109,113,115,138,
			165,292,300,328,340
Knowledge	acceptor		47
Knowledge	acquisition		5,7,20,42,47,70
Knowledge	acquisition	interviews	64
Knowledge	assimilation		42,47
Knowledge	base		10,19,23,66,81,114,154,292
Knowledge	editor		66
Knowledge	element		8,37,67
Knowledge	engineering		9,19,55,64,371
Knowledge	engineering	knowledge	55
Knowledge	epistomology		63
Knowledge	processing	ability	47
Knowledge	processing	knowledge	50,55
Knowledge	processing	machine	47
Knowledge	processing	system	43
Knowledge	representation		15,24,25,65,67,102,121,166,
			328,355
Knowledge	representation	requirements	24,25
Knowledge	seeking		227
Knowledge	seeking	model	312
Knowledge	structure		8,22,25,70,108,161
Knowledge	synthesis		67,71
Knowledge	transducer		43
Knowledge-based	simulation	environment	81

L

Language	5,8,10,22,25,66,70,83,104,106,
	107,108,113,116,121,146,161,
	319,328,356

Language	structure		161
Large	scale	systems	334
Latent	knowledge		47
Lattice			31,32,38
Learning			3,41,42,47,50,51,53,55,154,211, 223,245,251,257,269,276
Learning	automata	theory	211
Learning	behavior		211
Learning	network		257
Learning	process		154
Learning	rule		245
Learning	simulation	environment	269
Learning by	abstraction		53
Learning by	analogy		53
Learning by	direct	memorization	53
Learning by	discovery		51
Learning by	experimentation		51
Learning by	generalization		53
Learning by	operationalization		53
Learning by	simile		251
Learning from	examples		53
Learning from	general	cases	53
Least	inclusive	category	252
Level of	hierarchy		256
Level of	knowledge		20,53
Level of	response		256
Liberal	learning		50
Linear	optimization		121
Linearized	model		103
Locality			170,171
Logic	programming		181,385
Logic	programming	specification	182
Logic	simulation		386
Logical	behavior	specification	400
Logical	dependencies		166
Logical	inference		182
Look	ahead	test	322
Low-level	knowledge		53
Lumped	model		106

M

Machine			43,47,133,140,146,148
Machine	learning		3,41,42,47
Macro			109
Macroscopic	level		102
Maintenance	facility		67
Management of	change		311
Marginal	utility	array	343
Martingale			214
Matching of	model	behavior	27,156
Mathematical	model		31,105,108,146,356
Mathematical	operations		31,106,133
Mathematical	problems		5,105
Mechanism to	handle	time	395
Mechanization			42
Mental	process		5
Message			393
Message	passing		326

Messages			65
Meta	knowledge		33
Meta	learning		50
Meta	model		6
Meta	rules		66
Meta	system	level	196
Micro-world			5
Microscopic	level		103
Mimicry			5,6
Minimum	state	machine	148
Mirror	modelling		230,312
Mixing of	formalisms		117
Mode			8,23,197
Mode of a	node		23
Model	base		30,33,105,113,114,115,129,160, 286
Model	based	advisor	299
Model	based	certifier	299
Model	behavior		27,156,250
Model	building	process	81,91,101,114,116
Model	composition		103,113,114
Model	connectivity		128
Model	construction		79,92,109,148,200,279,354
Model	definition		6,9,26,31,43,62,105,106,160, 402
Model	development	process	279
Model	formulation		8,67,105,124
Model	frame		109,115
Model	generation/	referencing	10,86,115
Model	inferencing		73
Model	information		290
Model	instantiation		95
Model	management	system	115,313
Model	module		87,114,117
Model	module	relationship	117
Model	processing		41,73,133,267
Model	referencing		267
Model	reliability		300
Model	restructuring		233
Model	searching		73
Model	specification		6,106,121,135,166
Model	storage and	retrieval	101,106
Model	structure		86,246,403
Model	synthesis		16,195,203
Model	translator		115
Model	validation		127,279,281
Modelling	epistemic	systems	241
Modelling	epistomology		64
Modelling	knowledge	elements	37
Modelling	support		358
Modelling	system		9,27,66,399
Modelling and	simulation	consultation	73
Modelling and	simulation	environment	42
Modelling and	simulation	knowledge	55
Modification of	models		156
Module			87,114,117,183
Monitor(ing)			10,51,66,325
Morphological	assessment		268
Mosaic	learning		55
Most-probable	candidate	model	313

Motivational	vector		343
Mouse			66
Multi-teacher	environment		213,218,219,220
Multicomponent	DEVS		181
Multifacetted	models		20,81,195
Multilayered	hierarchy		246
Multilevel	expert	system	286
Multilevel	systems	specification	136
Multiparadigm	computer		47
Multiple	association		167
Multiple	decomposition		78
Multiscenario	experiment		319
Multiserver			199

N

Named	group		252
Nand	module		183
Natural	language	interfaces	5,10,66,121
Natural	language	script	22,317,328
Nearly	decomposable	hierarchy	326
Need	vector		342
Negotiation	process		339,345
Network			37,116,136,159,246,257
Network	architecture		246
Network	specification		136
Network	traversal		37
Network of	processing	elements	159
Neural	discharge	activity	246
Neural	net	testing	256
Neural	system	model	245
Neuron	cluster		247
Node	objects		23,38
Non-procedural	model	description	160
Non-supervised	pattern	analysis	234
Nonstationary	multi-teacher	environment	219
Normal	mode		197
Normative	assessment		269
Numerical	data		70,72
Numerical	model	(in)validation	127

O

Object			15,22,25,35,38,62,65,108,133,
			161,166
Object	oriented	decomposition	122
Object	oriented	language	356
Object	oriented	modelling	230,386
Object	oriented	paradigm	166
Object	similarity		29
Object	specification		167
Objective of	simulation	study	79
Objectives	driven	methodology	79,81,97
Observational	learning		51
Open	ended	list	393
Operational	knowledge		65
Operational	validity		281,282
Operator			106,133

Optimal	path		222
Optimization	function		121
Optimization	model		360
Optimizing	algorithm		316
Organizational	behavior		327,341
Organizational	design		311
Organizational	system		340
Oscillatory	convergence		350
Oscillatory	divergence		351
Output	alphabet		140,149
Output	analysis		295
Output	function		140

P

Pairwise	interaction		237
Paradigm	systems		228,241
Parallel	processing		159
Parametrization			318
Partial	differential	equation	105
Partial	model		87
Partial	net		26
Partial	process		232
Partitioning			22,102,126,166
Passive	constraints		91,92
Passive	learning		51
Passive	perception		51
Pattern	analysis		234,312
Pattern	discovery		230
Pattern	matching		27,317
Pattern	recognition		245
Pattern of	interaction		229
Perception			41,51
Perceptual	variables		344
Performance			47,85,206
Performance	index		85
Permissible	model	behavior	250
Permissible	model	structure	246
Personal	acquaintances		237
Petri	net		169,369,370
Petri	net	graph	169,369
Petri	net	identifier	370
Phenomenological		fidelity	329
Pheromone	composition and concentration		239
Pipeline			200
Planning			311,322,385,387
Point	behavior		72
Policy	analysis		315
Policy	construction		311
Policy	evaluation		311
Possible	behavior		390
Post-	condition		177
Postprocessing			161
Potential	observables		227
Pragmatic	assessment		269
Pre-	condition		176
Precision			150
Predicate			65,125,387,395
Predicates for	simulation		395

Predicting 350
Predictive validation 358
Probability management 66,341
Probability vector 213
Probability of succeeding state 147
Problem decomposition assistance 67
Problem domain 6,10,81
Problem entity 280
Problem identification 355
Problem solving 4,5,15,20,42,133,134,353,361
Problem solving environment 361
Problem specification 354
Procedural knowledge 328
Procedural method 108
Procedure 33,121,126,128,133,160,282
Process 5,81,91,101,114,116,121,154, 199,214,232,279,339,346
Process definition 391
Process interaction 165,170,173
Process model 356,377
Process oriented approach 389
Process subgraphs 173
Processing time 257
Production rule 34,166,378
Program generator 10,73
Programming 4,25,181,182,385
Programming in conceptual way 4
Proof tree 388
Protocol 202
Prototype development 360
Prototyping 319,360
Proximity based interactions 231
Pruning 8,86,87,149,198,350
Pruning of input set 149
Pure system entity structures 87

Q

Qualitative heuristic rule 316
Qualitative heuristics 323
Qualitative model 381
Quality assessment study 268
Quality assurance of simulation 267
Quality of knowledge 47
Quantitative algorithm 323
Quantity of knowledge 47
Quasi deterministic state 160
Query system 9,117,360
Questionaire 129
Quiescent entity 228

R

Random environment 211
Range of input variable 305
Rational analytic model 319
Real world system 79
Realization transformation 137

Reasoning			4,6,34,35,41,66,391
Recurrence	equation		108
Recursive	application of	frames	35
Reduction of	output	set	149
Reformulation	procedure		121,126,128
Reinforcement	scheme		212,215
Relation			15,24,35,80,109,115,117,121, 122,126,198,229,315,366
Relation	oriented	decomposition	122
Relational	scheme		366
Relational	system	description	121
Relative	strength of	connections	250
Relative	time		157
Reliability			300
Representation	requirement		24,25
Resource	balance	vector	343
Response			256,257
Restructuring			233
Robot			42
Rote	learning		53
Rule			16,21,34,66,92,166,182,245, 316,322,378,381
Rule	base		381
Rule	based	system	81,91,276,381
Rule	scheme		92
Rule	development	methodology	91
Rule-based	decision	model	320
Rule	based	technique	320,377
Rules for	altering	system	196
Run	time	decisions	151

S

SOIBEAN			145
Scheduling			165,170,172
Scenario			108,315,317,356
Scheduling	procedure		160
Scheme			92,200,202,208,212,215,366,371
Scope of	learning		50
Scratchpad			66
Search	procedure		33,133
Search	space		73,91
Second	normal	form	370
Selection of	model	alternatives	91
Self	documenting	code	333
Self	monitoring		51
Self	sufficiency		230
Semantic	assessment		269
Semantic	data	model	365
Semantic	error		256
Semantic	net		22,26,108,368
Semantic	property		123
Semantically	related	concepts	249
Sending			367
Sensitivity			332,356
Sensitivity	analysis		356
Sequence of	actions		388
Sequence of	operations		4,157,160,169
Sequencing			4,107,157,160,169

Sequential   machine   146
Sequential   pyramid   248
Service   behavior   327
Service   model   323
Set of   possible   structures   199
Sets of   coherent   observations   228
Severity of   errors   254
Shadow   world   232
Signal   107,151,168
Similarity   7,27,29,31,33,245
Similarity   assessment   245
Similarity   net   27,33
Similarity of   models   7,21,29,30,31
Simplest   model   86,103
Simplification   86,103,149,165,174,175,176,280
Simplification of   specification   174,175,176
Simulation   41,43,267,269,386,395
Simulation   system   42,47,81,116,148,155
Simulation   design   55,83
Simulation   environment   42,81,269
Simulation   language   83,104,113,116,146
Simulation   mode   8
Simulation   objective   41,79
Simulation   program   84
Simulation   program   generator   10,73
Simulation   quality   assurance   268
Simulation   study   7,41,79,105
Simulation   support   system   400
Simulation   system   structure   154
Simulation in   Prolog   385
Simulation of   digital   logic   158
Simulative   learning   51
Single   interval   simulation   246
Slot   35,288
Slot   filling   condition   35
Smooth   convergence   350
Smooth   divergence   350
Societal   system   311
Software   10,55,113,133,286,292,335
Software   engineering   knowledge   55,113
Software   system   286,335
Solution   process   121
Solution   space   134
Space   26,33,63,73,91,133,134
Specialization   29,33,80,81,200
Specialization taxonomy   tree   29,33
Specific   knowledge   10,81,300
Specific   language   319
Specification   6,79,84,91,106,121,133,135,
                                                     136,155,158,165,166,167,171,
                                                     176,177,181,187,195,196,198,
                                                     299,354,400
Specification   of   models   6,106,114,121,133,135,155,158,
                                                     165,166,171,181
Specification   transformation   133
Stable   situation   346
Stalemate   349
Stand   alone   model   382
State   105,133,134,140,147,148,160,
                                                     166,185,196,197,201,388

State	changes		229
State	definition		160,166
State	function		140,147
State	machine		133,134,140,148
State	set		134,140
State	space		133
State	transformation		134
State	transition		147,185,197,201
State	variables		105
Static	analysis		166
Static	structure		306
Statistical	subroutine		150,292
Statistical	test		282
Stepwise	decomposition		401
Stochastic	automaton		211 ,212
Stochastic	process		214
Stochastic	sequential	machines	146
Stochastic	simulation	machine	148
Storage of	knowledge		47,101,106
Strategic	analysis		315
Strategic	behavior		327
Strategic	level	gaming	315
Strategy			66,88,203,311,315,327,340,390
Stratification	graph		138
Stratified	knowledge		21,138
Strict	hierarchy		23
Strict	uniformity		23
Strong	typing		321
Structural	(in)validation		126,127
Structural	behavior		196,198
Structural	change		199,201
Structural	constraints		88,199
Structural	similarity		7
Structural	specification		400
Structure			8,22,24,25,30,63,70,79,80,87,
			89,93,97,106,108,139,154,161,
			166,195,196,197,198,199,206,
			211,220,221,227,228,229,231,
			250,306,329,392,403
Structure	state	transition	197,201
Structure of	model	base	33
Structured	conceptual	objects	22,25,161
Structured	system		7,30,32,106
Structuring			25,92,200,220,326
Structuring	paradigm		22,32
Subject			62
Submicroscopic	level		103
Submodel	picture	hierarchy	402
Subordinate	response		257
Subroutine			146,150,165
Successfull	negotiation		345
Summary	variables		95
Superordinate	response		257
Supporting	evidence		23
Surrogate	concept		370
Symbolic	computation		4
Symbolic	model	processing	41,73,133
Symbolic	processing	software	10,133
Symmetry	group		146
Synchronization			107,329

Syntactic   assessment   268
Synthesis   16,67,71,91,134,137,195,203,354
Synthesis   problem   16,67,71,134,137
Synthesis   rule   specification   91
Synthesis of   complex   models   195,203
System   analysis   21,79,134,137,166
System   database   286
System   description   17,121,357
System   design   93,133,135,153,195
System   driven   dialogue   305
System   entity   structure   24,80,87,89,139,154,392
System   identification   155,196
System   information   290
System   knowledge   6,15,16,43,104,346
System   knowledge   structuring   8,22,25,70,108,161
System   monitor   325
System   relation   base   121,126
System   specification   79,121,133,135,136,195,196,245
System   specification algorithm   133
System   specification ,transformation   133
Systems   research   7,134,385

T

Taxonomic   knowledge   16,80
Taxonomy   16,29,33,41
Taxonomy of   machine   learning   50
Taxonomy of   synergies   9
Template   85,93,123,198
Temporal   knowledge   70,71,372
Testing   70,72,126,127,133,256,282,377
Theorem   proving   system   177
Theory   84,134,146,211,340,385
Tightness   128
Time   4,107,149,151,157,160,169,205,
                                                   229,257,368,391,392,395
Time   anticipation   149
Time   based   signal   107,151,168
Time   sequencing   4,107,157,160,169
Timing   regime   229
Top-down   synthesis   203
Tracer   51,66,403
Trail of   strengthened connections   248
Trajectory   72
Transaction   107,209
Transducer   43,84
Transformation   50,53,115,133,134,137,170,171,
                                                   208
Transformation   of   knowledge   50,53,115
Transition   147,185,197,201
Transition   graph   368
Transmittor   receptor   dissociation   255
Traversal   27,37,88
Tree   29,33,79,87,93,106,139,222,249,
                                                   250,317,329,388
Tree   structure   93,106
Trend   extrapolation   312
Troughput   205
Turn   around   time   205